THE SCHOOL OF PRAYER

An Introduction to the Divine Office for All Christians

JOHN BROOK

THE LITURGICAL PRESS
Collegeville, Minnesota

Imprimatur: Rt Rev. L. A. Boyle, Bishop of Dunedin, New Zealand
Dunedin, 22 May 1990

Nihil obstat: Father Anton Cowan, *Censor*
Imprimatur: Rt Rev. John Crowley, VG, Bishop in Central London
Westminster, 19 April 1991

First published in the United States of America in 1992
by The Liturgical Press
Collegeville, Minnesota

ISBN 0-8146-2028-0

The *Nihil obstat* and *Imprimatur* are a declaration that a book or pamphlet is considered to be free from doctrinal or moral error. It is not implied that those who have granted the *Nihil obstat* or *Imprimatur* agree with the contents, opinions or statements expressed.

Contents

Preface

This book is written for all who are learning to pray. It is written firstly for lay people, to introduce them to one of the Church's greatest treasures of prayer, the Divine Office. The word 'Office' comes from the Latin *officium,* meaning 'service', 'something done for someone'. The Divine Office is the service given to God in prayer. The Office is also called the Liturgy of the Hours, referring to the seven 'hours', or times of prayer for each day. It is part of the public liturgy of the Church.

The Divine Office is a pattern of prayer based on the psalms. In the early centuries of the Church the Office was the prayer of the whole Christian community, not just the clergy or religious. It was the Church's school of prayer. By medieval times the Office had, outside the monasteries, become the private prayer of the clergy. The Second Vatican Council revised the Office in such a way as to restore it to its original function as the prayer of the whole people of God. I hope that this book may help to fulfil that intention.

Secondly, this book is written for novices and seminary students who are just beginning to pray the Office. There are riches in the Office that need to be unlocked, and questions that need to be answered if beginners are to gain most benefit from it.

Part 1 gives a general introduction to the basic principles of praying the Office. Part 2 is a commentary which will help in putting the principles into daily practice.

The Divine Office is made up almost entirely of Scripture, and for this reason it is a form of prayer that should appeal to the deepest convictions of Protestant Christians. It is natural that Protestants would have reservations about using a Catholic form of prayer, and so the third purpose of this book is to commend the Office to them. I am convinced that the Divine Office could be one of the pillars on which the unity of the Church is rebuilt. My own Christian nurture was in Evangelical Protestantism, with its zeal for prayer but suspicion of written forms. I have tried to be sensitive to this antipathy to liturgical prayer and to commend such prayer to my Evangelical brothers and sisters in Christ.

I also hope that those who have been praying the Office for years may find something here to enrich their devotion. In praying the psalms it is possible to run through words, phrases, whole sections which we do not understand but we say just because they are there. Such prayer can become a heaping up of empty phrases. A return to the original meaning of the psalm and a deliberate attempt to pray the psalm with Christ can bring a freshness back into praying the Office.

I was introduced to the Divine Office by the late Father Leo Curry when he and I were chaplains at Massey University, Palmerston North. His friendship changed the whole direction of my life, a change which began when he encouraged me to begin praying the Office. His life was tragically cut short, and I hope that this book may in some way continue the ministry he began. I dedicate the book to him.

John Brook
Dunedin
Pentecost, 1990

Part 1
Introduction to the Divine Office

1 Learning to Pray

The desire to pray

The fact that you are reading this book is a clear sign that you already have the desire to pray. That desire may come from many sources. For many modern Christians the desire to pray and to grow in prayer finds its source in a fresh experience of the Holy Spirit. The Spirit is the love of God poured into our hearts, so it is not surprising that the gift of the Spirit inspires us to respond to God's love in prayer. When two people are in love they want to spend time with each other, time talking, time just being together. When we receive the gift of the love of God, the gift of the Holy Spirit, we want to spend time in communion with God, we want to pray.

The desire to pray may not come from any one experience, but from a deep-rooted yearning for God, a longing that is itself a gift of the Spirit. Retreat centres and courses on spirituality are multiplying in order to meet the needs of those who are serious about prayer.

But the desire to pray is not enough. Anyone who has tried to pray consistently knows that it is not as natural as breathing. We need help in learning to pray, and the Divine Office gives us this help.

Coming to know God

When we are beginning in prayer our first need is to come to know God. Prayer is love, and we can only love someone we know. God knows and loves us intimately. In prayer we come to know and love God in return.

We come to know God through his self-revelation in Jesus, and we come to know Jesus as we meet him in the Scriptures.

The whole purpose of the Scriptures can be summed up in the reason St John gives for writing his Gospel: 'These are written that you may believe that Jesus is the Christ, the Son of God, and that believing you may have life in his name.' (John 20:31). If we are to come to know God revealed in Christ we must come to know the Scriptures, and for this the Divine Office is a priceless gift. It gives us a daily diet of Scripture selected for the purpose of meditation and prayer. If we use the Office rightly it will lead us into the mind and heart of God. It will lead us to know God.

One of the Church's Doctors of the spiritual life, St John of the Cross, describes the prayer of beginners as 'meditation', where meditation means taking time to come to know God. The Divine Office provides us with the means for meditation.

The basic principle of the Office

A child learns to write by copying the shape of the letters the teacher has carefully written out. The teacher writes a line and underneath the child copies the example of the teacher. That is precisely how we learn to pray, how we come to know God. The Holy Spirit is our teacher. We learn to pray by taking the prayers inspired by the Spirit and copying them, following the movement of the Spirit with mind and heart. This is the fundamental principle of the Divine Office. The Office sets before us the prayers inspired by the Spirit in the psalms and canticles of Scripture, in the prayers of the saints and the Church's liturgy. As we take these prayers and copy them, with concentration of mind and heart, the same Spirit who inspired these prayers will inspire us to pray. The Spirit will teach us to pray.

Two very different experiences taught me the truth of this principle. The first was an experience of deep depression. For months on end I could not pray. If I tried to pray I only fell inward into despair and empty silence. During this time I picked up the Anglican Book of Common Prayer and began to read each morning the order for Morning Prayer. It was like being winched slowly out of a pit. The prayer of confession, the psalms and other prayers, expressed my own longing for forgiveness and for God's peace in a way I could never do on my own.

The second experience which showed me how the Spirit can teach us to pray as we follow the prayer of the Church was not depression but the opposite – an overwhelming experience of the love of God. I now longed to pray, especially to praise, but my vocabulary was so limited. Prayer was spontaneous, but undisciplined and erratic. A priest encouraged me to try using the Divine Office as revised by Vatican II. Initially I was daunted by the sheer size of the book, but as I began to use it I discovered that it was surprisingly simple, and more importantly, that it resolved some persistent difficulties in prayer.

The principle in practice

Learning to pray by following the prayers inspired by the Spirit, by praying the Divine Office, provides a unique solution to common difficulties everyone faces when beginning to pray.

The Office resolves the difficulty of finding words. When we make time to pray we may find that our mind goes blank. We may be depressed and unable to turn to God for help; or joyful, but not know how to express our praise and thanks to God. The Divine Office gives us the words of prayer, words inspired by the Spirit, the words of sacred Scripture. The psalms, which make up the substance of the Office, express the whole gamut of human emotion in prayer, and praying the psalms gives voice to the deepest movements of the soul.

The Office also helps to overcome the difficulty of making time to pray and establishing a daily discipline of prayer that lasts more than a few weeks or months. We face the constant temptation of leaving prayer to the fag end of the day, or forgetting about it in the pressure of everything else that has to be done. The Divine Office is an enormous help in tackling the problem of discipline in prayer, because it provides a pattern of prayer that can easily be built into our daily habits.

Praying the Office helps us to focus our distracting thoughts. We begin to pray, but within a minute we may be turning over some family problem, or reliving a vivid scene from last night's television. The Office focuses our thoughts in prayer by providing an objective text on which to concentrate. We are not left to our own resources.

The Office also enlarges our vision in prayer. Without the Office our prayers can follow the same old track, saying the same things over and over again, boxed in to our own small world. The Office explodes that box and opens us to experience the whole Church praying the mind of Christ, praying for the world for which he suffered and died.

The Divine Office provides a pattern of prayer which helps to solve the most common difficulties in prayer. It is a way of prayer rooted in the Scriptures, in the experience of Jesus, and in the life of his Church. It is a way that has been proved by countless Christians from the earliest times.

One of the most moving modern testimonies to the way a pattern of liturgical prayer such as the Divine Office can sustain and transform us comes from an Orthodox Christian in Soviet Russia. Anatoli Levetin was a teacher of Russian literature who was imprisoned for carrying out an informal religious education programme for young people. He describes his experience of daily prayer while in solitary confinement:

> The greatest miracle of all is prayer. I have only to turn my thoughts to God and I suddenly feel a force bursting into me; there is new strength in my soul, in my entire being . . . The basis of my whole spiritual life is the Orthodox liturgy, so while I was in prison I attended it every day in my imagination. At 8.00 in the morning I would begin walking round my cell, repeating its words to myself. I was then inseparably linked to the whole Christian world. In the Great Litany I would always pray for the Pope and for the Oecumenical Patriarch, as well as for the leaders of my

own church. At the central point of the liturgy . . . I felt myself standing before the face of the Lord, sensing almost physically his wounded, bleeding body. I would begin praying in my own words, remembering all those near to me, those in prison and those who were free, those still alive and those who had died. More and more names welled up from my memory . . . The prison walls moved apart and the whole universe became my residence, visible and invisible, the universe for which that wounded, pierced body offered itself in sacrifice . . . After this, I experienced an exaltation of spirit all day – I felt purified within (From Michael Bordeaux, *Risen Indeed*, London, DLT, 1983, p. 59).

Jesus learns to pray

Learning to pray by following the prayers inspired by the Spirit is the way Jesus learnt to pray. The Jewish practice of daily prayer was the school in which Jesus learnt. Following Jewish custom he prayed three times a day: morning prayer at sunrise, afternoon prayer at the time of the evening sacrifice in the Temple in Jerusalem (3 p.m.), and evening prayer at nightfall. These three 'hours' of prayer were the daily habit of every devout Jew.

Morning prayer consisted of two main parts: the *Sh*^{e}*ma'* and the *T*^{e}*philla*. The *Sh*^{e}*ma'* is the basic Jewish creed, taken from Deuteronomy 6:4—7.

> Hear, O Israel, the Lord our God is one Lord, and you shall love the Lord your God with all your heart, and with all your soul, and with all your might. And these words which I command you this day shall be upon your heart; and you shall teach them diligently to your children, and you shall talk of them when you sit down in your house, and when you walk by the way, and when you lie down, and when you rise.

Before and after reciting this creed the worshipper prayed a number of benedictions or blessings.

The second part of morning prayer was the *T*^{e}*philla*, meaning 'The Prayer'. The *T*^{e}*philla* was a hymn made up of a series of benedictions, fixed at eighteen by the end of the first century. The first benediction ran:

Blessed art thou, O Lord,
God of Abraham, God of Isaac and God of Jacob,
most high God, Lord of heaven and earth,
our shield and the shield of our fathers.
Blessed art thou, O Lord, the shield of Abraham.

Jesus' way of speaking of God as 'the God of Abraham and the God of Isaac and the God of Jacob' (Mark 12:26) and 'Lord of heaven and earth' (Matthew 11:25) comes directly from this first benediction.

Afternoon prayer (3 p.m.) consisted only of the *T^e^philla*.

The third 'hour' of prayer, evening prayer, was identical to morning prayer: the *Sh^e^ma'* and the *T^e^philla*. Private petitions were added by each person following the offering of the set prayers.

In addition to these three daily hours of prayer Jesus learned the traditional Jewish prayers before and after each meal, with special graces for Sabbath and Passover, and he participated in the regular Sabbath worship with its liturgical cycle of psalms, Scripture readings and prayers. The influence of the psalms in Jesus' prayer can be seen most clearly in his prayer from the cross, *'My God, my God, why have you forsaken me'*, a direct quotation from Psalm 22:1.

This then was the rich cycle of prayer which Jesus learned and used. The Divine Office has its roots and its fundamental principle set firmly in the prayer of our Lord. He learned to pray by following the prayers inspired by the Spirit and set before him in the daily liturgy of Israel, and that is the way the Church teaches us to pray.

Of course there was far more to Jesus' prayer than the traditional Jewish model he grew up with. In his intimacy with God and his habit of spending hours alone with his Father, Jesus went far beyond the traditional Jewish practices of prayer, but this tradition was his school of prayer. The prayers which Jesus was taught at home and in the synagogue, prayers from the liturgical tradition of his people, laid the foundation for his unique prayer relationship with his Father.

The Gospels show us Jesus praying at the critical moments of his life: at his baptism when he was commissioned by the Father for his ministry; on the night before he chose his apostles; at his transfiguration; before he healed the deaf man; when he raised Lazarus from the dead; before he asked his disciples the crucial question 'Who do men say that I am?'; when he taught his disciples to pray; when they returned from their first mission; on the night before his passion; at the Last Supper; on the cross. Prayer animated his whole ministry, prayer that was learnt first of all from the liturgical tradition of Israel, in the three daily hours of prayer and in the Sabbath synagogue services.

When we pray the Divine Office we are learning to pray as Christ did.

Jesus teaches his disciples to pray

It was the example of Jesus at prayer that led the disciples to ask him, 'Lord, teach us to pray.' Luke's account of Jesus' answer (Luke 11:1—13) gives us the heart of his teaching on prayer. Jesus begins by giving the disciples a model to copy. 'When you pray, say this: . . . ' (Luke 11:2). He teaches them to pray by giving them a prayer which he expects them to learn off by heart and use every day. He teaches them to pray in the same way a school teacher teaches a child to write. It is the basic principle of the Divine Office in action again.

When the disciples asked Jesus to teach them to pray he did not reply by saying: 'Go away and pour out your heart to God. Pray as the Spirit moves you.' That may be good advice, but it is not the place to begin in a school of prayer. It would leave us at the mercy of ou r own limited capacity to tap the resources of the Spirit. Instead, Jesus gives us a model. He teaches us to pray in the same way he himself learnt to pray.

The Church prays as Jesus did

Jewish Christians followed the example of Jesus and the Jewish tradition in praying three times a day. The Acts of the Apostles twice refers to the afternoon prayer at 3 p.m. (Acts 3:1; 10:3,30). Paul's instruction to pray 'continually', 'without ceasing', 'day and night', may well be a reminder to the early Christians to observe the regular hours of prayer. The command: 'Pray constantly' in Romans 12:12 can mean: 'be faithful in observing the rite of prayer'.

By the end of the first century the Church had replaced the traditional Jewish prayers said at the three hours of prayer with the Lord's Prayer. The Didache (an early Christian manual of Church practice) says: 'Three times daily you shall pray thus', and goes on to cite the Lord's Prayer. (*Didache* 8:3).

It is possible that the Church modelled its own pattern of daily worship on the pattern of Jewish synagogue prayer. In the larger towns daily prayer may have been held each morning and evening in the synagogue, with readings from the sacred Scriptures, various prayers and psalms. The first evidence of daily prayer in local churches has this pattern.

There was far more to the early Church's practice of prayer than observing regular hours of prayer, but these hours were the framework around which the practice of daily prayer was built, the bones which gave strength and form to the body.

It is from the example of Jesus and the early Church that the pattern of prayer developed that today is known as the Divine Office. The story of that development is told in the next chapter.

2 The Divine Office is the Prayer of the Whole People of God

The Divine Office is usually assumed to be the private prayer of clergy and religious. Its roots are quite the opposite. In the early Church it was the prayer of the whole Christian community. The reform of Vatican II is a deliberate attempt to recover those roots, as Pope Paul VI said when promulgating the revised Office: 'This complete revision of the official prayer of the Church, taking into account both the oldest traditions and the needs of modern life, will, it is hoped, renew and vivify all Christian prayer and serve to nourish the spiritual life of the People of God.' (*Apostolic Constitution Promulgating the Divine Office, Laudis Canticum.* Henceforth cited as LC).

The roots of the Divine Office

It is helpful to examine the oldest traditions of the Office to see how the essential purpose of the Office was 'to nourish the spiritual life of the People of God' (LC n. 8), clergy and laity alike. We have already seen how those traditions go right back to Jewish disciplines of prayer, taken up and transformed by Jesus and his disciples. By the end of the second century this transformation had produced a pattern with some remarkable parallels to the modern Office. The principal times of prayer were at daybreak and sunset, what we now call Morning and Evening Prayer. These two 'hours' of prayer were assumed to be obligatory for all Christians. If possible, the faithful were encouraged to meet to pray at these times, to gather before work (before daybreak) to pray and listen to the reading of the Scriptures. If it was not possible for them to come together, they were to pray alone.

Hippolytus, a prominent theologian in the Church in

Rome in the early part of the third century, exhorted the Christians to morning prayer:

> And let every faithful man and woman, when they rise from sleep at dawn, before they undertake any work, wash their hands and pray to God, and so let them go to their work. But if there should be an instruction in the word, let each one prefer to go there, considering that it is God whom he hears speaking by the mouth of him who instructs.
> For he who prays with the Church will be able to avoid all the evils of that day. The God-fearing man should consider it a great loss if he does not go to the place in which they give instruction. (*Apostolic Tradition*, ¶ 41, written about AD 215).

Cyprian, Bishop of Carthage in north Africa, writing in the middle of the third century on the subject of prayer, strongly insists that all Christians must pray early in the morning, 'that the Lord's resurrection may be celebrated by morning prayer. . ., also at the sunsetting and at the decline of the day of necessity we must pray again.' (*De Oratione Dominica*, PL IV, 560).

The seven Hours of prayer

In addition to these two basic times of prayer, morning and evening, Christians in Rome were encouraged by Hippolytus to pray:

1. At 9 a.m. (the third hour, called Terce). 'If you are in your own home, pray at the third hour and praise God. If you are elsewhere at that moment, pray in your own heart. Because at this hour Christ was seen nailed upon the tree.' (Hippolytus, *Apostolic Tradition* ¶ 41. All the following quotations (2—5) are from the same source).
2. At noon (the sixth hour, Sext). 'Pray as well on the sixth hour. Because when Christ was nailed to the wood of the cross, daylight was suspended and a great darkness came upon the land.'
3. At 3 p.m. (the ninth hour, None). 'Let there also be full prayer and praise at the ninth hour . . . At that hour Christ

was pierced in his side and shed forth both water and blood.'

4. At midnight. 'At about midnight rise and wash your hands with water and pray. And if you have a wife, both of you pray together. Be not slothful to pray . . . At this hour all creation pauses for a brief moment to praise the Lord.'

5. At cockcrow, 'our eyes looking towards that day in the hope of eternal light at the resurrection of the dead.'

Hippolytus implies that prayer at seven times during the day (the seven 'hours' of prayer) was a well-established custom among the early Christians. It was a pattern expected of all Christians, not just the clergy. If it seems daunting to us, think of how much time we can spend watching TV.

In the early centuries of the Church Christians in different countries observed different patterns of daily prayer, but all seem to have included morning and evening prayer as part of the cycle. While at most of these times Christians prayed alone, morning and evening were times when, if possible, they came together to pray. There is evidence throughout the third century of daily morning and evening prayer services in the larger towns.

One other important feature highlighted by Hippolytus is the fact that the hours of prayer are a way of recalling Christ's passion. Each of the seven hours is linked to an aspect of Christ's death on the cross. Praying the Liturgy of the Hours is one way of participating in the salvation won in the cross and resurrection of Christ.

Morning and Evening Prayer

By the fourth century daily Morning and Evening Prayer in the local cathedral (the 'cathedral office') had become a universal custom. Eusebius, Bishop of Caesarea and the eminent historian of the early Church, says:

> The very fact that in God's churches throughout the world hymns, praises and truly divine delights are arranged in his honour at the morning sunrise and in the evening is surely no small sign of God's power. These 'delights of God' are the hymns sent up in his

Church throughout the world both morning and evening. (*Commentarius in Psalmos*, PG XXIII, 639).

The fact that both clergy and laity were encouraged to attend daily Morning and Evening Prayer is witnessed in the *Apostolic Constitutions,* a manual of Church order written about AD 380.

When you instruct the people, O Bishop, command and exhort them to make it a practice to come daily to the church in the morning and in the evening, and on no account cease to doing so, but to assemsble together continually; neither to diminish the Church by withdrawing themselves, and causing the body of Christ to be without its members. For it is not only spoken concerning the priests; but let everyone of the laity hearken to it as concerning himself, esteeming what was spoken by the Lord: 'He who is not with me is against me and he who does not gather with me, scatters.' . . . Assemble yourselves every day, morning and evening, singing psalms and praying in the Lord's house, in the morning saying the sixty-second psalm, and in the evening the one hundred and fortieth psalm. (Book 2 § LIX. PG I, 741—744.)

The influence of the monks

Throughout this period, from the end of the third century on, a lay spiritual movement was growing which was to have a decisive influence on the whole Church, and particularly on Christian prayer. Hundreds of devout Christians fled the world and went into the desert to live lives dedicated to prayer. Gradually some formed themselves into communities with distinctive patterns of prayer. Their most notable characteristic in common prayer was the praying of the entire book of Psalms, one psalm after the other, sometimes in the course of a single day. Each psalm was followed by prostration for private prayer. The most notable contribution of these monks in the development of the Divine Office was the practice of systematically reciting the psalms at the hours of prayer. Some of the monastic communities also developed a cycle of common prayer at the times of the 'lesser hours' (the five hours additional to Morning and Evening Prayer).

As the influence of the monastic communities grew, some of the cathedral churches took up the practice of the public, common prayer of the seven hours of daily prayer. This was a decisive development in the pattern we now know as the Divine Office, or the Liturgy of the Hours. Those who attended the lesser hours were clergy who lived a common life centred around the cathedral Church, and in some places they were joined by groups of fervent lay people who lived a monastic lifestyle in an urban setting. Some monasteries became linked to local churches, and the monks played a leading role in the daily liturgy, and in assigning particular psalms to particular hours and liturgical days.

Lay people still came daily to Morning and Evening Prayer, and these two hours were geared to encourage their full participation. The services were comparatively short, consisting of psalms, Scripture reading (sometimes a homily), hymns, intercessions, and concluding prayers. In subsequent centuries the monastic influence in the Office became stronger and stronger, with a corresponding decline in the participation of the laity.

In the Western Church by the twelfth century the Divine Office had become by and large private prayer, read in Latin from a book (the breviary), confined basically to priests and religious. The communal character of the prayer of the Office was preserved chiefly in the monasteries. It is obvious from its beginnings that this is far from what the Liturgy of the Hours was intended to be.

The reform of Vatican II

It was the example of the early Church, where the basic hours of Morning and Evening Prayer were the common prayer of the whole people of God, that was the inspiration for the reforms Vatican II made to the Divine Office. The purpose of the reform was to recover the essential traditions of daily prayer as practised in the early Church, making Morning and Evening Prayer from the Office accessible to all

Christians.

Some principles which guided the revision and are expressed in the new form of the Office, published in 1974, are:

1. The needs of lay people are to the fore. The Office has been composed so that 'it is the prayer not only of the clergy but of the whole people of God, and religious and lay people can take part in it'. (LC n.1)

2. The pattern of the Office is designed to fit the pattern of people's daily lives by making Morning and Evening Prayer the most important 'hours' of the day. Anyone who prays these hours prays the heart of the Office.

3. The weekly recitation of the whole psalter has been replaced by a four-weekly cycle of psalms and Scripture canticles.

The roots of the Office and the reforms of Vatican II witness to the fact that Liturgy of the Hours is the prayer of the whole Church.

The Liturgy of the Hours is the Church's school of prayer

The fruits of praying the Office were introduced in Chapter 1 and will be taken up again in Chapter 9, but at this point it is important to appreciate that the Divine Office is the Church's school of prayer. Robert Taft, a leading historian of the Liturgy of the Hours, describes the Office as:

> a novitiate in which she [the Church] teaches her age-old ways of how to glorify God in Christ as Church, together as one body, in union with and after the example of her head. No other form of prayer is so rooted in the mysteries of salvation history as they are unfolded day by day in the Church's annual cycle. Through this constant diet of Sacred Scripture not only does God speak in his Word to us, not only do we contemplate over and over again the central mysteries of salvation, but our own lives are gradually attuned to this rhythm, and we meditate again and again on the history of Israel, recapitulated in Jesus, that is also the saga of our own spiritual odyssey. (*The Liturgy of the Hours in East and West*, Minnesota, The Liturgical Press, 1986, p. 368).

3 Morning and Evening Prayer from the Divine Office

In the last chapter we saw how the fathers of the Second Vatican Council acted to restore the tradition which made Morning and Evening Prayer the two chief hours of prayer for the day. The Council described Morning and Evening Prayer as 'the two hinges on which the daily office turns.' (*Constitution on the Sacred Liturgy, Sacrosanctum Concilium,* henceforth cited as CSL, n. 89).

The other hours became: The *Office of Readings,* which includes both a substantial reading from Scripture and from the Church's greatest spiritual authors; *Prayer During the Day,* to be said before noon, at midday, and in the afternoon; *Night Prayer*, to be said just before going to bed.

The revision was completed in 1970 and an English translation published in 1974. In what follows, the text referred to is that published by Collins, *Morning and Evening Prayer,* 1976, an edition expressly designed to be used by lay people. It contains Morning and Evening Prayer for every day of the year exactly as it is in the full edition of the Liturgy of the Hours.

The Various Parts of Morning and Evening Prayer

1 Invitation to prayer

Morning prayer begins with what is technically called the invitatory (pronounced with the accent on the second syllable, 'invi´tatory'). The invitatory is an invitation to pray. It serves to focus our minds on what we are about to do. It brings us into the presence of God, it helps us to set aside the concerns that crowd in at the beginning of the day, and it calls us to give our full attention to God. It is like the warm-up that an athlete does before the actual event, a slow flexing of the spiritual muscles. The invitatory begins the dialogue with God which continues throughout the whole Office.

There are three parts to the invitatory.

Firstly, the versicle from Psalm 50(51):15:

> Verse: *Lord, open our lips:*
> Response: *And we shall praise your name.*

We call on the Lord, asking for his help in our prayer. The opening verse is an acknowledgement that without the Lord we can do nothing. The effectiveness of our prayer depends on his grace. This is symbolized in the action that accompanies the versicle - making the sign of the cross on the lips with the thumb.

The versicle also reminds us that our primary purpose in coming to prayer is to praise God's name. Everything else – listening to Scripture, intercession, petition – is within the context of praise. Praise comes first, and permeates the whole.

The second part of the invitatory is a psalm, usually Psalm 94(95), sometimes Psalm 99(100), 66(67), or 23(24). (The double numbering of the psalms is explained in section 3 of this chapter). Psalm 94 is a striking call to prayer. It begins with a call to give joyful thanks to the Lord; it reminds us that he is the creator of the world in all its beauty; it affirms our duty to worship the God who made us and cares for us; it concludes with a sober challenge to listen with a sensitive and obedient heart to God's word if we are to find the rest, the salvation, we long for.

The third part of the invitatory is the antiphon, which changes each day and serves to focus our attention on either one theme of the invitatory psalm, or on the theme of the particular day in the Church's liturgical calendar. The invitatory antiphon is always given at the very beginning of each day's prayer. The antiphon can be said just at the beginning of the invitatory psalm, or after each verse of the psalm. The invitatory antiphons for the different seasons of the Church's year are found on p. 369 in *Morning and Evening Prayer*. The psalm itself is on p. 371, or may be on the inside cover. Alternative invitatory psalms are on pp. 372—3.

Evening Prayer begins with a simpler invitation:

Verse: *O God, come to our aid.*
Response: *O Lord, make haste to help us.*

Glory be to the Father and to the Son and to the Holy Spirit, as it was in the beginning, is now, and ever shall be, world without end. Amen. Alleluia.

2 Hymn

From earliest times hymns have had a special place in the Office. Their use in Christian worship is clearly alluded to in the New Testament: 'With gratitude in your hearts sing psalms and hymns and inspired songs to God' (Colossians 3:16), and there are several extracts from early Christian hymns quoted in the New Testament, e.g. Philippians 2:5—11, Revelation 4:8,11.

The poetry of the hymn helps to move both mind and heart, drawing us into prayer, whether we are praying on our own or in community.

In addition to the hymn set down for each day there are special hymns for the different seasons of the liturgical year. These are found in Appendix II, pp. 1102 ff. As well as the hymns given in the book, any suitable hymn can be used. Even if you are saying the Office on your own, and you enjoy singing, sing the hymn aloud.

3 Psalmody, or Psalter

'Psalmody' means 'a collection of psalms arranged for singing'. 'Psalter' can refer to the Book of Psalms, or to a book of psalms arranged for liturgical use. When used of the Office both words refer to the collection of psalms arranged for prayer.

The psalms for Morning and Evening Prayer have been carefully selected and arranged to best aid Christian worship. The psalmody of Morning Prayer consists of three psalms. First is a morning psalm, that is, a psalm whose mood and content fit the beginning of the day. Take Psalm 142(143) for example,

In the morning let me know your love
for I put my trust in you.
Make me know the way I should walk:
to you I lift up my soul.

Or Psalm 56(57):

My heart is ready, O God,
my heart is ready.
I will sing, I will sing your praise.
Awake my soul,
awake lyre and harp,
I will awake the dawn.
O God, arise above the heavens;
may your glory shine on earth!

Second is a canticle. A canticle is a song, a hymn of praise, a psalm which comes from somewhere else in Scripture other than the book of Psalms. At Morning Prayer the canticle is always from the Old Testament and is often a classic passage from the prophets, especially Isaiah.

Third is another psalm, traditionally a psalm of praise. To begin the day with praise is one of the greatest antidotes to self-interest or self-pity. Praise lifts our minds to God and to his glory, and puts our own lives in their proper perspective.

The psalmody of Evening Prayer consists of three passages: two psalms or two sections of a longer psalm chosen because of the way they express prayer at the close of the day, followed by a canticle from the New Testament (from the Epistles or Revelation). The dominant note of the evening psalms is thanksgiving. In the evening we give thanks to God for the gift of the day.

The version of the Psalms used in the Office is the Grail version, a new translation designed especially for liturgical use. It is a translation which captures the poetry of the Hebrew original, and expresses the meaning in clear English. It is an excellent version because it has a simplicity and flow which make it a great aid to praying the psalms.

The numbering of the Psalms in the Office is different from the numbering in most versions of the Bible. The Office preserves the numbering system followed by the early Church, which used the Greek and Latin translations of the Hebrew text. The Greek (Septuagint) and Latin (Vulgate) versions join the Hebrew Psalms 9 and 10 together, and join Psalms 114 and 115 together, but divide Psalms 116 and 147 in two. The result is that for most of Psalms 10 to 148 the numbering in the Office is one behind that of a modern translation of the Bible. That is why most Psalms in the Office have two numbers. The first number is the liturgical number, following the Greek and Latin versions. The second, in brackets, is the number of the Psalm in any modern Bible.

The psalms in the Office are accented for singing and chanting, hence the accent mark ´ over certain words, and the * and † signs at the end of the lines. These are necessary for the antiphonal chanting of the psalms in community, but can be ignored for individual prayer.

When the Office is prayed in community, the community can be divided into two groups. The first group says the first two lines of the psalm, and the second group says the next two lines, and so on through the psalm. For each pair of lines, the group pauses for a moment at the * mark. So it runs like this:

> Group 1: O *Lord, you once favoured your land** (pause)
> *and revived the fortunes of Jacob,*
> Group 2: *you forgave the guilt of your people** (pause)
> *and covered all their sins.*

And so on through the psalm. The † sign means: 'Don't pause here; carry straight on and pause when you get to the * mark.'

Each psalm has an antiphon adapted from a verse in the psalm and designed to highlight a dominant theme in the psalm. The antiphon is said at the beginning of the psalm, or sometimes after each verse. Occasionally the antiphon is the first line of the psalm, in which case it is followed by the † sign. The † sign in this case also appears at the point where the recitation of the psalm is to begin. For example, Psalm 26(27) (Week 1, Wednesday Evening). The antiphon is: *'The Lord is my light and my help; whom shall I fear?*†' and the †sign is found at the beginning of the line †*The Lord is the stronghold of my life.* After reciting the antiphon, move straight to the words: *The Lord is the stronghold of my life.*

At the conclusion of each psalm, before the final antiphon, the ascription of praise is used:

> *Glory be to the Father and to the Son and to the Holy Spirit, as it was in the beginning is now and ever shall be, world without end. Amen.*

The psalms are distributed over a four-week cycle. The praying of the psalms and canticles is one of the chief parts of the Office, and Chapters 6 and 7 are devoted to this subject.

4 Scripture Reading

A short reading is given according to the liturgical day, season, or feast. The readings have been chosen with the purpose of expressing succinctly an important biblical theme. At Morning Prayer the reading is usually from the Old Testament. In the evening, it is always from the New Testament. During the seasons of Lent, Easter, Advent and Christmas the readings present a selection of the major Scripture passages on the central Christian mysteries. The readings can be varied, using, for example, the readings from the day's Eucharist, or from another Bible reading calendar.

The Scripture readings can be prayed following the pattern of what St Benedict called *lectio divina,* 'sacred reading'. *Lectio divina* has four steps (1) Read the passage. (2) When a word or phrase strikes you, stop reading and meditate on the phrase, allowing it to speak to you, to take root in you. (3) Turn the meditation into brief prayer. (4) *Contemplate* the Lord: be still in God's presence. Then continue reading and repeat the cycle.

5 Silence

The silence following the psalms and readings is an integral part of the prayer. In any attentive conversation between friends, after our friend has spoken we often pause, to absorb what they have said before we reply. To pause, to be silent after each psalm, allows the word of God to germinate in us. It gives us time to meditate on the word of God, and to listen to the voice of the Spirit in our hearts.

6 The response

The short verse and response is another way of absorbing the word of God by putting into words a proper response to the Scripture reading. The response is designed to turn the reading into prayer and contemplation. Although it is designed for corporate prayer, the response has great value in individual prayer, because it encourages our careful listening to God's word. The response 'enables the word of God to penetrate more deeply into the mind and heart of the person reciting or listening.' (*General Instruction on the Liturgy of the Hours*, henceforth cited as GILH, ¶172).

7 Gospel Canticles

At Morning Prayer the Gospel canticle, the Benedictus (Luke 1:68—79), follows the Scripture reading and response. At Evening Prayer the canticle is the Magnificat (Luke 1:46—55). 'These canticles express praise and thanksgiving for our redemption.' (GILH ¶50). The sign of the cross is made at the beginning of the canticles.

8 The Intercessions

The letter to Timothy advises that 'there should be prayers offered for everyone – petitions, intercessions and thanksgiving . . . To do this is right, and will please God our Saviour, who wants everyone to be saved and reach full knowledge of the truth' (1 Timothy 2:1—4).

In the morning the intercessions are designed to consecrate the day and our work to God. In the evening, the intercessions focus on the needs of the world. When praying alone, each intercession offers direction for our own personal prayer, bringing before the Lord our specific needs and the needs of those who are known to us. The final intercession each evening is always for the departed.

The intercessions of the Office are a constant stimulus to us to form our own intercessions, to bring to God the needs we carry on our own hearts, and to enlarge our hearts to pray for the needs of the world. The wording of the intercessions in the Office can seem a little vague, but that is because it is designed to be universal, and it is precisely that universal quality which opens our horizons in prayer. We can add our specific prayers at any point in the intercessions.

The intercessions were written at a time when 'men' and 'man' were understood to include the whole human race, male and female. It is a simple matter to bring the wording into line with current usage.

9 The Lord's Prayer

The Lord's Prayer has place of honour at the end of the intercessions and it sums up the whole prayer.

St Cyprian, a third century bishop of Carthage, in his treatise *On the Lord's Prayer*, said: 'Let us pray as our God and Master himself taught us. Our prayer is friendly and intimate when we petition God with his own prayer, letting the words of Christ rise to the Father's ears. When we pray, may the Father recognize his Son's own words. He who dwells in our breast should also be our voice.'

10 Concluding prayer

A concluding prayer completes the Hour. On Sundays and feast days, this concluding prayer is the same as the opening prayer at Mass.

11 Blessing

In prayer on one's own, or without a priest or deacon present, the conclusion is:

> *The Lord bless us, and keep us from all evil, and bring us to everlasting life. Amen.*

One peculiar feature of the structure of the Office is that each Sunday has two evening prayers. This is a remnant of the Jewish way of reckoning time, where the new day begins at sunset, not at midnight. Evening Prayer I is said on Saturday evening, and Evening Prayer II on Sunday evening.

Structure of Morning and Evening Prayer

Morning Prayer	**Evening Prayer**
INTRODUCTION	
V *Lord, open our lips.* R *And we shall praise your name.* [Invitatory psalm (Pss 94, 99, 66 or 23) with its antiphon]	V O *God, come to our aid.* R O *Lord, make haste to help us.* *Glory be . . .*
HYMN	
PSALMODY	
A 'morning' psalm Old Testament Canticle A psalm of praise	A psalm A psalm New Testament Canticle
SCRIPTURE READING	
(Silent Prayer)	
SHORT RESPONSORY	
GOSPEL CANTICLE	
Benedictus	Magnificat
INTERCESSIONS	
Consecrating the day to God	Intercession for the needs of the world
The Lord's Prayer	
CONCLUDING PRAYER	
BLESSING	

Getting Started

1 On your own

There are two editions of the Divine Office designed with the needs of lay people in mind.

Firstly, there is the *Shorter Morning and Evening Prayer* (London, Collins, 1983). For most of the year this edition gives the full form of Morning and Evening Prayer, but it has simplified the texts for the special seasons of Lent, Easter, Advent and Christmas, and does not include the texts for saints' days.

Secondly, *Morning and Evening Prayer* (London, Collins, 1976). This edition gives the full text of Morning and Evening Prayer for the whole year, with all the variations for each season, feast day and saint's day. To work out where to begin, use the table on p. xxviii.

If you have not used the psalms regularly in prayer before, then whichever edition you use the full form of the Office can be daunting. At first sight it looks complex, with lots of different parts and too many different Scriptures for prayer. There seems to be more than one can possibly take in or pray with concentration, and many who start praying the full form of Morning and Evening Prayer by themselves give up after a few weeks either because they cannot work out how to follow all the seasonal texts, or because they feel that they are saying a lot of words rather than praying to God. It feels like trying to run a mile when you are only fit enough to go once round the track.

One practical way of overcoming this problem is to start slowly, to take as much as you can handle and leave the rest until later. For example, if you have never prayed the psalms before, cut out the invitatory and the opening hymn, and begin morning prayer by praying either the first psalm (the 'morning' psalm), or the third psalm (the 'praise' psalm). Go on to the Scripture reading and the responsory, then conclude with the intercessions and the Lord's Prayer. That may be plenty to begin with. After a few weeks or months, when you feel you are able to expand your daily diet of praying the Scriptures, add the second psalm of the day. After some time, you will be ready to move on to the full form of Morning and Evening Prayer. The most important thing is not to try too much and so become discouraged and give up. Start slowly, and work up to the full form at your own pace.

Whether you decide to begin with the full form of Morning and Evening Prayer, or with a simplified version, the following suggestions may help.

1. Choose a time for prayer that fits in with your daily routine. If you are a mother with a baby or small children you may find time to say Morning Prayer while you are breast feeding, or as soon as the children have gone off to school for the day. If you are working outside the home, you may find time while you commute to or from work. It may be necessary to adjust your daily routines to make time for prayer, by getting up earlier. It is important to think creatively about where in your day you can be sure to make time to pray. Whatever time you choose, it will take discipline and perseverance to stick to it.

2. Find a place where you can be quiet and still. (It may help to set a small table, with a cloth, a candle, and a cross). Consciously recall the presence and love of God, the one whose presence fills the world, and fills the hearts of those who turn to him in humility. The invitatory and the opening hymn are a real help in 'practising the presence of God'.

3. Read the antiphon, the heading, and the sentence for the psalm and let them guide you as you seek to be sensitive to the movement of the Spirit when you pray the psalm.

Read each psalm slowly and seek to enter into the heart of the psalm, into the experience it comes out of. *If a phrase or word catches you, stay with it, savour its meaning before moving on.* You will find your own prayer emerging out of the prayer of the psalmist. The same Spirit who inspired the psalmist will inspire you as you pray. He will teach you to pray.

When we receive a letter from someone we love, we linger on certain phrases and go back and re-read a sentence that brings them close. God's word of love needs to be received and read in the same way.

The psalm may reflect your own experience, or it may be a door into the experience of others, into the prayer of the universal Church. Most importantly of all, it may give you entry into the heart of Christ and his prayer to the Father. Chapter 8 takes up this aspect of praying the psalms.

4. Read the Scripture Reading as the word of God addressed to you for that day. Let it soak in, then respond to the word, guided by the responsory.

5. In the intercessions bring your own needs and the needs of others to the Lord, guided by the intercessions given for each day. As you do so, the Spirit will teach you to intercede. Because the intercessions given in the Office are the prayers of the Church, the Bride of Christ, praying in complete harmony with his will, we can be sure that these prayers will be answered. Pray with that confidence and faith.

6. The Lord's Prayer sums up the whole experience of Christian prayer. One of the Church's greatest teachers on prayer, St Teresa of Avila, said: 'Whoever prays the Lord's Prayer with complete attention and devotion of heart rises to the heights of prayer.'

7. The concluding prayer and blessing complete the Hour, and lead us into the day or night.

Remember that the Office is a community prayer, and take any opportunities you can to pray the Office with others. Some parishes have Evening Prayer on Sundays. Some religious communities welcome others to pray the Office with them. If you know of someone else who is praying the Office, pray it together when you can.

2 In community

If you begin by praying the Office in community, as a novice or seminary student, you will begin immediately to use the full form of Morning and Evening Prayer. Your starting place is given to you in the prayer life of the community. It is an immense advantage in beginning to pray the Office to pray it with a community. The Liturgy of the Hours *is* common prayer, and the discipline of community prayer carries a beginner along while you are growing into a new form of prayer.

Two things can help as you begin to pray the Office in community. First, take a little time the night before Morning Prayer, or in the afternoon before Evening Prayer, to prepare one of the psalms or the Scripture reading. Prepare by reading it over, consulting the commentary which follows in Part 2, clarifying the meaning of the Scripture before you come to prayer.

Secondly, take time after each hour (if possible before you leave the chapel) to savour any words or phrases which may have stood out for you during the Office. Let the dialogue with God begun in the Office continue.

4 Night Prayer

Night Prayer is found in both *Shorter Morning and Evening Prayer* (p. 319) and *Morning and Evening Prayer* (p. 689), after the four-weekly cycle of psalms. In contrast to Evening Prayer, Night Prayer is brief, a prayer to be said at bedtime. It is the last act of the day, and its purpose is to consecrate the night hours to God. From the very earliest times night was a symbol of death. In Night Prayer we anticipate our death, we prepare for death by trusting our lives wholly to God. The psalms and Scriptures of Night Prayer all serve to strengthen our hope in the risen Christ, and to help us rest with him in peace.

In Night Prayer we entrust our lives to the Lord who directs us even while we sleep.

> *I will bless the Lord who gives me counsel,*
> *who even at night directs my heart.* (Psalm 15)

The Scriptures are full of examples of God directing people through dreams and visions in the night. While our conscious mind is asleep, our unconscious can become the vehicle through which the Lord gives us guidance or brings to the surface things we may be avoiding or unwilling to face.

The Structure of Night Prayer

1 Verse

Verse: O *God, come to our aid.*
Response: O *Lord, make haste to help us.*

Glory be to the Father and to the Son and to the Holy Spirit; as it was in the beginning, is now, and ever shall be, world without end. Amen. Alleluia.

2 Hymn

3 Examination of Conscience

When prayed in common this examination may take place in silence, or one of the penitential prayers from the Mass may be used. When prayed alone we can take time to recall particular words or actions which have broken God's law of love, and pray for the Lord's mercy. This is not a morbid exercise. A fundamental principal of learning in any area is to be able to recognise our faults and work at correcting them. The only way we will grow to maturity in Christian discipleship is by following this principle. It is as we take time regularly to examine our lives and see what needs to be put right that we will grow in love. We worship a God whose mercy is always sure, who came to be a doctor for sinners, not a friend of the self-righteous, and the nightly examination of conscience can be a golden opportunity to allow the heavenly physician to bring peace and healing to the wounds caused by our sin.

4 Psalmody

The psalmody of Night Prayer is simple. It is designed for those who are tired and weary. There is just a single psalm, or two very short psalms. Each of the psalms has been especially chosen for the way it expresses prayer at night.

The psalm given for Night Prayer for Sunday (Psalm 90(91)) can be used on any evening, to allow a person to learn it off by heart and recite it without the use of a book.

5 Scripture Reading

The Scripture reading is a brief sentence, well chosen for the hour.

6 Responsory

7 Canticle of Simeon

8 Concluding Prayer

9 Blessing

The same blessing is used every night:

The Lord grant us a quiet night and a perfect end.

10 Anthem to the Blessed Virgin

5 The Proper of Seasons and the Proper of Saints

The edition of the Office published by Collins as *Morning and Evening Prayer* is in three main sections:

1. The Proper of Seasons (pp. 3—367);
2. The Psalter (pp. 368—709);
3. The Proper of Saints (pp. 710—1098).

The second section (the Psalter) is the heart of the book. It contains the psalmody which is used all year (apart from solemnities and saints' days) as well as the Scripture readings, responsories, antiphons for the Benedictus and the Magnificat, intercessions, and concluding prayers for use in ordinary time.

The first and third sections contain the Propers. The word 'Proper' is a technical liturgical term referring to those parts of the liturgy which change according to the season of the Christian year or the saint's day being observed. 'Proper' comes from the Latin word *proprius*, meaning 'one's own', and so the Proper refers to those parts of the Office which belong specifically to a particular season or saint's day.

The Proper of Seasons

The Proper of Seasons contains the Scripture readings, responsories, Benedictus and Magnificat antiphons, intercessions, and concluding prayers for use during the seasons of Advent, Christmastide, Lent, Eastertide, and on the Solemnities of the Most Holy Trinity, the Body and Blood of Christ, and the Most Sacred Heart of Jesus.

Finding your way around the Office in these seasons is quite straightforward.

1. Find out which week of a particular season you are in, for example the second week of Advent (Advent 2) or the third week of Lent (Lent 3). The week of a particular season begins on the Sunday, so the second week of Advent begins on the second Sunday of Advent, and the third week of Lent begins on the third Sunday of Lent, and so on.

2. Turn to the Sunday of the week you are in, and there you will find instructions in italics which will tell you which week of the psalter to use for the appropriate week of the season. For example, if you are in the second week of Advent, turn to the Sundays of Advent (p. 3) and you will see under the heading PSALMODY that the Psalter for the week beginning on the second Sunday of Advent is the Psalter of Week 2. If you are in the third week of Lent, turn to the Sundays of Lent (p. 132) and there you will find that the psalter for the week beginning the third Sunday of Lent is the psalter of Week 3.

3. Now turn to the appropriate week of the psalter and to the appropriate day of the week and you will find the psalms with their proper antiphons. If you want to begin with a hymn suited to the season you will find a selection of hymns and poems in Appendix II, beginning on p. 1102.

4. At the conclusion of the psalter, turn back to the proper of seasons to the find the Scripture reading, responsory, Benedictus or Magnificat antiphon, and concluding prayer for the day.

One of the great blessings of the Office is that it presents a rich selection of Scriptures for meditation appropriate to the different seasons of the Church's year. In Advent, the Scriptures and intercessions prepare us for the second coming of Christ, as well as preparing us to celebrate his first coming. At Christmastide, the joyful mystery of the incarnation is taken up in prayer and meditation. In Lent, the

Scriptures and intercessions call us 'to repent and believe the Gospel'. As Holy Week approaches, the sufferings of Christ and the victory of the cross become the focus of our prayer. In Eastertide the Office brings before us the glories of the resurrection and life in the Spirit. Praying the Office through the seasons of the Christian year is one of the Church's most effective means of catechesis. It enables us to unite our lives with Christ, and to enter into 'every spiritual blessing' with which the Father has blessed us in Christ (Ephesians 1:3).

The Proper of Saints

The third section of *Morning and Evening Prayer* is the Proper of Saints, beginning on p. 709. This section is in two parts. The first part, Saints of the General Calendar, gives the date and the instructions necessary for each saints' day, directing us where to find the psalmody, readings, antiphons, intercessions, concluding prayers for the appropriate day. The second part, beginning on p. 965, is called The Common Offices. This part has the hymn, psalmody, antiphons, Scripture reading, intercessions and concluding prayer for each category of saints' day: the Blessed Virgin Mary, Apostle, Martyr, Pastor and so on. These Common Offices are the basic forms used to celebrate the saints' days. Any variations are given under the particular date in the first part of the Proper of Saints, Saints of the General Calendar.

The saints' days are in three categories: Solemnities, Feasts, and Memorias. The Office for Solemnities and Feasts takes precedence over the Office being followed at the time, but the Office for Memorias usually continues to follow the psalmody as it occurs in ordinary time or in the proper of seasons.

There are only 15 solemnities in the General Calendar (see pp. xlvii—lix) for the year. A solemnity is like a Sunday in that it has Evening Prayer I on the preceding day, and its own hymn, antiphons, reading, responsory and concluding prayer.

Feasts are more common (25 in the General Calendar), and they do not have Evening Prayer I, unless they are Feasts of the Lord occurring on a Sunday. As with a solemnity, the psalmody for a feast day is special to that day.

Memorias are more common still (over 60 in the General Calendar), but their psalmody is usually taken from the appropriate day of the week of the Church Year. Occasionally the hymn, reading, antiphons for the Benedictus and Magnificat, and the intercessions are proper for the memoria.

As with the Proper of Seasons, it is quite easy to find your way around and to discover the texts for a particular day's prayer. Turn to the date for the saint's day in the Proper of Saints. Immediately after the saint's name or the title of the day you will find in italics the status of the day, whether it is a Solemnity, Feast, or Memoria, and all the necessary instructions for finding the appropriate hymn, psalmody and so on.

1. Solemnities. For example, All Saints Day, 1 November, p. 920. Evening Prayer I is set out in the book. For the psalmody of Morning Prayer you are directed to Morning Prayer, Sunday, Week 1. The rest of the Office is on pp. 925—926. The psalmody for Evening Prayer II is set out in the book, pp. 926—928.

2. Feasts. Take, for example, the Feast of St Luke, 18 October, p. 913. For Morning Prayer the hymn is found in the Common of Apostles. The psalmody in that for Sunday, Week 1. The Scripture reading, intercessions, etc. are given. For Evening Prayer, the hymn and the psalmody come from the Common of Apostles, and the Scripture reading, intercessions and other parts are proper to the day.

3. Memoria. Take, for example, the Memoria for St Dominic, 8 August. The whole Office for the day, apart from the concluding prayer which is proper, can be found in the

Common of Pastors, or in the Common of Men Saints: Religious. Alternatively, the psalmody of the day of the week in ordinary time can be used.

The letter to the Hebrews brings before us the examples of the saints of the past in order to inspire us to greater faith in Christ (Hebrews 11—12). One of the purposes of celebrating the saints' days is to continue that tradition, to be reminded constantly of the holy men and women who have gone before us. Another reason for celebrating the saints' days is to invoke the prayers of the saints so that we may have their help in our own walk of faith, and that the fruits of the Spirit so evident in their lives may live in the Church in our time.

6 Prayer During the Day and the Office of Readings

The full form of the Divine Office includes three times of prayer during the day (Before Noon, Midday, Afternoon), plus the Office of Readings. The complete texts are found in the three-volume edition of the Office. Few people who are beginning to pray the Office will want to start off on the full diet of the seven hours of prayer, so I will only give a brief outline of Prayer During the Day and the Office of Readings.

Prayer During the Day

Prayer During the Day expresses the tradition of praying during the day's work, and the pattern of these three Hours is designed to meet the needs of those who say only one of the three Hours as well as of those who celebrate all three. Prayer During the Day has a simple structure: introductory verse, hymn, psalmody (three short psalms or parts of longer psalms), short Scripture reading, versicle, concluding prayer. As with Morning and Evening Prayer, Prayer During the Day has its own set of proper readings for the different seasons of the Christian year.

The Office of Readings

The Office of Readings follows a straightforward pattern of hymn, psalmody (three psalms or sections of longer psalms), two substantial readings (each with their own responsory) and concluding prayer. As with Morning and Evening Prayer, the psalmody of the Office of Readings follows a four-weekly cycle. The psalms of this cycle are not included in the commentary in Part 2.

The two readings are at the heart of this hour, and the

prime purpose of the Office of Readings is 'to present to the people of God . . . a more extensive meditation on sacred scripture and on the best writings of spiritual authors.' (GILH n. 55). The first reading is always from Scripture, and the second is either from the works of the Fathers or later spiritual writers. There is an extensive set of Proper readings for the different seasons of the Christian year and for the saints' days. The readings provide rich food from the Church's spiritual and theological tradition.

Anyone who has reached the stage of being at home with Morning and Evening Prayer should have no difficulty finding their way around Prayer During the Day and the Office of Readings.

7 Learning to Pray the Psalms

The psalms form a major part of Morning and Evening Prayer, therefore learning to pray the psalms is crucial to learning to pray the Office. The psalms have 'the power to raise men's minds to God, to evoke in them holy and wholesome thoughts, to help them give thanks in time of favour, and to bring consolation and constancy in adversity.' (GILH ¶100). The psalms reflect the whole range of human experience, from agony to ecstasy, and they speak with a sharp directness and honesty. 'Each psalm has a literal meaning which even in our times cannot be neglected. Though these songs originated many centuries ago in a semitic culture, they express the pain and hope, misery and confidence of men of any age and land.' (GILH ¶107).

Most importantly for prayer, 'The Holy Spirit, who inspired the psalmists, is always present with his grace to those believing Christians who with good intention sing and recite these songs.' (GILH ¶101). It is the promised presence of the Spirit that makes the psalms vital for anyone learning to pray. The same Spirit who inspired the psalmists is with us and in us, to move our own hearts and minds as he first moved the psalmist.

This means that anyone praying the psalms must come willing to be taught by the Spirit, willing to be blown where the wind of God moves. 'Whoever sings the psalms properly, meditating as he passes from verse to verse, is always prepared to respond in his heart to the movements of that Spirit who inspired the psalmist and is present to devout men and women ready to accept his grace.' (GILH ¶104). As we pray the psalms our heart is opened to the emotions which stirred the psalmist, both joy and anguish, praise and confession.

Anyone who has turned to the psalms knows that they present all sorts of difficulties to the Christian learning to pray. This chapter aims to bring out the richness of praying the psalms as well as identifying the difficulties and helping to resolve them.

The poetry of the Psalms

Poetry is very different from prose. The rhythm and metre of poetry are part of the meaning, because they determine the emphasis given to particular words. Poetry penetrates through the mind and moves the heart. Poetry translated from one language into another often loses its unique power, but in the case of the poetry of the Old Testament we are extraordinarily fortunate because the basic structure of Hebrew poetry survives translation and can be clearly picked up in English. Knowing something about the shape of Hebrew poetry can help in understanding the movement and development of thought in a psalm.

The basic rhythm of Hebrew poetry is a rhythm of meaning, and is called parallelism. Parallelism means that in any single verse the thought of the second line runs parallel to the first. The second line echoes the first. For example:

> *O praise the Lord, all you nations,*
> *acclaim him all you peoples.* (Psalm 116(117))

> *The Lord's is the earth and its fulness,*
> *the world and all its people.* (Psalm 23(24))

There are many different kinds of parallelism, but three of the most common are:

1. Repetitive parallelism (technically known as synonymous parallelism), where the second line simply repeats the first. The two examples just quoted from Psalms 116 and 23 are repetitive parallelism.

2. Contrasting parallelism (known also as antithetic paral-

lelism), where the second line makes a contrast with the first. For example:

> *Some trust in chariots or horses,*
> *but we in the name of the Lord.*
>
> *They will collapse and fall,*
> *but we shall hold and stand firm.* (Psalm 19(20))

3. Complementary parallelism (or synthetic parallelism), where the second line complements, develops, or fills out the meaning of the first line. For example:

> *If the Lord does not build the house,*
> *in vain do its builders labour.* (Psalm 126(127))

Understanding the different types of parallelism enables us to enter into the vibrant stream of thought flowing through a psalm. (Any major commentary on the Psalms will give a full analysis of the different types of parallelism).

The other main feature of Hebrew poetry is its metre, where a pattern of accented syllables gives the psalm a strong beat. Metre is obviously lost in translation from one language to another, but the English version of the Psalms used in the Divine Office (the Grail version) tries to reproduce something of the beat of Hebrew poetry.

The setting of the psalms

Most of the psalms appear at first sight to be poems written by and for an individual, and that is often how we understand them. In fact the reverse is true. The primary setting of the psalms is not individual prayer but corporate prayer, liturgical prayer, the prayer of the Temple liturgy. Even those psalms which most intensely portray the anguish or thanksgiving of an individual were used in Israel's liturgy. That is why they are in the Book of Psalms. The psalms (and so the Office) teach us that individual prayer and corporate prayer are not two radically different ways of praying. Corporate prayer can be intensely personal, even though it is not private. The psalms express the deepest movements of the soul in words that are designed to be prayed in common in the great congregation, not in private. When prayed in private, alone, the psalms by their very nature join us to the whole body of Christ.

Types of psalms

There are many ways of analysing the different types of psalms, but most of them can be put into two main groups: psalms of praise and psalms of lament. (See Claus Westermann, *Praise and Lament in the Psalms,* John Knox Press, Atlanta, 1981).

1 Psalms of Praise

Morning and Evening Prayer for each day always contain a psalm or canticle of praise. The third psalm of Morning Prayer is always a psalm of praise.

The psalms of praise fall into two groups, each reflecting a different style of praise, descriptive or declarative.

1. *Descriptive* praise means that the psalm offers praise to God by describing who he is and what he has done, *at all times and in all places.* These psalms praise God for the broad sweep of his actions in history. For example, take one of the most popular psalms in the Office, Psalm 112(113):

> *Praise, O servants of the Lord,*
> *praise the name of the Lord!*
> *May the name of the Lord be blessed*
> *both now and for evermore!*
> *From the rising of the sun to its setting*
> *praised be the name of the Lord!*
>
> *From the dust he lifts up the lowly,*
> *from his misery he raises the poor*
> *to set him in the company of princes,*
> *yes, with the princes of his people.*

2. *Declarative* praise means that the psalm declares God's greatness because of his *unique action* in the life of the nation or of an individual. This second group of psalms of praise is more particular and at times more personal in its praise than those in the first group.

Psalm 123(124) is a classic example of a psalm which declares God's power active in saving Israel from the particular threat of destruction in the Exile to Babylon.

Blessed be the Lord who did not give us
a prey to their teeth!
Our life, like a bird, has escaped
from the snare of the fowler.

Indeed the snare has been broken
and we have escaped.
Our help is in the name of the Lord,
who made heaven and earth.

Psalm 29(30) is an example of a psalm which declares God's mercy active in saving an individual:

I will praise you, Lord, you have rescued me
and have not let my enemies rejoice over me. . . .

Sing psalms to the Lord, you who love him,
give thanks to his holy name.

Setting

The psalms of praise are the prayers of God's people at worship in the Temple. The liturgy of the Temple and the festivals of Israel proclaimed the great events of Israel's salvation, and the psalms of praise of the people were the people's response to this revelation. A psalm like Psalm 117(118) was sung by the congregation at the Feast of Tabernacles.

The setting of the psalms of praise of the individual is still the worship of the Temple. The focus, though, is not on God's salvation of the nation but on his salvation of the individual. God's goodness to Israel was shown not only in the great events of her history, but also in his constant care for each person. An individual would give thanks to God for a personal deliverance (from illness or injustice) by bringing an offering to the priest. As the victim was sacrificed in the Temple a psalm would be recited as a public acknowledgement of the Lord's help, and the worshippers would be invited to join in the sacrificial meal. This is the setting of Psalm 115(116).

How can I repay the Lord
for his goodness to me?
The cup of salvation I will raise;
I will call on the Lord's name.

My vows to the Lord I will fulfill
before all his people,
in the courts of the house of the Lord,
in your midst, O Jerusalem.

Themes

The dominant themes of the psalms of praise sung at Israel's festivals are the themes of creation and redemption: God at work in nature, and God at work in saving his people, especially in the Exodus.

Those psalms which give thanks have a wide variety of themes: thanks for peace and prosperity, and thanks for deliverance from sickness, enemies, injustice or death.

Pattern

The psalms of praise all have a similar pattern: call to praise, reasons for praise, call to praise. Psalm 32(33) (Week 1, Tuesday Morning) is an example of a psalm of praise which takes up the theme of God's power in creation and in the Exodus. The call to praise begins the psalm:

Ring out your joy to the Lord, O you just;
for praise is fitting for loyal hearts.

Then comes the main body of the psalm, revealing the reasons why we should praise the Lord – for his wonders in nature and creation, and for his wonders revealed in Israel's history:

For the word of the Lord is faithful
and all his works to be trusted . . .

By his word the heavens were made,
by the breath of his mouth all the stars.
He collects the waves of the ocean;
he stores up the depths of the sea. . . .

A king is not saved by his army,
nor a warrior preserved by his strength.
A vain hope for safety is the horse;
despite its power it cannot save.

The Lord looks on those who revere him,
on those who hope in his love,
to rescue their souls from death,
to keep them alive in famine.

Finally, the call to praise is repeated and a brief prayer is offered:

May your love be upon us, O Lord,
as we place all our hope in you.

Another example of a psalm of praise which takes as its theme God's wonders in creation and in Israel's history is Psalm 97(98). It begins with a call to praise:

Sing a new song to the Lord

and immediately goes on to give the reasons for praise,

for he has worked wonders.
His right hand and his holy arm
have brought salvation.

The Lord has made know his salvation;
has shown justice to the nations.
He has remembered his truth and love
for the house of Israel.

Psalm 31(32) (Week 1, Thursday Evening) is a good example of a psalm of praise which takes up the experience of an individual. The psalm begins:

Happy the man whose offence is forgiven,
whose sin is remitted.
O happy the man to whom the Lord
imputes no guilt,
in whose spirit is no guile.

Then it goes on to the reason for thanksgiving:

But now I have acknowledged my sins;
my guilt I did not hide.
I said: 'I will confess
my offence to the Lord.'
And you, Lord, have forgiven
the guilt of my sin.

The psalm concludes with the call to praise:

Rejoice, rejoice in the Lord,
exult, you just!
O come, ring out your joy,
all you upright of heart.

Sometimes the psalms of praise (like this one) are not addressed to God but are psalms about God to be sung in his presence and in the presence of his people.

Praying the psalms of praise

The scriptures urge us 'to give thanks to God in all circumstances' (Ephesians 5:20), and the psalms of praise and thanksgiving certainly help us to do that. When our circumstances are joyful the psalms of praise turn our joy into worship and enable us to praise the one who is the source of all joy.

When our circumstances are difficult and trying, how can we pray the psalms of praise? In difficult times, praying the psalms of praise pulls us out of ourselves and enables us to live in the light of God's presence, guided by the one who makes 'all things work for good for those who love him' (Romans 8:28).

Praying the psalms of praise when we are sad or worried introduces us to one of the most profound mysteries of the Office. When we pray the Office we are not praying in our own name 'so much as in the name of the whole body of Christ.' (GILH ¶108). As we pray the Office we are joined to all God's people in their joy and sorrow. If we are depressed and the psalm we are praying is a psalm of praise we can pray the psalm for someone else, someone who is joyful, as a way of sharing their experience, as a way of learning to 'rejoice with those who rejoice' (Romans 12:15). It can be helpful to actually think of someone we know who is rejoicing, and pray with them in mind as we pray the psalm.

2 *Psalms of Lament*

Psalms of lament are by far the most common type in the Scriptures, and they are prominent in the Office.

Setting and Themes

Some of these psalms are psalms of national lament, expressing the cry of the people in times of national disaster. Psalm 76(77) is a fine example:

I cry aloud to God,
cry aloud to God that he may hear me.

'Will the Lord reject us for ever?
Will he show us his favour no more?
Has his love vanished for ever?
Has his promise come to an end?
Does God forget his mercy
or in anger withhold his compassion?

But most of the psalms of lament reflect the cry of an individual suffering some private grief, either sickness, the attack of enemies, or the consequences of personal sin.

Take Psalm 50(51) (Week 1, Friday Morning) for example. Psalms of lament usually begin by calling on God for his help:

Have mercy on me, God, in your kindness.
In your compassion blot out my offence.
O wash me more and more from my guilt
and cleanse me from my sin.

They move on to describe the plight of the psalmist, often using standard poetic images:

My offences truly I know them;
my sin is always before me...

Make me hear rejoicing and gladness,
that the bones you have crushed may revive.

They generally conclude with an expression of confidence in God and in his saving help:

A humbled, contrite heart you will not spurn.

Praying the psalms of lament

The psalms of lament put us in the same situation for prayer as the psalms of praise. If we are in trouble, they can enable us to express our anguish, our cry to God. They give us words at times when words fail us. They can winch us out of the pit. But what if we are joyful, and do not feel like praying a lament? Again, as with the psalms of praise, we can pray the lament as part of the body of Christ, entering into the experience of someone who is in despair, someone whose experience the words of the psalm describes. It is one way we can 'weep with those who weep' (Romans 12:15). In praying the laments we can pray with people throughout the world who are suffering for their faith, or suffering because of the injustice and greed of the rich and powerful.

It is the bringing of our own experience of life to the praying of the psalms which makes the four-week cycle of the psalms in the Office never pall. Because our life and the life of the Church are constantly changing we bring something fresh to the psalms every time we pray them. Over the years certain psalms will become etched into our memory because they come to be associated with particular events in our lives. These psalms shed God's light on the events and when we come to the psalm again in the four-week cycle, we bring a memory of meaning which greatly enriches our prayer.

As we bring our lives and the life of the world to God in praying the psalms a rich store of memory builds up, particular events being associated with particular Scriptures, and so the prayer of the Office brings us into a place where our past, present and future become one in prayer before the Lord.

The antiphon, heading, and sentence

The Office offers three further aids in learning to pray the psalms and in turning them into Christian prayer: the antiphon, the heading, and the sentence which go with each psalm. We have met them already.

The *antiphons* at the beginning and end of each psalm are carefully chosen: to help us turn the psalm into personal prayer; to pick out a line which is central to the psalm; to focus on the particular festival of the Christian Year which is being celebrated; and to provide variety in praying the psalms. The different antiphons help us to pray the same psalm in different ways at different times of the year.

On Sundays in *Morning and Evening Prayer* there is a piling up of antiphons which can be confusing. On Sunday Week 1 there are five antiphons given for each psalm, according to the particular Sunday of the Christian year. Looking at the antiphons between the psalms, the first antiphon goes with the preceding psalm and the second one with the following psalm. For example on Week 1, Sunday Evening Prayer I, between the first psalm (Psalm 140(141)) and the second psalm (Psalm 141(142)) the antiphons are listed under different Sundays of the year.

> Advent, Antiphon: *Proclaim it, say to the peoples: Behold, God will come and save us.*

This antiphon goes with the preceding psalm, Psalm 140.

> Advent, Antiphon 2: *Behold the Lord will come, and all his holy ones with him. On that day a great light will appear, alleluia.*

This antiphon goes with the following psalm, Psalm 141.

The *headings* are intended to highlight the meaning of the psalm, and its importance in Christian life.

The *sentence* at the beginning of each psalm is always a phrase from the New Testament or the Fathers of the Church and is designed to show how the psalm is to be prayed in the light of the new revelation of Christ.

Here are some examples from Week 1, Sunday, Morning Prayer, for illustration. The first psalm is Psalm 62(63).

Five antiphons are given. The first antiphon (Advent) expresses the Old Testament prophets' vision of the age of the Messiah.

> *On that day the mountains will run with sweet wine. The hills will flow with milk and honey.*

We pray the psalm in Advent with longing for the coming of Christ.

The second antiphon (Lent, Sunday 1) picks up the central theme of the psalm as an offering of praise and adoration to God, an offering of our life which we seek to make more complete during the season of Lent.

The third antiphon (Lent, Sunday 5) highlights one line from the psalm, *You, my God, have become my help*, and teaches us to pray the psalm with Christ on the eve of his passion.

The fourth antiphon (Eastertide) links the psalm's theme of thirst for God with Jesus' promise to give the water of life, the water of the Spirit, to anyone who comes to him and drinks (John 7:37—39):

> *Let anyone who is thirsty come and drink the water of life, a free gift for those who desire it, alleluia.*

The fifth antiphon (Through the Year) is used on the other Sundays of the Christian year. This antiphon begins the psalmody on Sunday morning, the day when we recall the power of God in raising Christ from the dead.

> *To you, O God, I keep vigil at dawn, to look upon your power, alleluia.*

The *heading* identifies the main theme of the psalm as:

> *A soul thirsting for God.*

The *sentence* reminds us that the Christian is to be constantly seeking God, ready for the Day when we will each give an account to God for our lives:

> *Let the man who has put away the deeds of the night watch for God.*

The third psalm is Psalm 149.

Again, there are five *antiphons*. The first (Advent) looks forward to the renewal of Jerusalem which was begun with the first coming of Christ and the creation of the Church, and will be completed with the triumphant return of Christ at the end of time.

> *Behold, a great Prophet will come and he will renew Jerusalem, alleluia.*

The second antiphon, *The Lord takes delight in his people. He crowns the poor with salvation*, is for use on the first Sunday of Lent. This antiphon comes straight from the psalm itself, and encourages the 'poor in spirit', those who know they need God, with the promise of salvation.

The third antiphon is for use on the fifth Sunday of Lent. We pray with Christ as he is glorified through his death and resurrection.

> *Now the hour has come for the Son of Man to be glorified.*

The fourth antiphon is for Eastertide, *Let the saints rejoice in glory, alleluia.* Through the psalm we express our joy in the resurrection of Jesus.

The fifth antiphon, *Let Sion's sons exalt in their king, alleluia*, is for use on other Sundays of the year. It is a line straight from the psalm. We, Sion's sons and daughters, exalt in the risen Christ, our king.

The *heading* describes the general nature of the psalm:

> *The song of joy of the saints.*

The *sentence* is from one of the Fathers, Hesychius, and indicates that the psalm is the song of the new community of God's people, the Church, rejoicing in Christ:

> *The members of the Church, God's new people, will rejoice in their king, who is Christ.*

Anyone who has turned to the psalms knows that they present all sorts of difficulties to the Christian learning to pray. What do we do with all the references to Israel, Jerusalem, the temple, the calls for vengeance on one's enemies? The next chapter aims to show how each of these obstacles to prayer turns out to be a blessing.

8 The Psalms: Prayer of Israel and Prayer of the Church

The psalms are obviously the prayer of Israel. How can they also be the prayer of the Church, Christian prayer? Part of the answer was given in the previous chapter. The psalms reflect the universal experience of humankind: joy, suffering, work, family, enemies, death, and in and above all this, our relationship with God. The psalms of praise and the psalms of lament become our prayer as they either reflect our own experience or enable us to enter into the experience of others. But there is more to praying the psalms than this.

In Acts 4 we have a striking example of how the early Church prayed the psalms. Peter and John had been hauled before the Sanhedrin and told to stop preaching the Gospel. On their release the Church gathered to give thanks to God, and the substance of their prayer was a psalm, Psalm 2.

> *Why this uproar among the nations,*
> *this impotent muttering of the peoples?*
> *Kings on earth take up position,*
> *princes plot together*
> *against the Lord and his Anointed.*
> (Acts 4:25—26, citing Psalm 2:1—2)

The Church gathered in prayer interprets the kings of Psalm 2 as a reference to Herod and Pontius Pilate, the nations as the gentiles (Rome), and the peoples as meaning the Jews. The *Anointed* of Psalm 2 is understood as referring to Jesus (Acts 4:27). Thus the early Church interpreted Psalm 2 as a prophecy about Jesus, the Messiah, as well as a prophecy about the experience of his Church facing opposition in the world.

We have here the key to understanding the psalms as Christian prayer. The Church sees in the psalms the experience of Christ and the experience of his Church. These two, Christ and his Church, are two parts of the one whole. The psalms are the prayer of the Church as the Body of Christ. They are the prayer of the whole Body, head and members, Christ and his people. St Augustine expressed this truth in his typically profound way:

> When we speak to God in prayer for mercy, we do not separate the Son from him; and when the body of the Son prays, it separates not its Head from itself: and it is the one saviour of his Body, our Lord Jesus Christ, the Son of God, who both prays for us, and prays in us, and is prayed to by us. He prays for us, as our Priest; he prays in us, as our Head; He is prayed to by us, as our God. Let us therefore recognize in him our words, and his words in us . . . Therefore we pray to him, through him, in him; and we speak with him, and he speaks with us; we speak in him, he speaks in us the prayer of this psalm. *(On Psalm 85* PL XXXVII, 1081*)*.

The next chapter is devoted to exploring how the psalms take us into the heart of Christ, the head of the Body, and into his prayer to the Father. The rest of this chapter will show how the psalms can be understood as an expression of the experience of the members of the Body, the experience of every Christian.

Israel and the Church

The fact that the psalms are the prayer of Israel and the nation of Israel is the theme of so many of them presents such an obstacle to some Christians that they have deliberately cut out the name *Israel* from parts of their psalter. Such a radical solution is a denial of our history. Israel's history is the Church's history. As Christians we praise God for his covenant with Abraham, Isaac and Jacob; for the Exodus, Jerusalem, the Temple, the return from Exile. But we reinterpret the ancient history of Israel in the light of its fulfilment in Christ. The Old Testament itself shows how

Israel re-interpreted its past history in the light of new revelations of God's love and power. The Exodus was re-interpreted as foreshadowing the return from Exile. The Davidic monarchy was re-interpreted as foreshadowing the reign of the Messiah. The New Testament authors, following the lead given by Jesus himself, took this process even further and re-interpreted the whole of Israel's history in the light of Christ, the supreme revelation of God.

St Paul calls the Church 'the Israel of God' (Galatians 6:17), the community of the new covenant, the community which has inherited the promises made to Israel of old (Galatians 3:6—9,29; 4:21—31). But he sees the Church not as the replacement of Israel so much as the transformation of Israel. He underlines our unity with Israel by drawing a humbling picture. Israel is an olive tree, and the Church is 'a wild olive shoot' grafted onto the tree. He says to the Church: 'Remember, it is not you who support the root, but the root that supports you' (Romans 11:18).

John's Gospel, too, reveals Jesus to be the fulfilment of Judaism, of all its institutions and festivals. John tells of how Jesus came to 'his own' (Israel), but his own people did not receive him. He then formed a new 'his own', made up of all those who received him, who believed in his name, who were born of the Spirit in baptism (John 1:11—12; 3:5—8).

The rest of this chapter takes up key events and institutions in the life of Israel which feature prominently in the psalms, and looks at the way in which they can be understood in the light of Christ, and the meaning which they can take on in Christian prayer.

1 The Creation

The psalms abound with references to the creation. The most characteristic theme is that the Lord who has revealed himself as Israel's saviour is the same Lord who made heaven and earth. God's relationship of love for his people began at creation. He is the source of the world's beauty and bounty.

The world is a constant revelation of his glory and of his goodness to all people. These are themes which every Christian can take up in prayer, especially because the world is for us a revelation of Christ. He is the one through whom 'all things were made' (John 1:3), and for whom all things were created (Colossians 1:16).

When we come to the way in which the psalms speak of creation three things may strike us as unusual. First, the psalmist simply identifies the forces of nature with the actions of God. It is the Lord who *showers down snow white as wool, scatters hoar-frost like ashes, hurls down hailstones like crumbs* (Psalm 147). We think of the weather in a much more impersonal way. There is obviously some poetic licence in the psalmist's language, but more importantly there is a conviction which we in our age need to recover: the world in which we live is God's world. While we understand far better than the ancient Israelites the way the world of nature works, if we lose the sense that the world is God's gift, and that we are responsible to him for what we do with it, we will extinguish life on the planet.

Linked to this simplicity with which the psalmists speak of God's action in sending rain, sun, wind and weather is a second feature which seems strange to us – the way in which creation is invited to praise God.

> *Let the heavens rejoice and the earth be glad,*
> *let the sea and all within it thunder praise,*
> *let the land and all it bears rejoice,*
> *all the trees of the wood shout for joy.* (Psalm 95(96)).

When the psalms call on all creation to praise the Lord, this is not just poetical imagination, but a profound insight into the link between the creator and the creation. All created things, including humankind, are made by God and so must respond to their creator with praise. Praise is the response of creatures to their creator. Men and women can praise God consciously, with heart and mind and voice. The rest of creation praises God simply by the fact of its existence, as a work of art praises the one who painted it simply by being what it is, a thing of beauty. All creation praises the Lord by the fact of its existence and the psalms call on creation to go on doing what it has always done – praise the Lord.

A third feature of the references to creation in the psalms which puzzles us is the picture of the world the psalmists assume. We know that the earth is round, that it moves through space in orbit around the sun, that it is basically made of rock, with a thin crust and a molten core. The psalmist's picture is very different. The ancient Hebrew understanding of the world, as found in Genesis 1 for example, is of the earth resting on water ('the waters under the earth') but supported firmly by pillars which are the bases of the mountains. Above the earth is a solid dome called the firmament. The firmament is like an up-turned basin dividing 'the waters above the firmament' (from which the rain, snow and hail come) from 'the waters under the firmament' (the sea). When it rains, God is said to open 'windows' in the firmament to release the waters above the earth.

While Israel's account of creation as found in Genesis 1 is radically different from the myths of her neighbours, there are some allusions to these ancient myths in the language of the psalms. The most common one is the idea that at creation God brought order out of chaos by taming the sea. The sea sometimes appears in the psalms as a symbol of the forces of chaos which threaten to break out again and engulf God's people, and the Lord is the mighty Creator-God who restrains the sea and protects his people.

2 The Covenant

Covenant is not a word we use much today, but the idea of covenant is central to modern life. A covenant is a binding agreement between two parties. A treaty between two nations is a covenant. A commercial contract is a covenant. The marriage vow is a covenant. The whole basis of Israel's life was the covenant God made with his people. It was God's covenant that made Israel his people. Time and time again the psalmists appeal to the covenant as the basis of their prayer for God's help for the nation and for the individual.

The psalms constantly allude to God's covenant with Abraham and his covenant at Sinai. God's covenant with Abraham marked the beginning of Israel as a nation. Genesis tells how the Lord appeared to Abraham and said to him:

> Behold, my covenant is with you, and you shall be the father of a multitude of nations . . . I will establish my covenant between me and you and your descendants after you throughout their generations for an everlasting covenant, to be God to you and to your descendants after you. And I will give to you, and to your descendants after you . . . the land of Canaan, for an everlasting possession; and I will be their God (Genesis 17:1—8).

When Israel was under threat of invasion, when it looked as if her enemies would wrest the land from them, it was to this covenant with Abraham that Israel appealed.

God renewed this covenant with Jacob, Abraham's grandson (Genesis 28:10—17), and when the psalmists refer to the nation of Israel as 'Jacob' it is Jacob as the heir of the covenant with Abraham that is in mind. To call Israel 'Jacob' or to refer to God as the 'God of Jacob' is to refer back to the covenant God made with Abraham and renewed with Jacob.

The next covenant God made with Israel was the covenant at Sinai. The covenant God made with Abraham promised him a lot and asked of him very little, just that he circumcise his sons as a sign of the covenant. But the covenant at Sinai (sometimes called the Mosaic covenant, although the covenant was not with Moses but with the whole nation) demanded much more of the people. Obedience to the Law enshrined in the Ten Commandments was Israel's obligation under the covenant. At Sinai the Lord said to Moses:

> Thus you shall say to the house of Jacob, and tell the people of Israel: You have seen what I did to the Egyptians, and how I bore you on eagles' wings and brought you to myself. Now therefore, if you will obey my voice and keep my covenant, you shall be my own possession among all peoples; for all the earth is mine, and you shall be to me a kingdom of priests and a holy nation
>
> (Exodus 19:3—6)

At the making of the covenant the Lord revealed himself in words that are echoed on every page of the psalms:

> The LORD, the LORD, a God merciful and gracious, slow to anger, and abounding in steadfast love and faithfulness, keeping steadfast love for thousands, forgiving iniquity and transgression and sin, but who will by no means clear the guilty . . .
>
> (Exodus 34:6—7).

The psalms of praise praise the Lord because of his commitment to the covenant. The psalms of lament appeal to him on the basis of the covenant. The words *mercy, grace, steadfast love, faithfulness, forgiveness* are the notes out of which the music of the psalms is written. God's *mercy, love,* and *faithfulness* all refer to God's commitment to the covenant.

Israel's failure to keep the covenant led to its collapse. Ezekiel and Jeremiah prophesied a new covenant made not on tablets of stone, as was the covenant at Sinai, but written instead on the hearts of the people. This new covenant came into effect with Christ's sacrifice on the cross, his resurrection from the dead, and his gift of the Holy Spirit. The Lord's *mercy, grace, steadfast love, faithfulness* and *forgiveness* have been poured out in superabundance through Christ in the new covenant, and as we pray the covenant language of the psalms it is the new covenant which is our praise and the basis of our prayer for help.

3 The Exodus

The Exodus was the founding event of the nation of Israel, and the story of the Exodus resounds again and again in the psalms. To understand the psalms one must read the book of Exodus. Exodus tells how the Hebrews were in slavery in Egypt, and God 'remembered his covenant with Abraham' (Exodus 2:24) and sent Moses to lead them out of bondage into the promised land. Pharaoh proved to be stubborn and he refused to let the people go, so the Lord sent a series of plagues on Egypt to persuade him to change his mind. The climax of these plagues was the death of all the first-born in Egypt. Pharaoh let the people go, but quickly changed his mind and pursued them with his army to the shores of the Sea of Reeds. The Lord parted the waters of the sea by means of a strong east wind (Exodus 14) and the Israelites crossed to safety, leaving the pursuing army of Pharaoh trapped in the mud, to be engulfed by the returning waters.

The Israelites journeyed to Mount Sinai and there received the covenant and the Ten Commandments (see the previous section). At Sinai the Lord appeared to Moses and Israel in a way which is recalled in every account in the psalms of God's coming to save his people. When the Lord appeared on Sinai Exodus records how:

> There were peals of thunder and flashes of lightning, dense cloud on the mountain and a very loud trumpet blast; and, in the camp, all the people trembled. Then Moses led the people out of the camp to meet God; and they took their stand at the bottom of the mountain. Mount Sinai was entirely wrapped in smoke, because the Lord had descended on it in the form of fire. The smoke rose like smoke from a furnace and the whole mountain shook violently. Moses spoke, and God answered him in the thunder . . .
>
> (Exodus 19:16—19).

This appearance of the Lord (known as a theophany) on Sinai etched itself into the consciousness of Israel, and when the psalms speak of God's appearing, it is usually in terms of earthquake, fire, thunder and lightning.

Immediately following God's appearance is the account of the giving of the Ten Commandments, Israel's obligation under the covenant. One of the distinctive features of the psalms is their appeal to God as a God of justice, a God who is concerned above all for the widow, the orphan and the stranger. This revelation of God as a God of justice is inherent in the law given at Sinai.

From Mount Sinai the Israelites wandered for forty years in the wilderness, and several incidents from those desert wanderings make their appearance in the psalms, especially the giving of water from the rock (Exodus 17:1—7) and the constant grumbling of the people against Moses and Aaron. (See the commentary on the invitatory, Psalm 94(95)).

Finally, the Israelites approached the promised land, the land of Canaan. Their first victories were over Sihon king of the Amorites and Og king of Bashan, and Israel's victory over these two kings features in the psalms as a symbol of God's power to bring his people into the promised land and to give them victory over all their enemies. (See the commentary on Psalm 135(136)).

This whole experience of the Exodus, the giving of the Law at Sinai, the wilderness wanderings, and the entry into the promised land is reinterpreted by the New Testament in the light of Christ. The sentence and the antiphons of the psalms in the Office indicate the way in which these events are taken up in Christ and so in Christian prayer.

For the Church, the Exodus from Egypt foreshadows the Cross and Resurrection of Christ, the founding events of the new covenant, the mighty acts of God by which he delivered his people from slavery to sin and fear of death.

Jesus' commandments become the Christians' law – Matthew's Gospel presents Jesus as the new Moses who delivers his teaching in the Sermon on the Mount, a teaching which supersedes the Law given on Mount Sinai.

The wandering in the wilderness becomes a symbol of the Christian's journey through this world on the way to the promised land, to the presence of God in heaven. On this journey we are fed with the manna of the eucharist and the water from the rock is none other that the gift of the Holy Spirit.

The commentary takes up these themes as they occur in particular psalms.

4 The King

After the conquest of the promised land, the next significant event as far as the psalms are concerned is the anointing of David as king, and the covenant God made with David. The Lord said to the prophet Nathan concerning David: 'I will establish the throne of his kingdom for ever. I will be his father, and he shall be my son.' To David he said: 'Your house and your kingdom shall be made sure before me; your throne shall be established for ever' (2 Samuel 7:13,16). The role of the king in the life of the nation and the covenant God made with the house of David is reflected in many of the psalms. There are prophetic psalms addressed to the king on his accession to the throne, prayers for the king before he goes into battle, thanksgiving for the victories of the king, prayers of the king himself, a royal processional song and a bridal ode for the marriage of the king. The fate of the king was inseparable from the fate of the nation, and God's faithfulness to his covenant with the house of David was vital for the peace and prosperity of the whole nation.

The significance of these psalms for Christian prayer is brought out in the next chapter, Christ in the Psalms.

5 The Exile

Some time after the entry into the promised land the Israelite tribes divided into two separate kingdoms: the northern kingdom known as Israel, and the southern kingdom known as Judah, although the unity between the two was such that at times both kingdoms together were known as 'all Israel'.

David and Solomon ruled over 'all Israel', but after Solomon's death the division became permanent. Both kingdoms shared the same faith in the Lord God, but their traditions were different and their system of kingship was different.

The northern kingdom fell to the armies of Assyria in 721 BC, just over two hundred years after the death of Solomon. The Assyrians deported the inhabitants, brought in foreigners to populate the land, and these foreigners brought with them their own gods. This was effectively the end of the northern kingdom of Israel. The story is told in 2 Kings 17.

The southern kingdom of Judah survived until 587 BC when it too was conquered, by the armies of the Babylonian king Nebuchadnezzar. He deported the inhabitants of Jerusalem to Babylon, and it seemed as if the southern kingdom was about to go the way of the north and disappear off the map. For fifty years the people of Judah (hence their name, 'the Jews') were held captive in Babylon, but then with the fall of Babylon to Cyrus king of Persia in 539 BC they were allowed to return home and to begin rebuilding their ruined nation. This period of captivity in Babylon is known as the Exile, and it exercised a profound influence on the whole faith of Israel, and on the psalms. The anguish of the Exile and the joy of the return to Jerusalem form the background to a great many of the psalms, as is brought out in the commentary.

The impact of the Exile and the way in which we can pray the psalms of the Exile can be illustrated from a psalm which may express the prayer of the people of the northern kingdom after its destruction by the Assyrians, or the southern kingdom after it fell to the Babylonians. Psalm 79(80) is a national lament, a prayer of Israel calling on God for help. The walls of the city are broken down, and the city has been plundered and razed to the ground.

O shepherd of Israel, hear us,
you who lead Joseph's flock
shine forth from your cherubim throne
upon Ephraim, Benjamin, Manasseh.
O Lord, rouse up your might,
O Lord, come to our help.

God of hosts, bring us back;
let your face shine on us and we shall be saved.

In the psalm Israel is referred to by the names of some of its leading tribes, Ephraim, Benjamin, Manasseh.

A Christian can pray this lament for the Church today wherever God's people are suffering destruction and hopelessness, whether it is the Church suffering under a totalitarian state, or the Church suffering under military dictatorship, or the Church ravaged by materialism and greed. The antiphon, heading, and sentence introducing this psalm guide us to pray the psalm for the suffering Church.

Antiphon: *Lord, rouse up your might and come to our help.*
Heading: *Lord, come to visit your vine.*

The vine is a Scriptural metaphor for both Israel (Isaiah 5) and the Church (John 15).

Sentence: *Come, Lord Jesus* (Revelation 22:20)

is the cry of the early Church suffering under the oppression of Rome and longing for the return of the Saviour.

6 The Temple

The Temple features in the psalms as the centre of Israel's worship. Solomon's temple was a simple stone structure, about thirty metres long, twenty metres wide, and fifteen metres high, beautifully decorated inside with cedar panelling and gold inlay. The heart of the temple was the holy of holies, a room which was a perfect cube, about ten metres in each dimension. Inside the holy of holies was the ark of the covenant, the object which above all symbolized for Israel the presence of the Lord.

The ark of the covenant was a wooden chest about 1200 mm. long, 800 mm. wide, and 800 mm. high. On top of the ark was a sheet of gold called the mercy seat, and at each end of the mercy seat stood two golden cherubim, covering the seat with their wings. Inside the ark were two tablets of stone on which were written the Ten Commandments, Israel's obligation under the covenant, hence the name 'ark of the covenant'. There are various interpretations in the Old Testament of the spiritual significance of the ark, but one thing is clear: the ark was a physical symbol of the very presence of the Lord, the 'seat' of his presence, his throne on earth. The ark is called 'the ark of the LORD of Hosts who sits above the cherubim' (1 Samuel 4:4), the 'footstool of God' (1 Chronicles 28:2).

The presence of the ark in the holy of holies symbolized the presence of the Lord. The temple was the house of God because the ark of God was there. Israel's worship was centred around the temple because the temple was the place of God's presence. Hence the psalmist's devotion to the courts of the Lord and the pilgrim's joy in going up to Jerusalem. Further, the temple was a sign of God's choice of Israel and of Jerusalem. God chose to live in this city, in his temple. Sion was the mountain God chose for his home. It was the awesome significance of God's promise to dwell in the temple in Jerusalem that made the destruction of the city and its temple in 587 BC so devastating. The destruction of the temple seemed to be the end of God's presence with his people.

What do we do with the many references to the temple as we pray the psalms? In some cases, where the psalmist speaks of the temple the Christian understands the Church. For example, in Psalm 47(48):

O God, we ponder your love
within your temple.

Or Psalm 121(122):

I rejoiced when I heard them say:
'Let us go to God's house.'

But there is something more. Jesus spoke of his body as the new temple. When he said to the Jews: 'Destroy this temple, and in three days I will raise it up', St John comments: 'He was speaking of the temple that was his body.' (John 2:21). Therefore, as we pray the psalms, some references to the temple can be understood as references to Christ, the new temple, the true locus of God's presence.

7 Sion, Jerusalem

Closely linked to the temple is the city of Jerusalem and the particular hill on which the temple was built, Mount Sion. Sion was significant for two reasons: it was the site of both the temple and the palace of the king. It was the city of God and the city of the king. It is natural then that Sion and love of Sion are favourite themes of the psalms.

What is the Christian to do with such references in praying the psalms? The essential clues are again given to us in the New Testament. St Paul speaks of the Church as the new Jerusalem, the Jerusalem which is free 'and is our mother' (Galatians 4:26). The book of Hebrews says: 'You have come to Mount Zion and the city of the living God, the heavenly Jerusalem.' (Hebrews 12:22): so references to Jerusalem in the psalms can be understood by the Christian as references to the Church.

But Jerusalem in the New Testament came also to be a symbol for heaven. Revelation 21 and 22 give John's vision of the heavenly Jerusalem.

> I saw the holy city, the new Jerusalem, coming down out of heaven from God, prepared as a bride dressed for her husband . . .
> Here God lives among human beings. He will make his home among them; they will be his people, and he will be their God, God-with-them. He will wipe away all tears from their eyes, there will be no more death, and no more mourning or sadness or pain.
> (Revelation 21:2—4).

It is the reality of heaven, the heavenly city, that the Christian longs and prays for as the psalmist longs and prays for Zion, the earthly city.

Psalm 47(48) (Week 1, Thursday Morning) is a psalm which extols the wonders of Sion. In the Office, the sentence indicates that the psalm be prayed as an expression of the Christian's longing for the new Jerusalem.

Antiphon: *The Lord is great and worthy to be praised in the city of our God.*
Heading: *Thanksgiving for the salvation of God's people.*

Sentence: *He took me to the top of a great mountain, and showed me the holy city of Jerusalem* (Revelation 21:10).

Jerusalem, then, is a symbol of the Church on earth and in heaven.

8 Israel's Festivals

The worship of the temple revolved around three great annual festivals, later known as Passover, Pentecost, and Tabernacles. Many of the psalms were composed for and sung at these festivals. A whole group of psalms became know as the 'Psalms of Ascent' (Psalms 120—134) because they were sung by the pilgrims as they travelled up to Jerusalem to celebrate the great religious festivals.

According to the Law every male Israelite was bound to go up to Jerusalem three times a year to celebrate the major feasts (Deuteronomy 16:16).

Passover and Unleavened Bread

Unleavened Bread and Passover were originally two separate feasts which later merged into one, Unleavened Bread being at first the more important of the two. (Regulations governing the feasts can be found in Exodus 12:1—13:16 and Deuteronomy 16:1—8). The feast of Passover was a solemn feast during which the paschal lamb was sacrificed and eaten. The feast of Unleavened Bread lasted for the next seven days, during which time the people were forbidden to eat anything with leaven (yeast) in it. While the origin of these festivals lies in the customs of the nomadic tribes, they were later given a very specific meaning by being associated with the Exodus from Egypt. Passover and Unleavened Bread became the great festival celebrating the Exodus, and the psalms which specifically remember the Exodus were sung at Passover. Psalm 135(136) (Week 4, Monday Morning) was sung at the conclusion of the Passover meal.

The connection of this feast with the Christian Easter is obvious. Christ was crucified as the Lamb of God whose sacrifice takes away the sins of the world. The Eucharist is the festival in which we enter into the salvation won by his sacrifice, and in communion we participate in the sacrificial meal.

Pentecost, or Weeks

The feast of Weeks was a harvest festival, to celebrate the ingathering of the cereal harvest, and to give thanks to the Lord for the fertility of the land and the gift of food. (See Leviticus 23:15—21 for the regulations for this feast). It came seven weeks after Passover, hence the title, feast of Weeks. The Greek name is Pentecost meaning 'fifty' days after Passover. The Lesser Hallel (Psalms 113—118) were sung at this feast, as well as psalms like Psalm 103(104) which praise God for the gifts of the earth.

This feast also has obvious Christian connections. It was at Pentecost that the Holy Spirit came, and at Pentecost we celebrate the gift of the Holy Spirit as the Lord and giver of life, the source of spiritual fruitfulness and joy.

Tabernacles, or Shelters

At the end of the autumn came the feast of Tabernacles, which was again a harvest festival celebration, this time for the grape harvest. The pilgrims would live in shelters made out of branches for the seven days of the festival, a custom which was interpreted as recalling the wilderness journeyings of Israel's ancestors. Tabernacles was Israel's favourite festival, a time of eating, drinking and dancing, of magnificent processions and ceremonies in the temple. Sometimes it is just called 'The Feast'. A popular saying went: 'The man who has never seen the joy of the night of this feast has never seen real joy in all his life.' Psalm 117(118) (Week 2, Sunday Morning) is a processional psalm for the feast of Shelters.

9 Israel's Enemies

Perhaps the greatest difficulty a Christian has in praying the psalms is what to do with the hatred they sometimes heap on their enemies.

The Office deliberately cuts out some of the fiercest expressions, and even three whole psalms, 'because of their imprecatory character' (GILH ¶131). In Psalm 109(110), for example, verse 6 is omitted:

He judges nations, heaping up corpses,
he breaks heads over the whole wide world.

But other expressions which seek God's vengeance on one's enemies, prayers for victory over them and for their destruction, are left intact and are expected to form part of the Christian's prayer. How can this be, when our Lord commanded us to love our enemies, to bless, not curse them?

It is important first to ask: who were these enemies? In the national psalms of lament the identity of the enemies is clear: they are either the foreign kings and armies that constantly threatened Israel's existence, or the natural disasters of drought, famine, and plague. In the psalms of individual lament, the identity of the enemies is far from clear. The psalmists resort to generalized metaphors when describing their plight. Their enemies attack like *wild beasts*; the *waves* of the sea crash over them; the bottomless *pit* threatens to swallow them – all traditional ways of describing sickness, imminent death, or attack and ridicule by personal foes.

In the Old Testament justice was achieved by the law of

retribution, 'an eye for and eye and a tooth for a tooth'. This may seem barbaric to us, but in its original setting, this law drastically limited the destruction and death wrought by tribal feuds. The vengeance a wounded party could take was strictly limited, so that if the law was followed a minor crime would not lead to a major blood bath. With the coming of Jesus the old law is transformed, and instead of vengeance against one's enemies, Jesus commands us to love our enemies and pray for those who persecute us (Matthew 5:43—44). On the cross he sets the example for all Christians to follow.

A Christian facing injustice or malicious attack prays the psalms which cry for justice and for deliverance from enemies, but purges the psalm of any trace of personal resentment. Some of the prayers of the psalmist surrounded by his enemies will always form a part of the prayer of a Christian facing injustice. In those circumstances we pray for vindication and for the work of our enemies to be confounded, at all times remembering the New Testament teaching that the believer must not take judgement into his own hands, but look to the Lord for vindication. St Paul says:

> Never try to get revenge: leave that, my dear friends, to the Retribution. As Scripture says: *Vengeance is mine – I will pay them back,* the Lord promises. *If your enemy is hungry, give him something to eat; if thirsty, something to drink. By this, you will be heaping red-hot coals on his head.* Do not be mastered by evil, but master evil with good. (Romans 12:19—21).

St Paul's counsel leads us into another aspect of praying the psalms which cry out to God for help in the face of attack by enemies. Romans 12:21 reminds us that the ultimate enemy we face is not a particular person or group, but evil itself. The enemies against which we struggle and pray are the traditional trio of the world, the flesh, and the devil. The world is not the people of the world, whom 'God loved so much that he gave his only Son' to save them (John 3:16), but the structures of oppression and injustice which are implacably opposed to Christ and to Christian values. The flesh is not the body, but the evil which hides in our hearts and wills, and the passions which threaten to hurt and destroy others, enemies against which we struggle all our lives. The devil is the devil, the father of lies.

St Paul speaks of the enemies of humankind as being sin and death, and of Christ as the one who 'must reign until he has put *all his enemies under his feet* . The last enemy to be destroyed is death.' (1 Corinthians 15:25—26).

When we pray with Psalm 58(59):

> *Rescue me, God, from my foes;*
> *protect me from those who attack me.*

and with Psalm 107(108),

> *Give us help against the foe:*
> *for the help of man is vain.*
> *With God we shall do bravely*
> *and he will trample down our foes.*

it is these traditional foes of sin and the devil which we come against as we pray the psalms. St Paul speaks of prayer as the way in which the Christian puts on armour so 'that you may be able to stand against the wiles of the devil.' (Ephesians 6:11). Praying with the psalmists as they wrestle with their enemies is one way in which we can put on our armour.

9 Christ in the Psalms

Within the two main psalm-types (praise and lament) there is one group of psalms which has had a profound influence on Christian use of the psalms – the Royal Psalms. Scattered throughout the psalter are a number of psalms originally connected with the court or the person of the Davidic king. There are prophetic psalms addressed to the king, prayers for the king, thanksgiving for the king, prayers of the king himself, a royal processional song and a bridal ode for the marriage of the king.

In these psalms the king is proclaimed to be 'son of God', his reign is said to be without end, stretching to the bounds of the earth. He is to bring peace and justice to the world and to be a saviour to his people. The fact that Israel's king was the anointed of Yahweh, the 'Messiah' ('Anointed One'), meant that many of these psalms became part of Israel's messianic hope. Christians quickly came to see in them clear prophecies of Christ. Psalm 109(110) is the most quoted psalm in the New Testament. In the messianic psalms the Church came to hear 'Christ calling out to his Father, or the Father speaking to the Son.' (GILH ¶109). Hence, in the psalms we are led into the heart of the Trinity, into the inner relationship between Father and Son. Patristic exegesis of the psalms concentrated on discerning the voice of the Father, the voice of the Son, and the voice of the Holy Spirit speaking in the psalms.

To read the psalms as a prophecy of Christ and his relationship with his Father, and through them to enter into the heart of the relationship between Father and Son, is perhaps the most important dimension of learning to pray the psalms, but also the most difficult. We will look at several psalms from Morning and Evening Prayer to see how they can be understood as expressing the experience and prayer of Christ.

Prophetic Psalms addressed to the King

Psalm 109(110) occurs each Sunday, for Evening Prayer II, and is a prophecy addressed to Israel's king, a prophecy which Jesus applied to himself in Matthew 22:41—46. Because this psalm is the most quoted in the whole of the New Testament and because it occurs each week in the four-week cycle of psalms of the Divine Office, it is worth while studying it closely.

The psalm begins:

> *The Lord's revelation to my Master:*
> *'Sit on my right:*
> *your foes I will put beneath your feet.'*

There are two levels of meaning in the psalm. The first is historical. The psalm seems to have originally been composed for the coronation of Israel's king. The opening words are a prophecy delivered, by the high priest, to the king, called here '*my Master*'.

Sit on my right. In the prophecy the Lord invites the king to take the place of highest honour, at God's right hand. Some scholars have suggested that at the coronation ceremony the king's throne was placed on the right of the Ark of the Covenant in the holy of holies, symbolically seating the king at the Lord's right hand.

Your foes I will put beneath your feet. A victorious king would sometimes place his foot on the neck of his defeated enemy, symbolizing his total power over his foe. The prophecy promises the king victory over all his enemies.

The second level of interpretation came when the psalm was interpreted by Jewish scholars as a prophecy concerning the Messiah. Now, instead of being *addressed to* David the king, the psalm was interpreted as being *composed* by David the king, and addressed to the coming Messiah.

This is the way Jesus reads the psalm in Matthew 22:41—45.

> While the Pharisees were gathered round, Jesus put to them this question, 'What is your opinion about the Christ? Whose son is he?' They told him, 'David's.' He said to them, 'Then how is it that David, moved by the Spirit, calls him Lord, where he says:
>
> *The Lord declared to my Lord,*
> *take your seat at my right hand,*
> *till I have made your enemies*
> *your footstool?*
>
> 'If David calls him Lord, how then can he be his son?'

Jesus is pointing to the fact that while his human origins go back to David, there is something divine about the Messiah which sets him above David. The early Church followed this second level of interpretation, taking its lead from Jesus himself and interpreting Psalm 109(110) as a prophecy given by David concerning the Messiah.

The psalm continues:

> *The Lord will wield from Sion*
> *your sceptre of power:*
> *rule in the midst of all your foes.*

On the historical level, it may have been at this point in the coronation ritual that the king was invested with the sceptre, symbol of his might and authority. The psalm says that the Lord God will wield the king's sceptre. In other words, God will exercise his divine authority and power on behalf of the king. Sion is another name for Jerusalem, the holy city.

Rule in the midst of all your foes. The king is commanded to exercise his authority as God's representative over all peoples. The prophecy assures the king he will be triumphant.

It is easy to see how this verse came to be applied to the Messiah, and hence to Jesus. It is understood by the Church as being a prophecy of the way the authority and power of Jesus the Christ will be exercised over all the world. Sion is interpreted as referring to heaven, or to the Church, the new Jerusalem.

A prince from the day of your birth
on the holy mountains;
from the womb before the dawn I begot you.

This verse has a number of widely variant translations, each dependent on different textual variants. The version we have here continues the prophecy addressed to the king, and speaks of his royal dignity from birth, and of his being 'son of God' – *from the womb . . . I begot you.* Psalm 89:27 also speaks of the Davidic king as God's *first-born son.* When the psalms speak of the king in this way, as God's son, they mean much less than what the New Testament means when it speaks of Jesus as God's Son.

The Old Testament use of the title 'son of God' when applied to the king meant that there was a unique relationship between the Lord and the king, a relationship as close as father and son. It is the Lord who has created and chosen the king, and who will be his Father. The king for his part owes the Lord the obedience and love of a son. Again, it is easy to understand how the early Church read this verse as a prophecy of Christ, Son of God in a unique sense.

The Lord has sworn an oath he will not change
'You are a priest for ever,
a priest like Melchizedek of old.'

This prophetic oracle installs the king in the priestly office. Melchizedek was a mysterious figure described in Genesis 14:18 as king of Salem (possibly an early name for Jerusalem) and 'a priest of God Most High', who blessed Abram and to whom Abram gave a tithe of all he possessed.

Psalm 109(110) takes Melchizedek as a forerunner of the Davidic king, who, like Melchizedek, is invested with his authority not by an earthly power but by God himself.

The Second Book of Samuel, (6:13—19) describes King

David performing priestly functions of offering burnt offerings and communion sacrifices when the Ark was first brought into Jerusalem. The Church reads this verse as a clear prophecy of Christ's priesthood. Its relationship to Melchizedek is fully worked out in Hebrews 7.

> *The Master standing at your right hand*
> *will shatter kings in the day of his wrath.*

This verse appears to be addressed to God, and speaks of the victory David will have over all his enemies. Understood as a prophecy of Christ, it refers to the Day when he will come to judge the living and the dead.

> *He shall drink from the stream by the wayside*
> *and therefore he will lift up his head.*

The king during the coronation ceremony may have drunk water from the brook – possibly the spring Gihon in Jerusalem, mentioned in connection with the anointing of King Solomon in 1 Kings (1:33—45) – in order to be empowered with life and power. Or the reference may be to the king refreshing himself from a mountain stream in the midst of battle. To *lift up his head* is a metaphor for victory. In this verse the Christian can read of the way Christ was filled with the Spirit for his ministry, and was therefore triumphant over sin and Satan.

The different ways that this psalm can be prayed with reference to Christ are indicated by the antiphons that go with it.

Through the Year: *The Lord will send his mighty sceptre from Sion, and he will rule for ever, alleluia.*

This antiphon gives the basic interpretation of the psalm as a prophecy concerning Christ, through whom God rules for ever. The heading for the psalm (*The Messiah is king and priest*) and the sentence (*He must be king so that he may put all his enemies under his feet* (1 Corinthians 15:25)) emphasize this Christological interpretation.

Advent: *Rejoice greatly, daughter of Sion, shout with gladness, daughter of Jerusalem, alleluia.*

As we pray Psalm 109(110) in Advent we celebrate the coming of Christ the king.

Lent, Sunday 1: *You must worship the Lord, your God, and serve him alone.*

This antiphon takes the reply Jesus gave at his temptation in the wilderness (which is read on this Sunday) and underlines the sovereign rule of the Lord. He has authority over Satan, the ultimate enemy.

Lent, Sunday 5: *As Moses lifted up the serpent in the desert, so the Son of Man must be lifted up:*

reminds us that the Messiah reigns from the tree, that his victory over his enemies was won on the Cross.

Eastertide: *The Lord has risen and sits at the right hand of God, alleluia:*

celebrates the 'coronation' of Christ, his ascension to his rightful place as ruler of all.

Prayers for the King

Psalm 71(72) (Week 2, Thursday Evening) is a prayer for King Solomon, whose wealth, glory and just rule it extols. Jewish Messianic interpretation read it as a psalm celebrating the future ideal King foretold by the prophet Isaiah (9:6—7; 11:1—5). Christians soon applied it to Christ.

O God, give your judgement to the king,
to a king's son your justice,
that he may judge your people in justice
and your poor in right judgement.

May the mountains bring forth peace for the people
and the hills, justice.
May he defend the poor of the people
and save the children of the needy
and crush the oppressor.

The way as Christians we should pray the psalm is indicated by the antiphons, the heading and the sentence. The first set of antiphons for Holy Week and Eastertide highlights the theme of Christ the just ruler, the one whose final triumph we pray and long for.

Holy Week: *Christ is the First-born form the dead, the Ruler of the kings of the earth. He has made us a kingdom for his God and Father.*

Eastertide: *God has appointed him to judge all men, both living and dead, alleluia.*

The second set of antiphons highlights Christ's present work of bringing good news to the poor:

Ant. 2: *The Lord will save the poor; from oppression he will rescue their lives.*

And God's deliverance of Christ from suffering and death:

Holy Week: *The Lord will save the poor when they cry and the needy who are helpless.*

The theme of the Messiah's universal rule is picked up by the first antiphon for use during the year, Ant. 1: *I will make you the light of the nations to bring my salvation to the ends of the earth.*

The psalm celebrates this universal rule of the Messiah in verses like:

Before him all kings shall fall prostrate,
all nations shall serve him.

Every tribe shall be blessed in him,
all nations bless his name.

Finally, the sentence for the psalm indicates how the gifts of the wise men, the 'three Kings', to the infant Jesus are anticipated in the psalm. The sentence is: *They opened their treasures and offered him gifts of gold, frankincense and myrrh* (Matthew 2:11). The psalm has this verse:

The kings of Sheba and Seba
shall bring him gifts.
Before him all kings shall fall prostrate.

Thanksgiving for the King

Psalm 20(21) (Week 1, Tuesday Evening) is a thanksgiving for a king's victory, as the heading to the psalm says.

O Lord, your strength gives joy to the king;
how your saving help makes him glad!
You have granted him his heart's desire;
you have not refused the prayer of his lips.

The antiphons and sentence clearly indicate how the psalm can be prayed as a thanksgiving for Christ's victory over death, and when prayed as this we become witnesses to the resurrection, and join with the first disciples in their praise of God.

Ant. 2: *We shall sing and praise your power.*
Eastertide: *You have assumed your great power, you have begun your reign, alleluia.*
Sentence: *He accepted human life, so that he could rise from the dead and live for ever and ever* (St Irenaeus).

Prayers of the King himself

Psalm 143(144) (Week 4, Thursday Evening) is a psalm in which the king gives thanks for victory in battle (first part, verses 1—11) and prays for the prosperity of his people. The antiphons and sentence that go with the psalm direct our attention to Christ, as well as reminding us that we share in his victory and in the blessings won by his cross and resurrection.

Sentence: *His arms are well trained for battle, since he has overcome the world, for he says, 'I have overcome the world'* (St Hilary).

This takes up the words of the opening verse:

Blessed be the Lord, my rock
who trains my arms for battle,
who prepares my hands for war.

The Lord is my love and my refuge; in him I place my trust.

Ant. 1: comes straight from the psalm itself:

He is my love, my fortress;
he is my stronghold, my saviour,
my shield, my place of refuge.

Eastertide: *The Lord is my stronghold and my saviour, alleluia.*

Royal Processional Hymn

Psalm 131(132) (Week 3, Thursday Evening) is a psalm which was sung in Israel on the anniversary of the transfer of the Ark of the Covenant from a Judean village (Kiriath-Jearim) to its rightful place in Jerusalem. The Ark was the place where Yahweh manifested his presence, and so its transfer to Jerusalem made the city not just the political capital of Israel, but its religious centre. The story is told in 2 Samuel 6, with David the King featuring prominently.

The psalm celebrates the events of the transfer of the Ark:

At Ephrata we heard of the ark;
we found it in the plains of Yearim.
'Let us go to the place of his dwelling; [Jerusalem]
let us go to kneel at his footstool.

Then it moves into a prophecy to the house of David, promising the perpetual lineage of David, and the prosperity of his city, Jerusalem:

The Lord swore an oath to David;
he will not go back on his word:
'A son, the fruit of your body,
will I set upon your throne. . . .
on your throne from age to age.

The antiphons and sentence pick up the way the psalm is to be prayed as a prophecy concerning Christ.

Eastertide: *The Lord God gave him the throne of David, his father, alleluia.*
and:
Jesus Christ is the only Ruler over all, the King of kings and Lord of lords, alleluia.
Sentence: *The Lord will give him the throne of David, his father* (Luke 1:32).

Royal Wedding Song

Psalm 44(45) (Week 2, Monday Evening) is a song celebrating the marriage of the king to a foreign princess and is in two parts. The Office separates each part with different antiphons. The poet first addresses the king, crediting him with the attributes of Yahweh and of Emmanuel (Isaiah 9:5—6). Then he turns in the second part to address the queen.

Jewish and Christian tradition read the psalm as celebrating the marriage of the Messianic King with Israel (prefiguring the Church). The sentence and antiphons bring out this reference to Christ and his bride, the Church.

Sentence: *Behold, the bridegroom is coming; go out to meet him* (Matthew 25:6).

Antiphons for the first part of the psalm, referring to Christ:

Ant 1: *You are the fairest of the children of men and graciousness is poured upon your lips.*
Holy Week: *He had no beauty, no majesty to draw our eyes, no grace to make us delight in him.*
Eastertide: *Blessed is he who comes in the name of the Lord, alleluia.*

Antiphons for the second part, referring to the Church:

Ant 2: *Behold, the bridegroom is coming; go out to meet him.*
Holy Week: *I will grant him very many people as his own, for surrendering himself to death.*
Eastertide: *Blessed are those who are called to the wedding feast of the lamb, alleluia.*

All the Psalms refer to Christ

Following the path so clearly set out in the Messianic psalms, the Fathers of the Church took the whole psalter and explained it as a prophecy of Christ. Sometimes this led to a rather strained interpretation of the psalms, but in other cases it opened up profound depths which will always be treasured by Christians who pray the psalms.

One example of a general psalm which is read as interpreting the experience of Christ is Psalm 29(30) (Week 1, Thursday Evening). It is a psalm of thanksgiving after the psalmist has been rescued from a deadly threat to his life.

I will praise you Lord, you have rescued me
and have not let my enemies rejoice over me.

O Lord, I cried to you for help
and you, my God, have healed me.
O Lord, you have raised my soul from the dead,
restored me to life from those who sink into the grave.

Sing psalms to the Lord, you who love him,
give thanks to his holy name.

The psalm can obviously be prayed by anyone as a psalm of thanksgiving to the Lord for deliverance from serious danger, but the sentence at the head of the psalm indicates how it can be prayed as the prayer of Christ: *Christ gives thanks to his Father after his glorious resurrection.* (Cassian). When we pray the psalm in this way, we pray with Christ on the morning of his resurrection.

10 The Gifts of the Divine Office

In praying the Office we are engaged in a mutual exchange of gifts. God gives his gifts to us, and we in response make our gifts to God.

I God's Gifts to us in the Office

1 The gift of participation in the priesthood of Christ

In the letter to the Hebrews Christ is revealed as the supreme high priest who exercised his priesthood while on earth through his intercession 'with loud cries and with tears' (Hebrews 5:7) and through his perfect sacrifice on the cross. But his priesthood was not limited to his life on earth. His priesthood is eternal. In heaven Christ continues to act as our high priest. 'He is able for all time to save those who draw near to God through him, since he always lives to make intercession for them' (Hebrews 7:25). On earth his priestly ministry continues through his Church, through the ministerial priesthood of those ordained to Holy Orders and through the priesthood common to all believers.

By the anointing of the Holy Spirit in baptism Christ gives all his people a share in his priesthood. He makes us all priests. In the Catholic baptismal rite, immediately after a person is baptized they are anointed with chrism and the celebrant says: 'God the Father of our Lord Jesus Christ has freed you from sin, given you a new birth by water and the Holy Spirit, and welcomed you into his holy people. He now anoints you with the chrism of salvation. As Christ was anointed Priest, Prophet, and King, so may you live always as members of his body, sharing everlasting life.' The first letter of Peter (which may be a post-baptismal instruction) proclaims: 'You are a chosen race, a kingdom of priests, a holy nation, a people to be a personal possession to sing the praises of God who called you out of darkness into his wonderful light' (1 Peter 2:9). In baptism Christ makes us all priests and calls us to share in his priestly ministry by sacrificing our lives to the will of the Father; and by interceding with him for all humankind.

How do we do exercise this priestly work of intercession? How do we join in Christ's priestly ministry? One of the most effective ways is through praying the Divine Office. What was said in Chapter 7 about the psalms is true of the whole Office. The psalms are the prayer of the Church, the Body of Christ, and so is the Office. When we pray the Office we are praying the prayer of Christ, praying through him, with him, in him. In praying the Office we are joining our voices with Christ in his prayer to the Father; we are sharing with him in his priesthood. 'In the Liturgy of the Hours, the Church exercises the priestly office of her head and constantly offers God a sacrifice of praise, "a verbal sacrifice that is offered every time we acknowledge his name." (Hebrews 13:15). This prayer is . . . the very prayer which Christ himself, together with his Body, addresses to the Father.' (GILH ¶15).

As we exercise the priesthood of Christ in praying the Liturgy of the Hours we praise the glory of God and we enter into the sufferings of the world. Praise and intercession are the two poles of the Office, because they are the two poles of Christ's priesthood. In his life on earth, and especially in his death on the cross, Christ glorified his Father (John 17:4) and achieved the salvation of humankind. He offered praise and intercession in word and deed. As we pray the Office with him we too offer praise and intercession. We glorify the Father and we pray for the salvation of the world. These two functions always belong together in the liturgy, because the liturgy is the prayer of Christ. 'He [Christ] continues his priestly work through his Church. The Church, by celebrating the Eucharist and by other means, especially the celebration of the divine office, is ceaselessly engaged in praising the Lord and interceding for the salvation of the entire world.' (CSL n. 83). 'The liturgy, then, is rightly seen as an exercise of the priestly office of Christ. . . . Every liturgical action, because it is an action of Christ the Priest and of his Body, which is the Church, is a sacred action surpassing all others. No other action of the Church can equal its efficacy by the same title and to the same degree.' (CSL n. 7).

In the Liturgy of the Hours 'the Church continues to offer that prayer and entreaty which Christ offered during his life on earth, and which therefore has a unique effectiveness. Thus the Church community exercises a true motherhood towards souls who are to be led to Christ, not only by charity, example and works of penance, but also by prayer.' (GILH ¶17). In praying the Office we are brought into the heart of Christ's love for the world, of his longing for all people to be saved.

The General Instruction on the Liturgy of the Hours repeatedly assures us that as we pray the Office we are praying the prayer of Christ. It is not our own prayer but his. It is not our own words but his words we are using. For example: 'This prayer is . . . the very prayer which Christ himself, together with his Body, addresses to the Father.' (GILH ¶15). In the Liturgy of the Hours 'the Church continues to offer that prayer and entreaty which Christ offered during his life on earth, and which therefore has a unique effectiveness.' (GILH ¶17). This is one of the central mysteries and glories of the Office and it has special significance for the intercessions.

Christ repeatedly promises us that when we pray 'in his name' our prayer will always be answered. When we pray the Divine Office we can be absolutely sure that we are praying in the name of Christ, because the prayer of the Office is his prayer, the prayer of his Church. It is not our own individual prayer, but the prayer of his body. Therefore we can be sure when we pray the Office that all we ask we will receive. Praying the Office with this assurance is a source of constant joy. The intercessions of the Office are the intercessions of Christ, whose prayer is always heard by the Father. As we pray through him, they become our intercessions, and we can be sure that each one is heard and answered by the Father.

At this point it is important to underline the fact that the privilege of praying the Office is given by the Church to the whole people of God. It is not, emphatically not, the preserve of clergy and religious. The General Instruction states of the Office that 'the praise of the Church is not to be considered either in its origins or of its nature as the preserve of clerics and monks; it belongs to the whole christian community' (¶ 270). Under the heading: The Mandate of Celebrating the Liturgy of the Hours, after encouraging bishops, priests, deacons, and religious communities to celebrate the Office, the General Instruction concludes: 'The same encouragement is to be given to the laity' (¶32). The whole people of God have been given the mandate to pray the Office. The Constitution on the Sacred Liturgy says: 'The laity, too, are encouraged to recite the divine office, either with the priests, or among themselves, or even individually.' (n. 100). One of those involved in preparing the revision of the Office following Vatican II, Fr A-M. Roguet, OP, said:

> Whether it be a group of lay-brothers or nuns, a group of lay people, or even a lay person on his own - if they celebrate the Liturgy of the Hours, they are truly praying the prayer of the Church, with Christ, and their celebration is 'liturgical' in the fullest sense of the word. (Roguet, *The Liturgy of the Hours*, p. 96).

2 The gift of the presence of Christ

Praying the Office is a participation in the priesthood of Christ because 'Christ is always present in his Church, especially in her liturgical celebrations' (CSL n. 7). Whenever the Church celebrates the Liturgy of the Hours, Christ is present in two ways. 'He is present in his word since it is he himself who speaks when the holy scriptures are read in the Church', and 'he is present when the Church prays and sings, for he has promised "where two or three are gathered together in my name there am I in the midst of them" (Matthew 18:20)' (CSL n. 7).

The gift of the presence of Christ in the Church's liturgy in his word and in the community is an objective presence in the sense that it is not dependent of our feelings or state of grace. His presence as we pray the Office is a promised gift in which we can rejoice, and to which we can respond with love and adoration.

The presence of Christ in the Office leads us into the presence of his Father. The Office is above all the prayer of Christ 'calling out to his Father' and 'the Father speaking to the Son' (GILH ¶109). As we pray the Office we are led into the heart of the Trinity. In praying the Office we can be drawn into the heart of Jesus' relationship to the Father. The Fathers of the Church taught that in the psalms we can hear Christ calling out to his Father and the Father speaking to the Son. Chapter 8 expounded this reality. One of the most moving experiences in praying the Office comes when we are conscious that we are praying with Christ in his prayer to the Father.

> When we pray the Liturgy of the Hours, this prayer is 'truly the voice of the Bride herself addressing her Bridegroom. It is the very prayer which Christ himself together with his Body addresses to the Father. Hence all who take part in the divine office are not only performing a duty for the Church, they are also sharing in what is the greatest honour for Christ's Bride: for by offering these

praises to God they are standing before God's throne in the name of the Church, their Mother.' (CSL n. 84).

3 The gift of the word of Christ

At both Morning and Evening Prayer the word of Christ speaks to us and directs our lives. The Office sets up 'a dialogue between God and man, so that "God speaks to his people . . . and the people reply to God both by song and by prayer"'(GILH ¶14). This daily dialogue with God is a source of immense spiritual nourishment. 'The readings and prayers of the Liturgy of the Hours constitute a wellspring of the Christian life. From this table of sacred scripture and the words of the saints this life is nourished, and by prayer it is strengthened.' (GILH ¶18). 'The saving word of God has great importance in the Liturgy of the Hours, and should be of enormous spiritual benefit for those taking part.' (GILH ¶14). The Scriptures repeatedly urge us to strive for holiness. Praying the Office is one of the most effective ways we can work for that goal.

St Paul said: 'Let the Word of Christ, in all its richness, find a home with you.' (Colossians 3:16). As we pray the Office day after day, meditating on the word of God, the thought-forms and truths of that word take hold of us. Our minds are transformed so that we can discern what is the will of God, 'what is good, acceptable, and mature.' (Romans 12:2). The Scriptures begin to soak into our minds and hearts and become part of us. The way we are living is constantly brought into the light of God's word, to be guided and transformed. In particular, the Scriptures expounding the mystery of the birth, death and resurrection of our Lord Jesus and of the gift of his Spirit come to determine our thinking and our way of life.

4 The gift of freedom in Christ

As we pray the Office each morning and evening in a disciplined way, not just when we feel like it, we are set free from slavery to our feelings and from self-centredness in prayer. Self-centredness is the original sin and the source of all actual sin. To be set free from self-centredness is a glorious liberation, and praying the Divine Office is one of the ways in which we can begin to enter into that freedom. The psalms take us into the heart of God and into the depths of human experience. They teach us to express not only our own longing for God but also to share the condition of all God's people, particularly the plight of the poor and suffering.

5 The gift of the Spirit

As we pray the Office the Spirit teaches us how to pray. As we follow the movements of the Spirit who inspired the psalms and Scriptures of the Office, he brings our life, with all its sorrows and joys, to the Father. As we pray the Office with the Spirit as our teacher we will learn how to listen to the Lord and how to rejoice in his glorious action in creation and in Christ. This is the way Jesus and his disciples learnt to pray, and this is how he teaches us today through his Church.

The Scriptures exhort us to be filled with the Spirit. In praying the Office each day we are coming to 'ask, seek and knock', in the certainty that our 'heavenly Father will give the Spirit to those who ask him' (Luke 11:13). The Office fans the flame of the Spirit within and brings us into communion with the Lord.

6 The gift of the Church

As we pray the Office the Spirit leads us into deeper communion with the whole Church, because when we pray the Office we pray not as isolated individuals but as part of the living body of Christ, praying the prayer of Christ.

> When there is a truly liturgical action, the community which performs it represents the Church, it *is* the Church. However small and poor a community may be, when it celebrates the liturgy it is a particular Church . . . Whenever it celebrates the liturgy, each local church causes the universal Church to be present.
>
> (Roguet, *Liturgy of the Hours*, pp. 84—85).

Prayer expresses the very essence of the Church as a community, and the Liturgy of the Hours is not private prayer but the prayer of the Church. Even when prayed alone, the Office joins us to the universal Church. One of the dangers of the current revival of spirituality is that it can lead people off into a world of their own, a 'journey into self', which is not the destination of Christian prayer. Christian prayer is a journey into God, and because of God's love for the world that journey is also a journey into the suffering and cries of a broken world. Praying the Office can join us with that world, can unite us with the Church and with all humankind.

The Divine Office as revised by Vatican II is of profound importance for unity within the Catholic Church, and for unity between Catholic and Protestant. Within the Catholic Church the Office is an excellent means for groups to express their unity with the universal Church by praying the prayer of the Church. The Office can be prayed in a wide variety of styles, and different groups can express something of their own charism in the way they pray the Office, while at the same time expressing their identity with the whole Church.

For example, the Office is a gift for charismatic prayer groups. Its structure is flexible and its overall pattern is that followed by most prayer groups: (1) praise and thanksgiving; (2) listening to the word of God; (3) response in prayer, intercession, ministry. For groups working for justice and peace, the Office offers a pattern of prayer which constantly expresses their concerns. The psalms of the Office give voice to the cry of the poor. The psalms beat with God's passion for justice and peace for all the earth. At all times the Office reminds us that 'salvation is of the Lord.' We are co-workers with him. On our own we can do nothing.

Between groups of radically different points of view, the Office can be (as is the Mass) a common ground on which they kneel together. There is nothing like common prayer to begin to melt the divisions which so easily divide Christians within the one Church.

One of the stated purposes of the reforms of the Second Vatican Council was 'to foster whatever can promote union among all who believe in Christ.' (CSL n. 1). Vatican II was deliberately ecumenical in its vision. The Divine Office could play a significant role in helping to heal the division between Catholic and Protestant because the Office is composed almost entirely of Scripture, and is therefore based on a foundation which Catholics and Protestants share in common.

When I was first introduced to the Office I was an Evangelical Protestant. I was having problems in prayer, and spoke with my Catholic colleague in the chaplaincy at Massey University, Fr Leo Curry. He encouraged me to try using the revised edition of the Office which had just been published. I approached it suspiciously, expecting to find archaic prayers laced with frequent references to Mary and the saints. To my astonishment I discovered that the Office is composed largely of Scripture, and as an Evangelical Protestant I could pray the Office with hardly a single reservation. In fact, the Office quickly became a source of stability and joy in prayer and I delighted in its love for Scripture, a love which is at the heart of Evangelical Protestantism. It is important to note, for the sake of Protestant Christians, that out of the 168 psalms and canticles which make up the four-week psalter of the Office, only seven passages come from the deutero-canonical Scriptures of the Old Testament (the Apocrypha), all of them being canticles of praise for God's work in creation and his deliverance of Israel. The deutero-canonical books of the Old Testament were received by the early Church because they were included in the Greek version of the Old Testament used in Judaism. They were not part of the Hebrew Bible. The Protestant Reformers refused to accept the divine inspiration of the Greek writings of the Old Testament although most of the Reformers commended them as being 'useful and good to read' (Luther). None of the seven canticles used in the Divine Office offends Protestant doctrine or sensitivities.

There are two matters which will be of special concern to Protestant Christians praying the Office. The first is that the final intercession each evening is for the dead. For example, *Show your mercy to the dead; – may they find their rest in Christ.* (Week 1, Monday Evening). *Bring those who have died in your peace to that knowledge which fulfills faith and answers hope – grant them the fulness of your love.* (Week 3, Wednesday Evening). For those who object to such prayers on doctrinal grounds, the best solution is to use the opportunity to give thanks to God for the faithful departed, particularly those known to us, and to pray that we may share with them in the joys of Christ's kingdom.

The second matter of concern to Protestant Christians is prayer to Mary. It may come as a considerable surprise to discover that in the four-week cycle of Morning and Evening Prayer there is not a single example of prayer to Mary. In fact, of the 280 separate intercessions in the four-week cycle for prayer during ordinary time (outside of Lent, Easter, Advent and Christmas), there are only six references to Mary, and in every one it is her example as the first disciple which is to the fore. For example: *Teach us to respond to your word like Mary our Mother: – may your word be fruitful in us.* (Week 1, Saturday Morning). *Mary listened to your voice, and brought your Word into the world: – by answering your call, may we too bring your Son to men.* (Week 3, Saturday Morning). These are intercessions all Christians can pray.

7 The gift of heaven

'In the earthly liturgy we take part in a foretaste of the heavenly liturgy which is celebrated in the Holy City of Jerusalem.' (CSL n. 8). In speaking of the Divine Office the Constitution on the Sacred Liturgy says:

> Jesus Christ, High Priest of the New and Eternal Covenant, taking human nature, introduced into this earthly exile that hymn which is sung throughout all ages in the halls of heaven. He attaches to himself the entire community of mankind and has them join him in singing his divine song of praise. (CSL n. 83).

As we pray the Office we are joining with the choirs of heaven in their unending hymn of praise. Praying the Office joins us to heaven and anticipates the day in which all creation will be healed and the whole earth join to sing God's praise. 'In the Liturgy of the Hours we proclaim this faith, we express and nurture this hope, and we share the joy of giving unceasing praise in the day which knows no end.' (GILH ¶16).

II Our Gifts to God in the Office

1 The gift of each day

The General Instruction on the Liturgy of the Hours states that one of the purposes of Morning Prayer is to enable us 'to consecrate to God the first movements of our minds and hearts.' (GILH ¶38). In Morning Prayer we begin the day with praise, submitting our whole being to God and to his will, renewing our love for him, bringing our work before him, praying that his kingdom will come.

Prayer in the morning also brings to mind the morning on which Christ was raised from the dead. Morning Prayer, 'recited as the light of a new day dawns, recalls the resurrection of the Lord Jesus, the true light, enlightening every man . . . We should pray in the morning to celebrate the resurrection of the Lord with morning prayer.' (GILH ¶38). We begin each day remembering that Christ is risen, and so we can look to the day with hope and confidence in God, remembering that the 'power working in us is the same as the mighty strength which he used when he raised Christ from death' (Ephesians 1:20). Morning Prayer has a note of triumph and joy. It looks to the future, not only of the coming day, but of the whole world. It has a sense of mission which comes out explicitly in the Benedictus. The Benedictus reminds us that we go into the day 'to prepare the way of the Lord', to clear a path for him by making known to people, in what we say and do, the salvation of Christ, the forgiveness of sins, *the loving-kindness of the heart of our God, who visits us like the dawn from on high.*

In Evening Prayer, our evening sacrifice of praise, we end the day with thankfulness to God for his goodness and for the gifts of the day. The dominant mood of Evening Prayer is one of thanksgiving, although we also intercede for the needs of others, particularly those we have met in the course of the day. In the evening we place our hope in the Sun which never sets, Christ our eternal light. In praying the Office we offer God the gift of each day.

2 The gift of praise

All that was said about sharing in the priestly work of Christ by offering the sacrifice of praise could be said again under this heading. In the Office Christ joins our gift with his in prayer to the Father.

3 The gift of our lives

St Paul appeals to us: 'Offer yourselves as a living sacrifice to God, dedicated to his service and pleasing to him. This is the true worship you should offer' (Romans 12:1). Praying the Office is one tangible way in which we can 'offer ourselves to God.' If we make this offering of mind, heart and will at the beginning of the day, we are more likely to carry it through the whole course of the day. The Office achieves its full purpose as it enables us to offer our lives to God.

III The Office and the Eucharist

There is an intimate relationship between the Divine Office and the Eucharist, a relationship which is beautifully described in the General Instruction on the Liturgy of the Hours ¶12.

> The Liturgy of the Hours extends to the different hours of the day the praise and prayer, the memorial of the mysteries of salvation and the foretaste of the heavenly glory, which are offered us in the eucharistic mystery, 'the centre and culmination of the whole life of the Christian community.'
>
> The Liturgy of the Hours is in itself an excellent preparation for the fruitful celebration of the Eucharist because it fosters those dispositions necessary, such as faith, hope and love, devotion and a spirit of sacrifice.

The Office thus has a vital role to play before and after the Eucharist. Before we come to the the Eucharist, the Office prepares our lives so that our celebration of the Eucharist becomes more fruitful. The Office does this primarily because it is composed of the word of God, a word which stirs us to faith, offers us hope, and renews the love of God in our hearts. Thus our participation in the Eucharist is deepened. For those who pray the Office in community, it is usual for Morning Prayer to precede daily Eucharist, because the Office is an excellent preparation for Eucharist.

After the Eucharist the Office becomes a unique means of carrying on in our lives the fruits of the sacrifice of Christ. The Office can be said to 'extend' the spiritual benefits of the Eucharist. The taste of the Eucharist lingers as we pray the Office. The spirit of prayer and praise is continued, the mysteries of salvation continue to be brought before us in the Scriptures, and the presence of Christ is renewed, because he is present 'where two or three gather in my name' (Matthew 18:20). He says to us: 'When you call, I will answer.' The Office is a unique way of bringing the blessings of the Sunday Eucharist into every day of the week.

Glossary for Part 1

Antiphon Sentences, usually from Scripture, recited before and after the Psalms and Canticles of the Office. They vary with the season, and their purpose is to highlight one aspect of the Psalm or Canticle.

Benedictus The canticle from Luke 1:68—79 is called the Benedictus, after its opening word in Latin. The Benedictus is recited at Morning Prayer after the Scripture reading.

Breviary The book in which the text of the Divine Office is printed.

Canticle From the Latin *canticulum,* 'a little song'. Canticles in the Divine Office are songs from Scripture outside the Book of Psalms. In Morning Prayer the second passage of the psalmody is one of the Old Testament canticles. In Evening Prayer, the last passage of the psalmody is a New Testament canticle.

Common Those sections of the Office which belong equally to a particular group of saints are *common* to that group. For example, the Common of Apostles is the set of texts (psalmody, Scripture readings, intercessions, etc.) which can be used on all the feast days of apostles. The Common of Women Saints is the set of texts which can be used on all the days in which we honour women saints.

Divine Office The name given to the official daily prayer of the Church, made up of the seven 'hours': (1) Office of

Readings, (2) Morning Prayer, (3) Prayer Before Noon, (4) Midday Prayer, (5) Afternoon Prayer, (6) Evening Prayer, (7) Night Prayer. The word 'Office' comes from the Latin *officium,* meaning 'service', 'something done for someone'. The Divine Office is the service given to God in prayer. Other names for the Divine Office are: Liturgy of the Hours, Daily Office, Prayer of the Church. The preferred name used in Church documents is the Liturgy of the Hours.

Feast A feast day is a day commemorating an event in the history of salvation, or a saint. There are 25 Feast Days in the General Calendar of the Church.

Hour In liturgical language, an hour is one of the seven times for prayer which make up the Divine Office. These are: (1) Office of Readings, (2) Morning Prayer, (3) Prayer Before Noon, (4) Midday Prayer, (5) Afternoon Prayer, (6) Evening Prayer, (7) Night Prayer. The Latin names for the seven hours are : matins and lauds (reckoned as one hour), prime, terce, sext, none, vespers, compline. The hours are sometimes called the canonical hours, because they are governed by Canon Law. The two 'major hours' are Morning and Evening Prayer.

Invitatory means 'invitation'. The prayer of the Office begins each day with the invitatory, the invitation to payer, which is made up of three parts:

(1) The opening versicle and response *(Lord, open our lips: And we shall praise your name).*

(2) A Psalm, usually Psalm 94(95), sometimes Psalms 99(100), 66(67), 23(24). The psalm used at this point is called the invitatory psalm.

(3) An antiphon which changes each day and serves to highlight a theme from the invitatory psalm or from the particular day in the Church's calendar.

Liturgy In its broadest sense, liturgy is the public worship of the Church, and includes all the official acts of prayer and the celebration of the sacraments which make up the Church's worship. In a more particular sense, the word liturgy is often used of the Holy Eucharist, the very heart of the Church's worship.

The root meaning of liturgy (from the Greek *leitourgia*) is 'service'. In the Greek OT and NT liturgy is a technical term for worship.

Liturgy of the Hours See **Divine Office**

Magnificat The canticle from Luke 1:46—55 is called the Magnificat, after its opening word in Latin. The Magnificat is recited after the Scripture reading at Evening Prayer.

Nunc Dimittis The canticle from Luke 2:29—32 is called the Nunc Dimittis, after its opening words in Latin. The Nunc Dimittis is recited after the Scripture reading at Night Prayer.

Octave An eight-day celebration of a major feast, in particular the feasts of Easter, Pentecost, and Christmas.

Office See **Divine Office.**

Ordinary Time In liturgical language, ordinary time is time outside the special seasons and feast days of the Church's year.

Proper A term which refers to those parts of the Office (or any liturgical prayer) which vary according to the day or season of the Church year. The list of contents in the texts of the Office has *The Proper of Seasons* (those texts which are use on particular seasons of the Church year, e.g. Lent, Eastertide, Christmastide); and *The Proper of Saints* (those texts which are used on saints' days). From the Latin *proprius*, 'one's own'. The Proper texts belong to one particular day or season.

Psalm Psalms with a capital P means the Book of Psalms found in sacred Scripture. The word psalms (in Greek) means: 'songs sung to stringed instruments', and so psalms (small p) can refer to any songs found in Scripture, although the perferred way of referring to psalms outside of the Book of Psalms is to call them canticles.

Psalmody A collection of psalms arranged for singing. When used of the office, psalmody refers to the selection of Psalms and canticles used at each hour of prayer.

Psalter Can be used to describe the Book of Psalms in the Bible, or to a book of psalms arranged for liturgical prayer. In the Divine Office, the psalter is the selection of Psalms and canticles used at each hour of prayer. It is synonymous with psalmody.

Responsory From Latin *respondere*, 'to answer'. A responsory is a liturgical chant made up of a series of versicles and responses, designed for alternate singing by different people. In Morning and Evening Prayer the Scripture readings are followed by a short responsory consisting of a single versicle (V.) and a response (R.).

Solemnity A feast day of special importance. There are 15 Solemnities in the General Calendar of the Divine Office.

Through the Year In some editions of Morning and Evening Prayer, this expression is used to identify antiphons and texts which are used outside of the liturgical seasons and feast days.

Triduum A celebration lasting three days. The Easter Triduum begins with the evening Mass on Holy Thursday and ends with Easter Sunday.

Vatican II A Council of the Catholic Church called by Pope John XXIII in 1959. The council met from 1962 to 1965 and issued a number of documents which initiated a radical reform of the life and worship of the Church. The document which guided the reform of the Divine Office was the Constitution on the Sacred Liturgy, known by its Latin title as *Sacrosanctum Concilium.*

Versicle A sentence of prayer which forms one part of a responsory, the other part being the response. From the Latin *versiculus,* 'little verse'.

Abbreviations

CSL	Constitution on the Sacred Liturgy (Sacrosanctum Concilium)
GILH	General Instruction on the Liturgy of the Hours
LC	Laudis Canticum (Apostolic Constitution Promulgating the Divine Office)
PG	Patrologia Graeca
PL	Patrologia Latina

Further Reading

1 On the history and theology of the Divine Office

General Instruction on the Liturgy of the Hours, found at the beginning of Vol 1 of the 3 Vol edition of the Divine Office.

Bradshaw, P., *Daily Prayer in the Early Church*, London, SPCK, 1981.

Crichton, J.D., *Christian Celebration: the Prayer of the Church*, London, Geoffrey Chapman, 1978.

Flannery, A. (ed), *Making the Most of the Breviary*, Dublin, Dominican Publications, 1975.

Jeremias, J., *The Prayers of Jesus*, London, SCM, 1967.

Jungmann, J.A., *Christian Prayer through the Centuries*, New York, Paulist Press, 1978.

Roguet, A-M., *The Liturgy of the Hours: the General Instruction of the Liturgy on the Hours, with a Commentary*, Australia, E.J. Dwyer, and London, Geoffrey Chapman, 1971.

Scotto, D.F. *The Liturgy of the Hours: its history and its importance as the communal prayer of the Church after the Liturgical Reform of Vatican II*, Massachusetts, St. Bede's Publications, 1987.

Taft, R., *The Liturgy of the Hours in East and West: the Origins of the Divine Office and its Meaning for Today*, Minnesota, The Liturgical Press, 1986.

2 On praying the psalms

Bonhoeffer, D., *Psalms: the Prayer Book of the Bible*, Minneapolis, Augsburg, 1970.

Goldingay, J., *Songs from a Strange Land: Psalms 42—51*, Leicester, IVP, 1978.

Lewis, C.S., *Reflections on the Psalms*, London, Collins, 1961.

Merton, T., *Praying the Psalms*, Minnesota, Liturgical Press, 1990.

Stott, J.R.W., *The Canticles and Selected Psalms*, London, Hodder and Stoughton, 1966.

3 Commentaries on the Psalms

There is an abundance of literature on the Psalms. The following selection of commentaries is intended as a guide for those who want to delve further into the interpretation of particular Psalms.

Allen, L.C., *Psalms 101—150*, Waco, Word Books, 1983.

Anderson, A.A., *The Book of Psalms, Vols 1 & 2*, London, Oliphants, 1972.

Craigie, P.C., *Psalms 1—50*, Waco, Word Books, 1985.

Knight, G.A.F., *The Psalms, Vols 1 & 2*, Edinburgh, Saint Andrew Press, 1983.

Kraus, H-J., *Psalms 1—50*, Minneapolis, Augsburg, 1987.

— *Theology of the Psalms*, Minneapolis, Augsburg, 1986.

Rogerson, J.W. and McKay, J.W., *Psalms 1—50, Psalms 51—100, Psalms 101—150*, Cambridge, Cambridge University Press, 1977.

Westermann, C., *The Living Psalms*, Edinburgh, T. & T. Clark, 1989.

Weiser, A., *The Psalms*, London, SCM, 1962.

Part 2
Commentary on the Psalms and Canticles of Morning, Evening and Night Prayer

Introduction

In this commentary the general principles expounded in Part 1 on how to pray the psalms will be applied to each psalm and canticle. In giving advice on how to pray the psalms of the Divine Office, the General Instruction on the Liturgy of the Hours makes a direct link between the inspiration of the Holy Spirit as we pray and our actual understanding of the psalms and canticles.

> The Holy Spirit, who inspired the psalmists, is always present with his grace to those believing Christians who with good intention sing and recite these songs. It is necessary, however, for each according to his powers, to have 'more intensive biblical instruction, especially with regard to the psalms', and be led to see how and in what way he may be able to recite and pray the psalms properly. (GILH ¶102).

The General Instruction also stresses the importance of paying close attention to the literal meaning of the psalm: 'The person praying the psalms is conscious of their importance for Christian living by keeping to their literal meaning.' (¶107).

This commentary takes up the counsel of the General Instruction, and is specifically designed for those who are beginning to pray Morning and Evening Prayer. It is based on the actual text used in Morning and Evening Prayer (the Grail version for the Psalms), and brings out the main theme of each psalm as well as explaining difficult ideas and phrases in the psalm or canticle. The commentary does not include much of the technical information found in commentaries based on the Hebrew or Greek text, but it indicates how each psalm and canticle can be prayed as Christian prayer, something other commentaries often omit altogether or barely mention.

In particular, the commentary follows the patristic principle of exegeting the psalms in the light of Christ, hearing in them the voice of Christ and his Church. This patristic principle is the basis of the antiphons of the Office and the commentary shows how the antiphons help the Christian to pray the psalms with the Church. The practice of following the principles of exegesis developed by the Fathers is commended in the General Instruction:

> Whoever says the psalms in the name of the Church should pay attention to the full meaning of the psalms, especially that messianic understanding which led the Church to adopt the psalter. The messianic meaning is made completely manifest in the New Testament; it is in fact declared by Christ our Lord himself when he said to the apostles: 'Everything written about me in the Law of Moses, in the prophets and in the psalms, has to be fulfilled' (Luke 24:44). . . .
>
> Following this path, the Fathers took the whole psalter and explained it as a prophecy about Christ and his Church; and for this same reason psalms were chosen for the sacred liturgy. Even if certain artificial interpretations were sometimes accepted, generally both the Fathers and the liturgy rightly heard in the psalms Christ calling out to his Father, or the Father speaking to the Son; they even recognized in them the voice of the Church, the apostles and the martyrs. (n. 109).

The voice of Christ, the voice of the Father, and the voice of the Church need to be discerned in the psalms if we are to pray them with greatest benefit.

Seeking to discern the literal meaning of the text and reading that text in the light of Christ are the two principles of exegesis which the Church gives a commentator on sacred Scripture, and I have tried to be faithful to them both. (See *Dei Verbum* n. 12).

Invitatory: Psalm 94(95)

For nearly 3,000 years this psalm has called God's people to worship at the beginning of each day. It is a call to sing God's praise and to listen to his word, and therefore it is the perfect beginning to the Divine Office. The psalm is in two parts: a psalm of praise, followed by a prophecy.

Come, ring out our joy to the Lord;
hail the God who saves us.
Let us come before him giving thanks,
with songs let us hail the Lord.

As the priests and people of Israel gather to worship, they exhort each other to sing with joy the praises of God. Even when we pray the Office alone we are not praying alone, for we are praying the prayer of the Church. We are praying with millions of other Christians throughout the world; we are praying with the Church in heaven and on earth; we are praying in, with, and through the head of the Church, our Lord Jesus Christ.

A mighty God is the Lord,
a great king above all gods.

Israel was surrounded by nations who worshipped a host of gods. At times the Scriptures declare these gods to be nothing, to be mere inventions of the human imagination. At other times (as here) the reality of other gods is acknowledged, but they are declared to be totally subservient to the Lord who is the *great king above all gods*. As members of a society which still worships a host of gods – greed, power, pleasure – we are called by this psalm to put them in their place: under the feet of the Lord.

In his hand are the depths of the earth;
the heights of the mountains are his.
To him belongs the sea, for he made it,
and the dry land shaped by his hands.

Nothing in the whole created world is beyond the rule of the Lord, for he created every part of it. All of creation is upheld and sustained by him, *in his hand*. Colossians affirms that the *hand* which holds the world is the nail-pierced *hand* of our Lord Jesus: 'In him, all things were created, in heaven and on earth, visible and invisible, . . . all things were created through him and for him' (1:16).

Come in; let us bow and bend low
let us kneel before the God who made us
for he is our God and we
the people who belong to his pasture,
the flock that is led by his hand.

The God who made the earth is the God *who made* us. The *hand* which holds the world is the *hand* which leads his people to pasture, the hand of the good shepherd. We worship God with *joy*, but also with reverence and humility: *let us bow and bend low*. We worship him because we are his creatures, he *made* us; and we worship him because we are his *flock*, the people Christ died to save, to unite into one family. We praise the God of creation and the God of the covenant.

O that today you would listen to his voice!
'Harden not your hearts as at Meribah,
as on that day at Massah in the desert
when your fathers put me to the test;
when they tried me, though they saw my work.

With this verse we come to the second part of the psalm – the prophecy. Worship is a dialogue with the Lord. We come to speak his praise and to *listen to his voice*. In the opening call to worship the Lord speaks directly to us and reminds us of

Israel's failure to listen and obey him during its journey to the promised land. We are on the same journey, to heaven, and if we are to reach our destination we must *listen to his voice*.

The reference to Meribah and Massah goes back to an incident recorded in Exodus 17:1—7 and Numbers 20:1—13. On their journey through the wilderness, the Israelites came to on oasis where there was no water. They cried out to Moses: 'Why did you bring us out of Egypt only to make us, our children and our livestock, die of thirst?' Moses prayed to the Lord, who told him to strike the rock (Exodus 17:6), and water began to flow. The story concludes with the line, '[Moses] gave the place the names of Massah and Meribah because of the Israelites' contentiousness and because they put the Lord to the test by saying, "Is the Lord with us, or not?" ' (Exodus 17:7). In Hebrew the name *Massah* means 'trial', and the name *Meribah* means 'contention'.

Israel put God *to the test* by doubting his power to save and deliver them, despite all he had done for them in the past. It is important not to misunderstand the kind of doubt referred to here, because the lesson of Massah and Meribah is basic for anyone who wants to follow the Lord.

There are at least two kinds of doubt. One is the doubt experienced by any honest seeker after God. At times the circumstances of our life may lead us to question the most fundamental truths of the faith. The second kind of doubt is the wilful refusal to believe despite the evidence. We will *not* believe, in spite of all we have seen and known of God. We doubt God's love and goodness despite overwhelming evidence of his care. It is this second kind of doubt, the wilful refusal to believe in spite of the evidence, which was Israel's sin at Meribah and Massah. They *tried* the Lord, even *though they saw his work*. In spite of the astonishing miracles God had worked for them in delivering them from Egypt and feeding them in the wilderness, they refused to believe. It is this kind of doubt which cuts us off completely from any growth in grace. This doubt is the result of a hard heart, a heart cynically closed to any possibility of being touched by God's love. *Harden not your hearts as at Meribah.* In its interpretation of this incident (and of the whole psalm) the New Testament book of Hebrews describes the sin of Israel at Meribah as 'this example of refusal to believe' (4:11).

Psalm 94(95) gives us a solemn warning against the cynicism which closes our ears and makes any communion with God impossible. Israel's cynicism arose out of suffering, and suffering can harden the heart against God more than anything else. In the midst of his own experience of suffering the Apostle Paul looked to the suffering of Christ and came to the conclusion: 'If God is for us, who is against us? He who did not spare his own Son but gave him up for us all, will he not also give us all things with him? . . . I am sure that neither death, nor life, nor angels, nor principalities, nor things present nor things to come, nor powers, nor height, nor depth, nor anything else in all creation, will be able to separate us from the love of God in Christ Jesus our Lord' (Romans 8:31—32,38—39).

For forty years I was wearied of these people
and I said: "Their hearts are astray,
these people do not know my ways."
Then I took an oath in my anger:
"Never shall they enter my rest."'

The *forty years* refers to the time Israel spent wandering in the wilderness on their way from Egypt to Canaan. *Their hearts are astray* because they are hardened, deliberately shut against God's word, refusing to believe. It is this rebellion of heart which stirs God's *anger*. His anger is not an impulsive reaction but his judgement on sin. His judgement was to leave Israel where they wanted to be, wandering in the wilderness. The *rest* they were forbidden to enjoy was the promised land, the land flowing with milk and honey. Of the generation which experienced the miracle of the Exodus, none entered the land of promise except Joshua and Caleb. The letter to the Hebrews interprets the *rest* as the experience of God's salvation in Christ. Hebrews warns Christians against the same kind of unbelief which brought judgement on Israel, unbelief which is the refusal to believe and which leads one 'to turn away from the living God' (Hebrews 3:12).

Benedictus: Luke 1:68—79

Luke places this canticle on the lips of Zechariah, father of John the Baptist, on the occasion of John's circumcision. Luke leads into the canticle with the words: 'His [John's] father Zechariah was filled with the Holy Spirit and spoke this prophecy.' Thus the canticle is more than a hymn of thanksgiving. It is a prophetic vision of the ministry of John and of the Messiah for whom he will prepare the way. The Benedictus celebrates God's salvation in Christ as the fulfilment of the Old Testament hope. It celebrates the coming of the Messiah promised to David, the possession of the land promised to the patriarchs, and the light seen by the prophets. The first part of the canticle focuses on the mission of the Messiah, and the second part on the ministry of his forerunner, John the Baptist. The canticle abounds in Old Testament quotations and allusions, and may well have been an existing psalm which Luke adapted for his purpose.

Blessed be the Lord, the God of Israel!
He has visited his people and redeemed them.

The Old Testament often speaks of God visiting his people to bring deliverance. When Moses and Aaron spoke to the Israelites of the Lord's plan to come and set them free from their slavery in Egypt, Scripture says that the people worshipped 'when they heard that the Lord had visited the people of Israel and that he had seen their affliction' (Exodus 4:31). Zechariah praises God because he has come in Jesus as he came at the Exodus to set his people free. Redemption means 'setting slaves free'. Jesus came 'to save his people from their sins' (Matthew 1:21), to set us free from the slavery of sin, to redeem us.

Some of the tenses in the first part of the Benedictus are in the past (*he has visited his people, he has raised up for us a mighty saviour*), but the events they refer to, the events through which God will redeem his people, are in the future – the birth, life, death, and resurrection of Jesus. This style of speech is common to the prophets. They express the absolute certainty of a future event by speaking as if it had already happened. All that has happened up to this point in Luke's Gospel is the conception of Jesus, but as a prophet Zechariah foresees the future significance of Mary's child while the child is still in her womb.

He has raised up for us a mighty saviour
in the house of David his servant,
as he promised by the lips of holy men,
those who were his prophets from of old.

The opening lines of the canticle spoke of the Lord launching a new Exodus in Jesus. Here we learn how Jesus is the Messiah, the fulfilment of God's promise to David. Through the prophet Nathan the Lord said to David: 'I will raise up your offspring after you, who shall come forth from your body, and I will establish his kingdom. . . . I will establish the throne of his kingdom for ever' (2 Samuel 7:13,14). After the end of the monarchy and during the exile the prophets of Israel understood this promise to David to be a promise of the coming Messiah. The Benedictus proclaims that in Jesus all the promises of the Old Testament prophets concerning the Messiah will be fulfilled. He is the Messiah of the house of David which Israel has been longing for. Luke will later (chapter 3) trace Jesus' lineage back to David. He comes from *the house of David his servant.*

A saviour who would free us from our foes,
from the hands of all who hate us.
So his love for our fathers is fulfilled
and his holy covenant remembered.

The meaning of Jesus as saviour begins to be unfolded. He is *a saviour who* will *free us from our foes*. The *foes* are all those who attack the people of God, all those who oppose God's salvation. Historically Zechariah and his generation (including the disciples) would have assumed that the occupying Roman forces were their *foes*, but Luke's Gospel will go on to reveal how Jesus came to set us free from the far more deadly and universal *foes* of sin and Satan.

This coming salvation is God's fulfilment of his holy covenant with Israel. When Israel cried out to the Lord for help during their slavery in Egypt, the book of Exodus says: 'God heard their groaning, and God remembered his covenant with Abraham, with Isaac, and with Jacob' (2:24). The covenant was later renewed in the promise: 'You shall be my people, and I will be your God' (Ezekiel 36:28).

He swore to Abraham our father to grant us,
that free from fear, and saved from the
hands of our foes,
we might serve him in holiness and justice
all the days of our life in his presence.

The oath to which the canticle refers is found in Genesis 22:16—17, where the Lord promises Abraham: 'I will indeed bless you, and I will multiply your descendants as the stars of heaven and as the sand which is on the seashore. And your descendants shall possess the gate of their enemies, and by your descendants shall all the nations of the earth bless themselves.' ('To possess the gate of your enemies' means to take over their towns, to have victory over them.) Luke's canticle interprets the Lord's promise in a broad sense as meaning deliverance from enemies and the freedom to worship and serve the Lord in obedience to his commandments, to live a life characterized by *holiness and justice*, a life lived in *his presence*. God's oath to Abraham is fulfilled in Jesus and in the salvation he brings.

As for you, little child,
you shall be called a prophet of God, the Most High.
You shall go ahead of the Lord
to prepare his ways before him,

The canticle now turns to the role which John the Baptist will play in this mighty deliverance God will bring. John is the *little child* who will *be called a prophet of God*. Luke has earlier spoken of Jesus as the Son of the Most High (Luke 1:32). John is to be *a prophet of the Most High*. His task will be *to prepare* the way of the *Lord* (Jesus), a task which is more clearly defined in the next verse.

To make known to his people their salvation
through forgiveness of all their sins,
the loving-kindness of the heart of our God
who visits us like the dawn from on high.

John's task is spelt out. He is not the saviour. He is *to make known to his people their salvation*, a task he fulfils when he points people to Jesus. Salvation is defined as the *forgiveness of sins*, and *the loving-kindness of the heart of our God*. John's message as described in Luke 3 was a strong call to repentance and the promise of baptism in the Holy Spirit and fire. This message was proclaimed again by Peter at Pentecost, when he called the people to 'Repent, and be baptized every one of you in the name of Jesus Christ for the forgiveness of your sins; and you will receive the gift of the Holy Spirit' (Acts 2:38).

The *dawn from on high* is Jesus, whose coming breaks the darkness of sin and brings the light of God's forgiveness and peace.

He will give light to those in darkness,
those who dwell in the shadow of death,
and guide us into the way of peace.

It is the Messiah, Jesus, *the dawn from on high*, who banishes the darkness of sin and brings the light of God's revelation. By his life, death and resurrection Jesus sets us free from the power of death, and *guides us into the way of peace. Peace* means the whole richness of God's salvation in Jesus.

Magnificat: Luke 1:46—55

When Mary went to visit her cousin Elizabeth, Elizabeth was filled with the Holy Spirit and exclaimed: 'Of all women you [Mary] are most blessed, and blessed is the fruit of your womb . . . Blessed is she who believed that the promise made her by the Lord would be fulfilled' (Luke 1:42—45). In response, Mary praises God in the words of the Magnificat.

Both the Magnificat and the Benedictus may have come from the circle of the Poor Ones (in Hebrew, the *Anawim*), a Jewish Christian group of lowly people whose faith was characterized by intense devotion to the Lord as the one who defends the poor and opposes the proud.

My soul glorifies the Lord,
my spirit rejoices in God, my Saviour.
He looks on his servant in her lowliness;
henceforth all ages will call me blessed.

Mary extols the Lord God and acknowledges him as her *Saviour*. Through the birth of her child Jesus God's decisive act of salvation will begin. Mary is overcome with the extraordinary honour the Lord has given her, because she regards herself as unworthy to be the mother of the one who will be the long-promised Messiah, Son of David and Son of God (Luke 1:32,35). This awesome privilege given to Mary means that all Christians of all time will count her as *blessed*. One of the intercessions from the Office expresses the attitude of the Church of all ages to Mary. 'From all eternity God chose Mary to be the Mother of Christ. Therefore she is above all other creatures both in heaven and on earth. With her we proclaim: My soul glorifies the Lord.' (Week 3, Saturday Morning Prayer).

The Almighty works marvels for me.
Holy his name!
His mercy is from age to age,
on those who fear him.

The word *marvels* is used in the Old Testament to describe God's action in delivering Israel from Egypt (Deuteronomy 10:21). The birth of the Messiah will begin the greatest of all God's *marvels* of salvation, the greatest act of *mercy* the world will ever see. Those who recognize God's sovereignty (*those who fear him*) are the ones who will rejoice in his *mercy*. Luke's Gospel is *par excellence* the Gospel which shows us the mercy of God in Christ to the sick, the poor, the broken-hearted, the outcasts.

He puts forth his arm in strength
and scatters the proud-hearted.
He casts the mighty from their thrones
and raises the lowly.

The *proud-hearted* are the enemies of God, those who oppose his salvation. Isaiah speaks of the day when the Lord will 'put an end to the pride of the arrogant' (13:11), and the Magnificat declares that that day has come with Christ. Luke tells how the Pharisees and rulers of the people, *the proud-hearted*, put Jesus to death; but in the resurrection and the gift of the Spirit at Pentecost a new Israel was born. The Church was led by those who were described as 'uneducated, common men' (Acts 4:13), but they *scattered the proud-hearted* with their boldness and the power of the Holy Spirit.

'God chose what is weak in the world to bring to shame the strong' (1 Corinthians 1:27). This same action of God is expressed also as the way he *casts the mighty from their thrones and raises the lowly.*

He fills the starving with good things,
sends the rich away empty.

The Gospels record how this promise was fulfilled in a very literal way. It was the wealthy elite of Israel who rejected Jesus and in the end were sent away *empty*. They refused the salvation offered by God and they ended up with nothing. It was the *starving*, the poor, who welcomed Jesus, believed in him, and were filled with the *good things* God gave in Christ, the gifts of forgiveness and the Holy Spirit. In the life of the kingdom it is those who continue to 'hunger and thirst after righteousness' who will be filled. It is those who are poor in spirit, those who know their need of God, who will be satisfied.

He protects Israel, his servant,
remembering his mercy,
the mercy promised to our fathers,
to Abraham and his sons for ever.

In the prophecy of Isaiah the Lord said to Israel: 'You are my servant, I have chosen you and not cast you off' (41:9). God came in Jesus to protect Israel, but Israel rejected him.

The canticle ends by recalling the promises the Lord made to the patriarchs, *to Abraham and his sons*. The Lord said to Abraham: 'I will establish my covenant between me and you and your descendents after you throughout their generations for an everlasting covenant, to be God to you and to your descendents after you' (Genesis 17:7). In Jesus God fulfilled the covenant made with *Abraham and his sons.*

Commentary on the Psalmody of Week 1

Week 1: Sunday

EVENING PRAYER I

Evening Prayer begins with a prayer for constancy in following the Lord (Psalm 140), and continues by asking for God's help in the face of overwhelming opposition (Psalm 141). The final canticle (Philippians 2) extols the glorious vindication of Christ who was obedient even to *death on a cross,* and who was rescued by God in the resurrection.

Psalm 140(141):1—9

Psalm 140 was written for evening prayer. It quickly became the classic evening psalm for Christian prayer. Thus it is a prayer that has been offered in the evening for well over 2,000 years. In praying the psalm we ask that we will be faithful to the Lord in the face of the temptation to compromise what matters most.

> *Let my prayer arise before you like incense,*
> *the raising of my hands like an evening oblation.*

The original setting of the psalm may have been the *evening oblation*, the evening sacrifice offered in the Temple at the end of each day. The burning of *incense* accompanied the offering. *The raising of . . . hands* is the traditional Jewish gesture accompanying prayer. It has been carried over into Christian prayer in the gestures of the priest presiding at the Eucharist. It is prayer in body language, the lifting of our life to God and the opening of our hands to receive his gifts.

Set, O Lord, a guard over my mouth

The psalmist recognizes how easy it is to let slip a word which will wound others or compromise the truth, and he prays that no such word will ever pass his lips.

Do not turn my heart to things that are wrong.

He prays that not only his lips but his innermost thoughts and intentions (*heart* in Hebrew refers to both mind and will) will be true to the Lord. The prayer is an expression of absolute trust in God, of giving one's whole being over to his direction. (It should not be misunderstood as implying that the Lord could ever lead anyone to do wrong). The psalmist makes a conscious rejection of evil, recognizing that evil begins in the heart and must be renounced in the heart if our actions are to be true to God. The psalm is the prayer of those who seek to obey our Lord's teaching in the Sermon on the Mount, with its radical penetration to the heart of morality.

Never allow me to share in their feasting. . . .
let the oil of the wicked not anoint my head.

The psalmist is tempted to join the company of those who reject the way of the Lord. They tempt him to follow their way by offering him lavish hospitality. Guests were traditionally anointed with perfumed olive oil as they arrived at a feast.

This is not the prayer of a self-righteous prig, or of a person unwilling to show our Lord's welcome to sinners by eating with them. It is the prayer of a man who knows the enormous power of bad friends, of peer pressure, to entice him into wrongdoing. C.S. Lewis described how 'There is a subtle play of looks and tones and laughs by which a mortal can imply that he is of the same party as those to whom he is speaking . . . . He will assume, at first only by his manner, but presently by his words, all sorts of cynical and sceptical attitudes which are not really his. But . . . they may become his.'

(*Screwtape Letters*, no. 10). St Paul warned that 'Bad company ruins good morals' (1 Corinthians 15:33).

> *Their princes were thrown down by the side of the rock:*
> *then they understood that my words were kind.*

This may refer to an ancient way of executing criminals – throwing them off a high cliff. Jesus himself nearly suffered the same treatment (Luke 4:29). These bad friends of the psalmist only come to their senses when they see the sticky end of their leaders, who suffer the ultimate disgrace of not even having a proper burial: *their bones were strewn at the mouth of the grave.*

> *To you, Lord God, my eyes are turned:*
> *in you I take refuge; spare my soul!*
> *From the trap they have laid for me keep me safe:*

Only the Lord can protect the psalmist from the force of the temptation to go with those who reject God's law and who are trying to entrap him and to entice him to join them. Every one of us faces subtle pressures to conform to the prevailing values and standards of our society, whether these are Christian or not. Psalm 140 is a prayer that we will resist that pressure and remain true to Christ.

The *antiphons* take up different aspects of the psalm, adapting it to the particular season of the Christian year. They all recognize that the psalm is a prayer for integrity and for faithfulness to the Lord.

The *heading* describes the psalm as Prayer in Time of Danger. The danger is the danger of being lured away from obedience to God.

The *sentence, The smoke of incense rose before God with the prayers of the saints from the hand of the angel* (Revelation 8:4), reminds us that this prayer, the prayer of the Church, ascends into the very presence of God.

Psalm 141(142)

This psalm is a lament of an individual. As with most of the laments it is difficult to determine the precise nature of the psalmist's trouble. Is the *prison* of the last part of the psalm meant to be understood literally or figuratively? Either way, the psalm is the cry of a person falsely accused by strong enemies, with nowhere to go for help but to the Lord. The psalm can be prayed by or on behalf of anyone undergoing severe persecution, but the sentence at the beginning of the psalm invites us to pray the psalm with Christ. The sentence from St Hilary, *All these things were fulfilled by the Lord at the time of his passion*, invites us to enter into the heart of our Lord in his suffering.

The psalm can thus be prayed in four ways.

1. It can express the prayer of anyone who is struggling for what is right, surrounded by overwhelming opposition from people determined to beat them down.

2. The opposition may not be from other people, but from within ourselves, from our own passions; so the psalm can be prayed by anyone struggling with crushing temptation or fear. St Francis was praying this psalm as he died.

3. The psalm leads us into the experience of men and women who are suffering injustice from governments or social structures whose power seems to be absolute. We pray with them as members of the same body, the Body of Christ, sharing through prayer in their struggle.

4. The psalm expresses the prayer of our Lord at his passion. We pray with and in our Saviour, in his prayer to the Father, as he suffered and died for the salvation of the world.

The antiphons take up these different ways of praying the psalm.

Most of the psalm is self-explanatory, but one or two phrases need some comment.

On the way where I shall walk
they have hidden a snare to entrap me.

As the psalmist sets out to do what is right he is aware that his enemies are lying in wait to trap him. Precisely how they intend to trap him we do not know.

Look on my right.

The *right* side was the traditional place taken by a friend or helper. When the psalmist looks to his right there is no one. He is alone, with none but the Lord to protect him:

'You are my refuge,
all I have in the land of the living.'

Around me the just will assemble
because of your goodness to me.

Despite the hopelessness of his situation, the psalmist still has hope that the Lord will vindicate him, and he looks forward to the time when he will come to the Temple to give thanks for his deliverance, surrounded by *the just*.

Philippians 2:6—11

This canticle is an early Christian hymn taken up by Paul in his appeal for unity in the Church at Philippi. Unity, he says, can only come as we each imitate the example of Christ in his humility.

Though he was in the form of God,
Jesus did not count equality with God
a thing to be grasped.

The hymn may be making a comparison between Christ and Adam. Adam, made in the image of God, grasped proudly at equality with God and lost the glory of communion with God. By contrast, Christ, *who was in the form of God*, in humility was obedient to the will of the Father and received the highest honour *in heaven and on earth*.

Jesus did not regard his *equality with God* as a privilege to be jealously clung to, *a thing to be grasped* at all costs. Instead,

He emptied himself,
taking the form of a servant,
being born in the likeness of men.

When Jesus became man he did not cease to be God, he did not empty himself of his divinity. He emptied himself of all the glory and status, all the privileges and honour which rightly accompanied his divine nature. (At the transfiguration the disciples are given a glimpse of the divine glory, the *form of God*, which Jesus put aside in becoming man). *A servant* was the lowest human status, and therefore the most dramatic contrast to *the form of God*. Jesus described his mission as that of a servant: 'The Son of Man came not to be served but to serve, and give his life as a ransom for many.' (Mark 10:45). His mission began when he was *born in the likeness of men*.

And being found in human form,
he humbled himself and became obedient unto death,
even death on a cross.

The hymn takes us down, down, down, each step involving a radical humility. Jesus not only became a human being, he suffered the ultimate fate of all humanity – death. His death was no ordinary death, but the most humiliating of deaths, death on a cross. The Old Testament Law pronounced a curse on anyone who died as Jesus did: 'Cursed be every one who hangs on a tree.' (Galatians 3:13, quoting Deuteronomy 21:23). This is as far from the glory of God as it is possible to go.

Therefore God has highly exalted him
and bestowed on him the name
which is above every name.

The hymn now lifts our gaze from the depths to the heights. Jesus humbled himself, God now acts to exalt him. This is the strongest appeal Paul can make for Christian unity – 'Follow the example of our Lord in his humility. Never hesitate to renounce your status or dignity in order to serve one another. If you follow the way of Jesus, God will exalt you.'

The same message is given in 1 Peter (5:6), 'Clothe yourselves, all of you, with humility toward one another, for "God opposes the proud, but gives grace to the humble." Humble yourselves therefore under the mighty hand of God, that in due time he may exalt you.'

The *name which is above every name* is revealed to us at the conclusion of the hymn. It is the name of God himself, the name 'Lord'. In the Scriptures a person's name expresses their nature and character. By bestowing on Jesus the name 'Lord', the name of God, God is declaring to the world the nature, character and authority of his Son.

That at the name of Jesus every knee should bow,
in heaven and on earth and under the earth.

In Isaiah 45:23 the Lord God declares:

By my own self I swear it;
what comes from my mouth is saving justice,
it is an irrevocable word:
All shall bend the knee to me,
by me every tongue shall swear,
saying, 'In Yahweh alone
are saving justice and strength,
until all those who used to rage at him
come to him in shame.

Jesus begins to fulfil this prophecy of the saving justice of God, a justice which will eventually triumph throughout the whole cosmos, *in heaven, on earth, under the earth.* (The underworld was the traditional place of the dead).

And every tongue confess that Jesus Christ is Lord,
to the glory of God the Father.

Lord is the name used in the Old Testament for God himself. The Hebrew name was YHWH (translated into English as Yahweh), for which the Jews substituted the word *Adonai, Lord,* because they believed the divine name was too holy to pronounce. The Septuagint (the Greek translation of the Old Testament) translated YHWH as *Kyrios,* Greek for 'Lord', and it is this word *Kyrios* which is used for Jesus here in the Philippian hymn.

The confession *Jesus Christ is Lord* was the earliest Christian creed, and is the climax of the hymn.

MORNING PRAYER

This morning's psalmody begins with the prayer of all those who come to worship in Spirit and in truth: *O God, you are my God, for you I long.* (Psalm 63). The longing for God turns into exuberant praise of God in the canticle from Daniel, and in the victory song of the saints (Psalm 149).

Psalm 62(63):2—9

With intense longing the psalmist expresses his desire for the presence of God. The psalm perfectly fits the day on which it is placed in Morning Prayer. It expresses the Christian's hunger for the presence of Christ in the Eucharistic meal.

O God, you are my God, for you I long;
for you my soul is thirsting,
my body pines for you
like a dry, weary land without water.

The psalmist is as thirsty for God as the land is for water in a parched desert. This thirst for God is the foundation of Christian life and growth. The New Testament repeatedly underlines the principle that only as we seek will we find. The hungry are filled with good things while the rich go away empty. The first beatitude promises blessings to the poor in spirit, to those who are thirsty for God.

So I gaze on you in the sanctuary
to see your strength and your glory.

The reference may be to a unique experience of God's glory, such as that described in Isaiah 6:1—10, when the prophet 'saw the Lord seated on a high and lofty throne; his train filled the sanctuary . . . and the Temple was full of smoke'. Or it may refer to a more common experience, where the psalmist sees God's strength and glory symbolized in the Ark of the Covenant, or in the Temple liturgy with its splendid music, drama, and sacrifice. The Christian coming to the Eucharist thinks instinctively of the presence of Christ in the consecrated bread, lifted up by the priest with the acclamation:

'This is the Lamb of God
who takes away the sins of the world.'

We gaze on him in the sanctuary to see his strength and glory.

For your love is better that life.

In the Old Testament life is regarded as the greatest gift of God, and yet the psalmist has come to see that the love of the Lord is even more precious than life itself.

In your name I will lift up my hands.

The psalmist knows that where the Lord's name is, there is his presence, so he begins his worship by calling the name of the Lord. The lifting up of both hands was the traditional posture of prayer, and a visible sign of the psalmist's longing that his empty hands would be filled with God's blessings.

My soul shall be filled as with a banquet.

In some of the Temple sacrifices the worshipper ate part of the sacrificial animal. This sacrificial meal becomes a sign for the psalmist of the spiritual refreshment he receives in the presence of the Lord. The *banquet* at which the Christian is filled is the Eucharist, where we feed on Christ in his word and in the sacrament, the sacrifice of his body and blood.

On my bed I remember you.
On you I muse through the night

The night hours have traditionally been a time of testing, a time when human defences are low and when the pull to evil seems stronger. So the psalmist deliberately decides to meditate in the night on the Lord, to turn to him for help. The need to turn to God for help in the night, to turn away from sin, is taken up in the **sentence**, *Let the man who has put away the deeds of the night watch for God.* The night is a symbol of ignorance and evil.

In the shadow of your wings I rejoice.

The *wings* may be the wings of a mother bird protecting her chicks, or the wings of the gold cherubim above the Ark of the Covenant in the sanctuary of the Temple. The psalmist rejoices in the protection of the presence of the Lord.

Your right hand holds me fast.

The right hand is the strong hand, the hand which protects (holds the sword) and the hand which works most powerfully.

Daniel 3:57—88, 56

This great canticle is inserted into the story of the three young men, Ananias, Azarias and Mizael who were thrown into the fiery furnace by the Babylonian King

Nebuchadnezzar. It is a hymn in which the whole of creation (*all you works of the Lord*), grouped into three choirs (*the heavens, the earth, children of men*), is called on to praise the Lord:

1. *The Heavens.* All heavenly beings and the heavens themselves (*angels, heavens, clouds, armies (spiritual powers), sun and moon, stars, showers and rain*) are called on to praise the Lord, together with all natural phenomena (*breezes and winds, fire and heat,* and so on).

2. *The Earth.* All features and creatures on earth (*mountains, plants, birds*, and so on), *O bless the Lord.*

3. *The children of men.* All the people of God (*children of men, priests, servants of the Lord, spirits and souls of the just*), *O bless the Lord.*

The order is the order of creation as described in Genesis 1.

Here is creation worshipping its creator, acknowledging that it owes its beginning and its continuing life to God. When the psalms and canticles call on all creation to praise the Lord, this is not poetical imagination, but a profound insight into the link between the creator and the creation. All created things, including humankind, are made by God and so must respond to their creator with praise. Praise is the response of creatures to their creation. Men and women can praise God consciously, with heart and mind and voice. The rest of creation praises God simply by the fact of its existence, as a work of art praises the one who painted it by being what it is, a thing of beauty. All creation praises the Lord by the fact of its existence, and this canticle (and other psalms like it) call on creation to go on doing what it has always done – praise the Lord.

This is a canticle to be prayed with imagination, bringing to mind some of the glorious beauty of creation as we have experienced it.

Psalm 149

This psalm of praise was sung originally to celebrate a victory by Israel's armies. It is sung by the Christian to celebrate the victory of Christ, who will come on the Last Day to judge the living and the dead.

Sing a new song to the Lord.

The *new song* may have been just that, a song especially composed for the occasion, or it may refer to a song sung to celebrate a new experience of God's action in Israel's history, saving Israel from her enemies. God's revelation of himself in Christ is the unique experience of salvation for which the Christian sings a *new song to the Lord.*

His praise in the assembly of the faithful.

For the Christian, *the assembly of the faithful* is the Church, and the placing of the psalm on Sunday leads us into the Eucharistic celebration where we rejoice in God's victory over sin.

Let Israel rejoice in its Maker.

The *Maker* refers not to creation but to the Lord's action in making a group of slaves and semi-nomads into a nation. The Church is the new Israel, made by the Lord. The Church was made through Jesus' action, when he called his apostles, died on the cross, rose from the dead, and baptized his disciples in the Holy Spirit. The Church is the People of God, called to *rejoice in its Maker.*

Let Sion's sons exult in their king.

The *sons of Sion* are those who worship the Lord on Sion, the holy mountain, Jerusalem. The *king* here is the Lord, not the Davidic king. It is the Lord who rules Israel and protects her. The early Christians quickly applied to Christ these references to the Lord as king. Christ was the true king of

Israel, the promised Messiah, the king who, according to John's Gospel, was enthroned on the cross. The sentence brings out this meaning: *The members of the Church, God's new people, will rejoice in their king, who is Christ* (Hesychius). (St Hesychius of Jerusalem was a fifth century Scripture scholar and monk).

Let them praise his name with dancing
and make music with timbrel and harp.

Dancing was common in Israel to express rejoicing after a national victory or to express joy during one of the great religious festivals. Jewish worship was very exuberant and festive, more like a black African ceremony than a white Anglo-Saxon liturgy.

Let the faithful rejoice in their glory,
shout for joy and take their rest.

After the joyful victory celebrations, the faithful will continue to celebrate by taking their rest, reclining at the feast.

Let the praise of God be on their lips
and a two-edged sword in their hand.

The combination of praising God while at the same time wielding a two-edged sword sounds incongruous and even offensive to us. The original scene was a victory dance, where the soldiers carried their weapons in the victory procession. The Book of Judith describes how Judith, following the victory over Holofernes, 'took her place at the head of the procession and led the women as they danced. All the men of Israel, armed and garlanded, followed them, singing hymns.' (Judith 15:13). We will consider how the Christian can pray this part of the psalm after looking at the last stanza.

To deal out vengeance to the nations
and punishment on all the peoples;
to bind their kings in chains

and their nobles in fetters of iron;
to carry out the sentence pre-ordained:
this honour is for all his faithful.

In its original setting, this section of the psalm continues the theme of victory over enemies, and turns from the victory of the recent past to look forward to the future victories of Israel's armies, when they will vanquish their foes, capture the enemy kings, and carry our God's judgement announced by the prophets against those who threaten to destroy his people.

How are we to pray this part of the psalm? The *antiphons* provide the crucial clues.

The antiphon for Advent interprets the psalm as a prophecy concerning the Second Coming, when Christ will return as judge of the living and the dead. '*Behold, a great Prophet will come and he will renew Jerusalem, alleluia.*' On that day the saints will share in Christ's work of judgement. St Paul said: 'Do you not realise that the holy people of God are to be the judges of the world?' (1 Corinthians 6:3). On that day the 'holy people of God' will fulfill the prophecy of this psalm, not in the bloodthirsty manner described, but in the way of the Lamb of God. According to John's Gospel (3:17—21) the judgement of the Last Day will be a matter of confirming the decision about Christ which people have already made in this life. In this sense, people judge themselves by the decisions they make here and now. As we pray the psalm guided by the Advent antiphon we rejoice in the hope of that day when Christ will come to bring true justice to the earth.

The antiphon for Lent, Sunday 1 gives a different slant to the psalm. '*The Lord takes delight in his people. He crowns the poor with salvation.*' Here we are directed to Christ as the judge who comes bringing perfect justice, salvation for the poor and oppressed. In Psalm 149 Israel represents the poor, surrounded by powerful foes, but rejoicing in God's saving help. The antiphon for Lent, Sunday 1 reminds us that the blessings of salvation are promised to the poor in spirit who cry to God for help. As St Paul urged the Ephesians, we must grow strong in the Lord, with the strength of his power, and put on the full armour of God, so as to be able to resist the devil's tactics. For it is not against human enemies that we have to struggle, but against the principalities and the ruling forces who are masters of the darkness in this world, the spirits of evil in the heavens. (Ephesians 6:10—12). The sword which we wield in this warfare is not a physical sword but the word of God, the sword of the Spirit. (Ephesians 6:17). We pray this psalm, then, conscious of the fact that we are engaged in a spiritual struggle, a struggle in which final victory is assured through Christ.

The antiphon for the fifth Sunday in Lent comes from John 12:23, *'Now the hour has come for the Son of Man to be glorified.'* John's Gospel interprets the cross as the beginning of the great hour of Jesus' victory. He is glorified when he is crucified. It is on the cross that he defeats the Prince of this world. *The sentence pre-ordained* of Psalm 149 is: 'God so loved the world that he gave his only son, so that everyone who believes in him may not perish but have eternal life.' (John 3:16). The cross of Jesus draws the military force out of Psalm 149, and replaces it with the force of love and the power of the Spirit. It was on the cross, not on the battlefield, that the great victory over our enemies, over sin and Satan, was won. As we pray the psalm we rejoice in the triumph of the cross.

The antiphon for Eastertide *'Let the saints rejoice in glory, alleluia'* looks forward to the day when 'there will be no more death, and no more mourning or sadness or pain. The world of the past is gone.' (Revelation 21:4). The victory of the resurrection is the first fruits of the final victory over all evil. We pray the psalm with this hope before us.

EVENING PRAYER II

The first psalm (109) is the most quoted psalm in the New Testament. It was loved by the early Church because Jesus himself read it as a prophecy of his role as God's Messiah. The second psalm (113A) celebrates God's power as the redeemer of his people, and the final canticle from Revelation joins our praise with the praise of heaven. In Lent the final canticle is from the First Letter of Peter, and is a hymn expounding the meaning of the cross.

Psalm 109(110):1—5,7

This psalm was studied in detail in Chapter 9, Christ in the Psalms, and the following exposition is an application and summary of what was said there. Psalm 109(110) occurs each Sunday, for Evening Prayer II. Jesus interpreted the psalm in Matthew 22:41—46 as a prophecy of King David concerning the coming Messiah, and that is the interpretation followed in the Office, as indicated by the **heading**: 'The Messiah is King and Priest'; and the **sentence**: *He must be king so that he may put all his enemies under his feet* (1 Corinthians 15:25). The psalm begins:

> *The Lord's revelation to my Master:*
> *'Sit on my right:*
> *your foes I will put beneath your feet.'*

Imagine David is speaking: when he speaks of *my Master* he is referring to the Messiah, to Christ, and is prophesying Christ's victory over his *foes,* over sin and death. The *right* was the side of honour and authority. When enemy kings were conquered they were sometimes forced to kneel while the conquering king put his foot on their neck, as a sign of his total victory over them. St Paul quotes this phrase with reference to Christ's resurrection, his victory over death. (1 Corinthians 15:25—27).

The Lord will wield from Sion
your sceptre of power:

The Lord God will wield the Messiah's sceptre. In other words, the Lord will exercise his divine authority and power through the Messiah. Sion is another name for Jerusalem, the Holy City.

rule in the midst of all your foes.

The Messiah is commanded to exercise his authority as God's representative over all peoples.

A prince from the day of your birth
on the holy mountains;
from the womb before the dawn I begot you.

The Messiah is given royal dignity from birth, and he is 'son of God' – *from the womb . . . I begot you.* The early Church read this verse as a prophecy of Christ, born Son of God in a unique sense.

The Lord has sworn an oath he will not change
'You are a priest for ever,
a priest like Melchizedek of old.'

This prophetic oracle bestows on the Messiah the priestly office. Melchizedek was a mysterious figure, described in Genesis 14:18 as king of Salem (possibly an early name for Jerusalem) and 'a priest of God Most High'. He blessed Abram and Abram gave him a tithe of all he possessed. Psalm 109(110) takes Melchizedek as a forerunner of the Messiah, who, like Melchizedek, is invested with his authority not by an earthly power but by God himself. The Church reads this verse as a clear prophecy of Christ's priesthood. Its relationship to the priesthood of Melchizedek is worked out in Hebrews 7.

The Master standing at your right hand
will shatter kings in the day of his wrath.

This verse appears to be addressed to God, and speaks of the victory the Messiah will have over all his enemies. In looking at the previous psalm, Psalm 149, we saw how this victory is to be understood. The earth's *kings* will be judged by Christ.

He shall drink from the stream by the wayside
and therefore he will lift up his head.

During the coronation ceremony the king may have drunk water from the brook, possibly the spring Gihon in Jerusalem, mentioned in connection with the anointing of King Solomon, (1 Kings 1:33—45), in order to be endowed with life and power. The Messiah will be filled with the Spirit, the water of eternal life, and will therefore be triumphant. To *lift up his head* is a metaphor for victory.

The different ways that this psalm can be prayed with reference to Christ are indicated by the antiphons. The antiphon Through the Year, *The Lord will send his mighty sceptre from Sion, and he will rule for ever, alleluia* gives the basic Christian interpretation of the psalm as a prophecy concerning Christ. God's authority and power are exercised through the rule of Christ. The Advent antiphon, *Rejoice greatly, daughter of Ṣion, shout with gladness, daughter of Jerusalem, alleluia* recalls Christ's triumphant entry into Jerusalem and looks forward to his second coming in power and glory.

The antiphon for Lent, Sunday 1, *You must worship the Lord, your God, and serve him alone* takes the reply Jesus gave at his temptation in the wilderness (the event which is recalled on this Sunday) and underlines the sovereign rule of the Lord. He has authority over Satan, the ultimate enemy. The antiphon for Lent, Sunday 5, *As Moses lifted up the serpent in the desert, so the Son of Man must be lifted up* reminds us that the Messiah reigns from the tree, that his victory on the cross opened the way to salvation for all people. Finally, the Eastertide antiphon: *The Lord has risen and sits at the right hand of God, alleluia* celebrates the 'coronation' of Christ, his ascension to his rightful place as ruler of all.

Psalm 113A(114):1—8

Israel's Exodus from Egypt and her entry into the promised land are the events celebrated with great vigour in this psalm. In Israel's liturgy the psalm was sung on the eighth day of the Passover Festival. The Christian interpretation is suggested by the **sentence:** *You, who have renounced this world, have also been led forth from Egypt* (St Augustine). Egypt is a symbol for the captivity of sin, and the Exodus is the Christian's liberation through the death and resurrection of Christ.

When Israel came forth from Egypt.

This verse proclaims that the birth of the nation, the time when it *came forth*, was at the Exodus

Jacob's sons from an alien people.

Jacob was regarded as the father of the nation of Israel. *Jacob's sons* means the family of Jacob which God has blessed and multiplied until it has become a great nation. The *alien people* are the Egyptians.

Judah became the Lord's temple.

Judah was the tribe centred around Jerusalem, the site of the Temple. As the tribe which gave Israel its greatest king, David, and in whose territory was the sacred Temple, Judah was sometimes synonymous with Israel. The verse implies that the nation of Israel is the people of God, the people amongst whom he dwells, his *temple*.

In praying this stanza, the Christian looks back to the

cross and resurrection as the moment when the new Israel, the Church, was born, and as the time when the Church became the temple of the Holy Spirit, the first fruits of the kingdom of God.

The sea fled at the sight

This is obviously a reference to the parting of the Sea of Reeds (as recorded in Exodus 14), enabling the Israelites to escape from the pursuing Egyptians. *Sea* in the Old Testament is often a symbol of the powers of chaos, and the psalm implies that these powers fled at the appearance of the Lord at the head of his people.

the Jordan turned back on its course

This refers to the occasion on the entry into the promised land when the river Jordan parted enabling the people to cross on dry ground. See Joshua 3—4.

the mountains leapt like rams
and the hills like yearling sheep

These two lines recall the appearance of the Lord on Mount Sinai when he made his covenant with Israel, and 'the whole mountain shook violently' (Exodus 19:18) with an earthquake.

Why was it, sea, that you fled etc?

Why did these great events happen? The last verse tells us:

Tremble, O earth, before the Lord,
in the presence of the God of Jacob.

It was the presence of the Lord which provoked these great events in Israel's history, the sea and the mountains in upheaval at his awesome presence.

who turns the rock into a pool
and flint into a spring of water

When Israel journeyed from Egypt to the promised land the Lord gave them water from the rock. See Exodus 17:1—7 for the story.

The antiphons again give the lead as to how to pray this psalm with the Church. At Advent as we pray the psalm we look forward to the final Exodus, when Christ will come and lead us to glory. At Eastertide we pray the psalm in the light of the Exodus of Christ on earth, his death and resurrection which won freedom from *the powers of darkness* for all who believe in him, and through which God brought us into *the kingdom of his Son, alleluia.*

Revelation 19:1,2,5—7

This canticle takes us into the courts of heaven. It is part of the song of victory sung after Babylon, symbol of all political powers which have persecuted the Church and murdered the faithful, is vanquished. The hymn is sung by the angels and martyrs, 'a huge crowd in heaven' (Revelation 19:1).

Alleluia is the Hebrew word meaning 'Praise Yah', that is, 'Praise Yahweh', 'Praise the Lord'. In the New Testament it occurs only in Revelation.

Salvation and glory and power belong to our God
His judgements are true and just.

God's justice finally triumphs over evil.

The Lord our God, the Almighty, reigns.

The constant prayer of God's people, 'Thy kingdom come', has finally been answered. The Lord reigns! Evil is vanquished.

The marriage of the Lamb has come,
and his bride has made herself ready.

The prophets spoke of Israel as the bride of the Lord (Hosea 2:18; Isaiah 54:6) and in the New Testament this imagery is transferred to Christ and his Church. Jesus described himself as the bridegroom (Mark 2:19), and St Paul speaks of the Church as the bride of Christ in a beautiful passage in Ephesians 5:25—27: 'Christ loved the Church and sacrificed himself for her to make her holy by washing her in cleansing water . . . so that when he took the Church to himself she would be glorious, . . . holy and faultless.' The bride has been made ready by the washing of baptism and the sanctifying power of the Holy Spirit. She is clothed in purity and splendour, ready to meet her spouse. In this canticle we celebrate that day when we, with all God's people, will be united forever with our Saviour, the one who loved us and gave himself for us.

1 Peter 2:21—24

During Lent this canticle takes the place of Revelation 19 and calls us to take up our cross and follow Christ. The context of the canticle in the First Letter of Peter is counsel to those who suffer unjustly, such as slaves under a harsh master.

Christ suffered for you,
leaving you an example
that you should follow in his steps.

The example of Christ in his suffering is the example the Christian is to follow in facing unjust treatment. This is not, as it has sometimes been interpreted, a call to ignore injustice, to stand by and let evil happen, to be a doormat. That is not what Christ did. Instead, 1 Peter (2:21—24) exhorts us, in our struggle for righteousness, personal and social, never to yield to hatred and bitterness, never to throw curses or threats, but to trust our cause to God, as Jesus did, knowing that God will vindicate his people in the end.

He committed no sin;
no guile was found on his lips.
When he was reviled,
he did not revile in return.

Peter has in mind the description in Isaiah 53 of the suffering servant of the Lord, and the actual behaviour of Jesus at his trial.

He himself bore our sins
in his body on the tree

Here are echoes of Isaiah, 'He was wounded for our rebellions, crushed because of our guilt; the punishment reconciling us fell on him.' (53:5).

that we might die to sin
and live to righteousness.

It is not enough for the Christian to know that Christ has borne our sins. The purpose of his death was that we too might die to sin and live a new life, a life not governed by the instinctive human law of tit for tat, of hatred and revenge in response to injustice.

By his wounds you have been healed

This verse speaks of the healing of forgiveness and the strength to live a new life, both of which flow from the cross.

Week 1: Monday

MORNING PRAYER

The day begins with humble worship of the Lord and prayer for deliverance from evil (Psalm 5), before moving on to praise (1 Chronicles 29) and awe at the mighty power of God's word (Psalm 28).

Psalm 5:2—10,12—13

The psalmist is oppressed by enemies, fellow Israelites who are destroying him with vicious slander. They are described as *bloodthirsty*, and would obviously not hesitate to do him physical harm. The psalmist begins his day by pleading with the Lord for help. For every Christian the struggle with our enemies (the world, the flesh, and the devil) is a daily business, and in Psalm 5 we turn to God with the prayer: 'Deliver us from evil.'

> *To my words give ear, O Lord,*
> *give head to my groaning.*

His anguish is so deep that his prayer is not just in *words*, but in *groaning*, in prayer that cannot find words but comes straight from the heart.

> *Attend to the sound of my cries,*
> *my King and my God.*

The king in Israel was also the chief judge, and so the psalmist appeals to the Lord, *my King*, to act as the supreme judge and give justice.

> *It is you whom I invoke, O Lord.*
> *In the morning you hear me;*
> *in the morning I offer you my prayer,*
> *watching and waiting.*

The psalmist is in the Temple, making his prayer in the morning, longing (*watching and waiting*) for a prophetic word from the Lord through the priest, a word which will give him hope. In Morning Prayer we come with a similar expectancy, knowing that the word of God is spoken to us afresh each day in the scriptures; hence the **sentence**: *Those who have received the Word of God which dwells within will rejoice for ever.*

> *You are no God who loves evil;*
> *no sinner is your guest.*
> *The boastful shall not stand their ground*
> *before your face.*

The *sinner* of this stanza is not the repentant believer, conscious of failure and weakness. Such a person is always welcome in God's presence. The sinner of this psalm is the person who loves evil, who arrogantly boasts of their own actions, who slanders the just (possibly giving false evidence in court), who is deceitful and ready to shed innocent blood. No such person can be God's guest, enjoying his hospitality and protection.

> *You hate all who do evil:*
> *you destroy all who lie.*

Those who do evil, as described in the psalm, will be judged by God. It is not up to us to take judgement into our own hands.

> *But I through the greatness of your love*

Love translates the Hebrew word *hesed*, which means covenant loyalty. God's *love* is his faithfulness to his promises of protection and blessing for Israel, assured by his covenant with them. It is this covenant love which the psalmist appeals to as the basis for his coming into God's house to pray for justice. As people of the new covenant, we have access into God's presence through the greatness of his love in Christ.

I bow down before your holy temple,
filled with awe.

The temple may remind us of the church where we worship, or more importantly of the one who is the new Temple, our Lord Jesus.

Lead me, Lord, in your justice,
because of those who lie in wait;
make clear your way before me.

At the beginning of the day we pray that we may avoid the Tempter, who 'is on the prowl like a roaring lion, looking for someone to devour' (1 Peter 5:8), and tread a clear path.

No truth can be found in their mouths,
their heart is all mischief,

further describes the enemies who are attempting to destroy the psalmist.

their throat a wide-open grave,

Their speech stinks, like an open grave in a hot climate. They may sound outwardly charming (*all honey their speech*), but inwardly their motives are deadly.

All those you protect shall be glad . . .

The psalm concludes with a joyful affirmation of God's protection, a marvellous certainty with which to begin the day. God's *favour* is like a *shield* which will protect the faithful from their enemies.

1 Chronicles 29:10—13

This canticle is self-explanatory. In the Book of Chronicles it comes as part of King David's thanksgiving prayer at the end of his life, as he looks forward to the building of the Temple. The **sentence** encourages us to bring the canticle up to date by offering it as praise for all the blessings the Father gives through our Lord Jesus.

As a prayer at the beginning of the day the canticle leads us to submit everything to God, to recognize that our life is lived under his rule.

Psalm 28(29)

The picture to keep in mind in reading this psalm is of a violent thunderstorm approaching the land (northern Israel) from the sea (the Mediterranean). The Lord comes in awesome majesty, like the approach of a thunderstorm, and the whole universe bows down in worship. This is generally agreed to be one of the oldest psalms in the psalter. It came to be part of the liturgy of the Feast of Tabernacles. (See Chapter 8, Israel's Festivals).

O give the Lord you sons of God,

The *sons of God* are the angels of the heavenly court, witnessing the appearance of the Lord, and called on to join in the great hymn of praise: *give the Lord glory and power.*

Adore the Lord in his holy court,

the court of heaven, where the *sons of God*, the angels, minister. The psalm begins with heaven giving praise to God, then moves to earth, where God comes in the storm.

The Lord's voice resounding on the waters,
the Lord on the immensity of waters.

The roar of the thunder is the voice of God booming out over the waters. The *waters* may refer to the Mediterranean sea, but more probably to the primeval waters of Genesis 1:2, 'Darkness was upon the face of the deep; and the wind of God was moving over the face of *the waters*.' In the Old Testament the waters, the sea, was a symbol of the forces of chaos which God tamed with his word at creation, as in Genesis 1: 'God said . . . and it was so.'

In Christian reflection, the *waters* came also to refer to the River Jordan, where Jesus heard the voice of his Father commissioning him for his mission. The **sentence** points us in this direction: *A voice was heard from heaven, saying, 'This is my beloved Son'* (Matthew 3:17).

The Lord's voice shattering the cedars,
the Lord shatters the cedars of Lebanon,

These trees were proverbial for their strength and grandeur. The Lord's voice is the lightning striking the cedars and splitting them open.

He makes Lebanon leap like a calf
and Sirion like a young wild-ox.

Lebanon means the mountains of Lebanon, the highest of which was *Sirion*, the Phoenician name for Mount Hermon. The mountains jump like a frightened calf at the coming of the Lord. The cedars and mountains of Lebanon were symbols of invincible strength and power, but they are as nothing compared to the power of the word of the Lord.

The Lord's voice flashes flames of fire

as bolts of lightning strike the earth, *shaking the wilderness. . . of Kadesh*, possibly the Syrian desert, *stripping the forest bare*, in the fierce intensity of the storm.

In his temple,

in heaven, where the angels cry: *Glory!*, the Lord sits

enthroned over the flood – a reference back to the *waters* of primeval times. Some commentators see here a reference to the flood of Noah, where God sat in judgement on the earth for its wickedness.

The Lord will give strength to his people,
the Lord will bless his people with peace.

The storm is over. The Lord who is so awesome in the wildest forces of nature is the same Lord who visits his people to give them strength and peace.

Seven times in this psalm we read of *The Lord's voice*, and this undoubtedly is the inspiration for the **heading** of the psalm, Public Praise of the Word of God. While in ancient Israel the voice of the Lord was associated with the storm, with thunder and lightning, for us the voice of the Lord is heard in the Word made flesh, in the Gospel of our Lord Jesus. It is this word which is 'living and powerful' (Hebrews 4:12), and which we praise in public worship as we respond to the reading of the scriptures:

'This is the Word of the Lord.'
'Thanks be to God.'

EVENING PRAYER

Psalm 10 is the prayer of someone surrounded by social chaos and looking to the Lord for justice. The second psalm (14) describes the quality of justice the Lord expects of those who pray for his help. The concluding canticle (Ephesians 1) gives glorious praise to God for his answer to all our prayers in the superabundant blessings he gives us in Christ.

Psalm 10(11)

This psalm seems to have been written by someone living in the midst of a general breakdown of law and order. His very life is threatened by ruthless men. In the face of this crisis the psalmist can either escape to the mountains or seek sanctuary in the Temple. The psalm can express the prayer of those who face similar social conditions today. It is the prayer of an innocent person seeking justice and God's protection. It is the prayer of all those *who hunger and thirst for what is right: they shall be satisfied* (Matthew 5:6) – the **sentence** for the psalm.

In the Lord I have taken refuge,

either by seeking protection in the Temple (under Israelite law the Temple was a place of sanctuary for the innocent), or by taking his fears to the Lord in prayer.

How can you say to my soul:

The *you* may refer to friends who have advised the psalmist, or *you* may refer to an inner voice, debating with the psalmist on how he should act in such a decadent society.

'Fly like a bird to its mountain.

He is tempted to flee from the chaos threatening him by escaping into the country, to the mountains, like a defenceless bird fleeing the hunter.

See the wicked bracing their bow;
they are fixing their arrows on the string
to shoot upright men in the dark.
Foundations once destroyed, what can the just do?'

His friends, or the inner voice, tell him to take a hard look at the threat. The *wicked* are preparing to destroy those who oppose their schemes, to do away with them by stealth. The very *foundations* of law and social order have broken down. What hope is there for the innocent? This psalm takes us into the plight of those whose lives are personally threatened in times of social upheaval. Should they escape to safety, or stand and resist? The psalmist looks to the Lord as his ultimate security.

The Lord is in his holy temple, in heaven, from where he rules the world, judging between the just and the wicked, preparing to destroy the wicked with *fire and brimstone* (traditional images of judgement, going back to the destruction of Sodom and Gomorrah) and save the innocent whom he loves. *Test* means to separate the bad from the good as a refiner of precious metals separates the dross from the gold.

The psalmist's confidence is restored by looking away from the evil surrounding him and looking to the Lord who reigns, whose kingdom will surely come. He turns to the Lord who is with him in his crisis (*In the Lord I have taken refuge*) and above him, ruling *in heaven*, and therefore in ultimate control. *The Lord is just and loves justice: the upright shall see his face* is the confident conclusion of the psalmist, the vision that gives him hope.

The psalm traces the movement of the soul from fear at the threat to life, to confidence in God who *loves justice.*

Psalm 14(15)

Psalm 14(15) has been called an 'entrance liturgy'. It is a psalm used by worshippers as they approach the Temple. The first verse is the people's question: *Lord, who shall be admitted to your tent and dwell on your holy mountain?* The rest of the psalm is the priest's answer, describing the conditions one must fulfil to be a guest of the Lord.

Lord, who shall be admitted to your tent?

The Temple at Jerusalem was sometimes called the *tent,* because the first tabernacle, erected during Israel's journey through the wilderness, was a tent.

and dwell on your holy mountain,

meaning Mount Sion, the actual site of the Temple building.

Sion was also a name used of the whole city of Jerusalem. To *dwell* has the sense of being a guest of the Lord, therefore enjoying the traditional friendship and protection that belongs to a guest.

The **sentence** gives the key as to how a Christian can pray the psalm: *You have come to Mount Sion to the city of the living God* (Hebrews 12:22). Our Mount Sion, our Temple, is the Body of Christ in heaven and on earth. The psalm prepares us to worship with the Church on earth, and it also prepares us to enter the Church in heaven. Jesus said, 'If your uprightness does not surpass that of the scribes and Pharisees, you will never get into the kingdom of heaven' (Matthew 5:20).

He who walks without fault

means the one who obeys the Law of the Lord. Psalm 119:1 speaks of those 'whose way is blameless, who walk in the Law of the Lord.' The second line puts the same idea in other words: *he who acts with justice* is he who is without fault. Justice is the pre-eminent concern of the Lord.

The requirement of walking without fault as a condition for fellowship with the Lord raises the question of self-righteousness in the psalms. Does the psalmist think that he can earn God's favour? No, not at all. The Israelite did not enter the people of God by being good, but by being born, and if male, circumcised. God's covenant love, his freely given grace, came first. But living as a partner to the covenant had clear obligations, and they are summed up in the requirement to keep the Law, or, in the words of this psalm, *to walk without fault*, to act with justice. St Paul said of his life before he became a Christian: 'as for the uprightness embodied in the Law, I was faultless' (Philippians 3:6). Paul was brought to see that this 'uprightness embodied in the Law' was not enough, because it did not lead to the blessings of the Spirit. Only faith in Jesus as Lord opened the way to life in the Spirit.

The Christian is first of all admitted into God's presence through faith and baptism in Christ. But once a partner to the new covenant, the Christian has clear obligations. We have been given a new commandment, a new righteousness even more demanding than the righteousness of the Law, because it asks for a radically new standard of love. To *walk without fault* according to the new commandment means that before we come into God's presence to worship we need to confess our sins and put on Christ, not as we might put on a coat over our dirty clothes, but by yielding to the cleansing and renewing grace of the Holy Spirit. The New Testament expects that Christians will strive to live a 'blameless' life. 'I charge you to keep the commandment unstained and free from reproach until the appearing of our Lord Jesus Christ' (1 Timothy 6:14). (See also Ephesians 5:25—27; 1 Thessalonians 5:23—24; 2 Peter 3:14).

The psalm goes on to spell out what it means to act with justice. It means first of all to speak *the truth from the heart.* If integrity is the first requirement for fellowship with the Lord, the second is truthful speech,

he who does not slander with his tongue.
he who does no wrong to his brother,
who casts no slur on his neighbour.

Who holds the godless in disdain

does not mean to despise atheists, but to refuse to honour those whose way of life is contrary to the Law of God. A society's values are revealed in those whom it honours, and the psalmist calls us to honour *those who fear the Lord.*

he who keeps his pledge, come what may

That is, the person who keeps their word, no matter what it may cost.

who takes no interest on a loan.

The Law did not ban interest because it was wrong in principle, but because it usually involved exploitation of the poor. An Israelite was permitted to charge interest to a foreigner in a business transaction, but not permitted to charge interest to a fellow-Israelite, because it was assumed that an Israelite would only need a loan to get him out of trouble, and charging interest would only compound his trouble.

and accepts no bribes against the innocent.

The taking of bribes in the course of justice was a serious temptation in Old Testament times, as it still is today in many societies. Again, the underlying concern is for justice, especially for the poor. Jesus said that only those who can be trusted with money can be trusted with true riches, with the kingdom of God (Luke 16:12).

such a man will stand firm for ever.

Come what may, the righteous will never fall, because they are assured of the Lord's protection.

Ephesians 1:3—10

This canticle is the first part of a glorious hymn of thanksgiving to God the Father for all he has done in Christ. The hymn unfolds the whole plan of salvation, from before time began, on into eternity. God's plan is revealed in six stages, of which four are given in the extract of the hymn presented to us for Evening Prayer.

Blessed be the God and Father
of our Lord Jesus Christ,
who has blessed us in Christ
with every spiritual blessing in the heavenly places.

The spiritual blessings about to be unfolded belong to heaven (*the heavenly places*), come from heaven, and lead us to heaven. We experience now the foretaste of these blessings, and in heaven the fulfilment of them, by being *in Christ*, one with him.

> *He chose us in him*
> *before the foundation of the world,*
> *that we should be holy*
> *and blameless before him.*

The first blessing is the blessing of being chosen by the Father to belong to Christ, to be in Christ. This choice was made in eternity, before the world was made. The purpose of God's choice, the reason why we have been chosen, is to *be holy*, to live a life set apart for God, wholly his. As in Psalm 14(15), the call of God must be matched by the response of a holy life.

> *He destined us in love*
> *to be his sons through Jesus Christ.*

The second blessing is the blessing of being made a child of God, of being born anew by the Spirit. This blessing is a gift of the Father's love. Jesus is the one who leads us into this relationship, the same relationship he shares with the Father, the relationship of sons and daughters. He is Son by nature, we by adoption.

> *according to the purpose of his will,*
> *to the praise of his glorious grace*
> *which he freely bestowed on us in the Beloved.*

Grace is God's gift of himself, his overwhelming generosity. All the blessings we receive in Christ are a result of God's grace. He is the source of all blessing, and he is also the one to whom all blessing leads. Everything comes from him and should lead to him, lead us to *praise his glorious grace* freely given in Christ, *the Beloved.*

In him we have redemption through his blood,
the forgiveness of our trespasses.

The third blessing is our redemption through the death of Jesus. Redemption means being set free. Slaves or hostages were redeemed, set free, when a ransom was paid. 1 Peter says, 'the price of your ransom . . . was paid, not in anything perishable like silver or gold, but in precious blood as of a blameless and spotless lamb, Christ.' (1:18—19). Christ won our freedom on the cross, the freedom which is the most fundamental of human freedoms, freedom from the guilt and power of sin. Redemption is here equated with *the forgiveness of our trespasses.*

We are a chosen people, an adopted people, a redeemed people,

according to the riches of his grace
which he lavished upon us.

He has made known to us
in all wisdom and insight
the mystery of his will.

The fourth blessing is being let into the secret purposes of God, being brought into *the mystery of his will. Mystery* means 'a secret long hidden in God', but now *made known to us* in Christ. Christ is the hidden mystery of God revealed to the world.

His purpose he set forth in Christ
as a plan for the fulness of time
to unite all things in him
things in heaven and things on earth.

The purpose of salvation is summed up in one word: *unity.* In a broken and divided world, God comes in Christ to bring unity, to reunite us to himself, to restore the break made at the Fall, to reunite the whole of creation *in him.* (This is the theme of the whole letter of Ephesians). This mystery has been made known *in the fulness of time*, that is, at the end of time, at the beginning of the climax of God's plan for the world. The story of the Fall (Genesis 1—4) tells how sin led to division: man and woman from God, man and woman from each other and from creation, the creation within itself, brother against brother. The purpose of God's coming in Christ is to undo the tragedy of the Fall, to reunite in Christ all that has been broken and divided. The task of building unity is absolutely fundamental to the Church's mission as it follows the purpose of God, the *mystery of his will*.

Week 1: Tuesday

MORNING PRAYER

Praise flows from the whole psalmody this morning. Psalm 23 leads us into the presence of the holy God who gives his blessing to the pure in heart. *He afflicts, and he shows mercy* (Tobit 13), and *in him do our hearts find joy* (Psalm 32).

Psalm 23(24)

This psalm may well have been sung during an annual procession with the Ark of the Covenant as it was brought into the Temple. The psalm opens with praise to the Lord the creator; then come the questions asked by the pilgrims as their procession approaches the Temple gates, the answers being given by the priest. It has the character of an entrance psalm, like Psalm 14(15) (Week 1, Monday Evening). The last part of the psalm continues the dialogue between people and priest as the worshippers pass through the Temple gates.

The Lord's is the earth and its fulness,
the world and all its peoples.
It is he who set in on the seas;
on the waters he made it firm.

The earth and everything in it (*its fulness*) belongs to the Lord because he made it. He *set it on the seas.* The Hebrews believed that the earth rested on a mighty ocean. At the beginning of time this ocean raged and heaved, but the Lord tamed it, and set the earth *firm* on the *waters.*

Who shall climb the mountain of the Lord?
(Mount Sion)
Who shall stand in his holy place?

The pilgrims shout these questions as they approach the gates of the Temple, the *holy place,* where the Lord makes his presence known to Israel.

The man with clean hands and pure heart.

The questions are answered by the priest. The first condition for entry into the Lord's presence is moral integrity in deed and in intention. *Clean hands* means blameless conduct, obedience to the Law, to the commandments of the Lord (as in Psalm 14(15)). *Pure heart* means obedience to the Lord not just in outward action but in inward thought. Jesus promised, taking up this line from Psalm 24, that the pure in heart would see God (Matthew 5:8).

Who desires not worthless things

This is the second condition for entry into the Lord's presence. *Worthless things* in this context are idols. In the New Testament greed for money and the things money can buy is exposed as idolatry (Ephesians 5:5). Money becomes an idol when we allow it to rule our lives. The insatiable desire for money must be renounced by those who wish to enter God's presence.

Who has not sworn so as to deceive his neighbour.

This refers to making a promise which we have no intention of keeping, or which is made deliberately to deceive. Honest speech is the third requirement for those who wish to enter the presence of the Lord.

He shall receive blessings from the Lord
and reward from the God who saves him.
Such are the men who seek him,
seek the face of the God of Jacob.

Those who seek God with integrity will be rewarded by the Lord's blessings. This experience of blessing is described in a very human and tender picture: seeing *the face of the God of Jacob*. To enter into the Lord's presence, to 'see' his face shine in blessing (Numbers 6:25, 'May the Lord make his face shine upon you'), is the longing of everyone who comes to seek the Lord.

O gates, lift high your heads;
grow higher, ancient doors.
Let him enter, the king of glory!

The worshippers accompanying the Ark reach the gates of the Temple and call on them to open. The gates will have to be opened to their fullest extent to make room for the king of glory, the glorious Lord who is king of heaven and earth, and whose presence is symbolized by the Ark.

The Second Book of Samuel (6:12—19), tells the story of the arrival of the Ark in Jerusalem, and this psalm may have been composed for that occasion. The arrival of the Ark marked the establishment of the sanctuary in Jerusalem as the chief sanctuary in Israel, and it also marked the end of Israel's wars of occupation of the promised land.

Who is the king of glory? (The priest's question)

The Lord, the mighty, the valiant,
the Lord, the valiant in war. (The people's reply)

The Lord is here described as a mighty warrior, the one who marches with Israel's armies. Israel carried the Ark into battle as a symbol of the Lord's presence with them. He is described in the last verse as *the Lord of armies,* the armies of Israel.

How is the Christian to pray this psalm, especially the last part? The **sentence** *The gates of heaven were opened to Christ because he was lifted up in the flesh* (St Irenaeus) directs us to the cross, resurrection and ascension of Jesus, his 'lifting up', as John's Gospel describes it. As we pray the psalm we praise Christ, *the man with clean hands and pure heart,* who entered heaven as the king of glory after defeating the foes of all humankind – sin, death, and Satan. Christ is the Lord *valiant in war,* the spiritual war. He is *the king of glory.*

The psalm can also be prayed as a preparation for worship. It is one of the psalms which can be used at the invitatory. It reminds us of the Lord as our creator, and of the absolute priority of personal integrity in those who come to *seek him.* The call to the gates to 'lift up their heads' can be addressed to our hearts, as we invite the king of glory, our Lord Jesus Christ, to dwell in us and rule over us.

Tobit 13:1—5B,7—8

The Book of Tobit is one of the deutero-canonical books of the Old Testament. Tobit was an exile from Israel living in Nineveh, capital of the Assyrian empire. Chapter 13 of the Book of Tobit, from which this canticle comes, is the song of an exile longing for Jerusalem and reflecting on the way the Lord has dealt with his people. The canticle is in the form of a psalm of praise and begins with a profession of faith in

God and in his eternal reign. Despite all that has happened to Israel in its near-annihilation, the Lord reigns: *Blessed is God who lives for ever, and blessed is his kingdom.*

The whole sad story of Israel's downfall and destruction at the hands of the Assyrians can be read in 2 Kings Chapters 14 to 17. Chapter 17 summarizes the reasons for the disaster: 'Israel despised God's laws and the covenant which he had made with their ancestors and the warnings which he had given them. Pursuing futility, they themselves became futile through copying the nations around them, although the Lord had ordered them not to act as they did. They rejected all the commandments of the Lord their God and cast themselves metal idols (2 Kings 17:15—16).

For he afflicts, and he shows mercy;
he leads down to Hades, and brings up again,
and there is no one who can escape his hand.

Tobit has in mind the destruction of Israel at the hands of the Assyrians, and he recognizes this destruction as God's punishment on a rebellious people. But he hopes for *mercy.* God is the one who not only brings men and nations close to death: he is also the one who *brings up again.* Everyone is subject to his reign, *there is no one who can escape his hand.*

Acknowledge him before the nations, O sons of Israel;
for he has scattered us among them.

Tobit appeals to his fellow-Israelites (*sons of Israel*) in captivity to praise God in the presence of the pagan *nations* amongst who they now live. Their exile, their being *scattered,* was God's doing. Israel has learned through her suffering that the Lord is always *our Father for ever,* the one who disciplines his children and the one who will show mercy to them:

He will afflict us for our iniquities;
and again he will show mercy,
but see what he will do with you.

I give him thanks in the land of my captivity (Nineveh)
and I show his power and majesty
to a nation of sinners.

The *sinners* may be the Assyrians, or Tobit's fellow Jews, whose unfaithfulness to the Lord led to the destruction of the nation. Tobit appeals to them to repent:

Turn back, you sinners, and do right before him;
who knows if he will accept you and have mercy on you?

If the Jews in exile repent, they will be forgiven, and God will gather them from among the nations, as prophesied in Deuteronomy 30.

The canticle concludes with a renewed affirmation of praise and faith in God's rule (*my soul exalts the King of heaven*), and the conviction that the exiles will one day *give him thanks in Jerusalem.*

We pray this canticle as members of the Church, the new people of God, scattered among the nations, called to praise God before them, sure of God's eternal rule, knowing him as our Father, and subject to the same discipline as Israel. In Romans Chapters 9 to 11 Paul warns Christians that they will not be treated any differently to Israel. *He will afflict us for our iniquities; and again he will show mercy, but see what he will do with you.* The canticle expresses our praise, assures us of God's mercy, and calls us to remain faithful to him in obedience to the new commandment.

Psalm 32(33)

The dominant theme of this psalm of praise is the word of God, powerful in creation, in history, and in the protection of his faithful people.

Ring out your joy to the Lord, O you just;
for praise is fitting for loyal hearts . . .

The *just* are those who are faithful to the commands of the covenant God made with his people.

A song that is new

is not necessarily a song which has just been composed, but a song which celebrates with ever-new freshness the acts of the Lord in the past and the present. A *new song* is sung by those who have experienced in a new way the faithfulness of the Lord.

For the word of the Lord is faithful

states the fundamental theme of the psalm. The *faithfulness*, dependability, of the word of the Lord will be shown in his work as creator and Lord of history.

The Lord loves justice and right,

and therefore his word will always be just and true. *Justice* in the Old Testament means 'being in right relationship with the Lord and his people', and in practical terms that means 'acting in obedience to the commandments of the covenant.' The Lord is just because he can always be counted on to fulfil his covenant with Israel.

By his word . . .

This takes up Genesis Chapter 1, with God creating the universe by the power of his word. The created universe is tangible proof of the effective power of God's word.

He collects the waves of the ocean;
he stores up the depths of the sea.

The *ocean* and *sea* referred to here are not the ocean and sea as we understand them, but the great cosmic waters which were present when God began to create 'the heavens and the earth' (Genesis 1:1). At creation God tamed the violent forces of the cosmic ocean, and brought order out of chaos. He put the waters in their place, some stored above the earth to be released as rain, others collected beneath the earth to become the waters of the sea on which the earth rested. (See Genesis 1:6—10).

The **sentence** *All things were made through him* (John 1:3) reminds as that the word of God which created the universe was the Word which became flesh, and lived among us (John 1:14), our Lord Jesus Christ.

Let all the earth fear the Lord,

not a cringing, terrified fear, but a holy reverence and awe inspired by the power of God's word.

He frustrates the designs of the nations,
he defeats the plans of the peoples.
His own designs shall stand for ever,
the plans of his heart from age to age.

The power of the word of the Lord is shown not only in creation but also in history. The *designs* and *plans* of the nations can never thwart the *designs* and *plans* of the Lord, *the plans of his heart.* No power on earth can frustrate his purposes.

They are happy, whose God is the Lord.
The people he has chosen as his own.

The fact that the Lord *chose* Israel was a constant source of praise and wonder, and a theme which became equally important to the new Israel, the Church. 'God . . .chose us in [Christ] before the foundation of the world, that we should be holy and blameless before him' (Ephesians 1:3—4).

He who shapes the hearts of them all
and considers all their deeds.

God is the creator of humankind, he is the one who creates (*shapes*) each life, and that is why ultimately all people will serve his plans, he will *shape the hearts of them all.* No one can thwart his plan for the world. He is the only one who knows the human heart; he is the judge of all the earth.

A king is not saved by his army,
nor a warrior preserved by his strength.
A vain hope for safety is the horse;
despite its power it cannot save.

Again, the message is that it is the plans of the Lord which *stand for ever,* not the will of kings and armies. Israel knew that victory came ultimately from the Lord, not from human might and weapons. Even the most formidable weapons of ancient warfare, *horse* and chariot, can not defeat the designs of the Lord. This was the lesson of the Exodus, when all Pharaoh's chariots and horsemen were thrown into the sea as they pursued an unarmed Israel.

The Lord looks on those who revere him,
on those who hope in his love,
to rescue their souls from death,
to keep them alive in famine.

The Lord is able to deliver his people out of the most desperate circumstances, even siege warfare, which brings *death and famine. Soul* in the Old Testament means 'life', not some part of a person distinct from the body. The resurrection of Christ means that even physical death has no hold over believers, that God will *rescue their souls from death.*

Our soul is waiting for the Lord . . .

The psalm concludes with a moving expression of faith in the word and will of the Lord. Because of his faithfulness in the past, we know he will be faithful in the future. We *wait for the Lord* rather that rushing ahead with our own designs and plans. *We trust in his holy name,* in his character revealed in his actions in creation and history. In the circumstances of our own lives, *we place all our hope in you.*

EVENING PRAYER

Everyone who follows Christ is committed to taking up their cross, to engaging in a life-long spiritual struggle. The first two psalms of Evening Prayer assure us that as we are united to Jesus we share in his victory. The final canticle foreshadows the reward of all those who persevere to the end. It takes us into the worship of heaven.

Psalm 19(20)

The two psalms for Evening Prayer are both Royal Psalms (see Chapter 9), psalms which centre on the person of the king and which were applied to the Messiah, the King of kings. According to the **heading** Psalm 19(20) is a Prayer For a King Before Battle. 2 Chronicles 20 describes a possible setting for the psalm. King Jehoshaphat went to the Temple before engaging the armies of Moab and Ammon. 'All the men of Judah stood before the Lord, with their little ones, their wives, and their children' (v. 13), as the king prayed for victory. The tense awareness of a life-and-death struggle colours the psalm.

The **sentence** and the **antiphons** direct us to pray for the victory of Christ in his struggle against our Enemy.

> *May the Lord answer in time of trial;*
> *may the name of Jacob's God protect you.*

The psalm begins with the prayer of the people for their king. The *name* of the Lord is not a magical formula, but the active presence of God, focused in the sanctuary in *Sion. Jacob* is another name for Israel. To call the Lord *Jacob's God* assured the king that the God who had chosen and blessed Jacob, who had pledged to protect Jacob's descendants, would surely come to the aid of the king and people *in time of trial.*

May he give you your heart's desire
and fulfil every one of your plans.

The king's desire is to see victory for God's people. The desire of Christ is to see his people not be overcome by evil, but overcome evil with good (Romans 12:21). We pray this psalm asking for the victory of Christ in the battle against evil in the world. As our lives are united with Christ, as his desire becomes our *heart's desire* we are assured that our deepest longings will be fulfilled.

I am sure now

Here we have a change of speaker: either the king himself (the Lord's *anointed*) or a prophet addressing the king.

Some trust in chariots or horses,

the ultimate weapons of war in the ancient world, *but we in the name of the Lord,* in the character of the Lord. The most powerful weapons are nothing against the power of the Lord.

They will collapse and fall,
but we shall hold and stand firm.

Give victory to the king, O Lord,
give answer on the day we call.

The psalm returns to the people, and their final prayer for their king. The *time* of trial has become a time for the nation to turn to God in prayer, a time for renewal of their faith in the Lord's power to save.

Psalm 20(21)

After returning from victory the king comes to the Temple to give thanks to the Lord. As in the previous psalm, the **sentence** and **antiphons** direct us to Christ, in this case inviting us to pray with him after the victory of the resurrection.

O Lord, your strength gives joy to the king;
how your saving help makes him glad!

The people give thanks to the Lord for the king's victory. His victories are their victories.

You have granted him his heart's desire;

implying that the king is a 'man after God's own heart.' All those whose wills are united with Christ know the joy of Jesus' promise: 'Ask, and you will receive.'

You have set on his head a crown of pure gold.

The *crown of pure gold* may have been a crown worn in a victory procession to celebrate the king's triumph. The reference to the *crown* has suggested to some commentators that this is a coronation psalm.

He asked you for life and this you have given,
days that will last from age to age.

Before going into battle the king asked the Lord to preserve his life. His prayer has been answered, and the future of his dynasty assured. *Days that will last from age to age* does not mean, in its Old Testament setting, eternal life, because the hope of eternal life as understood by the Christian was unknown in Old Testament times. What the king hopes for is the eternal continuity of the Davidic dynasty, a hope that was fulfilled in Christ.

Your saving help has given him glory.
You have laid upon him majesty and splendour,
you have granted your blessings to him for ever.

The gifts of *glory, majesty, and splendour* are all divine attributes. The king's glory, majesty and splendour are a reflection of God's glory, majesty, and splendour.

The king has put his trust in the Lord:
through the mercy of the Most High he shall stand firm.

We have here two of the most important words in the Old Testament, two words which take us to the heart of the covenant relationship between God and Israel: *mercy* and *trust.* The covenant has two partners: God, and Israel (represented by the king). God promises *mercy,* constant love, covenant loyalty which will never fail. The king's (and the people's) response must be one of *trust,* constant faith in God's steadfast love.

O Lord, arise in your strength;
we shall sing and praise your power.

The people pray for future victories for the king, through the strength of the Lord.

Revelation 4:11; 5:9,10,12

This canticle is made up of three separate canticles drawn from Revelation Chapters 4 and 5. These canticles may have been early Christian hymns sung at the Eucharist, but the scene in which they are set in Revelation is the court of heaven. The Lord God is seated on his throne surrounded by the hosts of heaven, who come in turn to worship God and to praise the Lamb, the crucified Christ. The worship of the Church on earth is a participation in the worship of the Church in heaven. In the Eucharist heaven and earth meet. The hymns of the Church on earth are sung by the Church in heaven.

Worthy are you, our Lord and God,
to receive glory and honour and power,
for you created all things,
and by your will they existed and were created.

This first canticle is introduced in Revelation 4:10 by the

words: 'The twenty-four elders prostrated themselves before him to worship the One who lives for ever and ever, and threw down their crowns in front of the throne, saying:' – then comes the canticle. The twenty-four elders represent the whole Church, the Church of the Old and the New Covenants: twelve elders represent the twelve tribes of Israel, and twelve represent the twelve apostles. Together they make up the whole of God's people. In Revelation the twenty-four elders have a priestly function in that they praise God and offer him the prayers of the faithful; and they have a royal function, in that they assist in the government of the world and share God's royal power.

These canticles are canticles of the persecuted Church at the end of the first century. They praise God because he is creator of all and therefore Lord of all, especially of the future. This is the hope of the suffering Church.

Worthy are you, O Lord,
to take the scroll and to open its seals,
for you were slain,
and by your blood you ransomed men for God
from every tribe and tongue and people and nation.

You have made us a kingdom and priests to our God,
and we shall reign on earth.

The second canticle is addressed to the Lamb, to the crucified Christ, sacrificed for the salvation of the world, for *every tribe and tongue and nation and people.* The *scroll* with its seven *seals* represents God's secret decrees regarding the future of the world and particularly the events before the end of history. The seals are broken and the contents revealed in the subsequent chapters of Revelation. Only the Lamb (Christ) is worthy to open the seals and unlock the future, only he is qualified to know and to put into effect God's plan for history, because it is through his death on the cross that the new people of God have come into being.

Christ is the key to history. The whole of creation and the whole of the Church now join to worship the Lamb who will inaugurate the new heavens and the new earth.

The Lamb, through his death on the cross, has founded a new Israel, a new *kingdom and priests to our God.* We share in Christ's priesthood as we offer this sacrifice of praise. We share in his kingship, as *we shall reign on earth.* Christ's functions as king and priest are continued on earth by his faithful people, who share his royal and priestly dignity. (The *earth* of the canticle may refer to the new earth of Revelation 21:1).

> *Worthy is the Lamb who was slain,*
> *to receive power and wealth,*
> *and wisdom and might,*
> *and honour and glory and blessing.*

In the final part of the canticle 'an immense number of angels' (Revelation 5:11) joins the created world and the Church to sing the praise of the Lamb. All heaven and earth sing his glory. The seven key words of the canticle suggest the fullness of power and glory. *Power, wealth, wisdom, and might* have to do with the Lamb's rule. *Honour, glory, and blessing* express the adoration of the whole universe. These seven 'gifts' of praise to the Lamb (with *wealth* replaced by 'thanksgiving') will be found later in Revelation 7:12 in a doxology addressed to God. In Christ dwells 'all the fulness of God' (Colossians 1:19). He possesses the full glory and authority of the Father.

Week 1: Wednesday

MORNING PRAYER

The psalmody begins with a meditation on the character and eventual fate of the evildoer (Psalm 35), moves on to a glorious hymn to the God who protects his people (Judith), and concludes with a psalm which celebrates God's reign over all nations.

Psalm 35(36)

Several psalms, like this one, reflect on the godlessness of the wicked who crush the poor, and the goodness of God who protects the righteous. This is a psalm of powerful contrasts, with its analysis of the depths of human evil and the heights of God's love.

> *Sin speaks to the sinner*
> *in the depths of his heart.*

In the rest of the Old Testament, the Hebrew word translated *speaks* nearly always refers to the Lord speaking to his prophets. In this psalm it is Sin which *speaks* to the sinner. Sin has become the wicked man's god, speaking *in the depths of his heart* to teach and inspire him to evil. St Paul quotes this text as the climax of his description of all humankind without God (Romans 3:18). We cannot remain neutral. If we refuse to listen to the word of God we begin to hear the voice of Sin.

> *There is no fear of God*
> *before his eyes.*

The *sinner* of this psalm is not the person who is loyal to God but has fallen to temptation. The *sinner* here is someone who scoffs at God and his Law, someone who has *no fear of God,* no fear of judgement, because for them God is irrelevant.

The *sinner* behaves as if God did not exist, in contrast to the righteous who can say 'I keep the Lord always before me' (Psalm 16:8). Dostoevsky, speaking of the brilliant young atheist revolutionaries in late nineteenth century Russia, said: 'If God is dead, anything is permitted.' The subsequent history of the Revolution proved him right.

He so flatters himself in his mind
that he knows not his guilt.

The godless man is so self-opinionated, so sure his way is better than God's, that he feels not the slightest twinge of conscience. He is so hardened that he never feels regret, *he knows not his guilt.*

In his mouth are mischief and deceit.

All wisdom is gone, wisdom not in the sense of intellectual learning, but wisdom which is the knowledge of God and his will. It is quite possible to be brilliant intellectually but to lack wisdom as defined in the Scriptures.

He plots the defeat of goodness
as he lies on his bed.

In the long night hours the righteous man meditates on the law of the Lord and sings God's praise, but the wicked man plans evil. At night our thoughts become like a compass needle, freely swinging to what attracts them most strongly, to what lies in the depths of our heart.

He has set his foot on evil ways,
he clings to what is evil.

Instead of being the free man he thinks he is, free of God, the godless person becomes the slave of evil, *he clings to what is evil.*

Your love, Lord, reaches to heaven;
your truth to the skies.

Your justice is like God's mountain, (Mount Sion)
your judgements like the deep.

Turning away from the evil of the godless, the psalmist now celebrates the wonder of God's love. His love is beyond human comprehension; it is inexhaustible; it reaches to the heights (the *skies*) and the depths (the *deep*). *Justice* here means God's faithfulness to his covenant, and his *judgements* are his actions which prove his faithfulness and bring about the salvation of his people.

To both man and beast you give protection.
O Lord, how precious is your love.
My God, the sons of men
find refuge in the shelter of your wings.

To *find refuge in the shelter of your wings* can be understood in two distinct ways, each of which is profound. Firstly, it can be understood as a poetic description of God's love. His love is not only vast and infinite; it is personal and intimate, like the warmth and security a mother hen gives her chickens nestled under the *shelter of* her *wings.* His tender love embraces the whole created universe, *man and beast* alike.

Secondly, finding *refuge in the shelter of your wings* may refer to the ark of the covenant in the Temple sanctuary. On top of the ark was the mercy seat, and at each end of the mercy seat sat a golden cherubim. According to Exodus, the cherubim 'spread out their wings above, overshadowing the mercy seat with their wings' (25:20). It was at the mercy seat that the Lord promised to meet his people: 'There I will meet with you, and from above the mercy seat, from between the two cherubim that are upon the ark of the testimony, I will speak with you of all that I will give you in commandment for the people of Israel' (25:22). To *find refuge in the shelter of your wings* then means to flee to the Temple, to the mercy seat, where God speaks to his people in love. The very next line assumes that we are in the Temple:

They feast on the riches of your house;
they drink from the stream of your delight.
In you is the source of life
and in your light we see light.

The Lord is like a generous host who feeds his guest with the very best of food and drink. The scene may be the thanksgiving sacrifice in the Temple, where the worshipper cooked and ate part of the sacrificial animal. *The stream of your delight* refers back to the river of the garden of Eden (*delight* translates the Hebrew 'Eden'), the source of life as God originally planned it; and it looks forward to the life-giving stream prophesied by Ezekiel 47, the stream which would flow from the side of the Temple bringing health and joy to all the world.

The stream of your delight is the water of the Spirit which flowed from the pierced side of Christ crucified, *the source of life.* It is the living water of eternal life. Jesus said, 'If anyone thirsts, let them come to me and drink. ". . . Out of his heart will flow rivers of living water." ' 'I am the light of the world, whoever follows me will not walk in darkness, but have the light of life.' (John 7:37—38; 8:12). In the book of Proverbs, the *source of life* is wisdom and the fear of God, both of which are unknown to the *sinner* of the first part of the psalm.

This psalm is alive with eucharistic meaning for the Christian. In the Eucharist we *feast on the riches* of God's house, we *drink from the stream of your delight.* Here is the source of life and light.

Keep on loving those who know you,
doing justice for upright hearts.
Let the foot of the proud not crush me
nor the hand of the wicked cast me out.

The psalm concludes with a prayer for protection from the wicked, who arrogantly 'trample the poor' (Amos 5:11) and seize their land. Such injustice will not go unpunished:

See how evildoers fall!
Flung down, they shall never arise.

Judith 16:2—3A,13—15.

The book of Judith tells the story of how a beautiful young widow, Judith, defeats the general (Holofernes) of a mighty Assyrian army which was threatening to destroy Israel. Holofernes is the incarnation of evil, and Judith (whose name means 'The Jewess') represents the cause of God. The story concludes with a great hymn of thanksgiving for Israel's victory over the Assyrian army, and part of the hymn is presented to us in this canticle. The canticle is largely made up of phrases from the psalms.

The Christian prays the canticle in thanksgiving for the Lord's power revealed in the creation and in redemption. The **sentence** directs us to the final victory of the Church at the end of time, when all heaven will *begin to sing a new song.*

Begin a song to my God with tambourines
sing to my Lord with cymbals.
Raise to him a new psalm;

The *new psalm* or *new song* (next verse) is a song which praises the Lord for the new way in which he has come to save his people. In response, the people say:

O Lord, you are great and glorious,
wonderful in strength, invincible.

For God is the Lord who crushes wars.

This phrase comes straight from the Song of Moses sung by Israel after the Exodus. Israel's God has again come to rescue his helpless people. No military force, no matter how overwhelming, can destroy God's chosen ones. This conviction sustains Christians today who live under the oppression of those who believe that political power comes out of the barrel of a gun.

Let all creatures serve you,
for you spoke and they were made.
You sent forth your Spirit, and it formed them.

The story of creation as recorded in Genesis Chapters 1 and 2 is the background to this passage. Because God has created all things, even Israel's enemies, they will all ultimately be subject to him.

There is none that can resist his voice.

For the mountains will be shaken to their foundations
with the waters;
at your presence the rocks shall melt like wax.

The awesome effect of the Lord's appearance as he comes to rescue Israel from her enemies is compared to a volcanic eruption, where the mountains are shaken and the rocks melt. God's appearances to Israel at Sinai were accompanied by such phenomena, and they became traditional in descriptions of a divine theophany. They find their way into St Matthew's account of the death and resurrection of Jesus (Matthew 27:51; 28:2), the greatest of all theophanies.

But to those who fear you
you will continue to show mercy.

Fear is the reverence shown by those who worship the Lord. *Mercy* is the Lord's faithfulness to his covenant. He will never abandon his chosen.

Psalm 46(47)

There is a small group of psalms (called Enthronement Psalms) which specifically celebrate the Lord as king. Psalm 46(47) is the first of these in the psalter. It has all the vivid excitement of a coronation day where the Lord is proclaimed king. Some scholars believe that these psalms were used in an annual ritual dramatizing God's enthronement as king and Lord of all creation, but there is great difficulty in trying to imagine how Israel would have staged such a ritual. Israel abhorred any visible representation of God, and it believed that the Lord was king from all eternity: 'Your throne is established from of old' (Psalm 93:2). It may be that the ark of the covenant was carried in procession to the Temple each year, and rather than an annual 'enthronement' of the Lord, Israel celebrated his eternal kingship in this ceremony, and renewed her allegiance to him. The psalm was later interpreted as celebrating the future establishment of God's kingdom on earth.

The Christian prays the enthronement psalms in celebration of Christ, who *is seated at the right hand of the Father; his kingdom will have no end* (**sentence**). Jesus was enthroned on the cross and in his resurrection and ascension.

All peoples, clap your hands
cry to God with shouts of joy!

This is exactly how Israel greeted a newly-crowned king (2 Kings 11:12). The invitation to acclaim the Lord as king is given to the whole world, *all peoples,* with the reason being:

For the Lord, the Most High, we must fear,
great king over all the earth.

The Lord is king of all nations, and therefore all should acknowledge his rule.

He subdues peoples under us
and nations under our feet.
Our inheritance, our glory, is from him,
given to Jacob out of love.

The reference is to the conquest of Canaan when the Israelites first entered the promised land, described here as *our inheritance.*

God goes up with shouts of joy;
the Lord ascends with trumpet blast.

Like a newly-crowned king, the Lord ascends his throne and is acclaimed with trumpets. The setting seems to be the Temple, where the Ark was the symbol of God's throne. The carrying of the Ark up to the Temple celebrates God's enthronement over Israel and over all nations. (The Temple was the earthly counterpart of God's heavenly dwelling). The Church sings this psalm on Ascension Day.

God is king of all the earth . . .

Here we have the central message of the psalm and of all the enthronement psalms: *God reigns*! We look forward to the final establishment of his kingdom as we pray: 'Thy kingdom come.'

The princes of the peoples are assembled
with the people of Abraham's God.

The psalm concludes with a vision of the goal of history and of the future kingdom of God. God's choice of Israel was not favouritism. He chose Israel so that in the end all nations would come to know and worship him, for he is *God who reigns over all.*

EVENING PRAYER

Three choice passages make up this evening's psalmody. The first two are from Psalm 27, and they give voice to the deepest longing of the soul: *to savour the sweetness of the Lord,* to *seek his face.* This longing is fulfilled in our relationship with Christ, which is unfolded with extraordinary power in the canticle from Colossians 1. *He is the image of the invisible God.*

Psalm 26(27)

This is the prayer of someone who is afflicted by pressure from without and within, someone who is feeling threatened by enemies and cut off from God. The psalmist makes this prayer in the Temple, possibly in the night hours, keeping vigil and waiting for the Lord.

> *The Lord is my light and my help;*
> *who shall I fear?*
> *The Lord is the stronghold of my life;*
> *before whom shall I shrink?*

As he prays in the night hours in the gloom of depression the psalmist looks to the Lord to be his *light,* to banish the powers of darkness as surely as the coming sunrise will drive away the night. The Lord is his *stronghold* protecting him from his enemies.

> *When evil-doers draw near*
> *to devour my flesh . . .*

We do not know who these enemies were (although we find out a little more about them in the second half of the psalm), but the psalmist here compares them to wild beasts out to tear him apart. In a change of metaphor, the enemies become an *army* encamped around him, waiting until daybreak to attack. Despite the overwhelming odds against him, the psalmist has no *fear,* because he has unshakable *trust* in the Lord, his *light,* his *help,* his *stronghold.* It is to the Lord that he now turns.

There is one thing I ask of the Lord,
for this I long,
to live in the house of the Lord,
all the days of my life,
to savour the sweetness of the Lord,
to behold his temple.

The psalmist is like Mary the sister of Martha, Mary who chose 'the one thing necessary' to life: to be still and listen to the word of the Lord. The psalmist's longing for the Lord is expressed in three ways. First, he seeks *to live in the house of the Lord all the days of my life,* to know the constant presence of God, to participate each day for the rest of his life in the worship of the Temple. Second, he longs *to savour the sweetness of the Lord,* to experience the beauty and glory of the Lord, to be 'lost in wonder, love and praise.' Third, he longs *to behold his temple,* either to see in the physical beauty and grandeur of the Temple a reflection of God's beauty and glory; or 'to see God's answer' to the prayer of his heart.

The **sentence**, *Behold, the place where God dwells among men* (Revelation 21:3) directs the Christian to heaven, where we will indeed *savour the sweetness of the Lord.* The prayer of the psalmist *to live in the house of the Lord* becomes the prayer of the Christian longing for heaven. The worship of the Church on earth should be a foretaste of the worship of the Church in heaven.

For there he keeps me safe in his tent:

The Temple was sometimes called the *tent,* because that is what it had been during the journey through the wilderness. The psalmist is sure he will be *safe* because he has sought refuge in the Lord, in his very dwelling-place.

And now my head shall be raised.

When someone is depressed or ashamed, they hang their head. When they are joyful, they lift their head. It is the Lord who will *raise* the psalmist's head by answering his prayer, and in response the psalmist will come and *offer within his tent a sacrifice of joy,* a thanksgiving sacrifice.

O Lord, hear my voice when I call;
have mercy and answer.

The psalmist now moves into the form of a lament and the nature of his problem becomes clearer. He has been falsely accused of some crime and become an outcast even to his own family. His very life may be in danger.

Of you my heart has spoken:
'Seek his face.'
It is your face, O Lord, that I seek;
hide not your face.

To 'seek the face of the Lord' means 'to consult the Lord', to seek to know his will in one's life, to seek his presence. The psalmist pleads with the Lord for help, for vindication and justice. For the Lord to 'hide his face' was a sign of his *anger* (Psalm 13:1).

Though father and mother forsake me

Possibly this refers to something that has actually happened to the psalmist, or it may be a poetic way of describing the experience of being completely abandoned. Even if those who love him most should desert him, the psalmist is sure that the Lord will always *receive* him, literally 'lift me up', as a parent lifts and hugs a crying child.

Instruct me Lord, in your way;
on an even path lead me.

The psalmist asks to be shown the way to act that will be

right in God's eyes, a way where he may walk securely and not be tripped up by his enemies who *lie in ambush,* and who are 'greedy' for his downfall. The attack against the psalmist is then described as slander:

False witnesses rise against me, breathing out fury.

I am sure I shall see the Lord's goodness
in the land of the living.

This is what the psalmist longs for above all else, to see the Lord, and he is sure God will answer his cry. *The land of the living* is this world, in contrast to Sheol, the world of the dead.

Hope in him, hold firm and take heart.
Hope in the Lord.

This may be a prophetic word addressed by the priest to the psalmist as he waits in prayer in the Temple, or it could be the psalmist exhorting himself to remain patient and full of hope. After Hannah's prayer in the Temple (1 Samuel 1:17), the priest Eli said to her: 'Go in peace, and the God of Israel grant your petition which you have made to him.' As we pray the psalm today it is a word of hope to us from God.

The **antiphon** for Eastertide, 'God has highly exalted him at his own right hand as leader and Saviour' invites us to pray this psalm with Christ as a way of entering into his experience as he faced the cross, and the slander of false witnesses and enemies who were out to destroy him. He faced his suffering with confident hope in God and a longing for the Father's presence as expressed in this psalm.

Colossians 1:12—20

The Pauline letter to the Colossians addresses a form of religious syncretism which had taken hold in the early Church. According to this teaching, Christ was one amongst many 'principalities and powers', 'elemental spirits' (Colossians 2:8) which inhabited the spiritual world and controlled the destiny of each person. Against this teaching Paul asserts the absolute supremacy of Christ and the utter uniqueness of his relationship to God.

Let us give thanks to the Father,
who has qualified us to share
in the inheritance of the saints in light.

The first part of the canticle is actually the conclusion of Paul's opening prayer for the Colossians. The *inheritance of the saints* is the salvation once reserved to Israel, to which the Gentiles are now called. The *saints* are the whole people of God, called to live in the light of salvation. The way in which the Father *has qualified us to share in the inheritance* of salvation is described in the next verse:

He has delivered us from the dominion of darkness
and transferred us to the kingdom of his beloved Son,
in whom we have redemption,
the forgiveness of sins.

In bringing us to salvation the Father has *delivered us, transferred us,* redeemed us; *delivered us from* the ruling force of darkness, from Satan's grip (as Israel was *delivered* from the grip of Pharaoh); *transferred us* to the rule of Christ, to the Church, which Christ rules as head. All who live in the Body of Christ, under the authority of *the head of the body,* live in the *kingdom of his beloved Son.* And in Christ *we have redemption,* defined as *the forgiveness of sins.* If someone was taken prisoner and enslaved they could be set free by payment of a ransom. The whole process of buying their freedom was called 'redemption', buying back what is your own. It is a wonderful picture of salvation. We belonged to God, we had been imprisoned by sin, 'slaves to sin' (Romans 6:17,20), but through the death of Christ we have been redeemed, set free, liberated from slavery, and are now free to serve God, to live in freedom in *the kingdom of his beloved Son.* The essence of this redemption is *the forgiveness of sins,* being set free from the power and penalty of sin.

The next part of the canticle is an early Christian hymn to our redeemer. It proclaims Christ's relationship to God, his relationship to creation, and his relationship to the Church.

He is the image of the invisible God.

He is not simply one expression of God amongst many, or the greatest prophet of God. He is *the image* of God. The Greek word for *image* is *eikon*, 'portrait'. When we look at Christ we see *the invisible God.* This is the fundamental conviction of the Christian faith. Christ is 'God from God, Light from Light, true God from true God.' In his teaching, his miracles, his cross we see the *image of the invisible God.*

the firstborn of all creation,

The *firstborn* son inherited by right his father's land, wealth, and titles. When Jesus is called *the firstborn of all creation* it does not mean that he was the first person to be created, but that the Father has given him all creation as his inheritance by right. Christ is the Lord of all creation. He has the rights of the firstborn.

for in him all things were created,
in heaven and on earth,
visible and invisible.

Christ has all the rights of the firstborn because he is the one in whom all creation was made, he is the Word through whom all things came into being (John 1:2). In the context of Colossians, the fact that *all things in heaven and on earth* were created *in* Christ is very significant, and is taken up in the next verse.

All things were created
through him and for him.
He is before all things,
and in him all things hold together.

There are no powers, physical or spiritual, in heaven or on earth, that are not ultimately subject to Christ. He is not one of the 'elemental spirits', but the Lord and maker of all powers. All were created *through him and for him. He is before all things,* that is, he existed before them and is therefore superior to them, and *in him all things hold together.* What an extraordinary vision! Christ is king of the whole universe. In him it all holds together; without him it all falls apart. All power, social, legal, political, spiritual belongs to Christ and will only *hold together* in him. This canticle explodes all boundaries which are set up to exclude Christ. 'Open wide the doors for Christ. To his saving power open the boundaries of states, economic and political systems, the vast fields of culture, civilisation and development.' (Pope John Paul II). Christ is the Lord of all human endeavour. The world is not a product of chance, not the result of random events, but was created through and for Christ.

He is the head of the body, the Church.

The canticle now moves in to the area of Christ's relationship to the Church. As in creation, so in the Church, all things exist through and for Christ. Earlier letters of Paul (Corinthians and Romans) described the Church as the body of Christ, but here Christ is revealed as the head of the body, the one who rules every part of the body. He exercises that rule through the action of his Spirit and through the office of his pastors.

He is the beginning

He is the source of the Church's life.

the first-born from the dead,

He is the first to be born again from the dead, the 'first-fruits of those who sleep' (1 Colossians 15:23).

that in everything he might be pre-eminent,

Here we have the theme of the whole canticle, and of the whole letter to the Colossians.

For in him all the fulness of God was pleased to dwell.

This translation echoes the opening phrase of the hymn: Christ is *the image of the invisible God.* An alternative translation, 'God wanted all fullness to be found in him' (New Jerusalem Bible) is probably more accurate. Christ is head not only of the Church, and of the whole of creation, but also of the entire cosmos, which he fills with his Spirit.

and through him to reconcile to himself all things.

It is the will of the Father that everything broken and shattered by the Fall should be reconciled in Christ, and only *through him.* The scope of God's redemption is not limited to the Church or to creation, but includes *all things, whether on earth or in heaven.*

making peace by the blood of his cross.

The final line of the canticle reminds us of the costly nature of this reconciliation. It was achieved by Christ's death on the cross. Through the cross God has reconciled all things to himself.

Week 1: Thursday

MORNING PRAYER

The movement of this morning's prayer is from hopelessness to heaven. Psalm 56 takes us into the experience of a man delivered from his oppressors. The Old Testament canticle (Jeremiah 31) sings the joy of a liberated people. Psalm 47 takes us into heaven, 'the holy city of Jerusalem', there to ponder the Lord's love.

Psalm 56(57)

This psalm is in two parts, each ending with the refrain: *O God, arise above the heavens; may your glory shine on earth!* The psalmist is afflicted by his enemies and in the first part of the psalm he cries to God for help. The second part is a surge of praise in response to God's answer to his prayer. The **sentence** from St Augustine directs us to pray the psalm to *celebrate the passion of Christ.* In the psalm we hear the voice of the Son in prayer to the Father on the eve of the cross.

> *Have mercy on me, God, have mercy*
> *for in you my soul has taken refuge.*
> *In the shadow of your wings I take refuge*
> *till the storms of destruction pass by.*

The psalmist has come to the Temple to make his prayer. Here he will find *refuge* from his enemies and *mercy,* God's saving help. The psalmist finds protection *in the shelter of your wings,* a reference either to the cherubim on the ark of the covenant in the Temple sanctuary, or to the Lord as being like a mother hen nestling her chicks under the protection of her outstretched *wings.* (See commentary on Psalm 35(36) Week 1 Wednesday Morning Prayer).

I call to God the Most High,

The *Most High* is a title for God which Israel took over from the previous inhabitants of Jerusalem for whom the Most High was the God who made heaven and earth (Genesis 14:19). It is a title which asserts God's universal rule, and so for the psalmist it expresses his faith that the God who made heaven and earth is the God who will come to save him from his enemies.

May God send his truth and his love.

Truth and *love* are the pivotal words of the covenant. God's *truth* is his utter faithfulness to the covenant. His word is *truth*. His *love* is his truth in action, his constant mercy which comes to rescue his people again and again.

my soul lies down among lions . . .

The enemies are pictured as wild beasts out to tear him to pieces and consume him. For teeth and tongues they have *spears, arrows,* and *sword.* Against such enemies the psalmist is helpless and can only *lie down* and wait for God's salvation.

O God, arise above the heavens;
may your glory shine on earth!

The original setting of the psalm may have been a night vigil. As the morning approaches, the psalmist sees in the rising of the sun a sign of God rising to come to his aid, his *glory* (the visible sign of his presence) shining on earth as the glory of the sun lights up the world at the start of a new day. For the psalmist, the glory of the Lord was not something abstract, but God's action in saving him from his enemies. The second part of the psalm radiates a sure confidence in God's salvation.

They laid a snare for my steps . . .

In a change of imagery, the enemies who were depicted as

wild beasts in the previous verse are now hunters who have been caught in their own trap. Evil is self-destructive.

My heart is ready, O God . . .

His fear is gone, his soul is no longer *bowed down,* but he is on his feet ready to praise God from the heart.

Awake my soul . . .

He calls on the instrumentalists to accompany him in his praise to God, as he sings to *awake the dawn.* The dawn is the symbol of God's coming salvation. It is the time when the long night of waiting is ended, the darkness is banished, and glory of the Lord appears. In this verse one can sense the thrill in the psalmist's heart as he anticipates God's salvation, symbolized in the rising sun.

The imagery of the psalm makes it obvious why the Church sings it to celebrate the resurrection. The Eastertide antiphon makes that theme explicit.

I will thank you Lord among the peoples . . .

He wants the whole world to know what God has done for him, and to join him in singing God's praise. God's covenant *love* and *truth*, infinite in their greatness, are the glorious themes of his praise.

Jeremiah 31:10—14

The prophet Jeremiah lived through the most traumatic events in the life of the nation. It was during his time as a prophet that the kingdom of Judah was utterly destroyed. Jerusalem was sacked, the Temple razed to the ground, and all the leading inhabitants of the city carted off to exile in Babylon. The northern kingdom of Israel had suffered a similar fate at the hands of the Assyrians only 130 years previously, and it never recovered. Jeremiah's initial task was to warn the people of approaching catastrophe, calling them to repentance, a message they totally ignored. After they were taken off into exile Jeremiah prophesied the restoration of the nation, and these prophesies of hope are largely found in chapters 30 to 33, a section of Jeremiah called the Book of Consolation.

This canticle, in Chapter 31:10—14, comes from the heart of the Book of Consolation. It is a prophecy of hope addressed to the exiles, assuring them that one day the Lord will bring them back to Sion and restore the prosperity of the nation. The **sentence** indicates how the Church reads the prophecy and how we can pray it: *Jesus had to die to reunite the children of God who had been scattered* (John 11:51,52). Apart from Christ all peoples are in exile, held captive by sin, scattered and without hope. Jesus died to bring us back to God, to bring us home. The canticle is sung with joy by all who know that the Lord has acted to 'ransom his people, alleluia' (Eastertide antiphon). Jeremiah's prophecy was fulfilled at Pentecost, and is still being fulfilled in the life of the Church.

O nations, hear the word of the Lord,
proclaim it to far-off coasts.

Jeremiah wants his message of hope to be heard in every corner of the world where the exiles now live.

Say: 'He who scattered Israel will gather him
and guard him as a shepherd guards his flock.

It was the Lord who *scattered Israel* into exile, because of their disobedience and unfaithfulness, but now he wants to gather his chastened people together again, as a shepherd goes out on the hills to search for his sheep, to gather his scattered flock into the safety and shelter of the fold.

For the Lord has ransomed Jacob.

The return from exile will be a new Exodus, when God will

ransom (redeem from slavery) the people of the promise, *Jacob*. The *overpowering hand* is the hand of Nebuchadnezzar, king of Babylon.

They will come and shout for joy on Mount Sion . . .

This whole verse portrays the prosperity of the redeemed people. The land is now devastated and barren, but when the exiles return it will begin to prosper and become what the promised land was for those who first entered it, 'a land flowing with milk and honey.' The Temple will be rebuilt and the returning exiles will *shout for joy on Mount Sion*. To the Christian these lines speak of the gifts of the Spirit and the nourishment given in the sacraments of the Church.

Then the young girls will rejoice and will dance . . .

In place of their present *grief*, the Lord will give *gladness* to the whole nation, *girls* and *men, young and old, priests* and *people*. All will be *filled with my blessings*.

Psalm 47(48)

This psalm is one of a group which have as their theme the praise of Sion, Jerusalem, site of the royal palace and the Temple. It may have been a psalm designed for the Feast of Tabernacles, because this feast celebrated (among other things) the Temple as the centre of Israel's worship. The psalm contrasts the reactions of two groups of people as they see Mount Sion: the enemies of Israel, and pilgrims coming to worship.

The key to praying the psalm in Christ is to understand Sion as a reference to the Church, especially the Church in heaven, as indicated by the **sentence**: *He took me to the top of a great mountain, and showed me the holy city of Jerusalem* (Revelation 21:10).

The Lord is great and worthy to be praised in the city of our God, in the Church in which we gather to praise the Lord.

Mount Sion, true pole of the earth is literally 'in the far north'. In Canaanite mythology 'the mountain of the north' or 'the far north' was the home of the gods, as Mount Olympus was in Greek mythology. The psalmist takes over the expression, applying it to Sion. Sion is the the home of the true God. Sion (the Church) is the true 'north', the *true pole of the earth*, the spiritual summit of the world.

God . . . has shown himself its stronghold

God is the true defence of Jerusalem, not the impressive physical battlements protecting the city. The Christian is reminded of Jesus' promise to the Church that 'the gates of hell can never overpower it.' (Matthew 16:18). The Church's defence is not in treaties or alliances with political powers, as the twentieth century of all centuries has shown us, but in God himself.

For the kings assembled together,
together they advanced.
They saw; at once they were astounded;
dismayed, they fled in fear.

This verse may refer to the miraculous deliverance of Jerusalem from the Assyrian armies during the reign of King Hezekiah, King of Judah from 715—687 BC. The Assyrian King Sennacherib besieged Jerusalem, but Isaiah prophesied that Sennacherib and his forces would suddenly leave. 'That same night the angel of the Lord went out and struck down a hundred and eighty-five thousand men in the Assyrian camp. In the early morning when it was time to get up, there they lay, so many corpses. Sennacherib struck camp and left; he returned home and stayed in Nineveh.' (Isaiah 37:36—37).

But the event in the psalmist's mind may not be an event in the past but an event in the future: the Day of the Lord, the great Day when God will come in power to bring justice on the earth. Prophets predicted (Psalm 2) that on this Day the kings of the earth would assemble together against Jerusalem to fight against the Lord and his anointed king.

They saw may refer to an awesome appearance of the Lord himself, such as is described in Isaiah 29:5—8:

> 'Suddenly, in an instant,
> you will be visited by Yahweh Sabaoth
> with thunder, tempest, flame of devouring fire'.

By the east wind you have destroyed
the ships of Tharsis.

These ships were among the largest vessels afloat, capable of sailing to Tharsis, a distant Phoenician colony in Spain. The kings are compared to these mighty ships, but the Lord shatters them on the rocks, like the east wind dashing the ships of Tharsis against the cliffs.

The powerful forces, political or social, which threaten to overwhelm the Church may at times gain the upper hand, but they will not ultimately triumph.

As we have heard refers to the prophecies concerning Jerusalem, prophecies that promise its security and prosperity. The New Testament speaks in like manner of the ultimate victory of the Church, the body of Christ.

In the heavenly Jerusalem 'there will be no more death, and no more mourning or sadness or pain. The world of the past has gone.' (Revelation 21:4).

the Lord of hosts.

The *hosts* may have referred originally to the armies of Israel, but later they were understood to be the hosts of heaven.

O God we ponder your love
within your temple.

Love translates the Hebrew word *hesed*, covenant love, the love by which the Lord binds himself to his people. We celebrate the love of God revealed on the Cross and mediated to us in the Eucharist by the Spirit.

your right hand

The right hand means the strong hand, the hand that brings victory.

Walk through Sion

The people are invited to join in a thanksgiving procession around the city, to rejoice in its physical strength seen in the *ramparts,* sloping banks protecting the foot of the walls; and her *castles,* the fortified towers of the palace.

The Christian rejoices in the wisdom and truth (the *judgements*) revealed in the Gospel, knows its invincible strength, and from personal experience of that strength evangelises *the next generation.*

EVENING PRAYER

This evening the psalmody begins with the experience of being set free from the deadly danger of self-satisfaction (Psalm 29). The joy of forgiveness is continued in Psalm 31, and the New Testament canticle (Revelation 11) takes us into heaven, to sing with the saints and angels of the victory of Christ over our Enemy.

Psalm 29(30)

This is a psalm of thanksgiving arising out of the experience of someone who has been critically ill. His sickness took him to death's door, and to make matters worse he was surrounded by 'Job's comforters' who come to judge him and accuse him of deserving to die because of his sin. These are the *enemies* of the first verse.

The **sentence** from Cassian (a monk and writer on monasticism in the early fifth century) indicates how the psalm is prayed by the Church as a celebration of Christ's resurrection, giving thanks with him to the Father after he rose from the dead.

I will praise you, Lord, you have rescued me
and have not let my enemies rejoice over me.

The *enemies* in this case are those who would have *rejoiced* if he had died, for then God would have shown his justice in condemning a sinner. The psalmist later admits that he had sinned in forgetting God as the source of his *good fortune,* but he has discovered God's mercy through his healing. God does not ever wish the death of the sinner, but rather that he should turn from his sin and live (Ezekiel 33:11). The *enemies* wanted judgement without mercy.

O Lord, I cried to you for help
and you, my God, have healed me.
O Lord, you have raised my soul from the dead,
restored me to life from those who sink into the grave.

Behind the language of this verse is the vivid picture of being let down into a well, into the pit of Sheol, and lifted up like a bucket of water. It is the Lord who has *raised* the psalmist *from the dead,* the Lord who has *healed* him. The verse does not mean that the psalmist actually died and was resurrected, but that he was so close to death he was as good as gone and at that point the Lord acted to heal him and restore him to life. When we pray the psalm with Christ we pray with one who did in fact die and rise again in the most literal sense, and with one whose burden of sin was not his own but ours. It was our sins he carried to the tree, by his stripes we are healed.

His anger lasts a moment; his favour all through life.
At night there are tears, but joy comes with the dawn.

The psalmist's sickness was a sign of God's *anger* with him. From the next verse it seems that his sin was one of smug self-satisfaction in his good times, not recognizing then that all he had was God's gift. But now, after his recovery, God's *anger* seems momentary compared with the joy he now knows.

The *tears* at night were tears of despair and remorse, *tears* of confession and repentance, as he realized his previous failure to recognize God as the source of his *good fortune*. His *joy* is the joy of one who has been healed, and whose healing is like the rising of the sun, banishing darkness and bringing life.

I said to myself in my good fortune:
'Nothing will ever disturb me.'
Your favour had set me on a mountain fastness,
then you hid your face and I was put to confusion.

In his prosperity the psalmist had forgotten that his good fortune was a gift from God. Deuteronomy warned the Israelites of precisely this sin: 'Beware lest you say in you heart, "My power and the might of my hand have gotten me this wealth." You shall remember the Lord you God, for it is he who gives you power to get wealth; that he may confirm his covenant which he swore to your fathers' (Deuteronomy 8:17—18). The psalmist was quite sure that in his riches he was totally secure, '*Nothing will ever disturb me.*' After his sickness and healing he came to see that what security he had came from God: *Your favour had set me on a mountain fastness.* When God's favour was withdrawn, his world crumbled: *then you hid your face and I was put to confusion.* When we forget that all we have is a gift, and begin to think it is all the result of our own effort, then the door is wide open to pride and self-satisfaction.

What profit would my death be, my going to the grave?
Can dust give you praise or proclaim your truth?

His death will serve no good purpose, for he cannot worship God from the grave.

The Lord listened and had pity . . .

The psalmist concludes as he began, praising God for his healing. His new awareness of the Lord as the source of life and health inspires him to a life of constant praise, *my soul sings psalms to you unceasingly*.

Psalm 31(32)

The joy of forgiveness is the theme of this psalm. In Christian tradition it is one of the seven penitential psalms. It was the favourite of St Augustine. The psalm is in three parts: the first is the personal testimony of the psalmist to his experience of God's forgiveness; the second is an instruction addressed to the congregation, possibly by the priest; finally there is a concluding call to rejoice in the Lord. The setting of the psalm is the worship of the Temple.

Happy the man whose offence is forgiven,
whose sin is remitted.
O happy the man to whom the Lord
imputes no guilt,
in whose spirit is no guile.

Woven into the exuberant joy of the psalmist is a profound analysis of the meaning of sin and forgiveness. Four different aspects of sin and forgiveness are described in the particular Hebrew words used in the opening verses of the psalm. First, sin is an *offence*, an act of rebellion against God, an act of disobedience which becomes a heavy burden. To be *forgiven* means to have the burden lifted and carried away. Second, sin is *sin*, wandering from God's way and going off on our own, making a mess of things. Forgiveness means that the mess is cleaned up, put right, *remitted*. A better translation would be *covered*, or *blotted out*. Third, sin involves *guilt*, which for the psalmist led to the breakdown of his health. Forgiveness means that the Lord no longer *imputes* the guilt to his account. The debt is cancelled. Fourth, sin is *guile*, deceit, cover-up; forgiveness means that inner purity is restored: in his *spirit is no guile*. Repentance and confession can only come when deceit is renounced.

I kept it secret and my frame was wasted.
I groaned all day long
for night and day your hand
was heavy upon me.
Indeed, my strength was dried up
as by the summer's heat.

Refusing to face up to our wrongdoing, keeping it *secret*, stifling our conscience, means that sin becomes like a festering sore which eats away at body and soul. We *groan* in self-pity. We loose all vitality and enthusiasm for living, and become like a wilting plant in the mid-*summer's heat*. The psalmist sees that even this self-imposed anguish is the discipline of the Lord: *your hand was heavy upon me*. Lovingly the Lord brings him to the point of repentance.

But now I have acknowledged my sins . . .

The same words which described the reality of sin in the first part of the psalm (*sin, guilt, offence*) are all used to show the completeness of the psalmist's confession. Honest confession, giving up deceit and pretence, leads to forgiveness. 'He who conceals his transgressions will not prosper, but he who confesses and forsakes them will obtain mercy.' (Proverbs 28:18).

So let every good man . . .

The psalmist now turns to the congregation to exhort them to turn from their sins to the Lord and find mercy.

The floods of water

Here we have a picture of the build-up of unconfessed sin and the trouble it brings as being like a torrent rushing down a dry stream bed after heavy rain, sweeping all before it. The *cries of deliverance* are the shouts of joy from the psalmist's fellow worshippers in the Temple.

I will instruct you and teach you
the way you should go;

Here begins the word of instruction from the Lord. It is the Lord who is speaking. He is the *I* in this verse. The verse is a prophetic word given by the priest to the newly-pardoned sinner (the *you* in this verse is singular) assuring him of the Lord's guidance, but it is a word spoken in the presence of the whole congregation and is intended to encourage and instruct them too.

Be not like horse and mule, unintelligent,
needing bridle and bit,
else they will not approach you.

It is better to submit willingly to the Lord than to need his heavy hand of discipline. If we do not *approach* the Lord readily, to confess our sins and receive his guidance, then we are like dumb animals (*horse and mule, unintelligent*) needing force to make us go in the right direction.

Many sorrows has the wicked
but he who trusts in the Lord,
loving mercy surrounds him.

This verse summarizes the Old Testament teaching on the two ways. The way of life is to trust in the Lord and experience his mercy. The way of death is the way of the wicked, the way of unrelieved sorrow.

Rejoice, rejoice in the Lord,
exult, you just!

The psalm concludes with a call to the congregation to join the psalmist in his joy.

Revelation 11:17—18; 12:10B—12A

This canticle is made up of two parts drawn from different scenes in Revelation. In both scenes we are present in eternity, and events which are past, present, and future are woven together and seen as a whole. The theme of the canticle is the kingdom of God, decisively inaugurated by Jesus and reaching its fulfillment on the Day when 'he will come again in glory to judge the living and the dead.'

The first part of the canticle, Revelation 11:17—18, comes from a scene which describes the climax of God's judgement on the world. In chapters 8 to 11 this judgement unfolds to the sound of seven trumpets. Each trumpet heralds the next stage in the judgement. With the sounding of the seventh trumpet in 11:15 the judgement reaches its climax: 'Then the seventh angel blew his trumpet, and voices could be heard shouting in heaven, calling, 'The kingdom of the world has become the kingdom of our Lord and his Christ, and he will reign for ever and ever." The Church's unceasing prayer, 'Thy kingdom come,' is about to be answered once and for all. This is the moment which all history has been leading up to: the glorious fulfilment of God's reign, inaugurated by Jesus in his life, death, and resurrection. At this point in the heavenly drama the twenty-four elders (representing the Church of the old and new covenants, the twelve tribes of Israel and the twelve apostles) burst into praise:

We give thanks to you, Lord God Almighty,
who are and who were,
that you have taken your great power
and begun to reign.

The kingdom of God has come. In the early chapters of Revelation God is described as the one 'who is, who was, and who is to come' (1:4,8). But here there is no 'who is to come.' He has come. His reign has begun.

> *The nations raged,*
> *but your wrath came,*
> *and the time for the dead to be judged,*
> *for rewarding your servants, the prophets and saints,*
> *and those who fear your name,*
> *both small and great.*

The judgement is pictured in terms taken from the Old Testament. The whole world, (the *nations*) is to be judged, and the righteous are to be rewarded. The *prophets* primarily refers to the Old Testament prophets, most of whom suffered hostility and rejection for their proclamation of the word of the Lord. The *saints* are the whole people of God, all who *fear* (reverence) his *name*.

The second part of the canticle comes from the next scene in Revelation, where the judgement begins with the defeat of Satan (symbolized by a dragon) by the archangel Michael. 'And now war broke out in heaven, when Michael with his angels attacked the dragon. The dragon fought back with his angels, but they were defeated and driven out of heaven' (12:7—8). This defeat is not in the future but in the past. It is an allegorical description of the victory won in the death and resurrection of Christ. In speaking of his coming death Jesus said: 'Now sentence is being passed on this world; now the prince of this world is to be driven out. And when I am lifted up from the earth, I shall draw all people to myself' (John 12:31). The judgement of God began in the ministry of Jesus and reaches a climax in his death and resurrection, his being 'lifted up.' Christ has won the first and decisive victory over

Satan. *Michael's victory is the victory in heaven which was effected by the victory of the cross.*

After Satan's defeat a voice from heaven proclaims the canticle:

Now the salvation and the power
and the kingdom of our God
and the authority of his Christ have come,
for the accuser of our brethren has been thrown down,
who accuses them day and night before our God.

This canticle interprets the meaning of the cross. On the cross the *kingdom of God* has *come.* The *accuser of our brethren has been thrown down.* In the Old Testament Satan is pictured as the one who accuses, who lays charges against the saints. The classic example comes in the book of Job, where Satan stands before God and accuses Job of being loyal to the Lord only so long as he lives in comfort and prosperity. The victory of Christ banished the accuser from heaven. In his place now stands Jesus, who continually intercedes for us to the Father (Romans 8:34).

And they have conquered him
by the blood of the Lamb
and by the word of their testimony,
for they loved not their lives even unto death.

The *they* of the first line are the martyrs, who by their own death (*they loved not their lives even unto death*) share in the death of Christ (*the blood of the Lamb*). Christ's victory on the cross is their victory. In their death they are joined to his death, and so share his victory over Satan. The martyrs also conquer Satan by *the word of their testimony,* their confession of faith in Christ as Lord made at their trial, before their earthly accusers. All heaven is called on to rejoice in their courage and faithfulness to Christ, even to death:

Rejoice, then, O heaven,
and you that dwell therein.

Week 1: Friday

MORNING PRAYER

The psalmody begins with a searching self-examination and prayer of confession (Psalm 50); moves on to a bold renunciation of idols and an acknowledgement that *In the Lord alone are victory and power* (Isaiah 45), and concludes with an invitation to all the earth to be *lost in wonder, love, and praise* (Psalm 99).

Psalm 50(51)

This prayer for God's mercy, cleansing, and renewal is the classic prayer of confession. It was traditionally regarded as the prayer of King David after he was exposed for his adultery with Bathsheba and the murder of her husband Uriah (see 2 Samuel 11—12), although the psalm is almost certainly a later composition.

> *Have mercy on me, God, in your kindness.*
> *In your compassion blot out my offence.*
> *O wash me more and more from my guilt*
> *and cleanse me from my sin.*

The psalmist begins in the only place where a sinner can begin, in humility pleading for *mercy,* casting himself on God's *kindness* and *compassion.* He appeals to the very nature of God, as God revealed himself to Israel, 'A God merciful and gracious, slow to anger, and abounding in steadfast love and faithfulness, . . . forgiving iniquity and transgression and sin' (Exodus 34:6—7). The psalmist knew how true God was to this revelation, because he knew the history of God's love for Israel, and so he casts himself on God's sure *mercy*. Throughout the Old Testament *mercy* means 'unearned favour'; God's *kindness* is his loyalty to his covenant with Israel, his promise to forgive their sin when they repent; *compassion* is the feeling a mother has for her own children, never ceasing to love them when they go wrong. In his opening prayer the psalmist thus appeals to God's revelation of his nature, to God's covenant with Israel, and to his tender love for his children.

The penitent describes his sin in three words: *offence, guilt, sin.* Each of them has in Hebrew a precise meaning, and reveals the psalmist's profound insight into the nature of human failure. An *offence* is an act of defiance in the face of authority. It was the root sin of Adam, his rebellion against God's command, his determination to live his own life according to his rules, not God's. *Guilt* here does not so much mean what we feel when we realize we have done wrong, but the act of deliberately choosing the wrong road. *Sin* is missing the mark, failing to live up to God's commandments. This is the most common word the psalmist uses to describe his failure. He has failed God, failed his community, and failed himself.

As he uses three distinctive words to describe his failure, so the psalmist uses three distinctive words to describe the forgiveness he seeks. He asks God to *blot out* his offence, to *wash* him from his guilt, and to *cleanse* him from his sin. Again, each of these words has a particular meaning. To *blot out* means 'to erase from the record.' The Old Testament speaks of a book which will be opened at the judgement, a book in which God has recorded all our deeds (Daniel 7:10). The psalmist appeals to God to *blot out* the record of his offence from this book. The word to *wash* is used for washing clothes by pounding them, giving them a thorough scrub to remove all the dirt. The psalmist prays for God to *wash* him *more and more,* to scrub him clean. Finally, he prays that God will *cleanse* him from his sin. *Cleanse* is a word used of ritual cleansing, when, for example, the priest declares a man 'clean' after the healing of some skin disease, like leprosy (Leviticus 13:6,34). His sin has banished him from God's presence, from the Temple, and he longs to be restored to fellowship.

> *My offences truly I know them;*
> *my sin is always before me.*
> *Against you, you alone, have I sinned;*
> *what is evil in your sight I have done.*

The psalmist is not wanting to deny that his sin had effected other people, but rather to get to the heart of the matter by acknowledging that all sin is ultimately sin against God, because it is a transgression of his command.

> *That you may be justified when you give sentence*
> *and be without reproach when you judge,*
> *O see, in guilt I was born,*
> *a sinner was I conceived.*

The psalmist acknowledges that God's sentence of 'Guilty' is just, because as he looks back to his birth he is conscious that his whole life has been corrupted by sin. He is not wanting to condemn his parents, still less the process of conception and birth, but rather to express his consciousness of a corruption that affects his whole being. To sin comes naturally. No one has to be taught to be a sinner. It is part of the human condition following the Fall.

> *Indeed you love truth in the heart;*
> *then in the secret of my heart teach me wisdom.*
> *O purify me, then I shall be clean;*
> *O wash me, I shall be whiter that snow.*

The *wisdom* which the psalmist seeks is the understanding that comes from being utterly faithful to God (this faithfulness is *truth in the heart*); *wisdom* which begins with reverence for God. Throughout the Old Testament 'The fear of the Lord is the beginning of wisdom.' Only God can teach such *wisdom;* only God can *purify* and *wash* him from his sin. This does not imply a radical individualism in our relationship to God. The words used in this verse allude to the ritual cleansing accomplished in the Temple. God alone can cleanse the sinner, but he acts through his Church, through its priests and sacraments.

Make me hear rejoicing and gladness,
that the bones you have crushed may revive.
From my sins turn away your face
and blot out all my guilt.

The psalmist is a broken man. He has been crushed by the enormity of his sin and longs to hear the word of forgiveness, the word which the prophet Nathan said to David after his confession: 'The Lord has removed your sin. You will not die' (2 Samuel 12:13). This assurance of God's forgiveness will bring *rejoicing and gladness* back into his life. He begs the Lord to look no longer on his sins.

A pure heart create for me, O God,
put a steadfast spirit within me.
Do not cast me away from your presence,
nor deprive me of your holy spirit.

As he has recognized the depth of his sin in the previous verses, so now he recognizes the radical cure he needs – nothing less than a new creation: *a pure heart create for me, O God.* This is the prayer of one who has plumbed the depths of his failure. He needs what the prophets promised and what Christ gave: 'A new heart I will give you, and a new spirit I will put within you; I will take out of your flesh the heart of stone and give you a heart of flesh. And I will put my spirit within you, and cause you to walk in my statutes and be careful to observe my ordinances' (Ezekiel 36:26—27). The **sentence** reminds the Christian that this renewal of the Spirit is a constant process: *You must be made new in mind and spirit, and put on the new nature of God's creating* (Ephesians 4:23,24).

A *steadfast spirit* is one that is determined to go God's way. Only God's presence, God's *holy spirit,* can give the renewal he needs. To be separated from God's presence is to be separated from the very source of life and joy.

Give me again the joy of your help;
with a spirit of fervour sustain me,
that I may teach transgressors your ways
and sinners may return to you.

One of the first signs of the Spirit's presence is joy, the joy of knowing God's *help,* but the psalmist knows he will need God to *sustain* the *spirit of fervour* in him so that his renewal will not be a flash-in-the-pan affair, but a permanent transformation. The renewal he seeks is not just his own individual reformation, but the *return* to the Lord of *sinners* and *transgressors* like himself. He will be able to *teach* them God's *ways,* to explain from his own experience how God is full of mercy and will always forgive those who repent.

O rescue me, God, my helper,
and my tongue shall ring out your goodness.
O Lord, open my lips
and my mouth shall declare your praise.

The psalmist promises to give public testimony to God's goodness if God will come and help him. His lips are now silent in God's presence because of his sin, but if the Lord will forgive and restore him he will then be able to *declare your praise.* These lines begin Morning Prayer each day. We acknowledge that our praise is given in response to God's grace.

For in sacrifice you take no delight,
burnt offering from me you would refuse,
my sacrifice a contrite spirit.
A humbled, contrite heart you will not spurn.

The psalmist's sins may have been so serious (murder or adultery?) that there was no atoning sacrifice prescribed for them in the Law. All he could do was throw himself on God's mercy, and come to God with a *humbled, contrite heart.*

Applied more generally, this verse is a classic statement of the emptiness of outward forms of religion which are not accompanied by inner integrity.

In your goodness, show favour to Sion:
rebuild the walls of Jerusalem.
Then you will be pleased with lawful sacrifice,
holocausts offered on your altar.

This last verse may have been added later, after the exile, when the walls of Jerusalem were broken down. The psalm then becomes the prayer not of an individual, but of the nation in exile, crushed because of their blatant disobedience to God, pleading for a new start, a new heart, a new Temple where the priests may once again offer *lawful sacrifice* on the altar. For the Christian, this verse is a prayer for the renewal of the Church, so that God's people will come with *a humbled, contrite heart* to offer *lawful sacrifice* on the *altar.*

Isaiah 45:15—25

This canticle comes from the second part of Isaiah (Deutero-Isaiah), and was written in the latter years of Israel's captivity in Babylon, just before the appearance on the world stage of Cyrus, King of the Persians. Cyrus conquered Babylon and allowed the first group of Jewish exiles to return to Jerusalem.

The immediate subject of the canticle is idolatry. In Babylon Israel was surrounded by idols, claimed by their makers to be more powerful than the Lord. The superior power of the idols has been demonstrated (according to their makers) by the destruction of the Temple of the Lord in Jerusalem by the armies of Babylon.

The canticle speaks strongly to those of us today who live in a society whose idols are money and power.

> *Truly, God of Israel, the Saviour,*
> *you are a God who lies hidden.*

In its immediate context this verse contrasts the presence of the Lord with the presence of idols. They can be seen by everyone, whereas the Lord cannot be seen. The *God of Israel, the Saviour, lies hidden.*

Another meaning of the verse is that the Lord does not act openly in history, but hides behind his instruments, such as Cyrus the pagan king of Persia. Cyrus was the instrument which the Lord used to rescue his people from captivity in Babylon.

> *They will be put to shame and disgraced,*
> *all who resist you.*
> *They will take themselves off in dismay,*
> *the makers of idols.*

The *makers of idols* are the Babylonians who hold Israel captive. *They will be put to shame* when they are defeated by Cyrus.

> *But Israel is saved by the Lord . . .*

The Lord will deliver Israel from captivity and carry her home to Jerusalem.

> *For this is the word of the Lord . . .*

In contrast to the idols who are dead and lifeless, the Lord is *the creator of heaven, the God who made the earth and shaped it.*

> *He did not create it in vain,*
> *he made it to be lived in.*

The other nations are in view here. They all form part of

God's creation, and God created the world for them to dwell in.

I have not spoken in secret, in some dark place,

as the gods of the nations do, giving advice from the underworld.

Assemble, all of you, draw near
you who have escaped from the nations.

From here on the canticle is addressed to all peoples of the world, not just to Israel. It is a call to everyone to turn from *idols made of wood,* and turn to the *God of justice, a saviour.*

To me every knee shall bow,
every tongue shall swear.

The last verse of the canticle looks to the future, when the Lord's rule will be established over the whole earth. Paul quotes this verse twice when speaking of the last judgement: once as proof that 'It is to God that each of us will have to give an account of himself' (Romans 14:11); and again in Philippians (2:10,11), as a prophecy of the universal character of salvation.

Psalm 99(100)

As the opening words imply, this is an entrance psalm, a psalm sung by worshippers as they begin their praise. It leads us into God's presence. As the third psalm in this morning's prayer, it lifts us out of the introspection and confession of Psalm 50(51) into joyful thanksgiving to God.

Cry out with joy to the Lord, all the earth.
Serve the Lord with gladness.
Come before him, singing for joy.

The psalm invites *all the earth* to praise the Lord, not just Israel. The Lord is Lord of *all*, and so *all the earth* should praise him. To *cry out with joy* means to openly acknowledge the Lord as king. It is a cry of homage, such as the people gave to their earthly sovereign.

Serve the Lord reminds us that worship is our duty. We are God's servants, and the first act of service we owe him is the worship of mind and heart and voice, a worship offered *with gladness*.

> *Know that he, the Lord, is God.*
> *He made us, we belong to him,*
> *we are his people, the sheep of his flock.*

To *know* the Lord means to be united to him, joined to him, loyal to him. He is our *God,* and we renounce all other gods. *He made us* is not so much a reference to the creation, but to the fact that God made Israel his people. For Israel, that 'making' began with God's choice of Abraham, Isaac and Jacob, and the deliverance from Egypt. For the Church, *he made us* his people through Christ's death on the cross. Jesus is the Good Shepherd who gave up his life for *the sheep of his flock*.

> *Go within his gates, giving thanks . . .*

As the worshippers enter the Temple *gates* and pass through its *courts* the call to praise and thank the Lord echoes back and forth in an exuberant chorus.

> *Indeed, how good is the Lord . . .*

The psalm concludes with three reasons why we should praise the Lord. All have to do with his character. He is *good,* meaning generous. His *merciful love* is *eternal. He is faithful from age to age.*

EVENING PRAYER

This evening's prayer celebrates the God who is *with us* as *our stronghold* and saviour in times of personal sickness (Psalm 40), natural disaster, and war (Psalm 45). We finish in heaven singing with the martyrs the hymn of the Lamb (Revelation 15:3—4) in praise of the final deliverance of the Lord when all evil will be vanquished and all nations *worship* the *Lord God the Almighty.*

Psalm 40(41)

This psalm has been described as a liturgy for the sick. The sick person comes to the Temple seeking God's healing. The Lord is his only hope, as he has been deserted by everyone, even his closest friend. They see his sickness as a sign that he is a great sinner and so has been rejected by God.

Happy the man who considers the poor and the weak.

The psalm begins with a word from the priest to the sick man as he comes to the Temple to pray for the Lord's help. The priest reminds the sick man of the character of the person whom the Lord saves – *the man who considers the poor and the weak.* Only someone who helps a fellow human being in need can expect to receive God's help in a time of need. This is exactly the same principle as we find in Jesus' teaching. 'Forgive us our sins as we forgive those who sin against us.'

The Lord will save him in the day of evil,
will guard him, give him life,
make him happy in the land
and will not give him up to the will of his foes.

To the one who gives help to the poor and the weak, the Lord will give protection, long life, and joyful life. In particular, he will give comfort and health to the sick:

The Lord will help him on his bed of pain,
he will bring him back from sickness to health.

The Lord is compared to a nurse who changes the sheets and cares for the sick man in his illness. We can pray the psalm in the light of Jesus' beatitude: 'Blessed are the merciful, for they shall obtain mercy' (Matthew 5:7).

As for me, I said: 'Lord, have mercy on me,
heal my soul for I have sinned against you.'

After hearing the word of the priest, the psalmist now speaks. He is conscious of a connection between his sickness and his sin, and so he prays for both physical and spiritual healing. He prays for health and for forgiveness. The healing Jesus brought was a healing of body and soul. His word: 'Your faith has made you whole', can be equally well translated, 'Your faith has saved you.' This reality is preserved in the Church's sacrament of the anointing of the sick. At the anointing, the priest says: 'Through this holy anointing may the Lord in his love and mercy help you with the grace of the Holy Spirit. May the Lord who frees you from sin save you and raise you up. Amen.'

But the trial the psalmist faces in his sickness is made a thousand times worse by the enemies and friends who turn against him.

My foes are speaking evil against me.
'How long before he dies and his name be forgotten?'
They come to visit me and speak empty words,
their hearts full of malice, they spread it abroad.

The *foes* may be inspired by greed as well as a gloating sense that he is getting his just deserts. They are waiting for the man to die because they expect to get hold of his property. He is the last of his line, and when he dies they will take his land. Their visits appear to be a sign of compassion, when in reality they are like vultures waiting for an animal to die.

My enemies whisper together against me.
They all weigh up the evil which is on me:
'Some deadly thing has fastened upon him,
he will not rise again from where he lies.'

The *enemies* assume that God will take the man's life because he has sinned and deserves death. The *deadly thing* may be a curse laid on the man, or it may refer to the deadly nature of his disease.

Thus even my friend, in whom I trusted,
who ate my bread, has turned against me.

To eat bread with a friend is a sign of close friendship. The psalmist's most bitter experience is betrayal by his friend. In John's Gospel (13:18) Jesus quotes these words with reference to his betrayal by Judas, who ate the bread of the Last Supper before going to the chief priests to arrange to hand Jesus over.

But you, O Lord, have mercy on me.
Let me rise once more and I will repay them.

The phrase may mean that the psalmist wants to recover in order to prove his enemies wrong in their predictions.

By this I shall know that you are my friend,
if my foes do not shout in triumph over me.
If you uphold me I shall be unharmed
and set in your presence for evermore.

If he is healed, and his enemies thus proved wrong, the psalmist will be sure of the friendship of the Lord. He is confident that he will be *set in your presence,* that he will come in future to the Temple to worship the Lord.

Psalm 45(46)

Psalm 45 takes up two of the most frightening events it is possible to experience: natural disaster and war. It sees these events as foreshadowing the judgement at the end of time, but sees also that through it all *God is for us a refuge and strength*. The psalm gives powerful encouragement to anyone facing upheaval and distress.

> *God is for us a refuge and strength,*
> *a helper close at hand, in time of distress.*

God is the one in whom we find protection, *refuge*, in the midst of suffering, and he is the one who gives us *strength* to win through and not be crushed. He is our *helper close at hand*, a phrase that reminds us of Jesus' promise of the Holy Spirit to be our Comforter, Counsellor, Paraclete.

> *So we shall not fear though the earth should rock,*
> *though the mountains fall into the depths of the sea,*
> *even though its waters rage and foam,*
> *even though the mountains be shaken by its waves.*

Ancient Israel did not take the world's stability for granted. It saw in the violence of volcanic eruption, earthquake, storm, and flood a sign that the universe contained vast forces of energy which could break loose. Israel understood creation as God bringing these forces under control, bringing order out of chaos, taming the sea and fixing the earth firmly on the waters. Psalm 45 describes the worst possible event: the forces of chaos begin to take control again and threaten the very foundations of creation. The world begins to fall apart. The sea takes over and the mountains crumble. The psalm has an uncanny relevance to our own time, when we are acutely conscious of the fragility of the planet earth and the threat to its existence from man-made pollution and nuclear weapons.

The psalmist may have been writing after some fearful natural disaster, or he may be describing in poetic language the worst that could happen to the world; or he may be thinking of the day of judgement. Whatever happens, he says: *We shall not fear,* because *God is for us a refuge and strength.*

> *The Lord of hosts is with us:*
> *the God of Jacob is our stronghold.*

The *Lord of Hosts* is the Lord of all the hosts of heaven and earth, of all 'thrones or dominions or principalities or authorities' (Colossians 1:16), the one who is ultimately in control. To him 'every knee shall bow.' The *God of Jacob* is the God who made a covenant with Jacob (Israel): 'I will be your God and you will be my people' (Jeremiah 31:33).

Our faith rests in the God to whom every power will submit, the God who has made a new covenant with us in Jesus Christ, a covenant which is renewed every time we celebrate the Eucharist. He is the God who is *with us, 'Immanuel'* (so the sentence), the God who is *our stronghold,* the one in whom we find refuge, as people found refuge from marauding troops by fleeing to a stronghold. God does not promise that trouble will not come to us; but he does promise that in the midst of trouble he will be *with us,* he will be *our stronghold.*

> *The waters of a river give joy to God's city,*
> *the holy place where the Most High dwells.*

In Jerusalem the gentle stream of Siloam ran from the Gihon spring into a pool inside the city walls, the pool of Siloam. These waters came to symbolize the Lord's provision for his people when they were besieged by enemies. But there is a more profound symbolism here. The prophet Ezekiel looked for the day when the river of God would flow from the Temple and bring life to the whole world (Ezekiel 47).

The Christian symbolism of the river is given in the Eastertide antiphon: 'The waters of a river give joy to God's city.' According to John's Gospel this river began to flow when the soldier pierced Jesus' side on the cross, 'and there came out blood and water,' symbols of the eucharist and baptism, through which the Spirit gives life to the people of God. The river of life flows also from God's throne in the new Jerusalem, in heaven (Revelation 22:1—2).

God is within, it cannot be shaken;
God will help it at the dawning of the day.

The *dawning of the day* may be an allusion to the Exodus, where the waters of the Red Sea returned to drown the Egyptian armies 'as morning dawned' (Exodus 14:27); or it may simply picture the coming of daylight which dispels the darkness.

Nations are in tumult, kingdoms are shaken:
he lifts his voice, the earth shrinks away.

From natural disaster the psalmist now turns to political turmoil. It is not the sea whose *waters rage and foam,* but the nations which *are in tumult.* It is not the mountains which are *shaken,* but *kingdoms.* The shaking is described as God's work. It all happens as *he lifts up his voice.* God's purpose in acting in history is now spelt out: he acts to bring an end to war.

Come, consider the works of the Lord
the redoubtable deeds he has done on the earth.
He puts an end to wars over all the earth;
the bow he breaks, the spear he snaps.
He burns the shields with fire.

The psalmist may have had in mind the occasion when the Assyrian armies were besieging Jerusalem, but one night they were smitten by a plague which annihilated the troops, and sent the remnant of the army fleeing. (2 Kings 18,19). Israel saw in this the clear hand of the Lord who *puts an end to wars.* But the words undoubtedly are meant to describe the future, the Day of the Lord, when evil will finally be conquered and peace will reign *over all the earth*. Every action which brings peace on earth today foreshadows the action of God who will bring eternal peace.

'Be still and know that I am God,
supreme among the nations, supreme on earth!'

It is the voice of the Lord which quells the tumult of the nations and the fears of his people, and brings peace on earth.

Revelation 15:3—4

Revelation 15 begins the prophecy of the destruction of the Roman Empire (called the Beast), symbol of all political regimes which claim totalitarian powers and persecute the Church. Before the destruction begins John sees a vision of the martyrs 'who had fought against the beast and won . . . They were singing the hymn of Moses, . . . and the hymn of the Lamb.' (Revelation 15:2,3). Then comes the canticle, verses 3—4. Its description as 'the hymn of Moses' goes back to the hymn the Israelites sung after crossing the Red Sea (Exodus 15). This hymn became Israel's great hymn of deliverance, and so it is the hymn the martyrs sing after their deliverance from the Beast. It was not a deliverance through military conquest, like Israel's, but a deliverance through death, the death of the Lamb (Jesus), and so it is 'the hymn of the Lamb', sung after he defeated death. The hymn is a mosaic of Old Testament phrases.

Great and wonderful are your deeds,
O Lord God the Almighty!
Just and true are your ways,
O King of the ages!

The *deeds* and *ways* are God's actions in Christ and his actions at the End, when his kingdom of justice comes in all its glory, when evil is destroyed and the saints reign.

Who shall not fear and glorify your name, O Lord?
For you alone are holy.
All nations shall come and worship you,
for your judgements have been revealed.

The *nations* will at the last recognize the salvation God has won for the world in Christ, in whom all God's *judgements* (his acts of saving justice) *have been revealed.*

Week 1: Saturday

MORNING PRAYER

Those who arranged the psalms and canticles of the Office understood human frailty. We are not usually at our brightest on Saturday morning, and the three passages for this morning have a refreshing simplicity. We sing the praise of God's word (Psalm 118), the praise of his action in delivering his people (Exodus 15), and invite all nations to join our praise of *his love* (Psalm 116).

Psalm 118(119):145—152 XIX (Koph)

Psalm 118(119) is the greatest expression in the Old Testament of love for God's law. As far as we can tell from the psalm itself, the psalmist was a young teacher of the law who stood firm against the indifference and laxity of his day. His psalm was composed according to a definite pattern. It is made up of twenty-two strophes, one for each letter of the Hebrew alphabet. Each strophe begins with the next letter of the alphabet, which makes the psalm an acrostic psalm. The extract of Psalm 118 which is presented for prayer this morning is the nineteenth strophe, and begins with the nineteenth letter of the Hebrew alphabet, Koph. Each strophe has eight verses, and each verse contains one of eight terms for the Law: law, commands, precepts, decrees, statutes, word, promise, will. (Different English versions translate these eight words in different ways, and the version used in the Office is not always consistent).

The meaning of the psalm can be followed quite easily, and needs no further explanation. The main purpose of the psalm is to engender in us the same deep love for the Lord and for his truth which fired the psalmist. Jesus said, 'If you love me, keep my commandments.'

Exodus 15:1—4A,8—13,17—18

The crossing of the Red (or Reed) Sea was for Israel the Lord's most glorious act of salvation on her behalf. The Exodus from Egypt was the founding event of the nation, in the same way that the Cross and Resurrection of Jesus are the founding events of the new Israel, the Church. In the story of the Exodus this canticle comes immediately after Israel has passed through the sea, and the water has closed in again swallowing the army of Pharaoh. The song begins by celebrating the destruction of Pharaoh's army, but goes on to speak of Israel's wanderings in the wilderness, the conquest of Canaan, and even the building of the Temple in Jerusalem. It is a song which has 'grown' over the centuries in which it was first sung, each generation adding a verse which celebrates God's salvation in their own time. Christians continued this tradition, and we find a version of this canticle in the last book of the Bible, in Revelation 15:3—4. The **sentence** (*Those who overcame the beast sang the hymn of Moses, the Servant of God*) comes from this version in Revelation, where it is the song of the martyrs who have been delivered through death from the power of the Beast, the Roman Empire. (See Week 1, Friday Evening). The Eastertide antiphon also connects the canticle with the song of the martyrs in Revelation 15: 'For the victors, theirs is the song of God's servant Moses, theirs is the song of the Lamb, alleluia.' Exodus 15 is a canticle to be sung by all who have experienced God's salvation, and can therefore sing in triumph with Israel old and new.

Most of the canticle describes the victory of the Exodus in vivid poetic language which needs no explanation, but the central theme of the canticle poses a problem for Christian prayer: *The Lord is a warrior!* The victory at the Red Sea is God's victory. It was he who *hurled the chariots of Pharaoh into the sea . . . You blew with your breath, the sea closed over them.* How are we to pray a canticle which so boldly paints the Lord as a mighty general wreaking destruction on his enemies? The Scriptures record how God chose a particular nation in order to reveal his will to all nations. Israel was constantly oppressed and attacked by the surrounding nations (beginning with the slavery in Egypt), and the only way she could be a free people and bear witness to the Lord's sovereign power was through defeating her enemies. Israel's victories were therefore God's victories, as he established the nation and progressively revealed his will to the people.

But the climax of God's revelation was Jesus, and Jesus brought a radical re-interpretation of God as a warrior. God's battle is no longer against Israel's enemies, but against Satan, against 'all his works and all his empty promises' (baptismal liturgy). Exodus 15 is transformed by Christ into a canticle of the God's victory over 'the ruling force of darkness' (Colossians 1:14).

The last part of the canticle moves from the Exodus to the settlement of Canaan and the building of the Temple in Jerusalem:

> *Your power has led them to your holy dwelling-place.*
>
> *You will lead them and plant them*
> *on your mountain,* (Sion)
> *the place, O Lord, where you have made your home,*
> *the sanctuary, Lord, which your hands have made.*

The final line announces one of the major themes of the Old

Testament, especially of the psalms: *The Lord will reign for ever and ever*. No power can thwart his plan for the salvation of the world.

Psalm 116(117)

This is the shortest psalm in the Old Testament but it's vision is universal and its message sums up God's will for the world. God's plan in saving Israel is to save *all you nations*. In his care for Israel the Lord has shown his *love,* shown that *he is faithful for ever,* and this love and faithfulness are for all nations, as in the **sentence:** *I ask the nations to give praise to God for his mercy* (Romans 15:8—9).

Commentary on the Psalmody of Week 2

Week 2: Sunday

EVENING PRAYER I

Each of the three passages for prayer this evening reveals the suffering and joy of a life wholly devoted to God. Psalm 118 is the prayer in affliction of one who can say of the Lord's will: 'It is the *joy of my heart.*' In the face of death, the psalmist prays to the Lord: *You will show me the path of life, the fulness of joy in your presence.* (Psalm 15). The Lord himself went through death to glory, and we worship him with every creature *in heaven and on earth.* (Philippians 2).

The cycle of prayer is so arranged that Week 2 is always used in Holy Week, and the antiphons are important in linking the events of Holy Week with the theme of each passage in the psalmody.

Psalm 118(119):105—112 XIV (Nun)

On the form and meaning of Psalm 118(119) as a whole, see Week 1, Saturday Morning.

> *Your word is a lamp for my steps*
> *and a light for my path.*

The psalmist treads a path through the traps set by his enemies (next verse), and looks to the word of God to guide him safely and securely. John's Gospel reveals Jesus as the Word who is the light of the world. Jesus said: 'Anyone who follows me will not be walking in the dark but will have the light of life' (John 8:12).

Lord, I am deeply afflicted:
by your word give me life.

The psalmist may have been a young scribe faithful to God's Law at a time when compromise and laxity had taken hold in society. Such a stand makes enemies, and so he is *deeply afflicted.* The *wicked try to ensnare* him. It is God's word which sustains and strengthens him, gives him *life.*

The **sentence** reminds us that the decree of the Lord which every disciple must obey is Jesus' commandment to love one another.

Psalm 15(16)

The psalmist prays for deliverance from two dangers: first, the danger of turning away from the Lord to worship other gods; second, the danger of death. This is one of the first psalms the Church interpreted as referring to Christ, and in praying the psalm we are praying with Christ to the Father who delivered him from death.

Preserve me, God, I take refuge in you.
I say to the Lord: 'You are my God.
My happiness lies in you alone.'

To take refuge in the Lord is to give one's ultimate loyalty to him alone ('*You are my God*'), and to find one's ultimate fulfilment in him alone ('*My happiness lies in you alone*').

He has put into my heart a marvellous love
for the faithful ones who dwell in his land.

Delight in God leads to delight in the people of God, his *faithful ones.* It is 'the love of God poured into our hearts by the Holy Spirit' which enables us to love one another.

Those who choose other gods increase their sorrows.
Never will I offer their offerings of blood.
Never will I take their name upon my lips.

Israel was surrounded by nations worshipping other gods, and she repeatedly gave in to the temptation to add these gods to the worship of the Lord. The psalmist knows the power of such a temptation, but he resolves to serve the Lord alone. He will never participate in idol worship, with its ritual pouring out of animal (and sometimes human) blood. *Never will I offer their offerings of blood.*

He will never pay homage to these gods by calling out for their help. *Never will I take their name on my lips.* The New Testament reveals how strong was the lure of idol worship for Gentile Christians, and modern Christians who live in a materialist consumer society, capitalist or communist, face a similar temptation.

O Lord, it is you who are my portion and cup;
it is you yourself who are my prize.

The psalmist resists the temptation to idol worship because he finds his spiritual hunger and thirst satisfied in the Lord. *You are my portion and my cup,* you are my food and drink.

The lot marked out for me is my delight:
welcome indeed the heritage that falls to me!

When Israel entered Canaan the land was divided amongst the tribes by ballot (by *lot*), and became the God-given heritage of that tribe. The psalmist may be referring to the plot of land that fell to his ancestors and which is his heritage; or he may be continuing the theme that the Lord alone is his heritage. The priests were given no land in Canaan because the Lord said: 'I will be your portion and your heritage' (Numbers 18:20). Thus *the lot marked out for me* may be the psalmist's way of describing his privilege of being a priest. As Christians our *heritage,* our inheritance, is the salvation won for us in Christ. 'It is in him that we have reveived our heritage' (Ephesians 1:10). The gift of the Spirit is the first installment, 'the pledge of our inheritance' (Ephesians 1:14).

I will bless the Lord who gives me counsel,
who even at night directs my heart.
I keep the Lord ever in my sight:
since he is at my right hand, I shall stand firm.

Many of the psalms commend the practice of the night vigil, meditating on the Lord in the night hours. In the stillness of the night and in the depths of my *heart* the Lord *gives me counsel.* As the psalmist thus keeps the Lord *ever in* his *sight,* ever before him, so the Lord *is at his right hand,* holding him firm in the midst of danger and death. It is this experience of the Lord's counsel and support that makes the psalmist so sure he will *stand firm* and not yield to idolatry or be given over to death.

And so my heart rejoices, my soul is glad;
even my body shall rest in safety.
For you will not leave my soul among the dead,
nor let your beloved know decay.

You will show me the path of life,
the fulness of joy in your presence,
at your right hand happiness for ever.

There are three levels of interpretation in these verses. At the primary level, they express the psalmist's confidence that he will not die, that his soul shall not be left *among the dead.* He is confident that the danger to his life will pass, and that he will remain among the living, on *the path of life.*

On the second level, this verse expresses the conviction that the *path of life* is much more than physical life. It is God's presence which brings *fulness of joy* and *happiness for ever.* Full life is life *in your presence.* This is as close as the Old Testament comes to the New Testament understanding of eternal life as communion with God, a union which physical death cannot destroy.

On the third level, these verses apply to the resurrection of our Lord Jesus. In his sermon on the day of Pentecost the Apostle Peter quoted these verses as a prophecy of Christ's resurrection (Acts 2:30,31). It is for this reason that Christians ever since have prayed the psalm with Christ as an expression of his confidence in the power of the Father to deliver him from death; hence the sentence: *God raised up Jesus, freeing him from the pains of death* (Acts 2:24).

The psalmist faced death and rose in confidence above that danger to know *the fulness of joy* in God's presence. Jesus faced death, went through death, and rose in triumph from the dead. The psalmist was not left *among the dead.* Jesus was delivered from the dead.

Philippians 2:6—11

See Week 1, Sunday Evening I.

MORNING PRAYER

The psalmody this morning prepares us for the celebration of the Eucharist. Psalm 117, like the Liturgy of the Eucharist, has many voices: people, priest, and king. The king is Christ, and in the psalm we pray with him before he is glorified in his cross and resurrection. The praise continues with the canticle from Daniel, in which we praise God who is present in the whole of creation. The crescendo of praise reaches its climax with Psalm 150. *Let everything that lives and breathes give praise to the Lord.*

Psalm 117(118)

Psalm 117 reveals extraordinary riches. For the Christian it evokes all the great events of Holy Week: Palm Sunday, the Last Supper (this psalm was part of the hymn Jesus and his disciples sang at the conclusion of the Lord's Supper,

Matthew 26:30), the Cross, and the Resurrection. In its original setting it seems to have been a hymn sung by the king together with priests and people, in thanksgiving for victory. The psalm begins as the procession approaches the gates of the Temple, and a priest at the gates cries out:

Give thanks to the Lord for he is good,
for his love endures for ever.

Let the sons of Israel say:
'His love endures forever.'
Let the sons of Aaron say:
'His love endures for ever.'
Let those who fear the Lord say:
'His love endures for ever.'

The whole nation is called on to give thanks to the Lord, with each group in the procession being addressed in turn: first the people, *the sons of Israel*; then the priests, *the sons of Aaron*; finally the whole procession, *those who fear* (reverence) *the Lord.*

The refrain *His love endures for ever* expresses the heart of God's covenant with Israel. His *love* (Hebrew, *hesed*) is his absolute loyalty to the covenant. Israel may be (and often was) unfaithful; the Lord is always faithful, *his love endures for ever.* The victory of the king for which this psalm gives thanks is another example of God's faithfulness to the covenant. Today we pray the psalm in thanksgiving for the supreme example of God's *love*: Jesus, who now speaks in the words of the psalm:

I called to the Lord in my distress;
he answered and freed me.
The Lord is at my side; I do not fear.
What can man do against me?
The Lord is at my side as my helper:
I shall look down on my foes.

The king now speaks, recalling before the people his prayer as he went into battle. It was the Lord who saved him, for no foe can stand against God. As we pray the psalm with Christ, we pray with him after the victory of the resurrection. His prayer becomes our prayer, his confidence our confidence.

> *It is better to take refuge in the Lord*
> *than to trust in men:*
> *it is better to take refuge in the Lord*
> *than to trust in princes.*

Human allies and counsellors (*men* and *princes*) can never compare with the help of the Lord. It is always *better to take refuge* in him.

> *The nations all encompassed me;*
> *In the Lord's name I crushed them . . .*

The king's enemies attacked like a swarm of *bees* and threatened to overwhelm him, but victory came as he put his trust in the *Lord's name,* in God's character and promises. On the cross Christ was attacked by his foe, the Prince of this world, but *in the Lord's name* he *crushed* him.

> *The Lord is my strength and my song;*
> *he is my saviour . . .*

This verse is a direct quotation from the Hymn of Moses (Week 1, Saturday Morning) sung by the Israelites after their victory over Pharaoh's army at the Red Sea. The king's victory is a continuation of the victory begun at the Exodus. As the Lord acted then, so he acts now. *His love endures for ever.*

> *The Lord's right hand has triumphed;*
> *his right hand raised me. . . .*

The king came face to face with death in battle but was delivered by the Lord. The resurrection of Christ fulfills the messianic prophecy of the psalm.

> *I was punished, I was punished by the Lord,*
> *but not doomed to die.*

The king interprets the intensity of the conflict as the Lord's discipline, bringing him to renewed faithfulness to the covenant. The *punishment* suffered by Christ was for us. 'He was wounded for our transgressions, he was bruised for our iniquities; upon him was the chastisement that made us whole, and with his stripes we are healed' (Isaiah 53:5).

> *Open to me the gates of holiness:*
> *I will enter and give thanks.*
> *This is the Lord's own gate*
> *where the just may enter.*

As the procession arrives at the Temple gates the king calls for the gates to be opened so he can *enter and give thanks.* The *just* are those who obey God's commandments. The gates of heaven opened to Christ, the *just* one, after his resurrection.

> *The stone which the builders rejected*
> *has become the corner stone.*

With this verse we hear the voice of the people celebrating the victory of the king. They begin by quoting a proverbial saying. In the pile of stones the builders were using (for the Temple?), one seemed to be useless. It would not fit anywhere and so the builders put it aside. Later they discover that the stone they rejected was exactly the right shape for a key part of the building, either the cornerstone which binds two walls together or the keystone in an arch. The people use the proverb to sum up the king's recent experience in battle. To his enemies the king appears to be so weak as to be useless. They reject him. But the Lord has given him victory and raised him to a position of highest honour. *This is the work of the Lord, a marvel in our eyes.* Even in Old Testament times the proverb had become associated with the coming Messiah (Isaiah 28:16).

Jesus, the Messiah, challenged his enemies to see in him the stone which they had rejected, the one who would become 'the head of the corner' (Matthew 21:42). St Peter applies this same verse to Jesus in his address to the Sanhedrin, as proof of how wrong they were about Jesus (Acts 4:11, the **sentence**: *This is the stone which was rejected by you builders, but which has become the corner stone*). By the time of the letter to the Ephesians Christ is called the 'cornerstone' of the Church, the one 'in whom the whole structure is joined together and grows into a holy temple in the Lord' (2:20,21).

> *This day was made by the Lord;*
> *we rejoice and are glad.*

The day is a day of rejoicing because of the victory *made by the Lord.* The Eastertide **antiphon** identifies this day as the day of Jesus' resurrection.

> *O Lord, grant us salvation;*
> *O Lord, grant success.*

The people pray for the Lord's blessing, which is then given by the priest:

> *Blessed in the name of the Lord*
> *is he who comes.*

The priest pronounces the Lord's blessing on all *who come* into the Temple. By the time of the New Testament the phrase *He who comes* had become a title of the Messiah. John the Baptist asked Jesus: 'Are you he who is to come?' (Matthew 11:3), and on Palm Sunday as Jesus enters Jerusalem the crowds hail him as the Messiah with the shout: 'Blessed is the King who comes in the name of the Lord!' (Luke 19:38). (See Palm Sunday **antiphon**). In the eucharistic prayer we take up this joyful cry and hail Christ as he comes in the consecrated bread and wine: 'Blessed is he who comes in the name of the Lord'.

> *We bless you from the house of the Lord;*
> *the Lord God is our light.*

The priestly blessing concludes. The *light* may be the light of God's presence (Numbers 6:24ff.) which gives joy and guidance to his people.

> *Go forward in procession with branches*
> *even to the altar.*

The priest now gives instructions to the worshippers as they approach the altar. On the Feast of Tabernacles the worshippers all carried a bundle of branches which they waved during the procession up *to the altar.*

> *You are my God, I thank you.*
> *My God, I praise you.*

The king speaks again, this time affirming his commitment to the Lord as his God and bringing the thanksgiving to a climax.

> *Give thanks to the Lord for he is good;*
> *for his love endures for ever.*

The psalm concludes with the opening verse being repeated. This is the grand theme of the whole psalm.

Daniel 3:52—57

This joyful canticle is a hymn in praise of the Creator. Apart from one phrase, it needs no explanation. It needs only a heart full of thankfulness for the blessings of the creation.

> *You are blest who gaze into the depths.*

Nothing escapes the Lord's eye, nothing is beyond his knowledge. He sees even into the world of the dead, *the depths.*

Psalm 150

The last psalm in the psalter is a call to the whole world, *everything that lives and breathes,* to praise the Lord. Ten times we hear the command 'Praise God', or 'Praise him.' The number may be deliberate, chosen to match the ten words of creation in Genesis 1 ('God said . . .') and the Ten Commandments. As with the previous canticle, it needs no explanation. It is a crescendo of praise.

EVENING PRAYER II

The Lord's power is supreme, in contrast to the things people worship as god's (Psalm 113B); but this power is the power of love, revealed in Christ's death and resurrection.

Psalm 109(110)

See Week 1, Sunday Evening II.

Psalm 113B(115)

This psalm builds the trust of God's people by praising the power of the Lord and mocking the impotence of idols. The idols are described as *the work of human hands,* reminding us that people in a materialist society can be as much caught up in idolatry as the nations surrounding Israel. The Church today is as exposed to the lure of idols as Israel was.

> *Not to us, Lord, not to us,*
> *but to your name give the glory*
> *for the sake of your love and your truth,*
> *lest the heathen say: 'Where is your God?'*

Israel is under threat of attack by foreign nations whose victory would only make their gods, their idols, appear to be more powerful than the Lord. The question of *the heathen: 'Where is their God?'* may have been a deliberate taunt thrown at Israel because she had no visible God. To those whose gods were idols, this meant that Israel's God did not exist. He was not visible therefore he did not exist.

The people come to the Temple to pray to the Lord for victory, not for their own glory, but for *the glory* of *your name*. The Lord's honour and commitment to the covenant (shown in his *love* and *truth*) are at stake, and this is Israel's concern rather than any self-seeking. Their hope for deliverance is founded on God's covenant *love* and *truth*.

But our God is in the heavens;
he does whatever he wills.
Their idols are silver and gold,
the work of human hands.

Israel's God may be invisible, *in the heavens,* but he is certainly not inactive. *He does whatever he wills.* His almighty power effects his will, in contrast to the idols of the heathen, who are visible all right, but dead, lifeless, *the work of human hands,* having neither the will nor the power to act.

They have mouths but they cannot speak. . . .

These idols seem to have all that is necessary for speech and action, but it is all a sham. Despite their *mouths, eyes, ears, nostrils,* they are dumb, blind, deaf, and *cannot smell.* They have *hands* that *cannot feel, feet* that *cannot walk, throats* that make *no sound.*

Their makers will come to be like them
and so will all who trust in them.

Idolatry is worse than useless. It makes those who worship idols less than human. This verse gives a prophetic warning to a society which makes the pursuit of wealth the supreme goal, the god. We become like the god we worship. St Paul said that those who worship idols become 'empty in their thinking' (Romans 1:21).

Sons of Israel, trust in the Lord;
he is their help and their shield . . .

A priest speaks to the whole congregation, to the laity (*Sons of Israel*), the priests (*Sons of Aaron*), and the whole nation (*You who fear him*), urging them all to *trust in the Lord* who *speaks* through priest and prophet, who *hears* the prayer of his people, who *sees* their plight, who *smells* the smoke of their sacrifices. He is *their help and their shield*, the one who will protect them against the attacks of their enemies.

He remembers us, and he will bless us.

In particular his blessing will bring an *increase* in the population, of enormous importance to Israel after the devastation of the Exile. The priest gives the blessing:

May you be blessed by the Lord,
the maker of heaven and earth.

The God who will bless them is no dumb idol, but the powerful creator of *heaven and earth.*

The heavens belong to the Lord (not to the idols)
but the earth he has given to men.

The earth and its fruits are God's gifts to humankind, not the gifts of idols.

The dead shall not praise the Lord,
nor those who go down into the silence.
But we who live bless the Lord
now and for ever. Amen.

The congregation replies to the priest's blessing. The living must praise the Lord for the blessings of the earth, because the dead cannot do this. To live is to *bless the Lord.*

Revelation 19:1—2,5—7

See Week 1, Sunday Evening II.

1 Peter 2:21—24

See Week 1, Sunday Evening II.

Week 2: Monday

MORNING PRAYER

The movement of this morning's prayer is from despair to praise. The first psalm is the cry of someone who feels cut off from God. The Old Testament canticle prays for God's glory to be renewed in the life and worship of his suffering people. The final psalm has been called 'the greatest poem in the psalter', and offers exuberant praise to God for his revelation through creation.

Psalm 41(42)

The **heading** of the psalm provides a key to it's interpretation: The Exile's Nostalgia for the Lord's Temple. The psalmist is in exile, probably in Babylon, far away from the Temple, surrounded by the enemies who had destroyed the Temple and the city he loved. The psalm divides into two parts, each part following a three-fold pattern: the psalmist pours out his sorrow, he then deliberately turns his mind away from his distress, and finally he turns to God in the words, *Hope in God; I will praise him still, my saviour and my God.* The psalm is a model of how to deal with spiritual depression, and some interpreters understand it to refer not to the desolation of the Exile but to the sense of desolation brought on by a severe illness.

The Holy Week antiphon takes us deep into the sorrow of

Jesus as we pray with him in Gethsemane. Jesus experienced the sense of being forsaken by God at the time of his greatest need, and in this he has undergone the most devastating experience which can come to anyone who loves God. In this psalm we pray with Christ and with all those who have felt abandoned by God. As we share in Christ's sufferings and the sufferings of his Body the Church, so we will share in his consolation.

(Prayed on a Monday, this psalm can express the prayer of priests and pastors who have led the celebrations of the previous Sunday).

Like the deer that yearns
for running streams,
so my soul is yearning
for you, my God.

In Palestine in the dry season the sun beats down for five long months, May to September. The land is baked dry, rivers cease to flow, and animals die of thirst. The psalmist longs for God with the same desperate intensity that *the deer* in the dry season thirsts for fresh water, for *running streams.*

Jesus promised 'living water', the water of the Spirit, to all who come thirsty to him (John 4:14; 7:37; and the sentence from Revelation 22:17). There is a true sense in which all who drink of the water of the Spirit are 'never thirsty again', the soul's deepest longing is satisfied; but there is another sense in which those who drink the water of the Spirit are always thirsty for more. They long to know more of the love and truth of their Lord. This thirst is the pre-requisite of all spiritual growth.

Soul in the psalms means the whole person.

My soul is thirsting for God,
the God of my life;
when can I enter and see
the face of God?

The Temple was the place where the Lord met with his people. There he spoke to them through priest and prophet; there the sacrifices for sin where offered; there the great events of Israel's redemption were celebrated in the feasts of Passover, Pentecost, and Tabernacles. The Temple was at the heart of Israel's relationship with God, and to be cut off from the Temple, as the psalmist was, was to be cut off from the wellsprings of spiritual life. He asks: *when can I enter* the Temple again, and know the intimate presence of God, *the face of God.* The psalmist does not limit God's presence to the Temple, otherwise he would not pray as he does, but the Temple is the place above all where God is revealed.

This verse can express the Christian's longing for heaven. We, like the psalmist, are exiles on this earth, for 'our homeland is in heaven and it is from there that we are expecting a Saviour, the Lord Jesus Christ' (Philippians 3:20).

My tears have become my bread,
by night, by day,
as I hear it said all the day long:
'Where is your God?'

The psalmist is depressed not only by the absence of God, but because of the presence of men who mock him, asking '*Where is your God?*' These men may be the Babylonians who have conquered Jerusalem and therefore believe that the God who protected the city, the Lord God of Israel, is nothing compared with their gods. They say to the Israelites in captivity: 'The Lord has been defeated. He is powerless to help you. *Where is your God?*' This was precisely the taunt hurled at Jesus by his enemies while he hung on the cross. 'He trusts in God; let God deliver him now, it he desires him.' (Matthew 27:43).

These things will I remember
as I pour out my soul:
how I would lead the rejoicing crowd

into the house of God,
amid cries of gladness and thanksgiving,
the throng wild with joy.

At this point the psalmist turns away from his present troubles and thinks back to the times when he led the processions into the temple on the great feast days. This may imply that the psalmist is Israel's king, or a leading priest. In remembering the feasts he begins to remember the events they celebrated: the Exodus from Egypt, the giving of the law and the covenant God made with Israel at Sinai, the entry into the promised land, the building and consecration of the Temple. This memory makes his present captivity even more painful, but at the same time renews his hope that the God who acted to deliver Israel in the past will act to deliver her in the future.

When we feel abandoned by God the memory of his past goodness can be a bittersweet experience. It may make our present trouble all the more painful, but it can also arouse hope. The God who acted in our past will come again to save us.

Why are you cast down, my soul,
why groan within me?
Hope in God; I will praise him still,
my saviour and my God.

The psalmist's hope is not a vague optimism but a conviction based on his memory of the way God has acted in the past. The Lord who saved Israel from Egypt will save her from this present captivity. He is *my saviour and my God.* It is this sure hope that gives rise to *praise.* In his depression the psalmist wills himself to praise and so begins to be lifted out of himself, to see life from God's perspective.

This is precisely the path St Paul followed in his own experience of suffering. In the midst of his suffering he looked back to the great events of Christ's death and resurrection, and then looked forward with unquenchable hope. 'What shall we say to this? If God is for us, who is against us? He who did not spare his own Son, but gave him up for us all, will he not also give us all things with him? Who shall bring any charge against God's elect? It is God who justifies; who is to condemn? Is it Christ Jesus, who died, yes, who rose was raised from the dead, who is at the right hand of God, who indeed intercedes for us? Who shall separate us from the love of Christ?' (Romans 8:31—35).

My soul is cast down within me
as I think of you,
from the country of Jordan and Mount Hermon,
from the Hill of Mizar.

The second part of the psalm follows the same three-fold pattern as the first: the psalmist expresses his anguish; he turns away from himself; he turns to God.

The geographical references in this verse imply that the psalmist is in the far north of Palestine, at the headwaters of the *Jordan* river, under the shadow of *Mount Hermon* and the *Hill of Mizar* (presumably also in the north, but a place unknown to us now). The psalmist may have actually been there in the procession of captives as they made their way in chains to Babylon, or he may be picturing the north of Israel as the furthermost point in the land from Jerusalem and thus a symbol of his present distance from the Temple.

Deep is calling on deep,
in the roar of waters:
your torrents and all your waves
swept over me.

The thought of Mount Hermon brings to mind the raging waterfalls which cascade off the mountain in winter. The psalmist feels as though he is in the midst of such a torrent, swept away, drowning. Behind this image there may be the thought of the ancient waters of chaos which God tamed at creation, but which now seem to be unleashed again. The psalmist's whole world has broken down. Chaos and evil reign.

By day the Lord will send
his loving kindness;
by night I will sing to him,
praise the God of my life.

This verse may be out of place, and belong at the end of the psalm, but it can be understood in its present position as an expression of hope. The psalmist has known the continual experience of God's grace in the past, *his loving kindness,* and this memory stirs hope that the *loving kindness* of the past will be renewed in the future.

I will say to God, my rock:
'Why have you forgotten me?
Why do I go mourning
oppressed by the foe?'

The image of the raging waters is taken up again, and in the midst of this wild river the psalmist clings to *God, my rock.* The most painful part of his whole experience is the thought that God has *forgotten* him. He has been abandoned to his foes.

With cries that pierce me to the heart,
my enemies revile me,
saying to me all the day long:
'Where is your God?'

The second part of the psalm finishes with the same question as the first, *'Where is your God?'*, and the same refrain, *Why are you cast down, my soul . . .*

The psalm is not finished here. Psalm 42(43) is a continuation of Psalm 41(42), and in some Bibles the two are printed as one (New Jerusalem Bible). Tomorrow, in Tuesday Morning Prayer, we pray Psalm 42(43).

Sirach 36:1—7,13—16

This prayer for Jerusalem comes in the book of Ben Sira (or Sirach), one of the deutero-canonical books of the Old Testament. Ben Sira was a godly scribe who was devoted to the Temple and to the Law. He writes in the tradition of the Wisdom literature, in about 190—180 BC, at a time when Israel was under Greek rule (the Seleucid dynasty) and the threat to her faith and institutions was growing. Thirty years later the Maccabaean revolt would break out.

The Christian prays in this canticle for the overthrow of 'the prince of this world' (see the Holy Week antiphon), and for the renewal of the Church (Eastertide antiphon).

> *Save us, God of all things,*
> *strike all the nations with terror;*
> *raise your hand against foreign nations*
> *that they may see the greatness of your might.*

Ben Sira is acutely conscious of the threat to Israel's faith and identity from the surrounding nations, especially the Greeks. His prayer is that Israel may be preserved from their attacks. The same prayer can be made for the Church, whose life and identity can be threatened by different political and cultural movements.

> *Our sufferings proved your holiness to them;*
> *let their downfall prove your glory to us.*
> *Let them know, as we ourselves know,*
> *that there is no other God but you.*

The *sufferings* he has in mind are the sufferings of the Exile, when God punished his people for their persistent rebellion. The writer of Chronicles describes how Israel kept on 'mocking the messengers of God, despising his words, and scoffing at his prophets, till the wrath of the Lord rose against his people, till there was no remedy' (2 Chronicles 36:16). The destruction of the city and the exile of the population was a dramatic sign to the nations that God is holy and he punishes sin. But in executing God's wrath, the foreign nations went too far (Isaiah 47:6), mocking God and nearly annihilating Israel, and so the people pray that the sin of the nations will be punished as was their own sin. This would be to Israel proof of God's *glory.* At times the Church in particular countries has been disciplined by God for unfaithfulness and has been threatened with destruction by the human instrument of discipline.

The **sentence,** *This is eternal life; to know you the one true God, and Jesus Christ whom you have sent* (John 17:3), picks up the last two lines of this stanza.

Give us signs again, . . .

As in the Exodus God worked *signs* and *wonders* for his people, so Ben Sira prays for such signs to be done in his own time.

Assemble all the tribes of Jacob . . .

He prays for all the exiles to be brought home, and for the nation (*Jacob*, the covenant people) to be restored to its former glory. Today we pray for the Church, broken into many pieces, to be restored to its true unity and holiness.

Have compassion on the holy city . . .

The attacks of Israel's enemies left Jerusalem devastated, and the returning exiles felt they would never complete the task of restoring the city and the temple to their former glory. Ben Sira longs for the *temple to be filled with* God's *glory.* Today we have the same longing for the Church.

Psalm 18(19)A

C.S. Lewis described this psalm as 'the greatest poem in the psalter and one of the greatest lyrics in the world' (*Reflections on the Psalms,* p. 56). God is praised as the creator of the heavens, and particularly of the sun, source of energy and light for the whole world.

> *The heavens proclaim the glory of God*
> *and the firmament shows forth the work of his hands.*
> *Day unto day takes up the story*
> *and night unto night makes known the message.*

In the Old Testament the *glory* of God is the splendour of his presence made visible. For the psalmist there is no more splendid evidence of God's glory than the heavens, whose stars are *the work of his hands*. The *firmament* was thought to be like an upturned basin separating the waters above the heavens from the waters beneath the heavens (Genesis 1:7). In our own time the vast order and mystery of the universe has been revealed to be far greater than anything the psalmist dreamed of, but our age has lost and needs to recover his sense of creation as a continuous (*Day unto day, . . . night unto night*) revelation (*message*) of God's glory. St Paul wrote of how 'ever since the creation of the world God's invisible nature, namely his eternal power and deity, has been clearly perceived in the things that have been made' (Romans 1:20).

> *No speech, no word, no voice is heard*
> *yet their span extends through all the earth,*
> *their words to the utmost bounds of the world.*

God's revelation of his glory through creation is a universal revelation. It is accessible to everyone, to all languages and cultures. Everyone, everywhere can read and hear its message. It is a picture that is worth a million words. St Paul quotes this verse as a prophecy of the universal proclamation of the gospel by the Apostles (Romans 10:18). God's revelation in Christ is to be as universal and plain to see as his revelation in creation.

There he has placed a tent for the sun;
it comes forth like a bridegroom coming from his tent,
rejoices like a champion to run its course.

The *sun* is the most spectacular sign of God's glory in creation. The *heavens* are like a tent from which the sun emerges every morning after its nightly rest. The sun *comes forth like a bridegroom* on his wedding day, dressed in dazzling robes, fresh, joyful, full of vigour; *like a champion* athlete ready *to run the course.*

The **sentence** *The Rising Sun has come to visit us to guide our feet in the way of peace* (Luke 1:78,79), points us to Christ, the Son of God, the ultimate revelation of God's glory. He is the light that 'shines in the darkness, and darkness could not overpower it' (John 1:4).

At the end of the sky is the rising of the sun;
to the furthest end of the sky is its course.
There is nothing concealed from its burning heat.

If the silence of the skies can speak to the deaf, the *heat* of the sun can speak to the blind. Everyone, no matter who they are, receives through creation the revelation of God's glory.

EVENING PRAYER

The praise of Christ and the blessings of his Bride, the Church, are the themes of all three passages in the psalmody this evening. Psalm 44(45) is one of the most beautiful of the messianic psalms, and the canticle of Ephesians 1:3—10 shows how the prophecy of the psalm is fulfilled in Christ.

Psalm 44(45)

This psalm is unique in the psalter. It is a royal wedding song in two parts. The first addresses the bridegroom, the king, dressed in all his *splendour and state.* The second addresses the bride, the queen, who comes escorted by her bridesmaids to be married in the royal palace. In Jewish tradition the psalm was read as a prophecy of the Messiah, God's anointed king. The Church readily applied the psalm to Jesus. He is the bridegroom (the sentence *Behold, the bridegroom is coming; go out to meet him* (Matthew 25:6)), and the Church is his bride, 'those who are called to the wedding feast of the Lamb' (Eastertide antiphon).

My heart overflows with noble words . . .

The poet, possibly a priest or a prophet, is exhilarated by his theme. The wedding of the king is an event of prime importance for the whole nation, as the king is God's viceroy.

You are the fairest of the children of men
and graciousness is poured upon your lips:
because God has blessed you for evermore.

The king's handsome appearance and gift with words are signs of the fact that God has blessed him from birth. A man's physical appearance was expected to reflect his inner qualities, and hence the bewilderment of Israel when they saw that the suffering servant of the Lord in Isaiah 53 'had no beauty, no majesty to draw our eyes, no grace to make us delight in him' (Holy Week antiphon). Those who see in Christ the suffering servant prophesied by Isaiah know that he is 'the image of the invisible God', 'full of grace and truth' (Colossians 1:15; John 1:14). *He is the fairest of the children of men.*

O mighty one, gird your sword upon your thigh;
in splendour and state, ride on in triumph
for the cause of truth and goodness and right.

The king is responsible for the protection of his people from the attacks of their enemies, and so he must be *mighty* in battle. His cause is not a selfish cause, but the cause of justice. He is to fight for *truth, goodness, and right.* As he engages in this battle for justice he shares the attributes of God, to whom belongs *splendour and state* (Psalm 96:6).

In his triumphant reign, Christ will 'put all his enemies under his feet. The last enemy to be destroyed is death' (1 Corinthians 15:25,26). The *sword* of Christ and his disciples is 'the sword of the Spirit, which is the word of God' (Ephesians 6:17). The weapons of Christ are spiritual, for his 'kingdom is not of this world' (John 18:36).

Take aim with your bow in your dread right hand . . .

Wherever the king fights for *truth, goodness, and right* his strong power (*dread right hand*) will bring him victory.

Your throne, O God, shall endure for ever.
A sceptre of justice is the sceptre of your kingdom.
Your love is for justice; your hatred for evil.

The king can be described as *God* not because he is divine, but because he has been adopted as God's son (Psalm 2:7), God's agent on earth. The king's throne can be called God's throne. It was part of God's promise to David that his throne would *endure for ever,* a promise which was fulfilled in Christ, Son of David and Son of God. The writer to the Hebrews read these verses as a prophecy describing the authority and the supreme glory of Christ, the unique Son of God (Hebrews 1:8,9).

The king was responsible for justice in the kingdom, and so the poet reminds the king of this solemn task laid on him. The kingdom of God is 'saving justice, peace and joy in the Holy Spirit' (Romans 14:17).

Therefore God, your God, has anointed you
with the oil of gladness above other kings:
your robes are fragrant with aloes and myrrh.

A king was anointed at his coronation, and thus became the

anointed one, the messiah, but the anointing here may be the king's anointing with fragrant oils at his wedding as a sign of abundant joy, *the oil of gladness.*

> *From the ivory palace you are greeted with music.*
> *The daughters of kings are among your loved ones.*
> *On your right stands the queen in gold of Ophir.*

The wedding music has begun and the new queen comes to stand at the king's *right hand,* signifying her superiority over all other women in the realm. The fact that the king's harem includes *the daughters of kings* indicates how powerful he is. In Christian interpretation these foreign princesses represent the Gentile nations converted to Christ and brought into the new Israel. The moment for the wedding has arrived, and *the queen* stands dressed in *gold of Ophir.* (Ophir may have been in the Arabian desert, the mine from which Solomon's gold came).

It is possible that the *queen* in this verse is the Queen Mother, standing with her son awaiting the bride. In Christian tradition this has prompted some interpreters to identify the queen with the Blessed Virgin Mary, Mother of Our Lord, Queen of heaven.

> *Listen, O daughter, give ear to my words:*
> *forget your own people and your father's house.*
> *So will the king desire your beauty:*
> *He is your lord, pay homage to him.*

The queen is a foreign princess, and the poet advises her to *forget* her *own people.* Foreign princesses sometimes brought with them their gods, and insisted on introducing them into the worship of Israel (this was one of the reasons for Solomon's downfall, 1 Kings 11), so the queen is told to leave all that behind, and be loyal to her husband and to his God. This is the way she will attract her new husband's devotion.

The Church as the bride of Christ is challenged to the same loyalty to her Lord.

> *And the people of Tyre shall come with gifts ,*
> *the richest of the people shall seek your favour.*
> *The daughter of the king is clothed with splendour,*
> *her robes embroidered with pearls set in gold.*

Tyre is the city just to the north of Israel, on the coast. The poet prophesies that the *richest of the people* of the surrounding nations will bring gifts to the new queen (a princess in her own right, a *daughter of the king*) in order to *seek her favour.* She may have to cut her ties with her *father's house,* but she will be rewarded with *splendour* and *gold,* and with *sons* (last verse), future *princes over all the earth.*

Again, these lines can be interpreted with reference to the Church. Her beauty and wealth are the fruits of the Spirit which will draw people to *seek her favour.* Her royal robe is holiness (Ephesians 5:27).

> *She is led to the king . . .*

As the bride enters the palace *amid gladness and joy,* so the Church will enter heaven for 'the marriage of the Lamb' (Revelation 21:9).

> *Sons shall be yours in place of your fathers:*
> *you will make them princes over all the earth.*

The Davidic king was to rule the earth in justice and truth, a prophecy that found its fulfilment in Christ. The union of Christ and his Church brings the blessing of sons and daughters through whom the name and honour of the king are revealed over *all the earth.*

> *May this song make your name for ever remembered.*
> *May the peoples praise you from age to age.*

The last two lines are the poet's address to the king, wishing him and his dynasty long life, honour and renown for all time.

Ephesians 1:3—10

See Week 1, Monday Evening.

Week 2: Tuesday

MORNING PRAYER

Today's psalmody is full of hope. It begins with the cry of an exile far away from the temple, praying in confident hope for God's light and truth to guide him. The Old Testament canticle gives thanks to God for deliverance from death, and the concluding psalm of praise gives thanks for deliverance from famine, extolling the lavish superabundance of God's gifts.

Psalm 42(43)

This psalm is a direct continuation of Psalm 41(42) and the introduction given to that psalm applies to this one. (See Week 2, Monday Morning). It follows the same three-fold pattern as the first two parts of Psalm 41: lament, turning from self, turning to God.

> *Defend me, O God, and plead my cause*
> *against a godless nation.*
> *From deceitful and cunning men*
> *rescue me, O God.*

The *godless nation* may well refer to the Babylonians who hold the psalmist captive. He feels he is on trial before them, and prays for God to come to his defence and *plead* his *cause*.

Since you, O God, are my stronghold,
why have you rejected me?
Why do I go mourning
oppressed by the foe?

It is the sense of being *rejected*, not just *forgotten,* by God which cuts the psalmist most deeply. Human friends have deserted him and now even God, the only one who could be his protection, his *stronghold,* seems to have *rejected* him.

O send forth you light and your truth;
let these be my guide.
Let them bring me to your holy mountain
to the place where you dwell.

When God led Israel out of Egypt into the promised land he went before them in a pillar of cloud by day and a pillar of *light* by night (Exodus 13:21). The psalmist prays for God's *light and truth* to guide him out of captivity back to Jerusalem, back to the Temple, to the *holy mountain, to the place where you dwell.* Despite feeling rejected by God he knows that God is his only hope, the only one who can deliver him.

And I will come to the altar of God,
the God of my joy.
My redeemer, I will thank you on the harp,
O God, my God.

One can sense in this verse a lifting of the despondency which has gripped the psalmist from the beginning of Psalm 41. He turned to God in prayer and poured out his soul to the Lord, praying for deliverance, and now he is sure that his prayer will be heard, that his joy will be restored and that he will once again praise God with music, *on the harp.*

Why are you cast down, my soul . . .

While the words of this last refrain are the same as the previous two (in Psalm 41) the meaning is different. Now there is a sense of light and confident hope that was missing before, there is a new determination: *I will praise him still, my saviour and my God.*

Isaiah 38:10—14,17—20

In about 700 BC Hezekiah, King of Judah, fell ill and was at the point of death. Isaiah 38 describes how he prayed to the Lord and was healed. The canticle expresses Hezekiah's thanksgiving. It begins with a lament which looks back to his illness, then goes on to a psalm of praise. The canticle reflects the dominant Old Testament understanding of death as the end, with no hope of eternal life. The canticle is transformed into Christian prayer by the antiphons and the sentence, *I was dead, and behold, I am alive and I hold the keys of death* (Revelation 1:17—18). We pray the canticle with Christ as he goes down into death and rises triumphant over death. We pray the canticle in Christ, knowing that as our life is lived in him we too will share the joy of the resurrection.

> *I said, In the noontide of my days I must depart;*
> *I am consigned to the gates of Sheol*
> *for the rest of my years.*

The *noontide* of his days is the prime of life. To die young was considered a sign of God's displeasure. For the little time left to him (*the rest of my years*) he has been *consigned to the gates of Sheol,* or as we might say, to death's door. *Sheol* is the world of the dead, silent, cut off from the world of the living, cut off from the Lord. Only late in the Old Testament do we find any hint of life after death. Death was thought to be the end, as the next verse states:

> *I said, I shall not see the Lord*
> *in the land of the living;*

I shall look upon man no more
among the inhabitants of the world.

The two most terrifying aspects of death confront Hezekiah: death will end his relationship with the Lord and his relationships with others.

My dwelling is plucked up and removed from me
like a shepherd's tent;
like a weaver I have rolled up my life;
he cuts me off from the loom.

His life will be over as quickly as a Bedouin's tent is packed up, or a weaver cuts his cloth off the loom.

From day to night you bring me to an end . . .

His condition is so acute that he is in constant pain, crying for help right through the night. The Lord has become to him like a lion crushing its prey.

Like a swallow or a crane I clamour . . .

His cry for help is like the never-ending sound of a bird call.

My eyes are weary with looking upward.
O Lord, I am oppressed; be my security.

He is smitten by God and can look to God alone for healing.

Lo, it was for my welfare
that I had great bitterness;
but you have held back my life
from the pit of destruction,
for you have cast all my sins behind your back.

Here we reach the turning point of the canticle. He is healed and forgiven, restored to life, and can see already that his life has been changed for the better through his suffering.

For Sheol cannot thank you . . .

For Hezekiah death is the end of everything: the end of life, the end of hope, and the end of any relationship with the Lord.

The living, the living, he thanks you . . .

He thanks God for his deliverance from death, and bears witness to God's faithfulness to the next generation, *the children.*

The Lord will save me . . .

His longing is to return to the Temple, the place of God's presence, and there sing God's praise *all the days of our life.*

Psalm 64(65)

This joyful psalm of praise celebrates three of God's greatest gifts: his gift of forgiveness to each individual sinner, the gift of his rule over the whole world, and his gift of fertility to the earth. It is a psalm which overflows with thanksgiving for the abundance of creation.

Its original setting may have been the Feast of Tabernacles, Israel's harvest festival, when the people came to the Temple to give thanks for the harvest and to pray for rain for the coming year. The Holy Week and Eastertide antiphons indicate how the psalm has been interpreted by the Church as a psalm of thanksgiving for the abundant blessings of the Spirit (the water of God) which flowed from the cross.

To you our praise is due
in Sion, O God.
To you we pay our vows,
you who hear our prayer.

The opening verses express our relationship to God as his servants. We owe him the *praise* of our hearts and the obedience of our lives. The *vows* may have been made in a time of drought, when the people turned to God who heard their *prayer.* As the concluding verses of the psalm testify, God gave them abundant rain, a vintage harvest, and fertile flocks.

To you all flesh will come
with its burden of sin.
Too heavy for us, our offences,
but you wipe them away.

In Israel a drought was sometimes interpreted as God's punishment for the nation's sin (1 Kings 8:35,36), and so forgiveness and the blessing of rain go together. Understood in the light of Christ the psalm speaks of the universal human need of God's forgiveness. *Our offences* are *too heavy for us,* and God alone can *wipe them away.* The assurance of forgiveness leads to the thought of the next verse.

Blessed is he whom you choose and call
to dwell in your courts.
We are filled with the blessings of your house,
of your holy temple.

God specifically chose and called the priests to service in the temple, but the privilege of every Israelite to come and worship was also described as God's choice and call. In the letter to the Ephesians St Paul speaks of how God chose us 'before the foundation of the world' (1:4), called us to a life of holiness and love (4:1,2), and blessed us 'in Christ with every spiritual blessing' (1:3). This psalm speaks for all who are 'in Christ'.

You keep your pledge with wonders,
O God our saviour,
the hope of all the earth
and of far distant isles.

God's *pledge* is his covenant with Israel, and he keeps his pledge with *wonders,* a word used specifically of God's mighty acts of deliverance in Israel's history, beginning with the Exodus. The *wonders* of the new covenant began with the life, death and resurrection of Jesus, who is the Saviour of the world, *the hope of all the earth.*

You uphold the mountains with your strength,
you are girded with power.
You still the roaring of the seas,
the roaring of their waves
and the tumult of the peoples.

Three images of God's power tumble over each other: he is creator, warrior, and king. He is the mighty creator who upholds *the mountains* in their grandeur. He is the warrior, *girded with power,* who tamed the waters of Chaos (*the roaring of the seas*) at the creation of the world (Genesis 1:2). The Israelites believed that the world was still threatened by these waters, and only the might of the Lord held them in check. He is the king of all the earth, the God who subdues all nations, all *peoples.* His power is not limited by national boundaries.

The ends of the earth stand in awe
at the sight of your wonders.
The lands of sunrise and sunset
you fill with your joy.

Psalm 18(19)A (Week 2, Monday Morning) spoke of the heavens proclaiming *the glory of God through all the earth.* The *wonders* at which *the ends of the earth stand in awe* are the wonders of creation and the *wonders* of God's action in salvation history, in Israel and in Christ.

You care for the earth, give it water,
you fill it with riches.
Your river in heaven brims over
to provide its grain.

The psalm moves on to its climax, the celebration of God's superabundant provision of fertility for Israel's crops and flocks. The Israelites explained the fall of rain as God opening windows in the heavens (Genesis 7:11) to release the 'waters which are above the firmament' (Genesis 1:7). The *river in heaven* later came to be a symbol of the abundant gift of the Spirit which would bring spiritual life and nourishment to the whole world (Ezekiel 47). The 'rivers of living water' flow from the heart of Christ (John 7:38).

And thus you provide for the earth;
You drench its furrows,
you level it, soften it with showers,
you bless its growth.

C.S. Lewis comments on how the psalmist conveys to us 'the very feel of weather – weather seen with a real countryman's eyes, enjoyed almost as a vegetable might be supposed to enjoy it' (*Reflections on the Psalms,* p. 67). There are two vital periods of rain in Israel, the early rain and the latter rain. The early rain is essential in the autumn (October-November) to soften the hard, dry ground so it can be ploughed and sown with seed. The latter rain is the spring rain (April-May), essential to swell the ripening grain. Without the early and the latter rain the crops fail and the people suffer famine. The psalmist describes both rains as God's special visitation. First, he comes to *drench its furrows,* then:

You crown the year with your goodness.
Abundance flows in your steps,
in the pastures of the wilderness it flows.

As God visits the earth with the latter rain, *abundance flows in* his steps. His bounty ensures a bumper harvest. The abundance spills over even to *the pastures of the wilderness,* which are usually unfit for cultivation.

God gives his Holy Spirit in the same way as this psalm describes his gift of rain. He gives his Spirit 'without measure' (John 3:34).

The hills are girded with joy,
the meadows covered with flocks,

the valleys are decked with wheat.
They shout for joy, yes, they sing.

The final verse pictures the fertile countryside *hills, meadows, valleys,* coming like a crowd of joyful pilgrims to the Temple feast, dressed in their best festive clothing, shouting *for joy,* as *they sing* God's praise.

In its universal scope, this psalm foreshadows three of the central petitions of the Lord's Prayer: forgive us our sins, deliver us from evil, and give us this day our daily bread.

EVENING PRAYER

Psalm 48(49) is a meditation on the futility of wealth. It challenges us to put first the kingdom of God, and to give thanks to God who *will ransom me from death.* The inauguration of God's kingdom is celebrated in the New Testament canticle from Revelation, where we give all *power, wealth, wisdom, and might* to Christ, *the Lamb who was slain* to ransom us for God.

Psalm 48(49)

This is a 'wisdom psalm'. It comes from the same tradition as the books of Proverbs, Job and Ecclesiastes. It is the work of an intellectual, a philosopher grappling with the same kind of problem that faced Job. Is there no justice in this world? The godless seem to be far more successful in terms of wealth and power than the righteous.

The Wisdom tradition takes up basic questions about the meaning of human life in the face of experiences which make us ask if there is any meaning. The Wisdom writers attempt to answer these questions without reference to God's covenant relationship with Israel, and in this way their writing has special relevance for our own age, when many people believe in God but live with no knowledge or experience of the gifts of the new covenant.

Hear this, all you peoples,
give heed, all who dwell in the world,
men both low and high,
rich and poor alike!

The psalm is addressed to all *peoples,* not just to the faithful, and it grapples with a question which all must answer, *rich and poor alike.* His words are an encouragement to the poor and a warning to the rich.

My lips will speak words of wisdom.
My heart is full of insight.
I will turn my mind to a parable,
with the harp I will solve my problem

While the psalmist is one of the *wisdom* writers, he writes not just as a philosopher, but as a man of prayer. Only as he sought God's inspiration did he solve his *problem.* The *parable* means the 'instruction' from God who alone can bring true wisdom. This instruction is given at a level deeper than the mind. It is heard in poetry, in song, with the harp.

Why should I fear in evil days
the malice of the foes who surround me,
men who trust in their wealth,
and boast of the vastness of their riches?

The psalmist states the essence of his problem. He is afraid, the days are *evil,* because he is oppressed by bullies whose wealth seems to give them the power to do what they like. Money is their god. They *trust* in their wealth as the righteous *trust* in the Lord. They *boast of the vastness of heir riches* as the righteous boast in the Lord. (Notice the antiphon, 'You cannot serve both God and wealth'). The *fear* of the psalmist is not just the *malice* of these men, but the fact that they seem to live a trouble-free, successful life, despite their pride and their arrogant rejection of all that God's Law teaches. The psalmist is afraid that his whole moral universe is unravelling. Is there no justice? Is morality a cruel joke?

> *For no man can buy his own ransom,*
> *or pay a price to God for his life.*
> *The ransom of his soul is beyond him.*
> *He cannot buy life without end,*
> *nor avoid coming to the grave.*

Here he begins the answer to his question. Wealth cannot protect a man from death. All the wealth of the rich man can never *ransom his soul* or *buy life without end.* According to Old Testament law, if a man accidentally killed another he could buy his life by paying the family of the dead person a large sum, a 'ransom' (Exodus 21). If he did not pay the price his life could be taken in just revenge by the family. The psalmist declares that this kind of transaction is impossible with God when it comes to death. No amount of money can ever ransom a man's life from death. Eternal life is not for sale. Those who *trust in their wealth* are in for a rude shock.

> *He knows that wise men and fools must both perish*
> *and leave their wealth to others.*
> *Their graves are their homes for ever,*
> *their dwelling place from age to age,*
> *though their names spread wide through the land.*

If wealth will not buy eternal life, neither will brains or fame. When it comes to death the wise and the foolish, the famous and the nobodies, are all in the same boat. All end up in the same place, the grave. The one certainty about wealth is that you can not take it with you. It is not the currency of heaven.

> *In his riches, man lacks wisdom:*
> *he is like the beasts that are destroyed.*

This verse could be the epitaph of the twentieth century, an age of unparalleled wealth and unparalleled destruction. Greed for power and wealth has been the driving force behind the wars and destruction for which this century is notorious. According to the psalmist, a man who *trusts* in money, who *boasts* in riches rather than in God, becomes little better than an animal. His moral judgement vanishes, and his spiritual capacities shrivel away to nothing. He lives only for the physical.

The antiphons and the **sentence** remind us that the temptation to trust in riches is always open for the Christian, and the only escape is to 'Look for the things of heaven, not for the things which are upon this earth' (Eastertide antiphon).

This is the lot of those who trust in themselves,
who have others at their beck and call.
Like sheep they are driven to the grave,
where death shall be their shepherd
and the just shall become their rulers.

Instead of trusting in God, the rich *trust* in their riches and *in themselves.* They have boundless self-confidence, and assume they have the right to rule the world, to have others jump to their every *beck and call.* They treat other people like animals, not realizing that in so doing they become like animals themselves, *sheep driven to the grave.* The psalmist upends a favourite Old Testament image of Israel as the flock of the Lord and the Lord as their *shepherd.* (Psalm 22(23)). To the rich who trust in themselves he says: *Death shall be their shepherd.*

At this point in the psalm we see the beginnings of faith in life after death. In that life the wrongs of this life will be put right, true justice will be done, *the just shall become their rulers,* that is, the rulers of the rich oppressors. When the Day of the Lord dawns the positions of the wicked and the righteous will be reversed.

With the morning their outward show vanishes
and the grave becomes their home.
But God will ransom me from death
and take my soul to himself.

The first two lines continue the theme of the futility of those who trust in riches. They vanish overnight and live in Sheol for ever. With the words *But God* we reach one of the high points of Old Testament faith. The fate of the godless and the righteous is not the same. Both are not confined to Sheol for ever. *God will ransom* the just *from death*. God will do what the wealthy man could never do. Psalm 48(49) shows how the hope of life after death developed in the Old Testament. This hope grew from an acute awareness that justice is not done in this life, that here the just may suffer while the wicked prosper. But God is above all a God of justice, and his power will ensure that one day, the Day of the Lord, the righteous will be rewarded.

The words *God will ransom me from death* take the Christian straight to the cross, where, as the letter of Peter says, 'You were ransomed from the futile ways inherited from your fathers, not with perishable things such as silver or gold, but with the precious blood of Christ' (1 Peter 1:18,19). Jesus said: 'The son of man came not to be served but to serve, and to give his life as a ransom for many' (Matthew 20:28).

Then do not fear when a man grows rich,
when the glory of his house increases . . .

The *fear* with which the psalmist began is cast away as he sees the futility of trusting in money and the reward of trusting in God. Wealth (*the glory of his house*) and fame (*'Men will praise me for all my success'*) do not go with us into the next life. Those who *flatter* themselves, *trust in themselves, will never see the light* of God's presence *any more*. They will be forever in Sheol, the land of darkness. This for the psalmist is the ultimate tragedy of those who boast in their wealth and refuse to trust in God.

Revelation 4:11; 5:9,10,11

See Week 1, Tuesday Evening.

Week 2: Wednesday

MORNING PRAYER

The psalmody begins with tears and with a sense of being rejected by the Lord and abandoned to life without him (Psalm 76). But the Old Testament canticle is the jubilant testimony of a woman (Hannah) who experienced the Lord's saving help in the midst of despair. The final psalm proclaims: *The Lord is king, let earth rejoice!*

Psalm 76(77)

The psalm is in two parts. First, a lament expressing either the cry of the exiles in Babylon, or the despair of those who returned to Jerusalem from exile only to meet harsh conditions in the ruined city. Second, a psalm of praise, recalling the *wonders of old* in which the Lord saved Israel.

I cry aloud to God,
cry aloud to God that he may hear me.

In the day of my distress I sought the Lord.
My hands were raised at night without ceasing;
my soul refused to be consoled.
I remembered my God and I groaned.
I pondered and my spirit fainted.

The anguish of the psalmist arises from the dramatic contrast between the state of the nation now, when it is humiliated and seems to be abandoned by God; and the state of the nation in the past, when God acted in power to make Israel great. As the psalmist *remembered God* he *groaned* and his *spirit fainted.*

You withheld sleep from my eyes . . .

The cause of the psalmist's trouble is again revealed to be the contrast between the present and the past. It is the *thought of the days of long ago,* when the nation was so obviously blessed by God, that makes him question God's ways in the present.

'Will the Lord reject us for ever? . . .'

This painful series of questions shows the depth of the exile's despair. All he believes in, the Lord's *favour, love, promise, mercy, compassion* is called into question. But even in the questions there is hope. All the questions will receive the same answer: 'No!' The Lord has not rejected us. He will *show us his favour* again. His *love* has not *vanished.* His *promise* stands. He will not *forget his mercy* or *withhold his compassion.*

I said: 'This is what causes my grief;
that the way of the Most High has changed.'

The doubt which has been in the psalmist's mind since the first verse is finally out in the open. The previous series of questions all adds up to this: *the way of the Most High has changed.* But as he thinks again on the past, as he *remembers the deeds of the Lord,* his *wonders, works, and mighty deeds,* something happens. He changes (not God!). His faith is restored.

Your ways, O God, are holy.
What god is great as our God?

You are the God who works wonders.
You showed your power among the peoples.
Your strong arm redeemed your people
the sons of Jacob and Joseph.

Israel's present distress is a sign that God is *holy*, that he disciplines his people. He has worked *wonders* in the past, and will do so again in the future. He *redeemed* his people, the *sons of Jacob and Joseph* by delivering them from slavery in Egypt.

The waters saw you, O God,
the waters saw you and trembled . . .

When God *redeemed* his people he led them *through the sea* (the Reed Sea). While it is the Exodus event which is in mind here, the psalmist describes it in language which recalls another great victory of the Lord, his victory over the waters of Chaos at the creation of the world. Creation and redemption are woven together to become one great act of God. Israel, along with other nations in the ancient Near East, believed that before creation the world was ruled by the primal Sea. God tamed the waters and put them in their place, bringing order out of chaos. His action was accompanied by lightning (*your arrows flashed to and fro*), *thunder*, and earthquake (*the earth was moved and trembled*), traditional signs of God's appearing on earth, signs which awed Israel at Sinai.

Even though God's salvation was dramatic and visible to all, faith and trust were necessary. *No one saw your footprints* means that although Israel experienced the power of God, they did not see God himself. In the present time of doubt and distress, the same faith and trust are needed.

You guided your people like a flock
by the hand of Moses and Aaron.

God guided his people to safety by these two leaders, and the implication is that he will continue to guide his *people like a flock* through their present humiliation.

The psalm counsels us in our troubles to take our most painful doubts and questions to the Lord in prayer, and to remember the *wonders of old* recorded for us in the Scriptures and re-lived in the Eucharist. In this way we will be restored in faith and hope. *We are in difficulties on every side, but never consumed* (2 Corinthians 4:8), (**sentence**).

1 Samuel 2:1—10

This canticle is called the Song of Hannah because it appears in the book of Samuel as her response to the Lord's promise to her that she will bear a son (the boy Samuel). The canticle is a prototype of the Magnificat. It is an exuberant, sometimes defiant canticle, whose theme is summed up in the **sentence** from the Magnificat: *He put down the mighty from their seats and exalted the lowly; he filled the hungry with good things* (Luke 1:52—53).

My heart exults in the Lord,
I find my strength in my God;
my mouth laughs at my enemies
as I rejoice in your saving help.

The Christian who prays this canticle does so knowing that 'it is not against human enemies that we have to struggle, but against the principalities, against the powers, against the world rulers of this present darkness, against the spiritual hosts of wickedness in the heavenly places' (Ephesians 6:12). In Christ we *laugh* at these enemies, rejoicing in his *saving help.*

For those who trust him the Lord is a *Rock,* on whom we stand absolutely firm and secure.

Bring your haughty words to an end . . .

The central theme of the canticle is that God is the ruler of the earth, not man. Man may *boast* proudly of his achievements, but it is the Lord *who knows all* and *weighs men's deeds.* He will adjust the balance in favour of the weak and the poor. Pride, the root sin according to Genesis 3, is rebuked.

The bows of the mighty are broken . . .

In Israel, as in many countries today, society was at times radically polarized between the rich and the poor, the powerful and the weak. The ruling class treated the peasants like dirt. (Read 1 Kings 21, and the book of Amos). For Hannah, the birth of her son was a glorious sign that the Lord was upending human injustice and restoring equity. Those who grow rich through brute force will be *broken.* Those who never do a day's work, living in luxury while their servants slave for a pittance, will have to *labour for bread* like everyone else.

The connections with Mary's Magnificat are powerful. For Mary, the birth of her son was also a sign that God 'casts the mighty from their thrones and raises the lowly. He fills the starving with good things, and sends the rich empty away.' Mary's son would reveal the true nature of the revolution God would bring on the earth. His beatitudes, according to Luke, begin: 'Blessed are you poor, for yours is the kingdom of God. Blessed are you that hunger now, for you shall be satisfied' (Luke 6:20,21). The God of Hannah, Mary, and Jesus is a God of justice, who acts to protect the poor and the weak.

The childless wife has children now
but the fruitful wife bears no more.

This verse connects the canticle specifically with the prayer of Hannah. To give children to the barren is seen in the Scriptures as one of the most astonishing signs of God's power and mercy. He did this for Sarah (Genesis 18:14;

Romans 4:19—21), for Hannah, and for Elizabeth, mother of John the Baptist (Luke 1:7,13).

It is the Lord who gives life and death . . .

The next few verses again sound the central note of the canticle: the whole of life is in the hands of the Lord. We are not proud masters of our own fate. Life and death are in God's hands. He has power to *bring men to the grave and back* (in its original context meaning to the very point of death and back, but for us the resurrection immediately comes to mind). God can lower the proud (bring them to *poverty*) and exult the lowly (give them *riches*).

He lifts up the lowly from the dust . . .

The theme of the canticle is restated. The *ash heap* is the village rubbish dump, where beggars and lepers lived (as in many cities today).

For the pillars of the earth are the Lord's,
on them he has set the world.

God is the creator of the world and therefore his power is unlimited. (The Hebrews believed that the world rested on giant pillars which were the bases of the mountains).

He guards the steps of his faithful . . .

In very strong language the canticle again asserts that God is sovereign, and his justice will triumph. He is the Lord of history, the judge of all the earth (*the ends of the earth*). He is the one to whom 'every knee shall bow'.

He will give power to his king
and exalt the might of his anointed.

The mention of the *king* may indicate that the canticle was originally a royal psalm of victory which the author of Samuel has put on Hannah's lips to bring out the significance of Samuel's birth. It was Samuel who anointed Israel's first king, Saul, and her greatest king, David. At the time of Hannah's prayer, Israel had no monarchy.

This reference to the *king* prompted the messianic interpretation of the whole canticle. The age of true justice is the age of the Messiah. The gospel of Christ reveals 'the saving justice of God' (Romans 1:17). Hannah's vision comes to its full realization in Christ.

Psalm 96(97)

This psalm is one of the Enthronement Psalms which celebrate the Lord's reign over Israel and over all the earth. For an explanation of the original setting of these psalms, see the introduction to Psalm 46(47), Week 1, Wednesday Morning.

The Lord is king, let earth rejoice,
let all the coastlands be glad.

The theme of the kingdom of God was central to Jesus' ministry. According to John's Gospel Jesus was enthroned on the cross and in his resurrection and ascension. Hence the **sentence**, *This psalm tell of the salvation of the world and of the faith all peoples would have in Christ* (St Athanasius). As we pray the psalm we rejoice in Christ's rule. The *coastlands* are the remotest parts of the earth.

Cloud and darkness are his raiment;
his throne, justice and right.

A fire prepares his path;
it burns up his foes on every side.
His lightnings light up the world,
the earth trembles at the sight.

The mountains melt like wax
before the Lord of all the earth.

The psalm begins by recalling God's covenant with Israel on Mount Sinai, where he revealed himself as Israel's king. When the Lord appeared on Mount Sinai 'the mountain burned with fire to the heart of heaven, wrapped in darkness, cloud and gloom. Then the LORD spoke . . . out of the midst of the fire' (Deuteronomy 4:11). The Lord's appearance was accompanied by earthquake (*the earth trembles*), volcanic eruption (*the mountains melt like wax, a fire prepares his path*), thunder and lightning (*his lightnings light up the world*). These physical signs point to the mighty power of the Lord to establish *justice and right,* to defeat his *foes,* to be *Lord of all the earth.* These signs of the Lord's appearance at Sinai became the signs used to describe the future Day of the Lord, when he would come in glory to establish true justice on the earth.

The writer to the Hebrews draws a contrast between the old and new covenants, a contrast between the way God appeared to Israel of old and the way he appears to the Church today (Hebrews 12:18—29). Today God does not appear on Mount Sinai in 'a blazing fire, and darkness, and gloom, and a tempest' (Hebrews 12:18), but he comes to the new Mount Sion, the heavenly Jerusalem, the Church on earth and in heaven. Here he speaks through word and sacrament to his covenant people. Here *the Lord is king.*

Let those who serve idols be ashamed,
those who boast of their worthless gods.
All you spirits, worship him.

Those *who serve idols* will be put to shame because they will never receive any help from *their worthless gods.* As Psalm 113B(115) (Week 2, Sunday Evening II) puts it: 'Our God is in the heavens; he does whatever he wills. Their idols are silver and gold, the work of human hands.' The *spirits* may refer to the idols, or to the spiritual beings in the heavens. All must bow down and *worship* the Lord.

Sion hears and is glad;
the people of Judah rejoice
because of your judgements O Lord.

The Lord's *judgements* are his victories over Israel's enemies. God judges those who seek to destroy his people.

For you indeed are the Lord
most high above all the earth
exalted far above all spirits.

The Lord is the supreme God, ruler of heaven and earth, before whom *all spirits,* all spiritual beings, must submit.

The Lord loves those who hate evil . . .

Those who obey the commands of the Lord will ultimately triumph over evil, they will not be ensnared by *the wicked.*

Light shines forth for the just
and joy for the upright of heart.
Rejoice, you just, in the Lord;
give glory to his holy name.

The psalm concludes on the same joyful note with which it began. Those who are loyal to the covenant (*the just*) will live in the *light* of God's presence, where there is 'fulness of joy.' They will *give glory to his holy name,* that is, they will honour God by their lips and their lives.

EVENING PRAYER

Tonight the psalmody leads us to renewed hope in God, who protects his people in their troubles (Psalm 61), guides the nations (Psalm 66), and is revealed in Christ, the one in whom all things hold together (Colossians 1).

Psalm 61(62)

The psalmist is under intense pressure from those who are out to destroy him, and in the psalm he reveals an unshakeable confidence in God. As with many of the psalms, there is little to indicate the precise nature of the opposition the psalmist faced. The mention of taking *refuge in God* may imply that the psalmist sought sanctuary in the Temple. The psalm is a call to trust in God and not in powerful men or in money.

The Holy Week antiphon ('The wicked men said: let us oppress the just man, since his ways are contrary to ours') leads us to pray the psalm with Christ, as those who plotted his death gradually closed in on him.

In God alone is my soul at rest;
my help comes from him.
He alone is my rock, my stronghold,
my fortress: I stand firm.

The word *alone* sounds throughout this psalm. *God alone* is the source of a person's security. He *alone* can be trusted. He is *my rock,* the one foundation on which I can stand firm and secure; *my stronghold,* who will save me from the relentless attacks of my enemies; *my fortress,* who gives refuge and protection to the oppressed. Therefore *I stand firm* in the midst of those who seek to topple me.

Under attack from the world, the flesh, and the devil, the Christian can find *rest,* protection, and a firm foundation in *God alone.* The Eastertide antiphon and the **sentence** both remind us that it is through faith that we overcome the world, faith in Christ our Saviour. *May the God of hope fill you with all peace as you believe in him* (Romans 15:13).

How long will you all attack one man
to break him down,
as though he were a tottering wall,
or a tumbling fence?

The psalmist feels like a city wall constantly battered by an enemy's siege machines. The only aim of his enemies is to destroy him, to crush him under the pressure of their relentless assault. (The psalmist may have been a prominent leader in Israel).

Their plan is only to destroy:
they take pleasure in lies.
With their mouth they utter blessing
but in their heart they curse.

His enemies are the most dangerous kind: hypocrites, all charm on the outside, but underneath out for his blood, willing to *destroy* him with *lies.*

In God is my safety and glory . . .

The psalmist turns to the congregation (evidence that he has sought refuge in the Temple?). From his own experience he urges them to *take refuge in God,* to *pour out* their *hearts before him,* to bring their deepest longings in prayer to the only one who can be absolutely trusted. Peace of heart comes from following this counsel of the psalmist, repeated by St Paul: 'Have no anxiety about anything, but in everything by prayer and supplication with thanksgiving let your requests be made known to God. And the peace of God, which passes all understanding, will keep your hearts and your minds in Christ Jesus' (Philippians 4:6,7).

Common folk are only a breath,
great men an illusion.
Placed in the scales, they rise;
they weigh less than a breath.

Compared to God, who is a *rock,* a *stronghold,* a *fortress,* people are so fickle. Their support (as every political poll shows) easily moves, like a *breath* of wind. When God *weighs* them in his scales they are nothing, empty of the justice, mercy, and love which God looks for.

Do not put your trust in oppression
nor vain hopes on plunder.
Do not set your heart on riches
even when they increase.

The natural human tendency is not to trust God, but to trust human power, whether the power of *great men,* or the power of popular opinion, (*common folk*). After warning against putting one's trust in people the psalmist warns against putting one's trust in money. 'Love of money is the root of all evils' (1 Timothy 6:10). Love of money invariably leads to *oppression* and *plunder* of the kind which many Third World countries have suffered at the hands of colonial regimes, multi-national companies, and dictators.

For God has said only one thing:
only two do I know:
that to God alone belongs power
and to you , Lord, love;
and that you repay each man
according to his deeds.

The *two* things which the psalmist has heard, either from the mouth of a prophet or from the Law, are that God alone is all-powerful and therefore the only one in whom we can ultimately *rest*; and that God alone is the source of *love,* the love which is God's loyalty to his covenant. 'If we are faithless, he remains faithful – for he cannot deny himself' (2 Timothy 2:13).

God's faithfulness means that he will bless those who love him and keep his commandments (Exodus 20:6).

Psalm 66(67)

This psalm is a prayer asking for God's blessing: on his people, on all nations, on the harvest. It may have been a harvest festival hymn sung at the Feast of Tabernacles, but its concern is far wider than the crops. The structure of the psalm (three verses, each with a refrain) can be clearly seen in the way it is set out in the Office.

> *O God, be gracious and bless us*
> *and let your face shed its light upon us.*

These words echo the Aaronic blessing found in Numbers 6:24—26. It is a prayer for the presence of God, with all the blessings which his presence brings. A shining face (*let your face shed its light upon us*) is an expression of joy and approval. When God delights in his people, when they know his approval, they will be richly blessed.

> *So will you ways be known on earth*
> *and all nations learn your saving help.*

God's people pray for his blessing not for selfish reasons, not just for their own good, but so that *all nations* will come to know God's will (his *ways*) and his salvation, his *saving help*. As the nations see how God blesses the people who love and obey him, they will learn that he is the true God, and come to worship him.

> *Let the peoples praise you, O God;*
> *let all the peoples praise you.*

May all nations, *all the peoples,* come to acknowledge God and worship him. Israel was chosen by God in order that through her he might bless all the nations.

> *Let the nations be glad and exult*
> *for you rule the world with justice.*
> *With fairness you rule the peoples,*
> *you guide the nations on earth.*

Israel rejoiced in God's just *rule* over her as her king, and in the way he guided the nation like a shepherd. Here, those blessings which were of crucial importance to Israel are extended to all the world. All nations can *be glad and exult* in

God's just rule and in his care and guidance. God will *rule the world with justice* and *guide the nations on earth.*

The **sentence,** *Let it be known to you that this salvation from God has been sent to all peoples* (Acts 28:28), and the antiphons for Holy Week and Eastertide show how the blessings promised in this psalm are given to the world in Christ, 'the light of the nations'.

The earth has yielded its fruit
for God, our God, has blessed us.
May God still give us his blessing
till the ends of the earth revere him.

At harvest time the people gave thanks to God for the bounty of the earth, and saw it as a sure sign of God's just rule and his shepherd-like care. God *blessed* his people by providing for their daily needs. As was proclaimed in the previous verses, the purpose of this blessing is not just for Israel, but so that *the ends of the earth* may *revere* God.

Colossians 1:12—20

See Week 1, Wednesday Evening.

Week 2: Thursday

MORNING PRAYER

This morning's psalmody arises out of the experience of the Exile. In Psalm 79 we can still smell the smoke from the fires which razed the cities of Israel. The people pray: *O God of hosts, bring us back; let your face shine on us and we shall be saved.* In the Old Testament canticle we share the joy of those who began to return from Exile. God has heard their prayer, and now they *sing and shout for joy.* The final psalm contains God's appeal to the people to learn the lesson of the

Exile, to turn from their disobedience and allow the Lord to feed them with *finest wheat.*

Psalm 79(80)

The disaster which lies behind this psalm was either the annihilation of the northern kingdom of Israel by the Assyrian army in 722 BC, or the capture and sacking of Jerusalem by the Babylonian army in 587 BC. It is a prayer for the restoration of Israel, a cry for help from a people who have suffered total devastation. They fear that because of their disobedience the Lord may have annulled his covenant with them.

The **sentence,** *Come, Lord Jesus* (Revelation 22:20) is the cry of the persecuted Church, overpowered by the brutal might of totalitarian Rome. Psalm 79(80) is the prayer of the Church wherever her children are persecuted and slaughtered by oppressive regimes.

The **antiphon, heading** and **sentence** introducing the psalm guide us to pray the psalm for the suffering Church.

> Antiphon: *Lord, rouse up your might and come to our help.*
> Heading: Lord, come to visit your vine

(The vine is a Scriptural metaphor for both Israel (Isaiah 5) and the Church (John 15)).

Sentence: *Come, Lord Jesus* (Rev 22:20), is the cry of the suffering Church.

> *O shepherd of Israel, hear us,*
> *you who lead Joseph's flock,*
> *shine forth from your cherubim throne*
> *upon Ephraim, Benjamin, Manasseh.*

Joseph was the collective name often given to Israel's northern tribes, comprising *Ephraim, Benjamin, Manasseh,* and several others. This may well indicate that the psalm is the prayer of the northern exiles after Assyria's conquest of their territory in 721 BC. The tribe of Joseph knew the Lord as

Shepherd right from the days of their ancestor (Genesis 49:24). The people's prayer for help is rooted in their faith that the Lord is still their Shepherd, despite their present desolation.

God was not only their shepherd, he was the transcendent king, the ruler of the earth, whose presence was promised in the sanctuary of the Temple where the ark of the covenant rested, watched over by the golden *cherubim*.

O Lord, rouse up your might,
O Lord, come to our help.

The prayer of the exiles is bold and desperate. In colloquial language they are saying to God: 'Wake up! Stir yourself! Do something!'

God of hosts, bring us back;
let your face shine on us and we shall be saved.

The *God of hosts* is the God who commands the *hosts* of heaven. The exiles implore him to act in power, to rout his enemies and *bring* the exiles *back* home, back to the land of promise. The second part of their prayer is a prayer for the blessing given by Aaron the high priest to Israel: 'May the Lord make his face to shine upon you' (Numbers 6:24). A shining face is a sure sign of delight and favour. The one thing the exiles long for is some sign that God has not deserted them, that his anger has past, that he now looks with favour on them and will come to save them. This prayer is the refrain of the psalm.

Lord God of hosts, how long
will you frown on your people's plea?
You have fed them with tears for their bread,
an abundance of tears for their drink.
You have made us the taunt of our neighbours,
our enemies laugh us to scorn.

Because there has been no answer to their prayer the exiles believe that the Lord is still angry with them and with their prayer. They ask: *How long will you frown on your people's plea?* The only answer they have had is *tears,* and the *scorn* of their captors (*the taunt of our neighbours*).

> *You brought a vine out of Egypt;*
> *to plant it you drove out the nations.*
> *Before it you cleared the ground;*
> *it took root and spread through the land.*

The vine was one of Israel's most prized plants, and it became a treasured symbol of the nation. The prophet Isaiah wrote a haunting song in which he described Israel's history in terms of the planting, growth, and destruction of a vineyard (Isaiah 5). This psalm does the same. It begins with the Exodus (*You brought a vine out of Egypt*), then tells the story of Israel's entry into the promised land (*to plant it you drove out the nations*) and gradual settlement (*it took root and spread through the land*). At each stage the psalm underlines God's initiative in Israel's history.

> *The mountains were covered with its shadow,*
> *the cedars of God with its boughs.*
> *It stretched out its branches to the sea,*
> *to the Great River it stretched out its shoots.*

The astonishing growth of the vine refers to the period of the rule of David and Solomon when Israel's empire was said to include Lebanon (*the cedars*) and to stretch from the Mediterranean (*the sea*) in the west to the Euphrates River (*the Great River*) in the east. Israel was at its zenith. From here the story takes a dramatic turn.

> *Then why have you broken down its walls?*
> *It is plucked by all who pass by.*
> *It is ravaged by the boar of the forest,*
> *devoured by the beasts of the field.*

Because of her persistent rebellion and idolatry God withdrew his protection from Israel, leaving her defenceless, like a vineyard whose *walls* were *broken down,* open to any passer-by to wander in and help themselves (*it is plucked by all who pass by*), and to destruction by wild animals (*the boar of the forest* and *the beasts of the field*). The *boar* was unclean according to the Law, and is probably a symbol of the foreign nation (Assyria or Babylon) which *ravaged* the land.

God of hosts, turn again, we implore,
look down from heaven and see.
Visit this vine and protect it,
the vine your right hand has planted.

The boldness of the psalm is shown again. The exiles plead with God to change his mind (literally, to repent!), to leave *heaven* and come down and *see* for himself the desperate trouble they are in, to pay a *visit* to *this vine*, and do something about *protecting it*. It is his *vine, planted* by his own *hand*. He must come to save it.

The Holy Week **antiphon** transforms this part of the psalm into the prayer of Christ on Holy Thursday as he faced the cross. 'Look, Lord, and answer quickly, for I am in distress.' Jesus drew on the image of Israel as the vine when he said: 'I am the true vine' (John 15:1). Jesus is what Israel was meant to be. He is the whole vine, and everyone joined to him is a branch of the one vine (Eastertide antiphon).

Men have burnt it with fire and destroyed it.
May they perish at the frown of your face.

The *fire* was quite literal. Cities were razed to the ground. The exiles pray that God's anger (*the frown of your face*) may be transferred from them (the psalm began with God *frowning* on his *people's plea*) to their enemies.

May your hand be on the man you have chosen
the man you have given your strength.

Who is *the man?* Historically, there are two possibilities. The reference may be to the king, who was regarded as God's *chosen* leader. His task was to defend the nation and the exiles pray that God will raise up a leader to restore them to their land. In praying for the Church this verse can be a prayer for the Pope and bishops, for all Christian leaders who are God's chosen shepherds of the flock.

The second possibility is that the *man* refers to Israel, *chosen* and strengthened by God to witness to the nations. Hence it can be a prayer for the Church.

And we shall never forsake you again:
give us life that we may call upon your name.

Without God's protection and presence, the people are as good as dead. They acknowledge that their present suffering is a direct result of the fact that they chose to *forsake* the Lord, and they pray that he will have mercy on them and give them *life,* that they may worship him.

Isaiah 12:1—6

In chapter eleven Isaiah has prophesied the return of the exiles from Babylon. He describes the return as a new Exodus, when God will again deliver his people from slavery and bring them back to the land of promise. The canticle in Isaiah 12 is a psalm of praise celebrating this new Exodus, as the Song of Moses (Week 1, Saturday Morning) celebrated the first Exodus.

I thank you Lord, you were angry with me
but your anger has passed and you give me comfort.

This is the voice of the whole nation giving thanks that God's *anger,* his punishment of Israel for her sins, *has passed.* Isaiah 1 to 11 catalogues Israel's oppression of the poor and the rampant injustice which finally provoked God to act. 'The anger of the Lord was kindled against his people, and he stretched out his hand against them and smote them' (Isaiah 5:25). Jerusalem and the Temple were destroyed and the people carried off into exile. But the time of God's *anger has passed,* and the Lord has come to *comfort* his people by restoring them to their land.

Truly, God is my salvation,
I trust, I shall not fear.
For the Lord is my strength, my song,
he is my saviour.

The theme of this verse is *salvation. Salvation* comes from God, he is *my saviour.* No other gods can save, no man can save. Salvation comes from God alone, therefore the only response of the people is to *trust,* and *not fear.* Isaiah later says to the exiles: 'In returning and rest you shall be saved; in quietness and trust shall be your strength' (30:15).

The last two lines, *For the Lord is my strength, my song, he is my saviour* come straight from the Song of Moses (Exodus 15), the hymn Israel sung after the crossing of the Red Sea. God's action in restoring the exiles to Jerusalem will be a new Exodus.

The Holy Week antiphon, 'See now that God is my salvation; I have trust and no fear', enables us to pray the canticle with Christ as he goes to the cross.

With joy you will draw water
from the wells of salvation.
Give thanks to the Lord, give praise to his name!
Make his mighty deeds known to the peoples.

As Israel journeyed through the wilderness to the promised land the Lord provided water from *wells* that sprang out of the rock. Another Exodus psalm describes how the Lord 'turns the rock into a pool of water, the flint into a spring of water' (Psalm 114:8). In the new Exodus the Lord will again sustain and nourish his people during their long and difficult journey home.

In John 4:14 Jesus our saviour promises to those who *trust* in him 'a spring of water welling up to eternal life.' He is the well of salvation from which we draw *with joy* the water of the Spirit which sustains us in our journey to heaven. In the **sentence** and the Eastertide antiphon Jesus call us to *come and drink*. Those who are filled with the Spirit will then be able to *give praise to his name* and in the witness of word and life *make his mighty deeds known to the peoples*.

Declare the greatness of his name,
sing a psalm to the Lord!
For he has done glorious deeds;
make them known to all the earth.

This verse again echoes the Song of Moses (*he has done glorious deeds,* Exodus 15:1), and is the hymn of praise of those who have returned to Jerusalem. It is also the hymn of praise of those who have experienced the *glorious deeds* of God in Christ.

People of Sion, sing and shout for joy
for great in your midst is the Holy One of Israel.

This is the song of those who know God's powerful presence in their *midst*. He is the *Holy One,* who has punished his people for their sins and now restores and comforts them. *Sing and shout for joy!*

Psalm 80(81)

The heading for this psalm, Solemn Renewal of the Covenant, puts it in the setting of the Feast of Tabernacles, the greatest of the three annual pilgrim feasts of Israel. At the Feast of Tabernacles the Law was read and the people were exhorted to renew their trust in God and their obedience to his commandments. (The Christian equivalent is the renewal of baptismal vows during the Easter liturgy). At Tabernacles the events of the journey through the wilderness were relived and celebrated in the temple liturgy. All of these threads are woven together in this psalm.

The major section of the psalm is a prophecy in which God urges his people to listen to his word and 'walk in his ways'. The prophecy is preceded by a call to worship:

Ring out your joy to God our strength,
shout in triumph to the God of Jacob.
Raise a song and sound the timbrel,
the sweet-sounding harp and the lute,
blow the trumpet at the new moon,
when the moon is full, on our feast.

Each autumn Israel celebrated a complex festive season which began on the first day of the seventh month (*the new moon*) and continued through to the fifteenth day (*the full moon*), when the Feast of Tabernacles began (see Leviticus 23:23—43). The beginning of the whole season was marked by the blowing of the ram's horn, *the trumpet,* on the day of the new moon. Tabernacles was a very joyful feast, as is clear from first verses of the psalm. It was a time for singing, shouting, dancing, and music.

For this is Israel's law,
a command of the God of Jacob.
He imposed it as a rule on Joseph,
when he went out against the land of Egypt.

The feast is appointed by God and has its beginning in the Exodus (Exodus 23:14ff) when God *went out against the land of Egypt,* when he sent the plagues on Egypt to persuade Pharaoh to let the people go. *Joseph* may refer to the northern tribes or to the whole nation.

A voice I did not know said to me:
I freed your shoulder from the burden;
your hands were freed from the load.
You called in distress and I saved you.

The prophet speaks as if he is Israel in Egypt hearing the voice of the Lord for the first time. It is a new voice, a *voice I did not know,* a voice that promised freedom from the *burden* of slavery, from the making and carrying of heavy *loads* of bricks to build the Pharaoh's cities. The Lord says to the people: *You called in distress and I saved you.* The present congregation and their ancestors who left Egypt generations ago are addressed as one people. The Exodus was the salvation of the whole nation for all time. As members of the new Israel, grafted on to the tree, the Exodus is our salvation, completed in Christ. In Christ our shoulders were *freed* from the *burden* of sin.

I answered, concealed in the storm cloud,
at the waters of Meribah I tested you.
Listen, my people, to my warning,
O Israel, it only you would heed!

The prophecy moves from the Exodus to Mount Sinai, where God spoke from out of *the storm cloud.* Later, at *Meribah*, he *tested* the people. It was at Meribah that the people ran out of water and accused Moses, and hence the Lord, of bringing them out of Egypt to die of thirst in the desert. The Lord's response was to make water flow from the rock. In Exodus the incident is described as Israel testing God (Exodus 17:1—7; see the comment on Psalm 94(95), the Invitatory psalm), but in this psalm it is put the other way round. At Meribah God was testing Israel, testing the depth of their faith.

The solemn call: *Listen, my people* introduces the next verse:

Let there be no foreign god among you,
no worship of an alien god.
I am the Lord your God,
who brought you up from the land of Egypt.
Open wide your mouth and I will fill it.

We are back at Mount Sinai, where God gave Israel the Law. The first commandment of the Law said: 'You shall have no other gods besides me.' (Exodus 20:3). *Let there be no foreign god among you.* It was Israel's repeated disobedience to this first commandment that was one of the major causes of her downfall. The commandments were not the way Israel earned God's favour. His salvation came first (the deliverance *from the land of Egypt*) and their obedience was to be a grateful response to God's grace.

The invitation *Open wide your mouth and I will fill it* is God's promise to bless the people physically and spiritually. If only they will be loyal to him they will have food aplenty. In Israel the Feast of Tabernacles was the festival at which the nation gave thanks for the harvest and prayed for rain for the coming season. It was on the last day of this feast that Jesus said: 'If anyone thirst let him come to me and drink' (John 7:37).

But my people did not heed my voice
and Israel would not obey,
so I left them in their stubbornness of heart
to follow their own designs.

These tragic words describe the attitude of Israel not only in the wilderness, but right down through her history. Time after time she 'seized [God's] servants, thrashed one, killed another and stoned a third' (Matthew 21:35). The sentence warns Christians against falling into precisely the same trap: *Take care that no one among you has a wicked, unbelieving heart* (Hebrews 3:12). When the people blatantly rejected God, he *left them . . . to follow their own designs.*

O that my people would heed me,
that Israel would walk in my ways!
At once I would subdue their foes,
turn my hand against their enemies.

At the end of the Law, in Deuteronomy 28, the Lord laid out two ways before Israel: the way of life and the way of death, blessing and curse. Blessing was promised 'if you faithfully obey the voice of the Lord your God, by keeping and observing all his commandments' (Deuteronomy 28:1). If they kept God's commandments, then the promise was: 'The enemies who attack you, the Lord will defeat before your eyes' (Deuteronomy 28:6). In our fight against 'the world, the flesh, and the devil' obedience to Christ's commands assures us of God's protection and victory.

The Lord's enemies would cringe at their feet
and their subjection would last for ever.
But Israel I would feed with finest wheat
and fill them with honey from the rock.

Another aspect of the blessing promised to those who obeyed God's commandments was blessing on 'the yield of your soil' (Deuteronomy 28:4), *the finest wheat. Honey from the rock* was wild honey, a choice delicacy.

In these lines the Christian cannot fail to be reminded of the blessing of the Eucharist, where 'The Lord has fed us with finest wheat' (Holy Thursday and Eastertide antiphon), with the bread which becomes the body of our Lord Jesus Christ. Each Eucharist is a renewal of the new covenant. We relive the saving events of the cross and resurrection, the events which prove to us that nothing can ever separate us from the love of Christ, and in the Eucharist we pledge ourselves to Christ as we hear and believe his Word, as we eat his body and drink his blood.

EVENING PRAYER

The psalm tonight is a prayer for a new king, a prayer that he will rule in justice. It is a prayer which extols the royal power of the Messiah. We pray: 'May your kingdom come'. In the New Testament canticle we give thanks to God that in Christ his kingdom has come.

Psalm 71(72)

The psalm is a prayer that Israel's king may rule in justice, and have a long and prosperous reign. The psalm prays that the decisions of the king will put into action God's passionate concern for justice for the poor and needy. It may have been a prayer offered at the time of the king's coronation, or at an annual festival celebrating God's covenant with the house of David. In both Jewish and Christian interpretation the psalm was understood as a prophecy concerning the Messiah, the coming king, who would establish God's rule throughout the world. Hence the **heading**: The Royal Power of the Messiah. All the antiphons lead us to pray the psalm with reference to Christ. He is 'the Ruler of the kings of the earth', 'God has appointed him to judge all men, both living and dead' (Holy Week and Eastertide).

O God, give your judgement to the king,
to a king's son your justice,
that he may judge your people in justice
and your poor in right judgement.

Israel's fundamental ideal for her king was that he should reflect the justice of God in all his actions. Only then could the nation be at peace. The psalm begins with the prayer that God would give his gifts of *judgement* and *justice* to the king, in order that he might *judge your people in justice and your poor in right judgement.* At the coronation ceremony this prayer may have accompanied the handing over of the

Law to the king, in much the same way as the book of the Gospels is handed to a deacon at his ordination.

(The *king's son* is the same person as the *king*. The point is that the new king is not a usurper, but the legitimate heir to the throne, *a king's son*.)

Luke's Gospel shows how this prayer was fulfilled in Christ. At the beginning of his ministry Jesus applied to himself the prophecy of Isaiah, 'The Spirit of the Lord is upon me, because he has anointed me to preach good news to the poor' (Luke 4:18). God gave Christ his *judgement* and *justice*.

> *May the mountains bring forth peace for the people*
> *and the hills, justice.*

In the Law God promised the people: 'If you walk in my statutes and observe my commandments and do them, then I will give you your rains in their season, and the land shall yield its increase . . . And I will give you peace in the land' (Leviticus 26:3—6). If the king acts justly, then the land (*the mountains and the hills* – most of Israel is hill country) will be peaceful and prosperous.

> *May he defend the poor of the people*
> *and save the children of the needy*
> *and crush the oppressor.*

The *children of the needy* are those who are most exposed to oppression and injustice, and the king has a special responsibility to *defend* them, to *save* them, and to *crush* those who oppress them.

> *He shall endure like the sun and the moon*
> *from age to age.*

This is a prayer that the dynasty of the king, the house of David, may endure for ever as the Lord had promised (Psalm 89:36) and as was fulfilled in Christ.

He shall descend like rain on the meadow,
like raindrops on the earth.

The just rule of the king will be to the people as life-giving rain is to the earth. A prophecy attributed to King David said: 'When one rules justly over men . . . he dawns on them like . . . rain that makes grass to sprout from the earth' (2 Samuel 23:3,4).

In his days justice shall flourish
and peace till the moon fails.
He shall rule from sea to sea,
from the Great River to earth's bounds.

As the Lord's representative on earth the king will *rule* forever, over the whole world. (The *Great River* is the Euphrates). Obviously such a claim was not realized by any king of Israel but came to be part of Israel's hope for the Messiah, a hope which was realized in Jesus who is 'far above all rule and authority and power and dominion . . . not only in this age but also in that which is to come' (Ephesians 1:21).

Before him his enemies shall fall,
his foes lick the dust.
The kings of Tharsis and the sea coasts
shall pay him tribute.

The kings of Sheba and Seba
shall bring him gifts.
Before him all kings shall fall prostrate,
all nations serve him.

These verses continue the theme of the king's universal rule. He will be victorious over all his enemies, and his supreme authority will be acknowledged by *all kings* and *all nations*. *Tharsis and the sea coasts* refers to the western boundaries of the earth as Israel knew it (*Tharsis* may have been on the west coast of Spain), *Sheba* and *Seba* refer to the southern most parts of the know world (they were both probably in southern Arabia).

The visit of the wise men to the infant Jesus began to fulfil these messianic prophecies of the homage that would be paid by the nations to the king of Israel. Matthew's Gospel tells us that when the wise men saw Jesus, 'falling to their knees they did him homage. Then opening their treasures, they offered him gifts of gold, frankincense and myrrh' (Matthew 2:11), all treasures of Arabia.

For he shall save the poor when they cry
and the needy who are helpless.
He will have pity on the weak
and save the lives of the poor.

From oppression he will rescue their lives,
to him their blood is dear.

The universal rule of the Messiah will not be like the rule of human emperors and kings who crush the poor, seize their land, and show no mercy. The Messiah's rule will bring justice for the *poor* and mercy for the *weak*. He said, 'Blessed are the poor in spirit, for theirs is the kingdom of heaven' (Matthew 5:3).

Long may he live,
may the gold of Sheba be given him.
They shall pray for him without ceasing
and bless him all the day.

Israel prays for the success of the Messiah's mission of bringing justice to the world, a prayer which the Church continues to the end of time. The *gold of Sheba* stands for all forms of tribute brought to the king from all over the world. (*Sheba* was noted for its gold mines). Tuesday evening's canticle from Revelation 5 speaks of how the Lamb will receive *power and wealth and wisdom and might* from *every tribe and tongue and people and nation.* (Week 3, Tuesday Evening).

May corn be abundant in the land
to the peaks of the mountains.
May its fruit rustle like Lebanon;
may men flourish in the cities
like grass on the earth.

A community which is ruled with perfect justice by the Messiah will be a prosperous community, with food to meet its own needs and to feed the hungry, a community like that described in Acts: 'The Lord added to their number day by day those who were being saved' (Acts 2:47). When the Church lives out the justice of the Messiah the physical and spiritual needs of the people are met, and the Church grows 'in grace and in numbers'.

The fertility of the crops and the population is described in gloriously extravagant terms. Instead of being limited to the plains, corn will grow everywhere, even to *the peaks of the mountains*. The stalks will be as strong and tall as *Lebanon* cedars. The population will grow *like grass* – a blessing in earlier centuries when a nation's population could be decimated by war and famine.

May his name be blessed for ever
and endure like the sun.
Every tribe shall be blessed in him,
all nations bless his name . . .

In the last verses of the psalm Israel, old and new, praises the Messiah and the *Lord God,* and her praise becomes caught up with the choirs of heaven in the next canticle, from Revelation 11,12.

The concluding verse formed a doxology for the Second Book of the Psalter. (The present book of Psalms is divided into five books, possibly modelled on the five books of the Law).

Revelation 11:17—18;12:10B—12A

See Week 1, Thursday Evening.

Week 2: Friday

MORNING PRAYER

Psalm 50 and the canticle from Habakkuk both speak of the pain we suffer when we are disciplined by God because of our sin, and both speak of the joy we find when we repent and come back to the Lord. The final psalm, Psalm 147, gives expression to that joy.

Psalm 50(51)

See Week 1, Friday Morning.

Habakkuk 3:2—4,13A,14—19

The prophet Habakkuk probably wrote in the years immediately preceding the first siege of Jerusalem by the Babylonians (597 BC). (See Chapter 8 on the Exile.) Surrounding countries fell like ninepins before the might and terror of King Nebuchadnezzar's armies, and Habakkuk knows that it is only a matter of time before Israel is attacked and subdued. He foresees the devastation which will come on his nation, but then in a most remarkable way he prophesies (60 years before it happened) the eventual downfall of their oppressor, Babylon. In this canticle he prays for God to intervene and save his people. But even if they are made to suffer, Habakkuk rejoices in the fact that God will eventually deliver Israel, as he delivered her out of slavery in Egypt.

Habakkuk expresses a remarkable faith in the face of coming tragedy. His example is set before Christ's faithful who have to endure tribulation before the return of their Lord; thus the **sentence,** *Lift up your heads, for your redemption is near at hand* (Luke 21:28).

Lord, I have heard of your fame,
I stand in awe of your deeds.
Do them again in our days,
in our days make them known!
In spite of your anger, have compassion.

The prophet recalls the mighty acts of God in the Exodus, where the *fame* of the Lord was established and where his awesome *deeds* delivered Israel from Pharaoh's army. He prays for the Lord to act in the same way now, as Israel faces annihilation at the hands of Nebuchadnezzar. *Do them again in our days.* According to Habakkuk there is one crucial difference between Israel at the Exodus and Israel now. At the time of the Exodus Israel had all the innocence of a new-born child. Now the nation stands before God as a rebellious and disobedient people who have tried him to the limit. In his *anger* the Lord is about to punish them for their sins. Habakkuk prays: *In spite of your anger, have compassion.*

God comes forth from Teman,
the Holy One from mount Paran
His splendour covers the sky
and his glory fills the earth.
His brilliance is like the light,
rays flash from his hands;
there his power is hidden.

Habakkuk has a vision of the Lord marching at the head of his people as they begin the Exodus and journey through the wilderness to the promised land. The prophet describes the coming of the Lord at the head of Israel as being like the coming of a thunderstorm, like the storms he has seen advancing from the south-east of Canaan (*Teman and Mount Paran* are in Edom, in the area between the Dead Sea and the Gulf of Aqaba), the very route Israel took in approaching Canaan. God's presence is identified with different features of the storm, the swirling clouds filling the horizon (*his splendour covers the sky*), and the lightning (*his brilliance is like the light, rays flash from his hands*).

You march out to save your people,
to save the one you have anointed.
You made a path for your horses in the sea,
in the raging of the mighty waters.

God marches at the head of his *people,* his *anointed.* The *anointed* does not refer to a particular individual but to the whole nation.

The crossing of the Red Sea is here intertwined with the Lord's victory over the gods of the primeval chaos. The Lord subdued the rebellious forces of *the sea*, and *the raging of the mighty waters* at creation. The same Lord who created the world is the Lord who delivered Israel at the Exodus, and the God who can now deliver Israel from the invading armies.

The Eastertide antiphon extends the mighty action of the Creator and the God of the Exodus to the resurrection of Jesus. The resurrection was the ultimate Exodus, when God 'came with strength to save' his people, when he came with his 'Anointed One.'

This I heard and I tremble with terror,
my lips quiver at the sound.
Weakness invades my bones,
my steps fail beneath me
yet I calmly wait for the doom
that will fall upon the people who assail us.

Habakkuk has seen in his vision God coming in awesome power to save his people and he is overcome with *terror*. His whole body turns to jelly, his *lips quiver, weakness invades* his *bones,* he cannot walk (*my steps fail beneath me*). He is so sure that God will come to save his people that he can see the eventual destruction of Israel's current enemy, although Nebuchadnezzar has not yet laid siege to Jerusalem.

For even though the fig does not blossom,
nor fruit grow on the vine . . .

This verse describes the famine that follows war. After Jerusalem fell and most of the population were carried off into exile, the land reverted to the wild and those who were left behind starved.

Yet I will rejoice in the Lord
and exult in God my saviour.
The Lord my God is my strength.
He makes me leap like the deer,
he guides me to the high places.

The reason why Habakkuk can *rejoice in the* Lord is because he is sure that whatever happens, the Lord will eventually come to restore and comfort his people. The Lord who saved his people from the Egyptians will not abandon them to the Babylonians.

This canticle is one of the most powerful statements of faith in the Old Testament. With his world collapsing around him the prophet not only stands firm, but *rejoices* in the certainty that the Lord will eventually save his people.

Psalm 147

The exiles have returned to Jerusalem and begun the work of rebuilding. With God's help, the walls have been rebuilt and the gates installed, and the land is beginning to return to its former prosperity.

The Church prays this psalm in praise of God's work in Christ to build a new city, the new Jerusalem, the Church on earth (the Eastertide antiphon: 'Sion, praise your God, for he has established peace in your land, alleluia') and in heaven (the **sentence:** *Come, and I will show you the bride that the Lamb has chosen* (Revelation 21:9)).

In modern translations of the Bible this psalm will be found as Psalm 147 verses 12—20.

O praise the Lord, Jerusalem!
Sion, praise your God!

He has strengthened the bars of your gates,
he has blessed the children within you.
He established peace on your borders,
he feeds you with finest wheat.

These verses sum up what God has done for the newly-returned exiles. The defences of the city have been rebuilt (*he has strengthened the bars of your gates,* the wooden bars which secured the gates when they were shut). The population, decimated by the exile, has begun to grow (*he has blessed the children within you*). Wars have ceased (*he established peace on your borders*). The fertility of the land has returned (*he feeds you with finest wheat*). Any genuine renewal of the Church brings the growth 'in grace and in numbers' of her children.

He sends out his word to the earth
and swiftly runs his command.

The rest of the psalm will praise God for the way in which *his word* directs and sustains the created world, and directs and sustains his people. God reveals his will in creation and in the Church. In a most striking phrase, God's word is likened to a messenger sent out, running to fulfil his command. In Jesus the Word through whom all things were made became flesh and lived among us (John 1).

He showers down snow white as wool . . .

The next lines give a vivid description of winter and spring.

We treat weather cycles in a more detached and impersonal way, but we need to recover the sensitivity of the psalmist to the fact that the earth and its forces are a gift of the creator who constantly sustains the world and its life.

He makes his word known to Jacob,
to Israel his laws and decrees.
He has not dealt thus with other nations;
he has not taught them his decrees.

The same word which created and sustains the universe is known to his covenant people (*Jacob*) in his *laws and decrees. Israel* alone among the *nations* has been blessed in this way, but as the prophets pointed out, the purpose of this unique blessing was to bring all nations of the earth to worship the Lord. This universal extension of God's blessing has been given through Christ in his Church.

EVENING PRAYER

The psalmody this evening celebrates God's protection of the *simple,* (Psalm 114) the ones Jesus called 'my little children'. The Lord will deliver us from evil (Psalm 120), and bring us to sing his praise with the saints and martyrs in heaven (Revelation 15).

Psalm 114(116)

When an Israelite had been delivered from trouble, such as a serious illness, he came to the temple to offer a thanksgiving sacrifice. This psalm (the first part of Psalm 116) describes the psalmist's trouble and the Lord's deliverance.

I love the Lord for he has heard
the cry of my appeal . . .

The psalmist's love for the Lord arises out of his experience of answered prayer. As the letter of John says, 'We love, because he first loved us' (1 John 4:19). Our love for God and for others is a response to God's overwhelming love for us, revealed in Christ.

They surrounded me, the snares of death,
with the anguish of the tomb;
they caught me, sorrow and distress.
I called on the Lord's name.

In his desperate illness the psalmist felt that death was a hunter in whose net he was about to be caught and dragged down to *the tomb.* There was no way he could escape. The *snares of death surrounded* him. Whichever way he turned he would be trapped. *Sorrow and distress* had already *caught* him.

The **sentence** encourages us to pray the psalm as an expression of thankfulness to God for the way he will deliver us from the *many hardships* we face as we journey to *the kingdom of God.*

How gracious is the Lord, and just;
our God has compassion.
The Lord protects the simple hearts;
I was helpless so he saved me.

Gracious is a word used in the Old Testament only of the Lord. It means the way he freely gives his protection and help to the needy. The Lord is not only *gracious,* he is also *just,* true to his covenant which promises salvation to the poor and oppressed. God is *gracious,* he is *just,* and he *has compassion. Compassion* is not just tender feelings, but tangible acts of mercy, shown by the one who is *our God,* who has bound himself by the covenant: 'I will be your God and you shall be my people.'

The *simple hearts* are those who trust without question, the naïve, the ones whom Jesus called 'little children'. They can say with extraordinary simplicity, I *was helpless so he saved me*.

> *Turn back, my soul, to your rest*
> *for the Lord has been good;*
> *he has kept my soul from death,*
> *my eyes from tears*
> *and my feet from stumbling.*

The Eastertide antiphon ('The Lord saved my soul from the power of death') teaches us to pray these verses with Christ after the triumph of his resurrection, and to pray them knowing that as we are joined to Christ we too will share in his triumph over death. Death for the psalmist was a prison into which one entered never to escape. For the Christian death is a door through which we pass on our way to God. The antiphon for use throughout the year (*Lord, keep my soul from death, my feet from stumbling*) understands *death* to be the spiritual death from which we are saved by Christ.

> *I will walk in the presence of the Lord*
> *in the land of the living.*

To *walk in the presence of the Lord* means to live in obedience to his will, to walk in harmony and fellowship with him. The *land of the living* stretches beyond this life into the life of the world to come.

Psalm 120(121)

This is the first of the Psalms of Ascent we meet in the psalmody of Morning and Evening Prayer. There are fifteen such psalms (120—134). They were sung by pilgrims on their way up to Jerusalem to celebrate one of the great annual feasts: Passover, Pentecost, and Tabernacles. Psalm 120(121) is best understood as a liturgy sung by priest and people as the pilgrims enter the holy city. (It can also be interpreted as a liturgy of blessing on the pilgrims as they leave the city to travel home).

I lift up my eyes to the mountains:
from where shall come my help?
My help shall come from the Lord
who made heaven and earth.

As the pilgrim approaches Jerusalem he lifts up his eyes and looks at the hills on which the city is built. The temple is the place of God's presence, the place where one can find his help, and so the pilgrim asks (rhetorically): *from where shall come my help?* and answers his own question, *My help shall come from the Lord.* The Lord whom he has come to worship, the Lord who will come to his help, is none other than the creator of *heaven and earth.*

May he never allow you to stumble!
Let him sleep not, your guard.
No, he sleeps not nor slumbers,
Israel's guard.

At this point a priest addresses the pilgrims, giving them assurance of the very help they need, the help of the Lord. The Lord will keep them faithful to his way, not allowing them *to stumble.* The Lord is a *guard* who never goes to *sleep* at his post, he never goes off duty. He keeps constant watch over his people to protect them from their enemies.

The Lord is your guard and your shade;
at your right side he stands.
By day the sun shall not smite you
nor the moon by night.

The Lord stands at the *right side* of his people, the side of favour and trust, to *shade* them from the fierce heat of the sun and the malevolent influence of the *moon.* The *sun* is a symbol of the physical dangers the people face, and the *moon* a symbol of the evil spiritual forces that can attack them. (The belief that the moon could exercises an evil spiritual influence was widely held in the ancient Near East).

The Eastertide antiphon, 'The Lord protected his people as the apple of his eye', reminds us that because of the death and resurrection of Christ, no force, physical or spiritual, can ever separate us from God's love (Romans 8:31—39).

The Lord will guard you from evil,
he will guard your soul.
The Lord will guard your going and coming
both now and for ever.

Wherever we go, to and from Church, to and from work, we can trust the care and protection of the Lord *both now and for ever*. He will 'deliver us from evil'.

Revelation 15:3—4

See Week 1, Friday Evening.

Week 2: Saturday

MORNING PRAYER

Those who live in God's presence will be filled with the Spirit right into old age (Psalm 91). Although our outer nature is wasting away, our inner nature is being renewed every day. The people God has chosen he cares for like a tender father, giving them only what is best. Let us not be ungrateful for his goodness and spurn his care as Israel of old did (Deuteronomy 32). Morning Prayer concludes with a glorious psalm (8) of praise for the majesty of God and the dignity of man, especially the man Jesus.

Psalm 91(92)

This classic morning psalm is full of the vitality of spring and joy in God's creation and rule. According to Jewish tradition it was a psalm for the Sabbath. The **sentence** from St Athanasius (*the deeds of God's only Son are praised*) invites us as we pray the psalm also to praise God for the wonders of his new creation in Christ.

It is good to give thanks to the Lord
to make music to your name, O Most High,
to proclaim your love in the morning
and your truth in the watches of the night . . .

The double theme of the opening verses is sounded throughout the psalms: the Lord's *love* and *truth*. His *love* is his loyalty to the covenant, and his *truth* is his absolute faithfulness. Every word he utters is to be trusted. *Morning* may refer to the hour of morning sacrifice in the Temple. The *watches of the night* means 'all through the night.' The night was divided into four *watches*. Many of the psalms mention the night as the time for vigil and prayer to the Lord.

Your deeds, O Lord, have made me glad;
for the work of your hands I shout with joy.
O Lord, how great are your works!
How deep are your designs!
The foolish man cannot know this
and the fool cannot understand.

Here we have the reasons for thanksgiving – the *deeds* of the Lord and the *work* of his *hands*, both terms used of God's work in creation and in saving Israel. The *designs* of the Lord take us a step further. The psalmist speaks of God's ways which can never be fully understood by human wisdom, 'For my thoughts are not your thoughts, neither are your ways my ways, says the Lord' (Isaiah 55:8). There is much in the history of the world and in our own personal history that may cause us to question God's *designs,* but there can be no doubt of the Lord's *love* and *truth.* Only *the fool,* the one who deliberately rejects true wisdom, cannot understand the mystery and wonder of God's ways. The *foolish man* in this psalm is the man who thinks that evil will ultimately triumph. Despite their blunt exposure of human sin and evil, both the Jewish and Christian faiths are ultimately optimistic about the future. The resurrection (recalled for us by the Eastertide antiphon) means that nothing, not even death itself, can thwart the good purposes of God. Because Christ is risen we can always look to the future with confidence.

Though the wicked spring up like grass
and all who do evil thrive:
they are doomed to be eternally destroyed.
But you, Lord, are eternally on high.
See how your enemies perish;
all doers of evil are scattered.

The thing that the *fool* cannot understand is that although the wicked seem to hold all the cards in this world, *they are doomed to be eternally destroyed.* God is a God of justice and he will punish the wicked and reward the righteous. The wicked in this context are those who act in blatant defiance of God's commandments.

To me you give the wild-ox's strength;
you anoint me with the purest oil.
My eyes looked in triumph on my foes;
my ears heard gladly of their fall.

The psalmist's confidence in the justice of God gives him renewed strength (like a *wild-ox*) and vitality (*the purest oil* is probably a symbol of overflowing blessing). He is sure of the ultimate triumph of God's cause. The psalmist's reference to the *fall* of his *foes* recalls for us Jesus words: 'I saw Satan fall like lightning from heaven' (Luke 10:18).

The just will flourish like the palm-tree
and grow like a Lebanon cedar.

The *doers of evil thrive* for a while, but they will *perish.* The *just* may suffer for their loyalty to the Lord, but they will eventually *flourish* and *grow.* The *palm-tree* is a symbol of bounty, a tree which gives both food and shelter, a tree of the oasis which can survive fierce storms. The *Lebanon cedar* is a symbol of might and splendour, some growing to thirty-five metres in height and living for over 2,000 years. The just will know spiritual vitality and strength right into old age.

Planted in the house of the Lord
they will flourish in the courts of our God,
still bearing fruit when they are old,
still full of sap, still green,
to proclaim that the Lord is just.
In him, my rock, there is no wrong.

The *just* receive their nourishment from the worship of the Temple, from the presence of the Lord. Those who find joy in his presence receive a freshness and vitality that never dies. Though their outer nature is wasting away, their inner nature is being renewed every day (2 Corinthians 4:16). They still bear the fruits of the Spirit, and their lives are a radiant testimony to the goodness of the Lord.

Deuteronomy 32:1—12

This great canticle of Moses is the climax to the book of Deuteronomy. The canticle seems to have been composed sometime after the Exile and inserted into its present context in order to contrast the faithfulness of the Lord with the disobedience of Israel. The canticle is in the form of a lawsuit between the Lord and Israel. After an introduction in which the witnesses are called, the canticle briefly states the charge against Israel. Then follows the address of the counsel for the prosecution, in which the Lord's care for Israel is declared. The extract we have in this morning's prayer stops at that point.

In Deuteronomy the canticle goes on to accuse Israel of apostasy, then to announce the sentence of 'Guilty' and the penalty of destruction. The **sentence,** *How often have I longed to gather your children as a hen gathers her young under her wings* (Matthew 23:37), puts the canticle in the context of Jesus' conflict with the Israel of his own time. In Jesus God made one last appeal to Israel to come back to him, but they would not.

Listen, O heavens, and I will speak,
let the earth hear the words on my lips.
May my teaching fall like the rain,
my speech descend like dew,
like rain drops on the young green,
like showers falling on the grass.

The witnesses to God's lawsuit with Israel are summoned. The *heavens* and *the earth,* representing the whole created order, are called to witness the covenant the Lord made with Israel which she has broken.

The lines beginning, *May my teaching fall like the rain,* are the words with which a teacher of wisdom in Israel began his instruction to his pupils. God's wisdom gives life to those who receive it. Later in the canticle the teacher (the counsel for the prosecution) will accuse Israel of being *senseless and foolish,* because she did not understand or obey the Lord. She lacked 'the fear of the Lord, which is the beginning of wisdom.'

For I shall praise the name of the Lord,
O give glory to this God of ours!
The Rock – his deeds are perfect,
and all his ways are just,
a faithful God, without deceit,
a God who is right and just.

The speaker begins to state the case against Israel, by making open declaration of the character of the Lord. He is *the Rock* (a favourite Old Testament title), unshakable and utterly faithful in contrast to fickle Israel. *His deeds are perfect,* in contrast to Israel's sin. *All his ways are just*: Israel is unjust. He is *faithful*: she is unfaithful. He is *without deceit*: Israel is full of deceit.

Those whom he begot unblemished
have become crooked, false, perverse.
Is it thus you repay the Lord,
O senseless and foolish people?
Is he not your father who created you,
he who made you, on whom you depend?

These verses paint the contrast between the character of God and the character of his people, but they do so by introducing what in the Old Testament is a rare and poignant theme – God as the *father* of his *people.* He *begot* them *unblemished* (that is, free of idolatry), *created* them, *made* them, they *depend* on him as a child does on its parents. And how do they repay him for all his love and care? They *have become crooked, false, perverse.* God is an anguished father who has done the very best for his child, and the child has broken his father's heart by turning out *senseless and foolish.*

Remember the days of old,
consider the years that are past;
ask your father and he will show you,
ask your elders and they will tell you.

The speaker now appeals to Israel to think back to her past, to recall God's goodness to her, to ask the *elders* who will be able to tell all the works of the Lord. Israel is *foolish* because she has forgotten her past, her traditions.

When the Most High gave the nations their heritage
and disposed men according to his plan,
in fixing the boundaries of the nations
he thought first of Israel's sons.
For Israel was the Lord's possession,
Jacob the one he had chosen.

God is the Lord of all the earth and all the *nations* have been given their allotted territory by him, but Israel was his favourite, his *chosen,* the one whom he considered *first.* Her rebellion and rejection of the Lord is all the more appalling.

God found him in a wilderness,
in fearful, desolate wastes;
he surrounded him, he lifted him up,
he kept him as the apple of his eye.

This verse continues the theme of the Lord as Israel's *father.* Israel was like an abandoned child, thrown out into the wilderness to die, until the Lord came and *lifted him up,* as a parent lifts up a crying child to comfort him. This child became immensely precious to the Lord, *the apple of his eye,* and in place of the *desolate wastes* he gave Israel a land flowing with milk and honey.

Like an eagle that watches its nest,
that hovers over its young,
so he spread his wings;
he took him,
placed him on his outstretched wings.
The Lord alone was his guide
and no other god was with him.

When an eagle stirs up its young to fly the nest it waits ready to catch them on its wings if they become tired and begin to fall. In the same way the Lord watched over Israel as she grew to maturity, ready to support and uphold *him* at the slightest sign of weariness. *The Lord alone was his guide,* but Israel chose to abandon the guidance of the Lord and worship other gods.

The Eastertide antiphon, 'It is I who give death and life; it is I who strike and also heal', comes from a later section of this same canticle, but in putting these words in the mouth of the risen Lord we are reminded that the Church will not be treated any differently from Israel. The letters to the churches in the book of Revelation show how Christ, the head of the Church, acts to rebuke and discipline his people. In speaking of Israel as the natural branches of the tree and the Church as the newly-grafted stock, St Paul said: 'If God did not spare the natural branches, neither will he spare you. Note then the kindness and severity of God: severity toward those who have fallen, but God's kindness to you, provided you continue in his kindness; otherwise you too will be cut off' (Romans 11:21,22). The canticle in Deuteronomy 32 goes on to describe how Israel abandoned the Lord when she became prosperous. The same could be said of many Christians in the West today.

Psalm 8

As the psalmist gazes up into the night sky he is overcome with wonder at the majesty of God and the insignificance of humankind, yet after praising the glory of God he recognizes the true glory of each person.

> *How great is your name, O Lord our God,*
> *through all the earth!*

God's *name* is his nature, his character. The psalmist extols the greatness of the Lord as he is revealed in the splendour of creation.

> *Your majesty is praised above the heavens;*
> *on the lips of children and of babes*
> *you have found praise to foil your enemy,*
> *to silence the foe and the rebel.*

The paradox is that despite his majesty, God 'chose what is foolish in the world to shame the wise, God chose what is weak in the world to shame the strong' (1 Corinthians 1:27). Amongst the nations of the ancient Near East Israel was weak, its people like *children and babes,* yet it was these *children and babes* that God chose to *foil* his enemies, to work out his purpose for the world. The *praise* offered by these insignificant ones will *silence the foe and the rebel,* all who resist God's will.

Jesus was 'weak' and 'foolish' in the eyes of the powerful of his time. On his last visit to the temple, in the week before he was crucified, Matthew records how he healed the blind and the lame, and the children cried out, 'Hosanna to the Son of David!', but the chief priests and the scribes were indignant. In answer to their hostility, Jesus quoted this verse from Psalm 8. The praise of the children silenced his enemies. (Matthew 21:14—16).

(This verse in Psalm 8 is obscure in the Hebrew, and capable of a number of different translations and interpretations. I have accepted the translation in the Office as it stands. Different versions offer other alternatives).

When I see the heavens, the work of your hands,
The moon and the stars which you arranged,
what is man that you should keep him in mind,
mortal man that you care for him.

Having thought of how insignificant Israel is amongst the nations, the psalmist goes on to reflect how insignificant *he* is in comparison with the awesome splendour of the night sky. Modern people may feel even more puny, given the fact that our solar system is so infinitesimally small in comparison with distant galaxies millions of light years away. How can the creator of the heavens and the earth be bothered with such an insignificant part of his creation? Yet he is:

Yet you have made him little less than a god;
with glory and honour you crowned him,
gave him power over the works of your hand,
put all things under his feet.

God not only considers *man*. He has given *him* a place of unparalleled *honour* and *glory* in creation. He has made *him little less than a god,* the *gods* in this instance meaning the beings that make up the heavenly court of the Lord, usually called 'angels'. *Man* is just a *little less* than the angels, and he has been blessed with the *glory and honour* which are usually reserved to God alone. God has also given him *power* over the created order, and *put all things under his feet.* The *all things* includes *sheep, cattle, savage beasts, birds, fish*. These verses recall the account of creation in Genesis, where man and woman are made in God's image and given dominion over all creatures (1:26—30).

The New Testament quotes these lines from Psalm 8 three times, and each time refers them to Christ. Hebrews 2:5—9 quotes this part of Psalm 8, and makes the astute observation that 'as it is, we do not yet see everything in subjection to [man]. But we see Jesus . . .' In other words, this glorious vision of man's authority in Psalm 8 finds its fulfilment in Christ, the perfect man, the one who has been given *power* over death and the devil. Hebrews 2 goes on to say that Christ shared our human nature 'so that by his death he might destroy him who has the power of death, that is, the devil, and deliver all those who through fear of death were subject to lifelong bondage' (2:14—15). St Paul quotes Psalm 8 with the same purpose of proving that in his resurrection the Father has given Christ power over death. 'For he must reign until he has put all his enemies under his feet. The last enemy to be destroyed is death' (1 Corinthians 15:25,26).

Ephesians 1:22 also quotes Psalm 8, as in the sentence, *He has put all things under his feet, and appointed him to be head of the whole Church*. The Risen Christ (see Eastertide antiphon) is the one to whom God has given all power and authority in this world and the next. He is the *man* whose glory we sing in this psalm, and whose glory we share. In prayer to his Father Jesus said of his disciples, 'The glory which you have given me I have given to them' (John 17:22).

Commentary on the Psalmody of Week 3

Week 3: Sunday

EVENING PRAYER I

God's help for the poor and suffering is the theme of tonight's psalmody. The first psalm has at its centre a succinct summary of the whole of the Old Testament revelation of God: his glory is above the heavens, and yet he comes to lift up the lowly. Psalm 115(116) is the personal testimony of one whom the Lord has 'lifted up', and who has come to make his sacrifice of thanksgiving. The ultimate example of how the Lord lifts up the lowly is presented to us in the final canticle from Philippians 2:6-11, the example of the humiliation, death, and resurrection of Jesus.

Psalm 112(113)

Psalm 112(113) is the first of a group of psalms (112—117) known to Israel as the 'Hallel', the 'Praise'. The Hallel was sung at the great feasts. Each psalm in the group begins in Hebrew with the cry 'Hallelujah!' At Passover, Psalms 112—113 were sung before the Passover meal, and Psalms 114—117 after it. Because of their association with the Passover feast, these psalms were sometimes called the Egyptian Hallel.

Psalm 112 has at its heart a magnificent expression of God's majesty and humility, of his glory and his gracious care for the poor. He is the one *who has risen on high to his throne,* yet *stoops from the heights to look down,* to *lift up the lowly.*

Praise, O servants of the Lord,
praise the name of the Lord!
May the name of the Lord be blessed
both now and for evermore!
From the rising of the sun to its setting
praised be the name of the Lord!

The *servants of the Lord* are not just the priests and the choir serving in the Temple but the whole congregation. They are God's *servants* who serve him with all their 'heart and mind and soul and strength.' The *servants of the Lord* are called three times to praise *the name of the Lord,* his being and character as he has revealed himself to Israel in mighty word and deed. The call to praise resounds not just at one particular time in the temple: it will sound for all time (*now and for evermore*) and in all places (*from the rising of the sun to its setting*), because the One who is to be praised is the creator and sustainer of the universe.

High above all nations is the Lord,
above the heavens his glory.
Who is like the Lord, our God,
who has risen on high to his throne
yet stoops from the heights to look down,
to look down upon heaven and earth?

Here we reach the kernel of the psalm, indeed the kernel of the whole Old Testament. God is revealed as the one *who has risen on high to his throne* (God's exalted majesty), *yet stoops from the heights to look down* (God's humility, his care for the earth and its suffering people). God transcends history (*all nations*) and creation (*the heavens*). It is impossible to confine him to one particular nation or place. God is incomparable. There is no one like him (*Who is like the Lord our God?*). He is beyond all our words and concepts. There is no one like him in his greatness and his mercy. But God is not known in the abstract, in his transcendence, but in the way he acts to restore and *lift up the lowly*. God's transcendence is intimately related to his care for the poor. It is because he is *high above all nations* that he is able to see and come to the aid of those who suffer. Whilst he is above creation and history he is also Lord of creation and history. Nothing can withstand his power.

The rest of the psalm goes on to unfold the nature of his mercy to the whole world, to *heaven and earth*.

> *From the dust he lifts up the lowly,*
> *from his misery he raises the poor*
> *to set him in the company of princes,*
> *yes, with the princes of his people.*
> *To the childless wife he gives a home*
> *and gladdens her heart with children.*

Two examples of God's mercy are given to show how he cares for the whole of suffering humanity. The first example is a man reduced to abject poverty, living at the city dump, in *the dust*, in *misery*. The Lord will act to *raise the poor* to the status of *princes*, giving them a place of honour and respect in the community. The second example is a woman who is *childless*, a state which was regarded in ancient Israel as a disgrace and a sign of God's rejection. God will do for the *childless wife* what he did for the man in poverty; he will raise her to a position of honour in her family, he will *gladden her heart with children*. This man and woman are chosen as typical of all suffering humanity, although behind them both is the example of Hannah, the mother of Samuel. These final verses of the psalm come straight from 1 Samuel 2:5—8, from the Canticle of Hannah (see Week 2, Wednesday Morning).

How does God act in mercy to the poor? The antiphons and the **sentence** bring us to Christ. Through him God *put* *down princes from their thrones and exalted the lowly* (Luke 1:52). The Church most clearly reflects the glory and being of God when she becomes the hand through which *he raises the poor,* lifting them from their *misery* and restoring their proper dignity within the community.

Psalm 115(116)

This is the second part of the psalm which we met on Week 2, Friday Evening. The psalmist was desperately ill, close to death, and in his affliction he cried to the Lord. The Lord heard his prayer and restored him to *the land of the living,* and now he comes to the Temple to present his sacrifice of thanksgiving. The sacrifice of thanksgiving was a form of communion sacrifice in which the worshipper ate part of the sacrifice as a sign of his communion with the Lord. To eat a meal with someone was an expression of brotherhood and of a mutual bond. The remainder of the sacrifice was burnt on the altar (see Leviticus 3; 7:11—15). In the communion sacrifice the worshipper both expressed thanks to God for his saving help, and bore witness to God's mercy before the congregation. The **sentence** calls us to offer this psalm as our sacrifice of praise: *Through him (Christ), let us offer God an unending sacrifice of praise* (Hebrews 13:15). The antiphons make the link between the psalm and the Eucharist *the* sacrifice of thanksgiving.

> *I trusted, even when I said:*
> *'I am sorely afflicted,'*
> *and when I said in my alarm:*
> *'No man can be trusted.'*

Even in the midst of his suffering, at a time when his faith was tested to the limit (*even when I said: 'I am sorely afflicted'*), the psalmist *trusted* in the Lord. '*No man can be trusted'* may describe his sense of the desperate nature of his illness (he was beyond human help), or it may refer to false accusations of sin thrown at him.

How can I repay the Lord
for his goodness to me?
The cup of salvation I will raise;
I will call on the Lord's name.

The psalmist has come into the temple to make his sacrifice of thanksgiving. Part of the ritual of the sacrifice involved taking a cup of wine, raising it before the Lord and pouring it out. (Numbers 28:7). The *cup of salvation* is thus the cup with which the psalmist gives thanks to the Lord for his salvation. In the communion sacrifice of the Eucharist the cup with which we give thanks to the Lord for his salvation is the cup over which Jesus said: 'This is my blood of the new covenant, which is poured out for many for the forgiveness of sins.'

To *call on the Lord's name* means to pray for his continued help and to proclaim the glory of his name in thanksgiving.

My vows to the Lord I will fulfil
before all his people.

In making his offering the psalmist is fulfilling a vow he made when he cried to the Lord for help during his sickness. He promised to bring a thanksgiving sacrifice to the Lord on his recovery. The fulfilling of the vow not only expresses the psalmist's gratitude to God; it also gives public testimony to God's grace *before all his people.* As we worship God each Sunday in the Eucharist we also are publically fulfilling the vow inherent in our baptism and confirmation, the vow of absolute loyalty of heart, mind, and soul to God.

O precious in the eyes of the Lord
is the death of his faithful.

The original meaning of this verse is that the untimely death of one of the Lord's *faithful* servants is not something he regards cheaply. It is *precious,* meaning 'costly'. God has delivered the psalmist from such a death. Prayed in the light of Christ the verse takes on a new meaning. It speaks of the immense cost of our redemption through the death of Christ, *his faithful* Son, a death that was *precious* to God in every way. All those who die united to Christ die 'in the Lord', and therefore their death becomes as his, *precious in the eyes of the Lord.*

> *Your servant, Lord, your servant am I;*
> *you have loosened my bonds.*
> *A thanksgiving sacrifice I make:*
> *I will call on the Lord's name.*

The psalmist brings with his *thanksgiving sacrifice* an even more costly sacrifice, the sacrifice of his freedom. He offers his absolute submission to the Lord, his obedience to his will in all things. *Your servant, Lord, your servant am I.* He makes the sacrifice of himself with such freedom and joy because he knows he is trusting his life to the one who has *loosened* his *bonds,* that is, delivered him from the *snares of death.* St Ignatius Loyola perfectly expressed this joyful sacrifice of one's freedom to God in his prayer, 'Take, and receive, O Lord, my entire liberty.'

Philippians 2:6—11

See Week 1, Sunday Evening.

MORNING PRAYER

This Sunday morning's psalms call on the whole of creation to join God's people in offering joyful praise. He is the One who rules the earth (Psalm 92), he is the Creator (Daniel 3 and Psalm 148), and he is the One who *comes close* to his people (Psalm 148). Praise the Lord!

Psalm 92(93)

This is one of the Enthronement Psalms which celebrate the Lord's reign over all the earth. (See on Psalm 46(47), Week 1, Wednesday Morning). Much of the imagery of the psalm comes from the enthronement of Israel's earthly king. Some scholars have suggested that the enthronement psalms were sung at an annual festival in which the Lord was proclaimed king and in which the people's allegiance to his rule was renewed. The **sentence** takes us into the future, to the time when evil will be finally vanquished and the Lord's reign established for ever: *The Lord, our God, the Almighty is king; let us be glad and rejoice and give him praise* (Revelation 19:6—7).

> *The Lord is king, with majesty enrobed;*
> *the Lord has robed himself with might,*
> *he has girded himself with power.*

When Israel's king was enthroned the people cried out with a great shout declaring their allegiance. (For Jehu for example: 'Jehu is king!' (2 Kings 9:13)). In this psalm the people cry out: *The Lord is king!* They own their allegiance to him alone. On Easter Sunday we acknowledge the Risen Christ with the acclamation: 'Christ is Risen!' and we renew our allegiance to him in the renewal of our baptismal vows.

At his enthronement Israel's king was clothed with magnificent robes, but the Lord is *enrobed with majesty* and *might* and *power*. God is ready to act with power to uphold his rule, and the psalm later tells how he has done this.

> *The world you made firm, not to be moved;*
> *your throne has stood firm from of old.*
> *From all eternity, O Lord, you are.*

At creation God subdued the forces of chaos (Genesis 1:2) and *made the world firm*. God's *throne*, his rule, is as unshakable as the earth, but in contrast to the earth his rule is *from all eternity.*

The waters have lifted up, O Lord,
the waters have lifted up their voice,
the waters have lifted up their thunder.

Greater than the roar of mighty waters,
more glorious than the surgings of the sea,
the Lord is glorious on high.

The psalm takes us back to the forces of chaos at creation, often described as *the waters* or *the sea,* the forces which the Lord by his *might* and *power* tamed, thus demonstrating that he is indeed *king.* The Canaanites and Babylonians believed that their gods had tamed the waters of chaos, but Israel declared the supremacy of her God by extolling him as the the one who stilled the *surgings of the sea* and *the roar of mighty waters. The Lord* (not Baal or Marduk, gods of Canaan and Babylon) *is glorious on high.*

These primeval forces of chaos also represented the hostile nations which surrounded Israel, and so there is a double meaning here. The Lord as *king* protects and delivers Israel (the Church) by his *might* and *power* from her enemies, even though at times they seem to overwhelm her like a thundering sea.

Truly your decrees are to be trusted.
Holiness is fitting to your house,
O Lord, until the end of time.

The psalm has proclaimed how the Lord by his power established the world: *you made it firm, not to be moved.* Now it speaks of his Law, his *decrees,* as established *until the end of time.* According to the OT, God's rule is shown both in the order of creation and in the revealed Law given to Israel. In the NT his *decrees* are revealed in the Gospel given to the Church. It is through his *decrees* that the Lord rules Israel as her king, and his *decrees* are always to be *trusted.* Those who trust his *decrees* will obey them and so become holy, and such *holiness* of life is required of those who worship in his *house,* because he is holy.

Daniel 3:57—88,56.

See Week 1, Sunday Morning.

Psalm 148

The pattern of Psalm 148 is identical to the previous canticle from Daniel 3. Heaven, earth, and all people are called on in succession to praise the Lord. The two parts of the psalm begin: *Praise the Lord from the heavens,* and *Praise the Lord from the earth.* The psalm is inspired by the first two chapters of Genesis and follows the order of creation as described there. This is Genesis 1 in poetry.

As we saw with the great canticle of creation from Daniel 3 (Week 1, Sunday Morning), praise is the response of creatures to their creator. Men and women can praise God consciously with heart and mind and voice. The rest of creation praises God simply by the fact of its existence, as a work of art praises the one who painted it by being what it is, a thing of beauty. Psalm 148 calls on creation to go on doing what it has always done – praise the Lord.

The meaning of the psalm is simple to follow, and only a few phrases need any explanation or comment.

> *Praise the Lord from the heavens,*
> *praise him in the heights . . .*

The *heights* refers to the dwelling place of God. The whole heavenly court is called on to *praise the Lord.*

The *waters above the heavens* reflects the ancient Hebrew idea of the sky (the 'firmament') being like an upturned basin separating the waters above the firmament from the waters below (Genesis 1:6—8). When it rains, the *waters above the heavens* are released.

> *Let them praise the name of the Lord.*
> *He commanded: they were made.*

This is the theological centre of the psalm. The *praise* of the creature is its response to being made by the *command* of the Lord, as in Genesis 1.

> *Praise the Lord from the earth,*
> *sea creatures and all oceans . . .*

Not only all things bright and beautiful, but all things fiercesome and ugly, all *sea creatures* and *stormy winds*, praise the Lord.

> *all mountains and hills,*
> *all fruit trees and cedars . . .*

Here we have our immediate environment. In contrast to the prevailing rationalistic world view which makes creation an object to be exploited by humankind, the psalms place us firmly within the created order, responsible for it and part of it. We more than any generation should know how essential the attitude of the psalmist is for the survival of the human race on planet earth.

> *all earth's kings and peoples,*
> *earth's princes and rulers . . . .*

All the inhabitants of the earth, from the greatest to the least, from *kings* to *children*, all alike are God's creatures, and all will find their joy in praising the Lord. Before God we are all equal, all responsible to him.

Let them praise the name of the Lord for he alone is exalted, in contrast to *earth's kings and princes*. He alone is the creator, he alone sustains the universe. The sentence rightly directs us *To the One who sits on the throne and to the Lamb, be all praise, honour, glory and power, for ever and ever* (Revelation 5:13).

He exalts the strength of his people . . .

The God who made the world comes to the aid of his people, and this is further reason why *he is the praise of all his saints.* The One who *alone is exalted* is the same one who *comes close* to his people. Praise the Lord!

EVENING PRAYER II

This evening's psalmody celebrates the triumph of Christ in his resurrection. Psalm 109 is a psalm of victory for the Messiah. Psalm 110 leads us to recall the *great and wonderful works of the Lord* which won our deliverance. In the final canticle we join with the angels and saints in heaven to sing *Alleluia! The Lord our God, the Almighty, reigns.*

Psalm 109(110):1—5,7

See Week 1, Sunday Evening II.

Psalm 110(111)

This psalm is an acrostic, each line beginning with the next letter in the Hebrew alphabet. The overall theme is of God's *great works* in Israel's history.

I will thank the Lord with all my heart
in the meeting of the just and their assembly.

The psalm was sung during worship at one of Israel's festivals, possibly at Passover. The *just* are those who are loyal to the covenant and keep God's commandments. The *assembly* is the whole nation of Israel.

Great are the works of the Lord;
to be pondered by all who love them.

This is the theme of the psalm. *Works* here mean the mighty deeds of the Lord acting in Israel's history, rather than the works of creation. The psalmist knows that faith in the Lord grows only as one *ponders,* 'studies', the way he has acted in the past. The **sentence** invites us to include in the praise of the Lord's *works* his work in Christ: *How great and wonderful are all your works, Lord God Almighty* (Revelation 15:3).

Majestic and glorious his work,
his justice stands firm for ever.

God's *justice* in saving the righteous and crushing the oppressor is a constant theme of Israel's praise.

He makes us remember his wonders.
The Lord is compassion and love.

The way that the Lord *makes* Israel *remember his wonders* is by instituting the great feasts of Passover, Pentecost, and Tabernacles. Here the events of the Exodus and the entry into Canaan are constantly relived, and the reality of the Lord's *compassion and love* is brought home. It was on Mount Sinai that the Lord revealed himself to Israel as 'a God merciful and gracious, slow to anger and abounding in steadfast love and faithfulness' (Exodus 34:6).

The great festivals of the Church – Easter, Pentecost, and Christmas – serve the same purpose, bringing before us the Lord's *compassion and love* shown in Christ. As we *ponder* these *great works of the Lord* faith grows.

He gives food to those who fear him;
keeps his covenant ever in mind.

The reference is to the way the Lord fed Israel with quails and manna during the journey through the wilderness. In providing for his people God was being faithful to his *covenant* with them made at Sinai. The food he gives today is the food of the Eucharist, through which he is faithful to his new covenant made in Christ.

He has shown his might to his people
by giving them the lands of the nations.

The land of Canaan was *the land of the nations*, the land the Lord gave to Israel.

His works are justice and truth:
his precepts are all of them sure,
standing firm for ever and ever:

they are made in uprightness and truth.

The Lord's *justice and truth* are shown by his faithfulness to his *precepts*, the Law God gave to Israel, the Law which will stand *firm for ever and ever.*

He has sent deliverance to his people
and established his covenant for ever.

The Exodus was the great *deliverance* of Israel, the act through which he *established his covenant* with them *for ever.*

Holy his name, to be feared.
To fear the Lord is the first stage of wisdom;
all who do so prove themselves wise.

This is one of the foundation principles of Israel's faith. The *fear of the Lord* is the absolute reverence and trust in the Lord which leads to wholehearted obedience to his will. *Wisdom* in this context does not mean great learning, but the practical knowledge of God's law and the way his law governs life.

Revelation 19:1—2,5—7

See Week 1, Sunday Evening II.

1 Peter 2:21—24

See Week 1, Sunday Evening II.

Week 3: Monday

MORNING PRAYER

All three scriptures in the psalmody revolve around the Temple. The first psalmist is a pilgrim longing for the presence of the Lord whom he will meet in the temple. The Old Testament canticle gives a vision of the Temple of the future, of Christ, who, as he was lifted up on the cross, drew all peoples to himself. The final psalm joyfully celebrates the day when all the earth will *worship the Lord in his temple,* in heaven.

Psalm 83(84)

The Temple was the centre of Israel's life and worship because there the Lord had promised his presence. The psalmist is a pilgrim coming up to Jerusalem for the feast of Tabernacles, the great New Year festival when the people gave thanks for the fruits of the year's harvest, prayed for rain for the coming season, renewed their allegiance to the covenant, and prayed for the outpouring of the Spirit on Israel. It was the greatest of the three pilgrim festivals, and the psalm expresses the longing of the devout Israelite to be in the Temple to celebrate this feast.

The **sentence** points the Christian to the city of God which is above, the new Jerusalem, the eternal dwelling place of the Lord: *We have no lasting city in this life but we look for one in the life to come* (Hebrews 13:14). We are pilgrims in this world, journeying to the city of God.

> *How lovely is your dwelling place,*
> *Lord, God of hosts.*

This is the language of love poetry. *Lovely* is a word used of people, rather than places, but for the psalmist the temple is a place of beauty because it is the *dwelling place* of the One whom he loves, the *Lord, God of hosts,* the God who is supreme ruler of the *hosts* of heaven and yet who has chosen to dwell with Israel

My soul is longing and yearning,
is yearning for the courts of the Lord.
My heart and my soul ring out their joy
to God, the living God.

Soul and *heart* refer to the very depths of one's being, the whole person, concentrated in *longing* and *yearning* for the Lord. It is in the Temple *courts* that the psalmist will participate in the inspiring liturgy of the feast of Tabernacles, and there sense the presence of *the living God.* The Christian shares the same *longing* and *yearning* for the Church in which we meet *the living God,* the Risen Lord, present to us in the Eucharist.

The sparrow herself finds a home
and the swallow a nest for her brood;
she lays her young by your altars,
Lord of hosts, my king and my God.

The psalmist longs to be like one of the birds which nest among the nooks and crannies of the temple courts, in the very presence of the Lord. They have the inestimable privilege of making their *home* and bringing up their *young* in the presence of the *Lord of hosts.*

They are happy, who dwell in your house,
for ever singing your praise.
They are happy, whose strength is in you,
in whose hearts are the roads to Sion.

From the birds we now move to the worshippers coming up to the festival, coming to *dwell* in the *house* of the Lord, coming to sing his *praise.* They will be truly *happy.* They will gain fresh *strength* from being in the Lord's presence. Their *hearts* are set on making the pilgrimage to Sion, travelling the *roads to Sion.* The next verse takes us through some of the hardships of this journey.

> *As they go through the Bitter Valley*
> *they make it a place of springs,*
> *the autumn rain covers it with blessings.*
> *They walk with ever growing strength,*
> *they will see the God of gods in Sion.*

The *Bitter Valley* was an arid valley through which the pilgrims had to pass on their way to Jerusalem. Even in such difficult places on their journey they are refreshed by their longing for the Lord. They *make the Bitter Valley a place of springs.* Their longing for God and for his gift of rain is answered when he sends down the first rain after the long, dry summer months. The *autumn rain* falls as they are on their way to Sion, and all around them they see fresh growth bursting from the soil. The Lord *covers the Bitter Valley with blessings.* And so the pilgrims *walk with ever growing strength,* filled with longing for God and surrounded by the blessings of the early rain. We can sense the mounting excitement of the pilgrims as they approach the holy city, refreshed by the early rains and joined by the swelling numbers of fellow pilgrims on the road to Jerusalem.

The expression: *they will see the God of gods in Sion,* is very bold, for it was stated in the Law that no one could see God and live (Exodus 33:20). The Temple building and liturgy are a visible expression of the *living God.*

For the Christian these verses speak of the power of the Eucharist, through which the Lord enables the faithful to transform the bitter and harsh experiences of life into *springs.* As we journey to the new Jerusalem we do so with *ever growing strength,* empowered by the Spirit, certain that there we shall *see God.*

O Lord God of hosts, hear my prayer,
give ear, O God of Jacob.
Turn your eyes, O God, our shield,
look on the face of your anointed.

The psalm now becomes a prayer for the king, (or possibly the high priest), the Lord's *anointed.* The king at times played an important role in the worship of the temple, and the welfare of the king was central to the welfare of the whole nation. The psalmist prays especially for the protection of the king in battle. God is *our shield,* the one who defends us from our enemies. Christ is our *annointed*, the one who pleads for us at the right hand of the Father.

One day within your courts
is better than a thousand elsewhere.
The threshold of the house of God
I prefer to the dwellings of the wicked.

The psalmist's longing for the temple is now reasserted in a beautiful way. He would rather spend *one day* in the presence of the Lord, in the temple, than a lifetime anywhere else. He would rather be standing as a supplicant at the entrance to the temple, on its *threshold,* than living in luxury with *the wicked* (who may be the surrounding pagan nations, or wealthy Israelites who have abandoned God). The next verse gives the reasons for his preference.

For the Lord God is a rampart, a shield;
he will give us his favour and glory.
The Lord will not refuse any good
to those who walk without blame.

The Lord is the one who will defend (as *a rampart*) his people and protect them (as *a shield*) from evil. He will give them *his favour and glory,* sharing with them his own being. These promises are for *those who walk without blame* meaning those who are loyal to the covenant, those who keep his Law. The Lord is the same 'yesterday, today, and forever' (Hebrews13:8). He always 'works for good with those who love him' (Romans 8:28).

Isaiah 2:2—5

The prophet Isaiah is writing at a time (740—700 BC) when the southern kingdom, Judah, is threatened with war from all sides. The Assyrians overthrew the northern kingdom of Israel in 721. The military power of the Babylonians, who were to sack Jerusalem in 587 BC, is growing. In the midst of this turmoil, Isaiah sees a vision of the future when God's peace will reign.

> *It shall come to pass in the latter days*

The prophecy looks forward to the day when the Lord himself will intervene in history to establish his kingdom of justice and peace. This prophecy of Isaiah began to be fulfilled in Christ but its complete fulfilment awaits the end of time.

> *that the mountain of the house of the Lord* (Sion)
> *will be established as the highest of the mountains,*
> *and shall be raised above the hills;*
> *and all the nations shall flow to it.*

In its physical setting Mount Sion is not especially grand, and is even overshadowed by the hills which surround Jerusalem. In his vision Isaiah sees Mount Sion *raised* up by the Lord until it is the *highest of the mountains*. Jerusalem is thus revealed to be the centre of the world, the point to which all peoples (*all nations*) will look, the place where God will appear as judge and saviour, the place where his word will be proclaimed. The nations will be drawn to

Jerusalem by the obvious fact that here dwells the God of all the earth.

> *And many peoples shall come, and say:*
> *'Come, let us go up to the mountain of the Lord,*
> *to the house of the God of Jacob,*
> *that he may teach us his ways*
> *and that we may walk in his paths.'*
> *For out of Sion shall go forth the law,*
> *and the word of the Lord from Jerusalem.*

Just as Israel once journeyed to the desert, to Mount Sinai, to receive the Law, so now the nations (*many peoples*) will come as pilgrims to Mount Sion because they will know that this is the only place where they can learn of God's *ways*. Only here will they find his *law*, only here will they hear his *word*.

> *He shall judge between the nations,*
> *and shall decide for many peoples;*
> *and they shall beat their swords into ploughshares,*
> *and their spears into pruning hooks;*
> *nation shall not lift up sword against nation,*
> *neither shall they learn war any more.*

Wars often begin when strong nations threaten the rights of weaker nations. God will *judge between the nations*, deciding the disputes which previously led to war. When the nations learn the *ways* of the Lord, when they *walk in his paths*, when they obey his *law*, then they will renounce their weapons of war and put their energies into the task God gave man at the creation, 'to till the earth', making it productive instead of destroying it by greed and violence. There is no more powerful statement in the Old Testament of the truth that war is a consequence of sin, and that people and nations who truly know God will bring an end to war.

This vision of Isaiah began to be fulfilled in the ministry of Jesus, whom God has 'raised from the dead and made him sit at his right hand in the heavenly places, far above all rule and authority and power and dominion' (Ephesians 1:20,21). He alone teaches the fulness of God's *ways.* In him we find the one whose teaching fulfils the *Law,* whose *word* goes out in the Church's preaching of the Gospel. Where his command to love our enemies is obeyed, wars cease. We long for the day when Christ's kingdom will reach its climax, when 'he will come again in glory to judge the living and the dead, and his kingdom will have no end'.

> *O house of Jacob, come,*
> *let us walk in the light of the Lord.*

In the light of the sun we can walk safely. In the *light of the Lord,* in the counsel of his word, we and the world can live in justice and peace.

Psalm 95(96)

As with the other Enthronement Psalms, Psalm 95 celebrates the universal kingship of God and looks forward to the Day when he will come to *rule the earth.*

> *O sing a new song to the Lord . . .*

A *new song* is not necessarily one which has just been composed, but a song sung to celebrate a new action of God, in this case his coming to deliver Israel from exile in Babylon. Just as the steadfast love of the Lord is 'new every morning' (Lamentations 3:22,23), so the praise of his people is to be renewed each day. In Morning Prayer we *sing a new song* to the Lord each day.

The **sentence** looks to the time when all heaven will sing *a new hymn in front of the throne, in the presence of the Lamb* (cf. Revelation 14:3). As we pray this psalm we anticipate that day. The call to *sing a new song* is made to *all the earth,* to all creation.

Proclaim his help day by day,
tell among the nations his glory
his wonders among all the peoples.

The psalm will go on to describe those *wonders*. They are the *wonders* of creation and redemption (*his help*), the glory of his rule.

The Lord is great and worthy of praise,
to be feared above all gods;
the gods of the heathens are naught.

The psalm brings together the two characteristic attitudes of the prophets to idols. They are vastly inferior to the Lord, and they are illusions, *naught*. Their power is nothing and worship of idols is futile.

It was the Lord who made the heavens . . ., not the idols. To him alone belong royal *majesty, state, power, splendour*, all of which are made known to Israel *in his holy place*, his sanctuary on earth (the Temple) and in heaven.

Give the Lord, you families of peoples . . .

The call to worship is renewed, and this time all *peoples* are specifically summoned to pledge their obedience to the Lord.

Bring an offering and enter his courts . . .

The nations are called to bring tribute (*offering*) such as an earthly king's subjects make, as a token of their submission to him. The outermost court of the Temple was the Court of the Gentiles, and it may be this *court* that the psalmist has in mind. The Temple was to be a 'house of prayer for all nations.'

Proclaim to the nations: 'God is king.'
The world he made firm in its place;
he will judge the peoples in fairness.

God's kingship is proclaimed with the same cry that accompanied the coronation of Israel's king: '*The Lord is king.*'

With this shout Israel calls on the whole world to bow the knee before the Lord because he is the creator of all and he will be the *judge* of all *the peoples.*

(It was at this point that the Old Latin translation had the phrase *Dominus regnavit a ligno,* 'The Lord has reigned from the tree', an early Christian gloss which later readers understood as a prophecy of the triumph of Christ on the cross. However it came into being, the phrase is a marvellous expression of the theology of the cross according to St John's Gospel).

Let the heavens rejoice and the earth be glad . . .

The whole world, *heavens, sea, land, trees* is invited to praise its creator joyfully, which it does by being itself, God's work of art which glorifies its maker.

at the presence of the Lord for he comes,
he comes to rule the earth.
With justice he will rule the world,
he will judge the peoples with his truth.

The Lord *comes* in many ways. The psalmist may have had in mind the Lord's action in leading the exiles back to Jerusalem. In Christ, the Lord came again to fulfil the vision of this psalm, to bring all *families of peoples* under God's rule. He will come again at the end of time 'to judge the living and the dead.' In every *coming* he acts with *justice,* in absolute fairness, and with *truth,* not according to some arbitrary standard but according to absolute truth.

EVENING PRAYER

The first psalm is a passionate cry for help (Psalm 122), which is answered by the second psalm (Psalm 123) and the New Testament canticle. In Christ *we have redemption through his blood, the forgiveness of our trespasses.*

Psalm 122(123)

The **sentence** catches the heart of the psalm perfectly: *The two blind men cried out, 'Lord, have pity on us, Son of David'* (Matthew 20:30). The psalm is an anguished cry for help, either from an individual or the community. The climax of the psalm is the plea, *Have mercy on us, Lord, have mercy.* The precise nature of the psalmist's trouble is obscure, but the call for help is crystal clear.

To you have I lifted up my eyes,
you who dwell in the heavens:
my eyes, like the eyes of slaves
on the hand of their lords.

The opening prayer for help evokes the greatness of God (*you who dwell in the heavens*), but also the sense of his distance. He seems far away, *in the heavens.* The dominant image of the psalm is that of the master-slave relationship. In Israel this was not necessarily a harsh relationship. Masters were responsible for giving justice to their servants, for providing their food, clothing, and shelter. Servants often became highly trusted employees, managing the master's property. The psalmist appeals to God as a servant to his master, humble, trustful, claiming God's protection and help.

Like the eyes of a servant
on the hand of her mistress,
so our eyes are on the Lord our God
till he show us his mercy.

The picture of the master-servant is repeated, this time as mistress-maid, to drive the point home and to lead up to the climax. We can feel the long, painful wait in the words *till he show us his mercy.* The psalmist acknowledges that he is utterly dependent on the Lord, the Lord who is *our God,* the Lord who has entered into a covenant with us.

Have mercy on us, Lord, have mercy.
We are filled with contempt.
Indeed all too full is our soul
with the scorn of the rich
with the proud man's disdain.

The psalmist as an individual (or the community as a whole) is under severe oppression, so severe that all they can say is: 'We've had enough.' 'We can't take any more.' *We are filled with contempt. Indeed all too full is our soul.* The *contempt* and *scorn* and *disdain* they suffer is difficult to define. (The translation here can be understood as implying that it is the psalmist who is guilty of *contempt, scorn, disdain.* The truth is the opposite. The psalmist and his community are the ones who are suffering from the *contempt, scorn,* and *disdain* of the *rich* and *proud*).

There are at least two historical circumstances which may lie behind this psalm. When the first exiles returned to Jerusalem from Babylon, they were treated with contempt and exposed to hostility by the surrounding peoples. Nehemiah records how the Gentile leaders 'derided us and despised us' (Nehemiah 2:19). Or the situation of the psalmist may reflect the glaring social inequalities of Israel before the exile, when the rich were described as those 'that trample the head of the poor into the dust of the earth' (Amos 2:7), those 'who are at ease in Zion' (Amos 6:1).

It takes little imagination to identify situations in our world where the rich and the proud (and how often wealth and arrogance go together) treat the poor with contempt. It happens between nations and within nations. In many nations the leaders and trendsetters treat the Church with *contempt* and *disdain,* taking every opportunity to pour *scorn* on its beliefs and practices. This psalm expresses the cry of God's faithful in such situations.

Psalm 123(124)

The kernel of this psalm is the shout of praise: *Blessed be the Lord who did not give us a prey to their teeth!* It is a psalm expressing the nation's praise and thanks to God after they have been delivered from an enemy who threatened to destroy them (*they would have swallowed us alive*). It is impossible to be more precise about the circumstances of the attack against Israel. It may be a prayer of the returning exiles.

'If the Lord had not been on our side' . . .

Here is the foundation statement of Israel's life and hope. Since their beginning as a people the Lord had watched over them.

they would have swallowed us alive

This may be the picture of a ravenous beast, or of Death waiting to devour its victims.

Then would the waters have engulfed us . . . like a flash flood in a wadi after heavy rains; or the reference may be to the waters of chaos which God tamed at creation, and which threaten to return and overwhelm his people.

Blessed be the Lord who did not give us
a prey to their teeth!
Our life, like a bird, has escaped
from the snare of the fowler.

The psalmist uses two dramatic images to portray their escape. Their attackers were like wild beasts about to rip their *prey* apart, or like hunters (*the fowler*) who have caught a bird and are about to kill it and cook it.

Indeed the snare has been broken
and we have escaped.
Our help is in the name of the Lord,
who made heaven and earth.

The Lord who is the creator of the universe is *our help,* our God, the one who has *broken the snare,* delivered us from our enemies. The Eastertide antiphon reminds us that through the resurrection of Christ we were set free from the snares of death and of Satan. In Christ's resurrection 'the snare has been broken and we have escaped, alleluia.' The sentence also gives us the assurance that the same Lord who delivered Israel is with us. *'Do not fear; for I am with you.'*

Ephesians 1:3—10

See Week 1, Monday Evening.

Week 3: Tuesday

MORNING PRAYER

This morning's psalmody reveals the wonder of our salvation. Salvation comes when God acts in *mercy and faithfulness,* with *justice and peace* (Psalm 84). Salvation is like an impregnable city where the *righteous* are sustained in *perfect peace* (Isaiah 12). Salvation comes when the Lord looks with delight and joy on his people (Psalm 66).

Psalm 84(85)

The psalm arises out of an experience of disillusionment caused by the apparent contradiction between God's promises and the present state of his people. The most likely setting for the psalm is some years after the return of the exiles from Babylon. The city is still not rebuilt and the land is very poor, having reverted to the wild during the long years of the captivity. Everything seems to be going against the exiles in their attempts to restore the land, and in this psalm they pray for the Lord's *mercy* and *saving help.*

O Lord, you once favoured your land . . .

The opening verse looks back to the recent deliverance of the exiles from Babylon, when the Lord showed favour to the *land* and revived the *fortunes of Jacob.* The psalm recognizes that the destruction of the land was God's punishment for *their sins,* and that the return from exile was the demonstration of his forgiveness.

Revive us now, God our helper! . . .

When the exiles returned to Jerusalem they faced very difficult conditions. The prophet Haggai described it like this: 'You have sown much and harvested little; you eat but never have enough, drink but never have your fill, put on clothes but feel no warmth. The wage-earner gets his wages only to put them in a bag with a hole in it . . . the sky has withheld the rain and the earth withheld its yield' (Haggai 1:6,10). The harsh reality of life seemed to contradict the glorious promises the Lord had made to the exiles through the prophet Isaiah (see Isaiah 40—55). They fear that the Lord is still angry with them. *Will you be angry with us for ever, will your anger never cease?* In their despair they pray for God's *mercy* and his saving *help,* and they are rewarded with a direct answer through the word of a prophet:

I will hear what the Lord God has to say,
a voice that speaks of peace
peace for his people and his friends
and those who turn to him in their hearts.
His help is near for those who fear him
and his glory will dwell in our land.

With these words the Lord begins to answer his people's prayer. A prophet in the Temple speaks, promising *peace* and *glory. Peace* (shalom) in the Old Testament is not primarily an absence of conflict, but a wholeness in relationships: between God and his people, between neighbours, and with the land. Peace grows out of justice and leads to prosperity. *Glory* is the very presence of God amongst his people, and is associated particularly with the Temple. The words may be a promise of the restoration of the Temple.

These blessings are promised to God's *people* (those to whom he is bound by covenant), *his friends* (those who are loyal to their commitments under the covenant), *those who turn to him in their hearts,* and those who *fear* (worship and obey) him. The prophets constantly warned the people to stop paying mere lip-service to the Lord, and called them to turn to him in their hearts. ('This people honour me with their lips, while their hearts are far from me' (Isaiah 29:13)). The return from exile would only be completed when the people had returned in their hearts to the Lord.

Mercy and faithfulness have met;
justice and peace have embraced.

This prophecy takes us into the heart of God's love for his people. In the midst of their despair he offers them again the priceless gifts of the covenant, gifts that in human terms are often opposites (like *mercy* and *justice*) but in God are joined in a profound unity. These words bring us to Christ, with the **sentence:** *When our Saviour came on earth God blessed his land* (Origen).

Mercy and faithfulness define God's unshakable commitment to his covenant with his people, a truth we need to be reminded of when circumstances go against us. *Justice and peace* define two of God's greatest gifts: *peace* is as described above, and *justice* is God's action to save the poor and defend them from their enemies. In God these gifts *embrace.*

Faithfulness shall spring from the earth
and justice look down from heaven.

God acts to bring in his kingdom by causing *faithfulness* to *spring from the earth* like a new shoot, and *justice* to come down like the rain *from heaven.*

The Lord will make us prosper
and our earth will yield its fruit.
Justice shall march before him
and peace in his steps

When the Lord comes in person to restore justice and peace amongst the people, then the land will begin to *prosper* and *yield its fruit.* The Old Testament constantly proclaims the unity between the land and its people. When the people act in justice and integrity the land prospers. When the people act selfishly, the land suffers. *Justice shall march before him* can be interpreted as a description of John the Baptist preparing the way of the Lord by preaching repentance; and the *peace* which *shall follow in his steps* as the Lord Jesus Christ, who came to bring 'peace on earth'.

Isaiah 26:1—4,7—9,12

This canticle comes in the middle of what is called Isaiah's Apocalypse (chapters 24—27). In his apocalypse Isaiah sees beyond the immediate events of his time, beyond the great social and political upheaval facing Israel, to God's final judgement. The canticle speaks of how, when God comes at the end of time to judge the world, Jerusalem will become a refuge for the upright. We pray the canticle with reference to the new Jerusalem, the Church. The **sentence** takes us to the Church in heaven: *The city walls stood on twelve foundation stones* (cf. Revelation 21:14), symbolizing the twelve apostles, the foundation on which the Church is built.

We have a strong city;
he sets up salvation as walls and bulwarks.

The earthly Jerusalem fell to the attacks of the Babylonian armies, but the Jerusalem to come will be impregnable, with defences that no enemy can breach. Its *walls and bulwarks* (*bulwarks* are great earth ramparts set up to strengthen the walls), its defence, is God's *salvation,* God's saving power.

Open the gates
that the righteous nation which keeps faith may enter in.

The scene shifts from the walls to the gates of the new Jerusalem. Isaiah sees the *righteous* standing before the gates calling out for admittance, just as the pilgrims used to do in the old Jerusalem when they came up to celebrate the feasts. The *righteous* are those who *keep faith,* who believe God's promises of salvation.

You keep him in perfect peace,
whose mind is stayed on you,
because he trusts in you.
Trust in the Lord for ever,
for the Lord God is an everlasting rock.

This is a classic theme in the whole of Isaiah's prophecy. *Peace* is the perfect restoration of all broken relationships: between the Lord and his people, between the people themselves, and with the land. *Peace* is fulfillment, abundant blessing, security. The first words of the risen Lord to his disciples were 'Peace be with you.' The peace longed for by the prophets is given by the risen Christ to those who *keep faith* in him, to those whose minds are *stayed* on him, firm in their commitment to him.

Those who so *trust in the Lord* will find him to be *an everlasting rock,* providing water in the desert (Exodus 17:6), shade in a thirsty land (Isaiah 32:2), safety when under attack (Psalm 40:2), and the only foundation on which we can build our lives (Matthew 7:24,25).

The way of the righteous is level;
you make smooth the path of the righteous.
In the path of your judgements, O Lord,
we wait for you. . .

This section of the canticle reveals the character of *the*

righteous. The righteous are those who walk in the *path of* the Lord's *judgements,* his commandments and decisions. The righteous *wait* for the Lord, instead of impatiently acting according to their own wisdom. They *yearn* for the Lord *in the night,* the time of vigil prayer; they *earnestly seek* the Lord and his presence. The Lord will *make smooth* and *level the path of the righteous,* he will clear away obstacles from their path and enable them to see his way in the confused course of history.

God's *judgements* are specifically his saving acts in history, the events which clearly reveal his *righteousness* to the world. For the Christian these acts are seen *par excellence* in Jesus.

O Lord, you will ordain peace for us;
you have wrought for us all our works.

God's people are defenceless in human terms ('How many divisions has the Pope?'), but the Lord himself will act for us, he will *ordain peace* and bring to completion *all our works.*

Psalm 66(67)

See Week 2, Wednesday Evening.

EVENING PRAYER

The Lord is the protector of his people (Psalm 124), and we must learn to trust him as a little child trusts its mother (Psalm 130). This trust is the door to the kingdom of heaven, whose anthem (Revelation 4) concludes Evening Prayer.

Psalm 124(125)

Israel is under the domination of a wicked regime, either a foreign power or an oligarchy of Israelites who care nothing for the Lord and his Law. (After the exile there were many periods of Israel's history which fit this description). Out of such a situation the psalmist cries to the Lord for help.

Those who trust in the Lord
are like Mount Sion, that cannot be shaken,
that stands for ever.

Sion is a massive rock that became for Israel a symbol of God's faithfulness. Despite the ascendancy of evil at this particular time in their history, *those who trust in the Lord* are sure that evil will not triumph. Their faith *cannot be shaken.*

Jerusalem! The mountains surround her,
so the Lord surrounds his people
both now and for ever.

From Sion itself the psalmist now looks to the mountains surrounding the city and sees in them another symbol of God's everlasting protection of his covenant people.

For the sceptre of the wicked shall not rest
over the land of the just
for fear that the hands of the just
should turn to evil.

The king's *sceptre* was the symbol of his power to rule. The *sceptre of the wicked* refers to the evil rulers who now control the land of promise, *the land of the just.* The psalmist is sure that the Lord will not allow their rule to last, because if it did then the *just* may be tempted beyond what they are able to bear. The *just* may cave in under social pressure and follow the fashion set by the ruling elite and begin to *turn to evil.* Foreign rulers often tried to introduce the worship of their gods to the local population. In the modern world foreign rulers or local oligarchies still do the same.

Do good, Lord, to those who are good,
to the upright of heart;
but the crooked and those who do evil,
drive them away!

The psalmist prays for the triumph of the justice of God, asking him to reward *the upright of heart* and to banish *those who do evil* from the land.

Psalm 130(131)

This is the psalm of a man in mid-life, an ambitious and strong-willed man who has come to terms with himself and learnt to trust in the Lord.

O Lord, my heart is not proud
nor haughty my eyes.
I have not gone after things too great for me
nor marvels beyond me.

This is the prayer of someone who has taken to heart the counsel of St Paul: 'I bid every one among you not to think of himself more highly than he ought to think, but to think with sober judgement' (Romans 12:3). Whereas in earlier days the psalmist had been a proud and ambitious man, he has learnt to be realistic about his gifts (*I have not gone after things too great for me*) and humble in the face of life's mysteries, *things too great for me.* Instead of trust in himself he has learnt to trust the Lord.

Truly I have set my soul
in silence and peace.
As a child has rest in its mother's arms,
even so my soul.

This 'coming to terms with life' has been a struggle. It has not come easily. He has had to *set* his soul, tame it, calm its passions. He compares himself now to a toddler, a three-year-old (in Hebrew, a 'weaned child'), contented, absolutely secure in its mother's care. It is the perfect trust of a child that Jesus commended when he said that we must become like little children in order to enter the kingdom of God. Jesus himself had learnt that trust, as the sentence tells us: *Learn from me, for I am gentle and humble in heart* (Matthew 11:29).

> *O Israel, hope in the Lord*
> *both now and forever.*

The experience of the psalmist is commended to the whole community. To *hope in the Lord* means to cast your life in complete confidence on him, to become like a child.

Revelation 4:11; 5:9,10,12

See Week 1, Tuesday Evening.

Week 3: Wednesday

MORNING PRAYER

Morning Prayer begins with a cry for God's help (Psalm 85). The answer to that prayer comes in the canticle (Isaiah 33) and final psalm (97), which both celebrate God's coming as judge and king. *Rejoice at the presence of the Lord, for he comes!*

Psalm 85(86)

This psalm is a lament, but as with most of the laments it is impossible to know the precise nature of the psalmist's difficulties. He is under attack from enemies of some kind, whom he describes as *ruthless men* who *seek my life.* There are numerous parallels to the language of other psalms. The author is someone deeply immersed in the liturgy of Israel, to the point where its language has become his own.

Turn your ear, O Lord, and give answer
for I am poor and needy.
Preserve my life, for I am faithful:
save the servant who trusts in you.

The psalmist describes himself as *poor, needy, faithful, the servant* of the Lord, all ways of appealing to the Lord for help, all ways of describing the same attitude of total loyalty to God. In later Israel the *poor* became a name for those who remained faithful to the Lord, while the *rich* were those who deserted their faith and compromised with whatever foreign power happened to be in control of the country. When Jesus said 'Blessed are the poor' he was speaking of the *faithful poor.*

You are my God, have mercy on me, Lord, . . .

In his covenant with Israel the Lord said to the people: 'I am the Lord your God' (Exodus 20:2). The psalmist appeals to God's covenant promise by calling him *my God.* God's *mercy* is his covenant loyalty, his promise to come to the aid of his people.

O Lord, you are good and forgiving, . . .

The psalmist is again recalling the promises of the covenant, where the Lord revealed himself as 'a God merciful and gracious, slow to anger, and abounding in steadfast love and faithfulness, . . . forgiving iniquity' (Exodus 34:6,7). The intercessions in the Eucharistic Prayers of the Mass appeal to God's promises in the new covenant:

Look with favour on your Church's offering
and see the Victim whose death has reconciled us to yourself.
Grant that we, who are nourished by his body and blood,
may be filled with his Holy Spirit,
and become one body, one spirit in Christ.
(Eucharistic Prayer III).

In the day of distress I will call
and surely you will reply. . . .

The psalmist is confident of God's help because of the promises of the covenant.

All the nations shall come to adore you
and glorify your name, O Lord: . . .

The later prophets of Israel looked forward to the day when all nations would come to worship the Lord, because he *alone* is *God.* The Eastertide antiphon brings before us the fulfilment of this prophetic longing in the resurrection of Christ and his gift of the Holy Spirit.

Show me, Lord, your way . . .

The psalmist recognizes that the *faithfulness* on which he based his cry for help is itself a gift of God. Only by God's grace is he able to *walk in* God's *truth.*

I will praise you, Lord my God, . . .

This verse introduces a new section in the psalm. Following his cry for mercy, the psalmist may have received a prophetic word from the priest in the temple assuring him that the Lord has heard and will answer his prayer; or the verse may be the psalmist's promise to bring a sacrifice of thanksgiving after his troubles are over.

To be delivered *from the depths of the grave* means to be restored to fellowship with God. In the *grave,* according to the Old Testament, such fellowship is lost.

The proud have risen against me . . .

This is the only clue we have as to the nature of the psalmist's trouble. It seems that he was under attack from a powerful and godless group who were determined to destroy him.

But you, God of mercy and compassion

Again we are taken back to the covenant promise of Exodus 34:6, quoted above.

O give your strength to your servant
and save your handmaid's son.

A servant born of a slave girl was permanently bound to his master (Exodus 21:4). By referring to this custom the psalmist affirms that he is bound to the Lord for ever.

Show me a sign of your favour
that my foes may see to their shame
that you console me and give me your help.

To ask for his foes to be put to *shame* is not personal vindictiveness. The issue at stake is loyalty to the covenant. The psalmist's enemies are godless men (*to you they pay no heed*) who are persecuting the *poor*. Their defeat will be the triumph of truth and righteousness.

Isaiah 33:13—16

This canticle is part of a long prophecy which speaks of the rise of a powerful enemy who is threatening Jerusalem, of the ultimate destruction of that enemy, then of the restoration of Jerusalem. The whole canticle reflects the situation of Israel after the exile. Verses 13—16 speak of God coming to restore Jerusalem and the sifting of good and evil that this will bring.

Hear, you who are far off,
what I have done;
and you who are near,
acknowledge my might.

The expressions *far off* and *near* are a way of saying: 'everyone'. The prophet calls on all people to prepare themselves for the mighty coming of God. The **sentence** from Acts 2:39: (*The promise that was made is for you and your children and for all those who are far away*) reminds us that at Pentecost God came in the power of the Spirit to bring salvation to all humankind.

The sinners in Sion are afraid;
trembling has seized the godless:
'Who among us can dwell with the devouring fire?
Who among us can dwell with everlasting burnings?

God's coming is compared to a *devouring fire,* ready to consume evil, beginning in Jerusalem. In the New Testament the book of Hebrews speaks of God as 'a consuming fire' (12:29) which will destroy evil. 'Judgement begins with the household of God' (1 Peter 4:17). The Advent and Eastertide antiphons point forward to the second coming of Christ, when he comes as judge.

Psalm 14(15) (Week 1, Monday Evening) begins with a dialogue between pilgrims to the temple and the priest standing at the gates. The people ask: 'Lord, who shall be admitted to your tent?' The priest begins his reply by describing the character of those who can stand before the Lord: 'He who walks without fault; he who acts with justice . . .' This canticle of Isaiah pictures the faithful asking the pilgrims' question: *Who among us can dwell with the devouring fire?* Who can enter the new Jerusalem? Who can live in the presence of God, whose holiness is a fire which consumes all sin? The answer begins with the next verse.

He who walks righteously and speaks uprightly,
who despises the gain of oppressions,
who shakes his hands lest they hold a bribe,
who stops his ears from hearing of bloodshed
and shuts his eyes from looking upon evil.

These qualities all have to do with social relationships. To *walk righteously* is to live in right relationship with God and others. To *speak uprightly* is to speak the truth. To *despise the gain of oppressions* is renounce the opportunity to make a profit by exploiting the poor. To *shake one's hands lest they hold a bribe* is to reject the taking of bribes, especially where it concerns the course of justice. To *stop* one's *ears from hearing of bloodshed* does not mean to be deaf to the cries of the oppressed, but to refuse to participate in, even to listen to, any plans which involve bloodshed and the taking of innocent life. To *shut* one's *eyes from looking upon evil* does not mean to turn a blind eye to injustice, but to turn away from participation in anything which may involve wrongdoing.

These verses foreshadow the Sermon on the Mount, and Jesus' word: 'Unless you righteousness exceeds that of the scribes and Pharisees, you will never enter the kingdom of heaven' (Matthew 5:20).

He will dwell on the heights;
his place of defence will be the fortresses of rocks;
his bread will be given him,
his water will be sure.

This begins the prophet's description of the new Jerusalem. Those who are granted entry will *dwell* with God, they will be secure from evil, they will be sustained by the bread and water of God. The prophet may have in mind the manna and the water with which God sustained Israel in the wilderness. For the Christian they speak of the eucharistic 'bread of life' and the 'water' of the Holy Spirit.

Psalm 97(98)

The previous canticle brought to mind the second coming of Christ. Psalm 97 *tells of the first coming of the Lord, and of the faith of all peoples* (St Athanasius): **sentence.** In style it is very similar to Psalm 95(96) (Week 3, Monday Morning), and requires little comment.

Psalm 97 celebrates a great victory which the Lord has achieved for Israel, probably the return from exile in Babylon, although some commentators see a reference to the Exodus. The threefold theme of the psalm is God the saviour, the king and the judge.

Sing a new song to the Lord . . .

As with Psalm 95, a *new song* is a song sung to celebrate a new action of God, in this case God's deliverance of Israel from exile. The exiles began to return in 539 BC and by the year 516 the temple was rebuilt. This is the *wonder* he has *worked* by his strength (*his right hand*) alone. A psalm like this may have been especially composed for the rededication of the temple.

The Lord has made known his salvation . . .

The deliverance is a public action of God (*All the ends of the earth have seen the salvation of our God*), an action which has revealed to all nations *his truth and love,* his covenant commitment to *the house of Israel.*

With trumpets and the sound of the horn
acclaim the King, the Lord.

The whole of creation is summoned to acclaim the Lord as *King,* as Israel acclaimed her kings at their coronation, with trumpet and horn (1 Kings 1:39).

Let the sea and all within it thunder . . .

The whole created *world* (*sea, rivers, hills, peoples*) is exhorted to pay homage to its King, the Lord God of Israel.

Rejoice at the presence of the Lord
for he comes to rule the earth.
He will rule the world with justice
and the peoples with fairness.

God's coming as King and Judge was awaited with great joy

in Israel, because it meant salvation for the poor and the punishment of their enemies. But the Lord's rule will not be partial. He will rule in perfect *justice, with fairness.* Jesus announced that the longed-for coming of the Lord to rule the earth had begun in his ministry. In Jesus 'The kingdom of heaven is at hand.' (Mark 1:15).

EVENING PRAYER

It is only as the Lord acts that anything of ultimate worth is achieved: that is the message of tonight's psalmody. The first psalm looks back to God's miraculous deliverance of Israel from exile in Babylon. The second psalm looks to his protection and care of the family. The New Testament canticle offers praise to Christ in whom *all things hold together.*

Psalm 125(126)

The experience behind this psalm is the restoration of Israel after the exile. When everything seemed hopeless, when it seemed as if God's promises had come to an end and Israel was finished, then the Lord acted to restore Israel to her land.

The sentence speaks of how those who share in the sufferings of the apostolic ministry will also share in its joy

When the Lord delivered Sion from bondage,
It seemed like a dream.
Then was our mouth filled with laughter,
on our lips there were songs.

The psalm begins by looking back with wonder on the miraculous deliverance of Israel from *bondage* in Babylon. To many of the exiles in captivity the possibility of their return did seem like a *dream,* and the prophets who foretold the return were often greeted with disbelief and outright scepticism.

The Eastertide antiphon points the Christian back to the miraculous deliverance God accomplished when he raised Christ from the dead. The disciples' sorrow was turned into joy when they saw the Lord.

The heathens themselves said: 'What marvels
the Lord worked for them!'

The return of Israel from exile made a profound impression on the surrounding nations, which recognized what God had done for his people. Many nations in the ancient Near East were wiped off the map by conquest and exile, and no doubt the conventional wisdom of the time was that puny Israel would go the same way.

Deliver us, O Lord, from our bondage
as streams in a dry land.

The return was not the answer to all their problems. The land had reverted to the wild, the city was defenceless and little more than a heap of rubble. The task of rebuilding was slow and painful. Therefore the psalmist appeals to the miraculous deliverance from Babylon and pleads with the Lord to act again, to *deliver* the people from the *bondage* of despair and discouragement. He prays that God's deliverance will be as swift and dramatic as the sudden rush of water in the dry stream beds of the desert after rain. These *streams in dry land* bring immediate growth.

Those who are sowing in tears
will sing when they reap.

They go out, they go our, full of tears,
carrying seed for the sowing:
they come back, they come back, full of song,
carrying their sheaves.

At this point the Lord speaks in answer to his people's cry and promises that although they *are sowing in tears,* they *will sing when they reap.* The work of replanting the fallow land, rebuilding the city, re-establishing the life and worship of the nation, proceeded slowly and painfully, *full of tears.* But the Lord promises that it will be fruitful work. It will not all come to nothing. At harvest time they will reap with joy because they will gather in a bumper crop.

This is a psalm for all those who are discouraged by the hard labour and meagre results of their apostolic work, whether it is raising a family, pastoring a congregation, or pioneering a difficult task.

Psalm 126(127)

The psalm begins with the general principle that success depends on God's blessing, and goes on to apply that principle to the family. The **sentence**, *You are God's building* (1 Corinthians 3:9), applies the principle to the growth and development of the Church, the family of God, and hence the psalm can be prayed as a prayer for the Church's growth in grace and numbers. In building the life of the Church, Jesus' word to his disciples sums up the lesson of this psalm: 'Without me you can do nothing' (John 15:5).

If the Lord does not build the house,
in vain do its builders labour;
if the Lord does not watch over the city,
in vain does the watchman keep vigil.

This may have been a well-known proverb in Israel. The *house* has a double meaning. It refers to the children and to the building, much as the word 'home' does in English. Without the Lord's blessing, the family will be weak and have no future.

What is true of the family is true of the city. Its defences are useless unless the Lord is protecting it.

In vain is your earlier rising,
your going later to rest,
you who toil for the bread you eat:
when he pours gifts on his beloved while they slumber.

This verse is not discouraging a person from hard work, but saying again that without trust in God we can achieve nothing. There is no point in toiling anxiously from the break of day long into the night, as if everything depended solely on our own efforts. Hard work is futile if God has no part in it. Those who trust in the Lord are able to take life at an even pace and be refreshed by the Lord in sleep.

Truly sons are a gift from the Lord,
a blessing, the fruit of the womb.
Indeed the sons of youth
are like arrows in the hand of a warrior.

These sentiments may sound offensive in a modern society where daughters are as valued as sons, but in ancient Israel (as in many countries still today) life was harsh and basic, without the blessings of modern medicine and machines. Sons were essential to continue the family name and to help defend and work the family lands. They *are like arrows in the hand of a warrior,* they are the first line of defence for the family when it is threatened. *Sons* born in one's *youth* were also crucial if the parents were to have anyone to support them when they reached old age. *Sons of youth* were their parent's superannuation. The psalm acknowledges that children are God's gift, that he is Lord of life and death.

O the happiness of the man
who has filled his quiver with these arrows!
He will have no cause for shame
when he disputes with his foes in the gateways.

The city gate was the place where the local court met. Anyone who had a law suit would bring it to the elders of the city gathered at the gate. Justice was often corrupt, and the judges open to bribes and threats, but the man who brought his dispute backed by a number of strapping sons was much more likely to get a fair hearing! The reason why widows and orphans were so vulnerable was because they had no family to back them up.

Colossians 1:12—20

See Week 1, Wednesday Evening.

Week 3: Thursday

MORNING PRAYER

The two keynotes of the psalmody are the holiness of God and his universal rule. All the nations, not just Israel, will *know* him (Psalm 86). The Lord is coming in power to carry out his plan of salvation and no one, no nation, can thwart him (Isaiah 40). *The Lord is king!* (Psalm 98).

Psalm 86(87)

This extraordinary psalm anticipates the time when all nations will look to Sion as the spiritual centre of the world. The New Testament sees in the psalm a prophecy of the Church: *The Jerusalem which is above is free and is our mother* (Galatians 4:26), **sentence.**

On the holy mountain is his city
cherished by the Lord.
The Lord prefers the gates of Sion
to all Jacob's dwellings.

The *holy mountain* is Sion, the site of the Temple, the place where the Lord 'has chosen to dwell' and therefore the place he *prefers to all Jacob's dwellings*. The gates of a city were the centre of its social and economic life, the place of trade and the place where justice was meted out.

Of you are told glorious things,
O city of God!

The prophets, especially Isaiah, are full of the promises God has made to Sion, the *glorious things* he has said of her. One of Isaiah's prophecies speaks of Sion as the mother of all peoples:

Rejoice with Jerusalem,
be glad for her, all you who love her! . . .
So that you may be suckled and satisfied
from her consoling breast,
so that you may drink deeply with delight
from her generous nipple . . .
As a mother comforts a child,
so I shall comfort you;
you will be comforted in Jerusalem. (66:10—13).

'Babylon and Egypt I will count
among those who know me;
Philistia, Tyre, Ethiopia,
these will be her children
and Sion shall be called "Mother"
for all shall be her children.'

This is one of the most astonishing prophecies in the whole of the psalter. Countries which were traditionally Israel's bitter enemies (Babylon and Egypt) are now going to come under the same protection and care which the Lord gives to Israel. They will *know* the Lord as Israel does, and through Sion the Lord will call them *children*. Sion will become the source of their life, their *Mother*. It is easy to see how the early Christians understood this to be a prophecy of the Church (Galatians 4:26), through whom God would bless all nations. In the new Jerusalem there will be 'people from every nation, race, tribe and language' (Revelation 7:9).

> *It is he, the Lord Most High,*
> *who gives each his place.*
> *In his register of peoples he writes:*
> *'These are her children'*
> *and while they dance they will sing:*
> *'In you all find their home.'*

The Lord who determines the *place* and destiny of each nation has determined that all nations will look with joy (*singing and dancing*) to Sion (the Church on earth and in heaven) as their spiritual mother, as the place where they are at *home.*

Isaiah 40:10—17

This canticle comes from the opening prophecy of Deutero-Isaiah (Second Isaiah, Isaiah chapters 40—55), who prophesied to the exiles in Babylon towards the end of their captivity, around 545 BC Deutero-Isaiah prophesied the end of the captivity and the return of the exiles to Jerusalem. The Advent antiphon and the antiphon for use throughout the year interpret the canticle as a prophecy of the second coming of Christ.

> *Behold, the Lord God comes with might,*
> *and his arm rules for him;*
> *behold, his reward is with him,*
> *and his recompense before him.*

In a quite remarkable way, Isaiah speaks of Israel's return as God's return. He *comes with might* to set the captives free. He exercises his power as Lord of all the earth, *his arm rules for him.* It is *the Lord God* who is coming; he is the one who is returning to Jerusalem and Israel is following in his train, like a line of captives in a king's triumphant procession home after victory. The returning exiles are described as the Lord's *reward* and *recompense,* the booty he has won in conquest. By describing the exiles' return as the Lord's return Isaiah implies that the whole event is the work of the Lord and him alone. At the same time he links up with the ancient tradition of the Lord appearing in power to save his people and reveal his will to them.

The **sentence**: *Behold, I come quickly, and my reward is with me* (Revelation 22:12) is the New Testament's application of this prophecy to the second coming of Christ. He will come as judge to *reward* the righteous, 'to repay everyone as their deeds deserve' (Revelation 22:12). The reward in this case is Christ's promised blessing to those who have been faithful to him.

He will feed his flock like a shepherd,
he will gather the lambs in his arms,
he will carry them in his bosom,
and gently lead those that are with young.

After the awesome picture of the Lord God in the first verse of the canticle, we have a complete contrast as Isaiah speaks of the Lord's tender care for his people. The *shepherd* is a royal title applied here to the Lord to depict his compassion for Israel as he leads them home to the fold. He will *feed his flock,* lifting up the new-born lambs (the children), and giving special protection to the ewes in lamb (the mothers of the newly re-formed nation?). As the good shepherd, the Lord protects the weak and the defenceless members of his flock, those who are especially vulnerable.

Who has measured the waters in the hollow of his hand
and marked off the heavens with a span,
enclosed the dust of the earth in a measure
and weighed the mountains in scales
and the hills in a balance?

No one! In this series of rhetorical questions the prophet seeks to build up the faith of his frightened and despondent countrymen. They are in awe of the gods and armies of Babylon. Isaiah calls them to consider the majesty of the creator of the universe and the lord of history. No one can begin to compare with him and with the wonders of his creation. Isaiah ranges over the whole universe, *waters* (the *waters* of chaos which God tamed at creation), *heavens, dust of the earth, mountains, hills*; and over every form of measure or weighing device, to prove that God's work is immeasurable. No one can describe the majesty of the creator or the scale of his work.

Who has directed the Spirit of the Lord,
or as his counsellor has instructed him?
Whom did he consult for his enlightenment,
and who taught him the path of justice,
taught him knowledge,
and showed him the way of understanding?

Isaiah challenges Israel with the question: Who is greater, the gods of Babylon or the Lord God of Israel? The *Spirit of the Lord* is the power by which God tamed the waters of chaos (Genesis 1:2) and the wisdom by which he made the world (Proverbs 8:22—31). In contrast to the supreme god of Babylon, Marduk, who needed a multiplicity of counsellor-gods to help him create and rule the world, the Lord God of Israel acts alone. He needs no *counsellor* to instruct him, or to give him *enlightenment, knowledge* and *understanding*.

Behold, the nations are like a drop from a bucket,
and are accounted as the dust on the scales;
behold, he takes up the isles
like fine dust.

The prophet moves from creation to history. As God is the master of creation, so he is the lord of history. When water is drawn from the well, a drop that falls from the bucket is not noticed; or when goods are weighed, no one bothers about dust on the scales. In God's plan, whole nations may be totally insignificant. Israel must not be intimidated by the grandeur and splendour of Babylon. Babylon will count for nothing in the Lord's plan for his people. The empires and powers of this world *are as nothing before him.*

Lebanon would not suffice for fuel,
nor are its beasts enough for a burnt offering.
All the nations are as nothing before him,
they are counted by him as less than nothing
and emptiness.

If God is so immeasurably great, as the canticle has proclaimed, then he must be worshipped with the greatest sacrifices and offerings man could conceive – all the *beasts* of *Lebanon* (a region famous for its sheep and cattle), with the fire of the altar fuelled by the great forests of *Lebanon.* But even this would not come near to honouring the greatness of God.

Nothing can stand in his path. Even the most powerful nations on earth *are as nothing before him.* None can thwart his plan for his people. Nations are like idols in God's sight: *emptiness.*

Psalm 98(99)

This is the last of the Enthronement Psalms, the psalms which celebrate the Lord as king. In these psalms Israel renews her allegiance to the Lord and her faith in his rule over all the earth.

The Lord is king; the peoples tremble,
He is enthroned on the cherubim; the earth quakes.
The Lord is great in Sion.

The *cherubim* were heavenly beings who were depicted in the Old Testament as winged creatures with a lion's body and a human or animal face. There were two carved cherubim above the Ark of the Covenant in the Holy of Holies, the innermost sanctuary of the temple. 'The cherubim spread out their wings over the place of the ark, so that the cherubim made a covering above the ark' (1 Kings 8:6). As the Ark of the Covenant was the locus of the glory of the Lord, the psalm speaks of the Lord as being *enthroned on the cherubim. The earth quakes* at the presence of the Lord, as on Mount Sinai when the Law was given. *Sion* is the earthly centre of God's universal kingdom.

The **sentence** from Athanasius (*You are higher than cherubim; you changed the bad state of the earth, when you came in a nature like ours*) encourages us to pray the psalm with the powerful ministry of our Saviour in mind.

He is supreme over all the peoples.
Let them praise his name, so terrible and great.
He is holy, full of power.

The Lord is king not only of Israel, but of the whole earth. *All the peoples* must bow before him and acknowledge his awesome power and majesty, his holiness.

You are a king who loves what is right;
you have established equity, justice and right;
you have established them in Jacob.

The quality of *justice* is essential to God's nature. He does not use his absolute power like an earthly dictator. The purpose of his gift of the Law to the people of God, to *Jacob,* was to *establish equity, justice and right* in the nation.

St Paul will describe the Gospel as being the revelation of the justice of God (Romans 1:17).

Exalt the Lord our God;
bow down before Sion, his footstool.
He the Lord is holy.

God is pictured seated on his throne in heaven with his feet resting on *Sion,* the place where he has chosen to place his name. The people are commanded to fall prostrate in humility before the Lord, to *bow down before* him.

> *Among his priests were Aaron and Moses,*
> *among those who invoked his name was Samuel.*
> *They invoked the Lord and he answered.*

These three great figures of Israel's history are brought together at this point in the psalm because they all at various stages interceded before the Lord for the nation. As their intercession was effective in the past, so will the intercession of their successors be in the present, the prayers of the priests and prophets of the temple.

> *To them he spoke in the pillar of cloud.*
> *they did his will; they kept the law,*
> *which he, the Lord, had given.*

The *pillar of cloud* was the symbol of God's presence with his people during their journey through the wilderness (Exodus 13:21ff). God spoke to Moses (Exodus 33:9) and to Aaron (Numbers 12:5) *in the pillar of cloud.* (The psalmist seems to have taken a little poetic licence in including Samuel at this point. The Lord certainly spoke to Samuel, but not, as far as we know, in a pillar of cloud).

These three great representatives of Israel's priestly and prophetic traditions not only heard the voice of the Lord, they obeyed it. *They did his will; they kept the law* of the covenant.

> *O Lord our God, you answered them.*
> *For them you were a God who forgives;*
> *yet you punished all their offences.*

Moses, Aaron, and Samuel succeeded through their intercession in gaining the Lord's mercy and forgiveness for his erring people, yet God also *punished all their* (the people's) *offences.* The Covenant was a two-way contract. When the people persisted in breaking their commitment to the

Covenant, the Lord disciplined them to bring them back to his ways, the way of life and blessing. *The Lord our God is holy.*

EVENING PRAYER

Christ the king is the theme of tonight's psalmody. Psalm 131 is a messianic prophecy of the blessings and authority of the Messiah, and in the canticle from Revelation we offer praise to God because *the authority of his Christ* has *come.*

Psalm 131(132)

This psalm expresses the significance for Israel of the Davidic kingship. The Lord made a covenant with David assuring him that 'Your house and your kingdom shall be made sure for ever before me; your throne will be established for ever' (2 Samuel 7:16). The continuity of the house of David became for the people a symbol of the Lord's favour. The sentence gives the Christian interpretation of this covenant: *The Lord God will give him [Christ] the throne of David, his father* (Luke 1:32). God's covenant with David was fulfilled in Jesus, the Son of David.

A pivotal event in the early days of David's reign was the bringing of the ark of the covenant up to Jerusalem, thus making Jerusalem not only the political capital but also the religious centre of Israel. It was the ark, the symbol of God's presence, that made Jerusalem the holy city. Psalm 131(132) celebrates the bringing of the ark to Jerusalem (an event recorded in 2 Samuel 6). The psalm may originally have been sung at the feast of Tabernacles to recall the dedication of the temple and the establishment of God's covenant with David. The psalm can be read as a liturgy enacting the story of the bringing of the ark to Jerusalem.

O Lord, remember David
and all the many hardships he endured,
the oath he swore to the Lord,
his vow to the Strong One of Jacob.

The speaker may well be the king, who begins his prayer by asking the Lord to *remember David,* and so implicitly to remember David's successor, the present king, and the covenant God made with David's line. David's *many hardships* refers to the hardships he underwent in bringing the ark to Jerusalem and in preparing to build the first Temple. At the end of his life David said: 'With great pains I have provided for the house of the Lord' (1 Chronicles 22:14).

Apart from this psalm, there is no other tradition of David making the following *oath to the Lord. The Strong One of Jacob* was an ancient title for God which has survived only in Israel's poetry.

'I will not enter the house where I live . . .

The psalm now quotes David's vow to find a place for the ark, symbol of the Lord's presence. The identity between the ark and the presence of the Lord was so close that in speaking of finding a place for the ark the psalm speaks of finding *a place for the Lord, a dwelling for the Strong One of Jacob.*

At Ephrata we heard of the ark;
we found it in the plains of Yearim.
'Let us go to the place of his dwelling;
let us go to kneel at his footstool.'

Before David's time the ark was in the little village of Kiriath-Jearim (*in the plains of Yearim*) in the district of Ephrata, south of Jerusalem. 2 Samuel tells how David took a force of thirty thousand troops to Kiriath-Jearim 'to bring up the ark of God' (6:2). At this point the congregation enacts the bringing of the ark to Jerusalem. They accompany it from Kiriath-Jearim up to the Holy City, and exhort each other with the words: *'Let us go to the place of his dwelling; let us go to kneel at his footstool.'* The ark was the place where the glory of the Lord was enthroned, and so the Temple could be called *the place of his dwelling* and the ark *his footstool.* The congregation proceed to the Temple to pay homage to the Lord, the king of all the earth.

> *Go up, Lord, to the place of your rest,*
> *you and the ark of your strength.*
> *Your priests shall be clothed with holiness:*
> *your faithful shall ring out their joy.*

The ark is being carried in procession to the sanctuary, and at this point the priest cries out: *Go up, Lord, to the place of your rest.* The sanctuary of the Temple was the place where the ark rested. It is called *the ark of your strength* because the ark was the symbol of God's strength which protected Israel from her enemies. *Holiness* is literally 'righteousness', and is here equivalent to God's salvation and blessing. The priests are the channel of God's blessing to the people, so when they are *clothed* with such blessing they will impart it to the people, who will then *ring out their joy.*

> *For the sake of David your servant*
> *do not reject you anointed.*

This is the underlying prayer of the whole psalm. The king and people pray that God will give the blessing he promised to David's house to the reigning monarch, the son of David, *your anointed.* David served the Lord faithfully, and for David's *sake* the nation prays for God to bless the present king.

> *The Lord swore an oath to David;*
> *he will not go back on his word:*
> *'A son, the fruit of you body,*
> *will I set upon your throne.*

The rest of the psalm is a prophecy given by a Temple

prophet in response to the prayer for God's blessing on the king. The prophecy begins by recalling God's covenant with David, 'Your throne will be established for ever' (2 Samuel 7:16). In Jesus the covenant was fulfilled. The Apostle Peter quoted this verse in his Pentecost sermon with reference to the resurrection of Christ (Acts 2:30). Christ was the Son of David whom God established as king for ever.

> *If they keep my covenant in truth*
> *and my laws that I have taught them,*
> *their sons also shall rule*
> *on your throne from age to age.'*

A covenant involves two parties. God promised to maintain David's dynasty: David's sons were bound to *keep my covenant in truth and my laws that I have taught them.*

> *For the Lord has chosen Sion;*
> *he has desired it for his dwelling:*
> *'This is my resting-place for ever,*
> *here have I chosen to live.*

It is the presence of the divine king in Sion which is the source of Israel's blessing. In bringing the ark to Jerusalem David was fulfilling the will of the Lord. It is in the new Jerusalem that these promises find their fulfilment.

> *I will greatly bless her produce,*
> *I will fill her poor with bread.*
> *I will clothe her priests with salvation*
> *and her faithful shall ring out their joy.*

The consequence of the Lord's presence with his people and their faithfulness to his *laws* is abundant blessing, physical and spiritual, of both land and people. The *priests* are the mediators of God's blessing, as explained earlier in the psalm.

There David's stock will flower:
I will prepare a lamp for my anointed.
I will cover his enemies with shame
but on him my crown shall shine,'

This last verse assures the king that the house of David will not die out. His *stock will flower* and his *lamp* will always shine. The *lamp* was a metaphor for the continuation of the dynasty. As long as there was a successor to the Davidic king, then David's *lamp* would continue to shine. In speaking of a later king (Abijam), the writer of the Book of Kings said: 'For David's sake the Lord his God gave him a lamp in Jerusalem, setting up his son after him' (1 Kings 15:4).

Later Jewish tradition read the whole of the second part of the psalm as a messianic prophecy, and the Church built on this interpretation in applying the psalm to Christ. The Messiah is a light to the nations (a *lamp*), the *anointed* of the Lord. On Christ the authority, the *crown,* of the Lord rests.

Revelation 11:17—18; 12:10B—12A

See Week 1, Thursday Evening.

Week 3: Friday

MORNING PRAYER

The first two parts of the psalmody form a comprehensive confession of sin, personal and corporate. It is a confession of the sin we are directly responsible for, and of the sin we are responsible for as members of a Church which is a community of sinners, with all-too-obvious weaknesses and failings. The final psalm of the morning is the praise of a forgiven people, who sing: *How good is the Lord, eternal his merciful love.* (Psalm 99).

Psalm 50(51)

See Week 1, Friday Morning.

Jeremiah 14:17—21

Jeremiah prophesied in the midst of the most tragic years of Israel's history, before and during the sack of Jerusalem in 587 BC. This canticle is a communal lament on the ravages of war and reflects both the physical and spiritual devastation of Judah following her capture. It is a canticle for the Church, wherever she is decimated by violence or faithlessness.

> *Let my eyes run down with tears night and day,*
> *and let them not cease,*
> *for the virgin daughter of my people is smitten with a great wound,*
> *with a very grevious blow.*

The *great wound,* the *very grevious blow,* was the destruction of Jerusalem by Nebuchadnezzar, King of Babylon. His armies 'slew their young men with the sword in the house of their sanctuary, and had no compassion on young man or virgin, old man or aged . . . They burned the house of God, and broke down the wall of Jerusalem, and burned all its palaces with fire, and destroyed all its precious vessels' (2 Chronicles 36:17—19). It is difficult for us to appreciate the catastrophic effect this destruction had on the faith of the people, as well as on their physical state. All the promises God had made concerning the temple, the city, the king, the people – all seemed to go up in smoke. As a people they thought they were finished. God had abandoned them because of their sin. Hence the *tears run down night and day.* The *virgin daughter of my people* is a way of describing the nation, the chosen bride of the Lord.

If I go out into the field . . .

We are given a vivid picture of the horror of war and the famine which follows. The crops were burnt and the families who farmed the land were carried off into exile. Famine quickly set in. But tragically, those who should be able to give hope and leadership to the people in their devastation, *prophet and priest,* are as lost as their flock. They no longer have any *knowledge* of the Lord and his truth, because for so long they had been telling the people lies, telling them that peace was just around the corner, that everything would be all right.

Have you utterly rejected Judah?
Does your soul loath Sion?
Why then have you smitten us
so that there is no healing for us?

The most dreadful questions anyone in Israel could ever ask are now uttered. Is this the end of everything? Do we have nothing left to hope for? At the time, there were no answers.

We looked for peace,
but no good came,
for a time of healing,
but behold, terror.

All Israel's prophets, except Jeremiah, predicted that there would be no catastrophe, that their enemies would not destroy them, that the temple and the city would be secure, and that they could look forward to a time of *peace* and *healing.* Only Jeremiah told the truth. The same kind of Pollyanna optimism can blind the Church in any time of crisis.

We acknowledge our wickedness, O Lord,
and the iniquity of our fathers,
for we have sinned against you.
do not spurn us, for your name's sake,

do not dishonour your glorious throne;
remember and do not break your covenant with us.

All the people could do was confess their sins, an action they had been glaringly reluctant to take until it was too late, but at last the truth is out. It was their own persistent rebellion and disobedience to the covenant which brought about their downfall, and all they can do is plead for mercy and appeal to the Lord to give them another chance.

The **sentence** brings before us the command of our Lord Jesus at the beginning of his ministry: *The kingdom of God is at hand. Repent, and believe in the gospel* (Mark 1:15), and the Eastertide antiphon is God's new covenant: 'Christ bore our sins in his own body on the cross, alleluia.'

Psalm 99(100)

See Week 1, Friday Morning.

EVENING PRAYER

Psalm 134 offers praise to the Lord for the key events of Israel's salvation. The concluding canticle from Revelation enables us to bring the praise of God up to date, to praise him for his *great and wonderful deeds* done in Christ.

Psalm 134(135)

This psalm was undoubtedly sung at one of Israel's festivals, probably the feast of the Passover. Although it includes parts of other psalms (notably Psalm 115 and 136), Psalm 134(135) has a real unity and development of thought. The psalm gives thanks to the Lord for his work in creation and in Israel's history, and contrasts this with the futility of pagan idols who can do nothing.

Praise the name of the Lord . . .

The psalm begins with a call to all the worshippers (*servants of the Lord*) standing in the temple courts to join together to praise the Lord.

Praise the Lord for the Lord is good.
Sing a psalm to his name for he is loving.
For the Lord has chosen Jacob for himself
and Israel for his own possession.

We begin to hear the reasons why we should praise the Lord. The first of them is because of the way he has shown his goodness and love by choosing Israel to be his people. Israel's identity and value rested solely in the fact that the Lord had chosen her *for himself*. Israel belonged to the Lord alone. The **sentence** carries over this fact to the new Israel, the Church: *You are a chosen race. Sing the praises of the one who called you out of darkness into his wonderful light* (1 Peter 2:9).

For I know the Lord is great,
that our Lord is high above all gods.

Creation becomes the next reason why we should praise the Lord. In creation his greatness is revealed. He *does whatever he wills.*

He summons clouds from the ends of the earth;
makes lightning produce the rain.

Lightning often accompanies heavy rain in Palestine, but to say that the lightning *produces* the rain is poetry, not science.

The first-born of the Egyptians he smote,
of man and beast alike.
Signs and wonders he worked
in the midst of your land, O Egypt,
against Pharaoh and all his servants.

From creation we move to the Exodus. The psalm rehearses only the bare outline of events. The death of the *first-born* was the climax of the plagues sent on Egypt to make Pharaoh change his mind and let the people go. It was the catalyst for the Exodus. *Signs and wonders* are events that specifically reveal the majesty and glory of God. St John takes up the word *sign* and uses it in the same sense to describe Jesus' miracles.

Nations in their greatness he struck
and kings in their splendour he slew.
Sihon, king of the Amorites,
Og, king of Bashan,
and all the kingdoms of Canaan.
He let Israel inherit their land;
on his people their land he bestowed.

We skip straight from the flight out of Egypt to the entry into the promised land, leaving out the crossing of the Red Sea and all the wilderness events. *Sihon* and *Og* are singled out because they were the first kings defeated by Israel in their march into the promised land. The *Amorites* lived in the territory we today call Jordan. *Bashan* is in this area too. The story of the conquests is told in Numbers 21:21—35. The description of the land as Israel's *inheritance* makes a link back to the Lord's promise to Abraham, to give him the land as 'an everlasting possession' (Genesis 17:8).

Lord, your name stands for ever,
unforgotten from age to age:
for the Lord does justice for his people;
the Lord takes pity on his servants.

God's character as revealed in the Exodus is of one who liberates the oppressed, *does justice for his people,* the implication being that he will always act in this way. His character is unchanging, his *name stands for ever.*

Pagan idols are silver and gold,
the work of human hands . . .

These verses are repeated in Psalm 113B(115) (Week 2, Sunday Evening II). In contrast to the Lord, who has acted so powerfully in creation and in saving his people, the gods of the nations (*pagan idols*) are worthless. They are dead, lifeless, *the work of human hands,* having neither the will nor power to act. These idols seem to have all that is necessary for speech and action, but it is all a sham. Despite their *mouths, eyes, ears,* they are dumb, blind and deaf.

Their makers will come to be like them
and so will all who trust in them!

Idolatry is worse than useless. Those who worship idols become less than human. The psalm gives a warning to a society which makes the pursuit of wealth the supreme goal, the god. We become like the god we worship.

Sons of Israel, bless the Lord! . . .

The whole congregation, laity (*Sons of Israel*), priests (*Sons of Aaron*), Levites (*Sons of Levi*) – all God's faithful people are exhorted to come and praise the Lord.

Revelation 15:3—4

See Week 1, Friday Evening.

Week 3: Saturday

MORNING PRAYER

Psalm 118 and Wisdom 9 are prayers for the grace and wisdom of God, without which we cannot do his will. Psalm 116 is a joyful acclamation of praise.

Psalm 118(119):145—152 XIX(Koph)

See Week 1, Saturday Morning.

Wisdom 9:1—6,9—11

The Book of Wisdom is the latest book in the Old Testament. It was probably finished only a few decades before Christ. It was written in the Greek-speaking Jewish community of Alexandria, Egypt, and reflects the Greek preoccupation with wisdom. The author follows a popular literary convention of the time by putting his words into the mouth of one of the great heroes of Israel's past, in this case king Solomon. The canticle is an eloquent prayer for the gift of Wisdom and can be linked to Jesus' promise to his followers: *I myself will give you an eloquence and a wisdom that none of your opponents will be able to resist* (Luke 21:15), **sentence.**

O God of my fathers and Lord of mercy,
who have made all things by your word,
and by your wisdom have formed man . . .

Wisdom was said to be the agent through whom God created the world (Proverbs 8), and therefore equivalent to his *word.* What the Old Testament affirms of wisdom the New Testament affirms of Christ (Colossians 1:16), who is the wisdom of God (1 Corinthians 1:30). The Advent antiphon thus transforms the canticle into a prayer for the return of Christ.

The canticle declares that man was created to *rule the world* in the same way that God rules, *in holiness and righteousness,* and to dispense justice with *uprightness.* This is another way of expressing the fact that man is made in the image of God.

For I am your slave
and the son of your maidservant . . .

The whole expression means 'I am bound to you for life'. The son of a slave girl belonged to her master in perpetuity.

With you is wisdom . . .

The rest of the canticle is a straightforward prayer asking for this most precious of God's gifts, his wisdom, the wisdom through whom he made the world and who understands his will perfectly, the wisdom who *knows and understands all things.*

Psalm 116(117)

See Week 1, Saturday Morning.

Commentary on the Psalmody of Week 4

Week 4: Sunday

EVENING PRAYER I

Tonight's psalmody prepares us to celebrate the Eucharist. The first psalm brings us to the heavenly Jerusalem. In the second psalm we confess our dependence on God's mercy. The final canticle is a hymn to Christ, the suffering servant whom we worship as our risen Lord.

Psalm 121(122)

This is a pilgrim psalm, sung at the moment when the pilgrims arrive at the Temple in Jerusalem. The **sentence** (*You have come to Mount Zion and the city of the living God, the heavenly Jerusalem*) invites us to pray the psalm as we enter the new Jerusalem, the Church of God. Our gathering for the Eucharist today foreshadows our gathering to sing the praise of the Lamb in heaven.

> *I rejoiced when I heard them say:*
> *'Let us go to God's house.'*
> *And now our feet are standing*
> *within your gates, O Jerusalem.*

The pilgrims have arrived at their destination, and for a moment they recall the day they set out, the glad day when the call went out in the village: *'Let us go to God's house.'* Now they are there, surrounded by the splendour of the holy city.

Jerusalem is built as a city
strongly compact.
It is there that the tribes go up,
the tribes of the Lord.

The pilgrims are proud of the strength of the city walls and of the splendour of the royal palace and the temple. They state the reason why they are there: Jerusalem was the centre which bound the various tribes of Israel together in their worship of *the Lord.*

For Israel's Law it is,
there to praise the Lord's name.
There were set the thrones of judgement
of the house of David.

According to *Israel's law*, all males were bound to travel to Jerusalem to celebrate the three main feasts: Passover, Pentecost and Tabernacles (Deuteronomy 16:16—17).

Jerusalem was the spiritual centre of the nation, the site of the temple, but it was also the judicial centre, the site of *the thrones of judgement.* The king was the supreme judge in the country, the final court of appeal.

For the peace of Jerusalem pray:
'Peace be to your homes!
May peace reign in your walls,
in your palaces, peace!'

The pilgrims salute the city with the traditional greeting given on entering a home or community. *Peace!* Jerusalem was the city of peace, the city whose name meant 'Shalom'. The peace of the city was crucial for the peace and prosperity of the whole country. If the government is in strife the people suffer.

for love of my brethren and friends
I say: 'Peace upon you!'

For love of the house of the Lord
I will ask for your good.

The pilgrims' prayer for the peace of the city is motivated by their *love of the house of the Lord.* Jerusalem is above all the city of the Lord.

Psalm 129(130)

The whole psalm is a petition for forgiveness made in the context of worship. It is a psalm that takes us to the heart of the Gospel, to Jesus, whose name means: *He will save his people from their sins* (**sentence**).

Out of the depths I cry to you, O Lord,
Lord, hear my voice!
O let your ears be attentive
to the voice of my pleading.

The psalmist's offence against God has effected every part of his being and his *cry* to God for help is a *cry* of deepest distress, a cry from *the depths.* He feels he is sinking in a bottomless pit. He knows he is guilty and all he can do is *plead* for the Lord's forgiveness.

If you, O Lord, should mark our guilt,
Lord, who would survive?
But with you is found forgiveness:
for this we revere you.

If God was to chalk up (to *mark*) all our sins, *our guilt,* and punish them as they deserve, no one could ever stand before him, no one would survive a moment in his presence. But the Lord does not do this. Instead, with him *is found forgiveness,* and for this *we revere* him. To *revere,* or 'fear', the Lord means to stand in wonder and gratitude in the presence of the God of mercy, the God whose very nature it is to show mercy. This is our only hope and it is a sure hope.

My soul is counting on the Lord,
I count on his word.
My soul is longing for the Lord
more that watchman for daybreak.

The psalmist's hope is centred wholly on God and his mercy. He waits patiently for the *word* of forgiveness to be pronounced by the priest. He waits for the Lord with the same mixture of anxiety and certainty that the *watchman* feels as he stays awake at his post, sensitive to danger, longing for the morning to come. And come it surely will, as surely as God's forgiveness:

Let the watchman count on daybreak
and Israel on the Lord.

Because with the Lord there is mercy
and fulness of redemption,
Israel indeed he will redeem
from all its iniquity.

The psalm moves from *the depths* of despair into the *fulness of redemption* experienced in Christ, 'in whom we have redemption, the forgiveness of sins' (Colossians 1:14), mercy not just for the individual but for the whole Church, the *Israel* of God.

Philippians 2:6—11

See Week 1, Sunday Evening I.

MORNING PRAYER

Psalm 117(118)

See Week 2, Sunday Morning.

Daniel 3:52—57

See Week 2, Sunday Morning.

Psalm 150

See Week 2, Sunday Morning.

EVENING PRAYER II

Jesus is Lord (Psalm 109), and those who worship him will be richly blessed, and in turn will be a blessing to others. They will be 'children of the light' (Psalm 111). They will rejoice with all God's saints at the marriage feast of the Lamb (Revelation 19).

Psalm 109(110)

See Week 1, Sunday Evening II.

Psalm 111(112)

This psalm is a companion to Psalm 110(111) (Week 3, Sunday Evening II). In structure it is an acrostic psalm, each new line beginning with the next letter of the Hebrew alphabet. The purpose of the psalm is to describe the blessings which will come to the one who is faithful to the Lord. The faithful are to reflect in their lives the character of God. *Be like children of the light; for the fruits of the light are seen in complete goodness and right living and truth* (Ephesians 5:8—9), **sentence.**

The psalm reflects a peaceful and settled era in Israel's history, and does not wrestle, as other psalms do, with the suffering of the righteous. The antiphon for use during the year (Blessed are those who hunger and thirst for justice, for they shall have their fill) interprets the psalm in the light of the beatitudes of Christ, whose blessings begin now with the gift of the Spirit, but only reach their perfection in heaven.

Happy the man who fears the Lord,
who takes delight in all his commands.
His sons will be powerful on earth;
the children of the upright are blessed.

It is the one who 'hears these words of mine and does them' (Matthew 7:24) who will be blessed, he and his whole family. Parents who seek to live in love and obedience to the Lord become the channels of God's blessing to their children.

Riches and wealth are in his house;
his justice stands firm for ever.
He is a light in the darkness for the upright:
he is generous, merciful and just.

In the Old Testament wealth and prosperity were accepted as signs of God's favour as long as they were honest gains. At the heart of God's covenant with Israel is a connection between obedience to God's commands and the prosperity of the land. The land and the people are a unity, and blessing for one means blessing for the other. But wealth is never to be selfishly hoarded. It is to be used to care for the 'orphans and widows'. And so the righteous man *is generous, merciful and just,* not a tight-fisted millionaire locked into his walled enclave. He is to be an example to others, *a light in the darkness.*

Jesus saw that *riches* could be a major obstacle to knowing God, and he shocked his disciples with his word that the rich would find it very hard to enter the kingdom of God (Luke 18:18—30). He promised to those who leave everything to follow him the richness and blessing (material and spiritual) of the community of faith.

The good man takes pity and lends,
he conducts his affairs with honour.
The just man will never waver:
he will be remembered for ever.

The rich man in the Old Testament was not, as is so common in our world, a greedy tycoon only out for profit. He was often a man of compassion, a man *who takes pity,* who *conducts his affairs with honour* and integrity.

He has no fear of evil news;
with a firm heart he trusts in the Lord.
With a steadfast heart he will not fear;
he will see the downfall of his foes.

The just man is not insulated from disaster and evil, but when it comes *he has no fear* because *he trusts in the Lord.* He knows that in the end the Lord will vindicate the faithful.

Open-handed , he gives to the poor . . .

Again, the generosity of the just is underlined, along with the ultimate downfall of the *wicked.* The God who is generous expects those who follow him to be generous too.

The psalm finishes with the warning that the plans of the wicked, their *desires,* lead to nothing.

Revelation 19:1—2,5—7

See Week 1, Sunday Evening II.

1 Peter 2:21—24

See Week 1, Sunday Evening II.

Week 4: Monday

MORNING PRAYER

This morning's psalmody offers a rich diet. The common theme of the three passages is the God who acts to save his people. Psalm 89 is a prayer which takes us into the heart of human weakness and frailty seen in the light of God's eternity. The canticle from Isaiah is an exuberant song of praise for the 'new thing' God will do in redeeming his captive people. The final psalm (134) invites us *to sing the praises of the one who called you out of darkness into his wonderful light.*

Psalm 89(90)

The psalm contrasts the eternal glory of God with the fleeting frailty of humanity. The language of the psalm has a solemn grandeur that enhances its message. It has the form of a communal lament, although it is impossible to discern the original nature of the distress. Behind much of the psalm lies the story of the creation and fall in Genesis 2—3. The psalm challenges us to face up to our limits, to acknowledge that we are God's creatures, and so to *gain wisdom,* a true perspective on what is important in life.

> *O Lord, you have been our refuge*
> *from one generation to the next.*

The psalmist looks back over the nation's history and recalls the ways in which the Lord has delivered his people from many dangers; he has been *our refuge* to successive generations.

> *Before the mountains were born*
> *or the earth brought forth*
> *you are God, without beginning or end.*

From his nation's history the psalmist turns to creation for signs of God's faithfulness. The mountains are creation's most dramatic examples of stability and permanence, but God preceded even these. He is eternal, in a way that his creatures can hardly grasp.

You turn men back into dust
and say: 'Go back, sons of men.'

From the eternal nature of God the psalm turns to the frailty of human life. God said to Adam and Eve the words repeated by the priest to each penitent in the Ash Wednesday liturgy: 'You are dust, and to dust you shall return' (Genesis 3:19). Death is acknowledged to be in God's hand. He it is who turns *men back into dust.*

To your eyes a thousand years
are like yesterday, come and gone,
no more than a watch in the night.

God's time and our time are dramatically different, like the contrast between a *thousand years* and a single day or a four-hour *watch in the night,* which for the lone watchman can seem like an eternity.

You sweep men away like a dream,
like grass which springs up in the morning.
In the morning it springs up and flowers:
by evening it withers and fades.

The whole of human existence, birth and death, is in God's hand. He is Lord of our coming into the world and our going from it. Compared to his eternity, our life is as fleeting as *a dream* or as *grass* in the searing desert.

So we are destroyed in your anger
struck down with terror in your fury.
Our guilt lies open before you;
our secrets in the light of your face.

The primal sin according to Genesis 3 was the sin of pride,

refusing to accept the limits God had set. The purpose of this psalm is to teach us to acknowledge those limits. After Adam and Eve disobeyed the Lord's clear command they were judged, and their punishment was given in the words the psalm has already quoted: 'You are dust, and to dust you shall return' (Genesis 3:19). Death is therefore understood as God's punishment for sin. It is an expression of his *anger* at human disobedience. The psalmist acknowledges this with the words: *Our guilt lies open before you.* In varying degrees we are all guilty of Adam's sin, of pride in the presence of God, of disobedience to his clear commands.

The link between sin and death is also made by St Paul in Romans 5: 'As sin came into the world through one man and death through sin, and so death spread to all men because all men sinned . . . As one man's trespass led to condemnation for all men, so one man's act of righteousness leads to acquittal and life for all men' (Romans 5:12,18). What we lost in Adam has been restored in Christ. In Christ God's *anger* has been turned away, and eternal life promised to all who are joined to Christ. 'As in Adam all die, so in Christ shall all be made alive' (1 Corinthians 15:22). The Christian still suffers the death of the body, but does so 'in sure and certain hope of the resurrection to eternal life, through our Lord Jesus Christ.'

All our days pass away in your anger.
Our life is over like a sigh.
Our span is seventy years
or eighty for those who are strong.

Not only our death, but also the frailty and shortness of our life is seen as a result of God's anger. Sin has torn the whole fabric of life, a theme which is continued in the next verse.

And most of these are emptiness and pain.
They pass swiftly and we are gone.
Who understands the power of your anger
and fears the strength of your fury?

Again the reference is to Genesis 3 and to God's punishment of Adam: 'Cursed is the ground because of you; in toil you shall eat of it all the days of your life . . . In the sweat of your face you shall eat bread till you return to the ground. (3:17,19).

The psalmist is not wanting to say that human life consists only of toil and trouble (although for some people this is all too true), but he is wanting to puncture self-sufficiency and pride, in order to bring us to a true realism about our life and its limits and our responsibility to God. The climax of his appeal comes in the words:

> *Make us know the shortness of our life*
> *that we may gain wisdom of heart.*
> *Lord, relent! Is your anger for ever?*
> *Show pity to your servants.*

The psalmist wants to engender in us true wisdom, an honest facing up to death, to the *shortness of our life,* and in the light of this to live in God's truth, to *gain wisdom of heart.* The psalm is a meditation on the foundation principle of Israel's Wisdom tradition: 'The fear of the Lord is the beginning of wisdom.' There may have been some particular distress which provoked the psalm and the prayer, *Show pity to your servants!*

> *In the morning, fill us with your love;*
> *we shall exult and rejoice all our days.*
> *Give us joy to balance our affliction*
> *for the years when we knew misfortune.*

The psalmist's prayer may have been offered in a night vigil, and so he asks for an answer *in the morning.* Or the morning may refer to the coming of the light which drives away the darkness of night, symbol of the present suffering of the nation. He prays for the Lord to *fill* them *with his love,* his covenant love, which will rescue them now as in the past. Their *affliction* has obviously lasted many years (the exile?), and so they long for a similar period of *joy*. Behind the urgent plea for God's *love* is an awareness of the shortness of life.

> *Show forth your work to your servants;*
> *let your glory shine on their children.*
> *Let the favour of the Lord be upon us:*
> *give success to the work of our hands*
> *give success to the work of our hands.*

God's work of salvation, his coming to deliver his *servants* from their troubles, is the *work* which the psalmist longs to see. He prays for God's *glory,* for the acts which show his majesty and power, to *shine on their children.* And despite his acute sense of the shortness and pain of human life, the psalmist concludes with a fervent prayer for the *success* of the *work of our hands,* our toil in the fields or in the city. When the Lord acts to *show forth* his *work,* then he will *give success to the work of our hands.* The only work which lasts is the work which is blessed by God.

Isaiah 42:10—16

Deutero-Isaiah has prophesied to the exiles in Babylon that the time of their captivity is drawing to an end, that the Lord will act as he did at the Exodus to deliver his people from their oppressors. As yet there are no signs of this redemption, but Deutero-Isaiah is so sure of the Lord's action that he calls on the exiles, indeed on the whole world, to join in praise for the Lord's deliverance.

> *Sing to the Lord a new song,*
> *his praise to the end of the earth!*
> *Let the sea roar and all that fills it. . . .*

The *new song* is necessary because the Lord is about to do a new thing, to come in sovereign power to save his people as he did at the time of the Exodus. The Lord goes as far as to say: 'Forget the past: look, I am doing a new thing!' (Isaiah 43:18,19). The **sentence** (*They were singing a new hymn before the throne of God* (Revelation 14:3)) brings into the praise the the new thing which God did in Christ.

The prophet calls on the whole world to join the exiles in praise of the Lord. He calls on *the sea* and all its creatures to *roar* their praise; the furthest islands (*the coastlands*) and their peoples to join in, with *the desert* peoples who live in the oases. Through the same desert which Israel travelled on the way to her captivity she will return in triumph. *Kedar* is the Arabian desert separating Babylon and Israel. *Sela* is a mountainous region on the southern borders of Israel, so its *inhabitants* are invited to *shout from the top of the mountains.* All Israel's neighbours are summoned to join in praise of the Lord, the creator of the earth and of its inhabitants, for his deliverance of his people. God's action is to take place in full view of the world, and the world is called on to *declare his praise.*

The Lord goes forth like a mighty man . . .

The Lord's coming to save his people is now described in terms drawn from Israel's earliest traditions, especially of the Exodus, in which the Lord appeared as a warrior ready to do battle on behalf of his people. The reason the prophet draws on this tradition is to say to the exiles: 'As God acted in the past, so he will act now. The God whose deliverance our ancestors praised is the God who is coming to our rescue now!'

For a long time I have held my peace,
I have kept still and restrained myself;
now I will cry out like a woman in travail,
I will gasp and pant.

From here to the end of the canticle it is the Lord who speaks through his prophet. During the long years of Israel's captivity the Lord has been silent (*I have held my peace*), but this has not been the silence of a God who could not care what was happening to his people, but of a God who could hardly restrain himself from acting. He had to wait until the time was right, until the 'new thing' had had time to grow like a baby in the womb. Now the time has come for the child to be born, for the deliverance to begin. *Now I will cry out like a woman in travail.* The rebirth of the nation is about to happen. God is a mother whose compassion for her children impels her to act, who gives birth to salvation.

> *I will lay waste mountains and hills,*
> *and dry up all their herbage;*
> *I will turn rivers into islands,*
> *and dry up the pools.*

These verses describe what will happen to the country which is holding Israel captive. The Lord's coming will bring salvation for his people but disaster for their oppressors, whose land will be turned into a desert.

> *And I will lead the blind*
> *in a way that they know not;*
> *in paths that they have not known*
> *I will guide them.*
> *I will turn the darkness before them into light,*
> *the rough places into level ground.*

Blindness and darkness sum up the present condition of the exiles. They see nothing ahead for them, no future. They think they have been forsaken by God, but he is about to *turn the darkness before them into light, the rough places* (which terrify the blind) *into level ground* on which they can walk secure and safe, on a *path that they have not known,* the path of deliverance.

Psalm 134(135):1—12

See Week 3, Friday Evening.

EVENING PRAYER

Psalm 135 was Israel's great hymn of praise sung at the conclusion of the Passover meal. It rehearses the *works of the Lord* in delivering his people and expresses the basic faith of the people of God in the confession: *his love endures for ever.* The glorious extent of God's love is celebrated in the final canticle, where we praise the one *who has blessed us in Christ with every spiritual blessing.*

Psalm 135(136)

This psalm was known to the Jews as the Great Hallel, the 'Great Praise' (in contrast to the Egyptian Hallel, Psalms 113—118). The Great Hallel concluded the Passover meal, and was the 'hymn' Jesus and his disciples sang at the conclusion of the Last Supper as he went to Gethsemane and to the cross (Matthew 26:30). Its use in the Easter liturgy continues this tradition.

In the Temple worship the psalm was probably sung antiphonally, with a priest or choir taking the first line and the congregation singing the response: *for his love endures for ever.* The theme of the psalm is God's wonders in creation, the Exodus, the entry to the promised land and the return from exile.

> *O give thanks to the Lord for he is good,*
> *for his love endures for ever. . . .*

The psalm opens with a call to worship the Lord who is *the God of gods,* the supreme God who rules over all other spiritual beings, all other *gods.* He is *the Lord of lords,* the ruler over all earthly rulers and kings.

The response: *for his love endures for ever,* is Israel's fundamental statement of faith. *Love* is the covenant love by which God bound himself to his people, the faithful *love* on which their whole life depends, the *love* to which they turn in their times of trouble.

who alone has wrought marvellous works . . .
whose wisdom it was made the skies . . .
who fixed the earth firmly on the seas . . .

These verses which begin the praise of God as creator are inspired by Genesis 1 and the Wisdom tradition of Israel. God's *marvellous works* are the works which reveal his nature and glory. *Wisdom* features in the Wisdom literature as the instrument by which God created the world. (See the canticle from Wisdom 9, Week 3, Saturday Morning). In creation, according to Hebrew thought, God tamed the waters of chaos (*the seas*) and *fixed the earth firmly* in place.

It was he who made the great lights . . .
the sun to rule in the day . . .
the moon and the stars in the night . . .

In contrast to Israel's neighbours, many of whom worshipped the sun, moon and stars as gods who controlled human destiny, Israel knew that these *lights* were created by the Lord God and under his control. He is the one who controls human destiny, not the *stars.* (A message that still needs to be proclaimed in an age of horoscopes).

The first-born of the Egyptians he smote . . .
He brought Israel out from their midst . . .
arm outstretched, with power in his hand . . .

We move from the Lord as creator to the Lord as redeemer of his people, the Lord who liberated Israel at the Exodus. The death of *the first-born of the Egyptians* was the climax of the plagues sent on Egypt to make Pharaoh change his mind and let the people go. It was the catalyst for the Exodus.

Arm outstretched, with power in his hand is a favourite phrase in the Book of Deuteronomy. It is a vivid way of describing the irresistible power of the Lord in delivering

Israel from her oppressors.

He divided the Red Sea in two . . .
he made Israel pass through the midst . . .
he flung Pharaoh and his force in the sea . . .

Here we have the central events of the Exodus. The psalm constantly underlines the action of God in every part of the drama.

Through the desert his people he led . . .
Nations in their greatness he struck . . .
Kings in their splendour he slew . . .

Despite their repeated failings in the *desert*, the refrain (*for his love endures for ever*) drives home the fact that the Lord never deserted his people, but continued to deliver them from their enemies, powerful *nations* and *kings*.

Sihon, king of the Amorites . . .
and Og, king of Bashan . . .

Sihon and Og are singled out because they were the first kings defeated by Israel in the conquest of the promised land. The *Amorites* lived in the territory we today call Jordan. *Bashan* is in this area too. The story of the conquests is told in Numbers 21:21—35.

He let Israel inherit their land . . .
On his servant their land he bestowed . . .

The description of the land as Israel's *inheritance* makes a link back to the Lord's promise to Abraham, to give him the land as 'an everlasting possession' (Genesis 17:8).

He remembered us in our distress . . .
And he snatched us away from our foes . . .

These two lines probably refer to the Lord's deliverance of Israel from exile in Babylon, although they could apply to many events in the nation's history.

He gives food to all living things . . .
To the God of heaven give thanks . . .

God's care for all the living was a theme of the feast of Tabernacles and may link the psalm to this feast. The *God of heaven* is a title for the Lord found only here in the psalms. It came into use after the exile as a way of expressing the supreme glory of God.

Ephesians 1:3—10

See Week 1, Monday Evening.

Week 4: Tuesday

MORNING PRAYER

The struggle for justice is the theme of today's psalmody. The first psalm is a ruler's vow of just government. The canticle (Daniel 3) is the prayer of a nation suffering injustice. The final psalm (143) is a king's prayer for help in the task of defending the realm. Anyone who is joined to Christ begins to walk a 'narrow way', a way that involves a struggle against sin and a struggle for righteousness.

Psalm 100(101)

At first sight this psalm seems to be a classic example of self-righteousness, and some of its phrases grate on our ears. But when the psalm is put in its original context it takes on a completely different complexion. The psalm is a king's vow, probably made on the occasion of his coronation and renewed annually, in which he makes a solemn commitment to just government and pledges his personal loyalty to the covenant God has made with Israel and the house of David.

The title is: Declaration of a Just Ruler. Underlying the psalm is the king's calling to be God's representative on earth.

In our prayer the psalm can become an expression of our commitment to the commandments of the new covenant. Jesus said: *If you love me, keep my commandments,* (**sentence**). Anyone who exercises authority, either as a pastor, parent, teacher, employer, is challenged by the vows made in this psalm.

> *My song is of mercy and justice;*
> *I sing to you, O Lord.*

The *mercy* and *justice* which are the themes of this song are the *mercy* and *justice* of the Lord, the Lord's covenant loyalty (*mercy*) to the house of David, and the *justice* which is the Lord's gift to the king to enable him to rule justly.

> *I will walk in the way of perfection.*
> *O when, Lord, will you come?*

The king vows to live with integrity, in complete harmony with the commandments of the law. *Perfection* does not mean absolute moral *perfection* but commitment to God's commandments. It is this loyalty which makes him bold to ask directly for God's help: *O when, Lord, will you come?*

> *I will walk with blameless heart*
> *within my house;*
> *I will not set before my eyes*
> *whatever is base.*

The king's *house* includes his family and his court, and in this the centre of his kingdom he promises integrity of *heart,* a heart and mind set on the ways of the Lord. The king recognizes that honest government begins with personal integrity.

Whatever is base is a reference to idols. Many of Israel's kings were entangled in by idol worship, sometimes introduced by their foreign wives. The king vows to eschew idols.

I will hate the ways of the crooked;
they shall not be my friends.
The false-hearted must keep far away;
the wicked I disown.

The king is resolved to banish from among his counsellors and advisors (*friends*) anyone who is *crooked, false-hearted,* or *wicked,* that is, anyone who is immoral, deceitful, or blatantly disobedient to the Lord.

The man who slanders his neighbour in secret
I will bring to silence.
The man of proud looks and haughty heart
I will never endure.

To *slander* one's *neighbour* refers to intrigue which can undermine government and to false testimony against someone charged with a crime. Such slanderers will get short shrift in the king's court. The *man of proud looks* is the man who exercises authority arrogantly, and so alienates the people from their king. Such men will not be tolerated.

I look to the faithful in the land
that they may dwell with me.
He who walks in the way of perfection
shall be my friend.

The king now describes the kind of men he will appoint to administer the land. *The faithful* are those who are faithful firstly to the Lord and then to the king. They will *dwell* with him, in his court. Those who walk *in the way of perfection* are those who share the king's commitment to the commandments of the Law.

No man who practices deceit
shall live within my house.
No man who utters lies shall stand
before my eyes.

The king singles out those who will not serve in his administration: the deceitful and liars. Honesty and truthfulness will be the hallmarks of his rule.

Morning by morning I will silence
all the wicked in the land,
uprooting from the city of the Lord
all who do evil.

The last verse of the psalm deals with the king as judge. The court in Jerusalem sat each morning (*morning by morning*). The king vows to administer true justice, to *silence the wicked,* those who have broken the law, and to uproot *all who do evil.* If only Israel's kings had lived by this vow!

Daniel 3:3,4,6,11—18

The book of Daniel was composed during the reign of one of the cruellest tyrants of all time, the Greek king Antiochus Epiphanes, who ruled Palestine from 175—164 BC In order to protect himself from the charge of writing subversive literature, the author of Daniel set his book during the reign of Nebuchadnezzar king of Babylon, some four centuries earlier. The canticle is a communal lament describing the desperate plight of the people who are without temple or sacrifice, both being forbidden by Antiochus. In the canticle Israel makes confession to the Lord for her sin, and prays for the Lord to remember his covenant and show mercy. As the **sentence** indicates, the canticle can express the Christian's confession, and the confession of the Church in the times of its unfaithfulness to the Gospel. *Repent and turn to God, that your sins may be wiped out.* (Acts 3:19).

Blessed are you, O Lord, God of our fathers . . .

The canticle begins by calling on the Lord who acted so powerfully in the past, for *our fathers.*

You are just . . .

The people confess that their present sufferings are a punishment for their past sins.

For your name's sake
do not give us up utterly,
and do not break your covenant.

Here we move into the heart of the prayer. As at the time of the exile, Israel's terrible fear is that the Lord has at last given up on his people. Because they have blatantly spurned their obligations under the covenant, they are afraid that God will decide to abandon his commitment to them. If this happens they will have nothing left to live for.

Do not withdraw your mercy from us
for the sake of Abraham your beloved . . .

The people now remind the Lord of his covenant, a covenant made with each of the patriarchs, with *Abraham, Isaac,* and *Israel.* To each the Lord *promised to make their descendants as many as the stars of heaven and as the sand on the shore of the sea.* (See Genesis 15 and 22:17).

For we, O Lord, have become fewer than any nation,
and are brought low this day in all the world
because of our sins;
and at this time there is no prince, or prophet, or leader,
no burnt offering, or sacrifice, or oblation, or incense,
no place to make an offering before you
or to find mercy.

The persecution of Antiochus Epiphanes threatened the very survival of the nation. He intended to wipe out the Jewish population of Jerusalem and colonize the city with Greeks, and to this end one of his generals entered the city on the sabbath, slaughtered most of the men, and carried off the women and children into slavery. Antiochus later decided to depopulate the whole of Judea and lay it waste. The guerrilla campaign of Judas Maccabaeus in 165 finally succeeded in turning back the holocaust, but only in the nick of time. The description of the state of the nation in this canticle is no exaggeration. Antiochus banned the worship of the Temple and built an altar to Zeus over the altar of burnt offering. Many Jewish leaders, including the high priest, capitulated to his demands.

Yet with a contrite heart and a humble spirit
may we be accepted,
as though it were with burnt offerings of rams and bulls
and with tens of thousands of fat lambs.

Although worship in the temple is impossible, the people pray that their acknowledgement of their sin and their sincere repentance will be *accepted* by the Lord as much as the most extravagant *burnt offerings.*

Such may our sacrifice be in your sight this day,
and may we wholly follow you,
for there will be no shame
for those who trust in you.

The people offer more than their repentance. They offer their resolve to *wholly follow* the Lord, to put all their *trust* in him.

Psalm 143(144):1—10

The psalm is the prayer of Israel's king, threatened by military attack from a nation which had previously pledged friendship. The treaty is broken, the enemy forces are forming, and the king pleads with the Lord to come to his aid.

The enemies against which we wrestle are not 'flesh and blood', but 'the wiles of the devil, . . . the spirits of evil' (Ephesians 6:10,12). The psalm becomes the prayer of all those who struggle against evil, against overwhelming temptation. The psalm enables us to say with St Paul: *I can do all things with the help of the One who gives me strength* (Philippians 4:13), **sentence.**

Blessed be the Lord, my rock
who trains my arms for battle,
who prepares my hands for war.

The king looks to the Lord for the skills he needs to defend the realm. The Lord is his *rock,* his secure defence, the one who comes to *train* and *prepare* him for the battle ahead. For the Christian this verse can be understood in the context of the spiritual warfare into which we are initiated by baptism and for which we are prepared by Christ.

He is my love, my fortress . . .

The king piles up a magnificent host of images, all of which speak of the Lord as his defence and his guarantee of victory.

Lord, what is man that you care for him . . .

This question brings out the psalmist's humility, and his sense of wonder that God in all his majesty and power should bother to come to his aid, he who is so frail and ephemeral, whose life is so short.

Lower your heavens and come down;
touch the mountains; wreathe them in smoke.
Flash your lightnings; rout the foe,
shoot your arrows and put them to flight.

The king now appeals for the Lord to come as he came of old on Mount Sinai, to the accompaniment of volcanic eruption, thunder and lightning (God's *arrows*). Such a coming will be sure to *rout the foe.*

Reach down from heaven and save me;
draw me out from the mighty waters,
from the hands of alien foes

whose mouths are filled with lies,
whose hands are raised in perjury.

Here we see the face of the foe and sense the strength of their forces. Against their armies the king feels as though he is in the grip of the waters of chaos (*the mighty waters*) which God conquered at the creation. His enemies have broken their treaty (*their mouths are filled with lies,* their *hands are raised in perjury*). When someone took an oath they raised their right hand towards heaven, appealing to God as a witness (Deuteronomy 32:40). His enemies have lied under oath.

To you, O God, will I sing a new song;
I will play on the ten-stringed harp
to you who give kings their victory,
who set David your servant free.

The king concludes by making a vow to return to the Temple after the *victory to sing a new song* to God, a song of thanksgiving for God's deliverance. The deliverance of the successor of David will be the deliverance of *David* himself.

EVENING PRAYER

The psalmody moves from despair (Psalm 136), to thanksgiving (Psalm 137), to the hymn of the redeemed in heaven (Revelation 4).

Psalm 136(137):1—6

Psalm 136 is the song of one of the exiles, possibly a Temple musician who was old enough to remember Jerusalem before its fall in 587 BC, one who has lived though the long years of captivity in Babylon. Some scholars go further and say the psalmist must have been one of the first to return to

Jerusalem, because the psalm seems to be written from Jerusalem looking back on the bitter past. The Christian prays the psalm as an expression of longing for the new Jerusalem, the Church, and for its renewal in times of disaster.

By the rivers of Babylon
there we sat and wept,
remembering Sion;
on the poplars that grew there
we hung up our harps.

Babylon was built close to the River Euphrates and the city was crossed by many canals which drew water from the Euphrates. The exile remembers how he and his countrymen sat beside these tree-lined *rivers of Babylon . . . and wept* with anguish as they *remembered Sion,* their home and the dwelling place of the Lord. They were so depressed that they *hung up* their *harps,* they could not even sing the hymns of their faith.

For it was there that they asked us,
our captors, for songs,
our oppressors, for joy.
'Sing to us,' they said,
'one of Sion's songs.'

The Babylonians taunted the exiles by asking them to sing *'one of Sion's songs,'* one of the psalms which extol Sion as the impregnable fortress, the city where the Lord God dwells, the city which he will deliver from all its enemies, the city they (the Babylonians) have conquered and reduced to rubble.

O how could we sing
the song of the Lord
on alien soil?

To sing one of the songs in praise of Sion's greatness when

Sion lies in ruins is impossible, especially amongst the very people who destroyed the city.

If I forget you, Jerusalem,
let my right hand wither!

O let my tongue
cleave to my mouth
if I remember you not,
If I prize not Jerusalem
above all my joys!

The psalmist makes a double vow never to forget Jerusalem. He would rather never play the harp (*let my right hand wither*) or sing (*let my tongue cleave to my mouth*) again, than forget Jerusalem and all it stands for. For many years after the return from exile the people got on with building their own houses and left the house of the Lord to lie in ruins (Haggai 1:9), and the psalmist may be lamenting such distorted priorities. What comes first?

Psalm 137(138)

The psalm begins with thanksgiving for the Lord's help, moves to praise of the majesty and glory of God, and concludes with the psalmist's confession of faith. The Eastertide antiphon shows how we can pray the psalm with Christ after his resurrection: 'In the midst of affliction you have given me life, alleluia.'

I thank you, Lord, with all my heart,
you have heard the words of my mouth. . . .

The psalmist has been in trouble of some kind, he has prayed to the Lord for help, and his prayer has been answered. He comes to the Temple where the Lord is present with all his *angels,* to *adore,* to worship the Lord with thanksgiving.

I will thank you for your faithfulness and love
which excel all we ever knew of you.
On the day I called, you answered;
you increased the strength of my soul.

The theme of his thanksgiving is the Lord's *faithfulness and love,* his unshakable loyalty to his covenant with his chosen people. The *strength of soul,* the restored vitality and hope the psalmist received in answer to his prayer, is the sign to him of God's love.

All earth's kings shall thank you
when they hear the words of your mouth.
They shall sing of the Lord's ways:
'How great is the glory of the Lord!'

On the basis of his own experience of God's grace, the psalmist looks forward to the day when all nations (*all earth's kings*) will praise the Lord and bow in adoration before him. The **sentence** declares that this day will indeed come when Christ's kingdom is established. *The kings of the earth will bring glory and honour to the holy city* (cf. Revelation 21:24). The *words of your mouth* are the promises God made to Israel, promises which are enshrined in the covenant.

The Lord is high yet he looks on the lowly
and the haughty he knows from afar.
Though I walk in the midst of affliction
you give me life and frustrate my foes.

The fulness of God is encompassed in these two characteristics: he is *high, yet he looks on the lowly.* The Lord is the majestic creator of heaven and earth, and yet he stoops to lift up the *lowly,* the helpless, the suffering, those who *walk in the midst of affliction.* The only ones he cannot help are the *haughty,* the proud, those who never ask for his help.

You stretch out your hand and save me,
your hand will do all things for me.
Your love, O Lord, is eternal,
discard not the work of your hands.

The one who is on *high* comes like a loving mother to *stretch out* her *hand* to *save* her child, the *work of your hands.* The psalmist entrusts his whole future to the *hand* that saves. *Your hand will do all things for me.*

The concluding confession of faith extols the Lord's *faithfulness and love* for which the psalmist has earlier given thanks. His *love is eternal,* ever sure, always to be trusted. The Lord will never *discard the work* of his *hands.*

Revelation 4:11, 5:9,10,11,12

See Week 1, Tuesday Evening.

Week 4: Wednesday

MORNING PRAYER

The first psalm is a prayer for help in the fight *against the foe.* The canticle gives a glorious vision of God's salvation, pictured as the Lord coming to marry Jerusalem. The Lord's coming always brings justice for the oppressed (Psalm 145).

Psalm 107(108)

Those who returned from the exile faced the task of rebuilding the nation. Psalm 107 became a vital expression of one aspect of that task – reclaiming the land of promise. The psalm joins together two sections of earlier psalms (57 and 60), the first offering praise for God's help in delivering

Israel, the second being a prophetic oracle defining the ideal boundaries of the land.

My heart is ready, O God;
I will sing, sing your praise.
Awake, my soul;
awake, lyre and harp.
I will awake the dawn.

The opening verses are a perfect beginning to morning prayer. In its original setting the first part of the psalm was the prayer of the king in the temple before daybreak praying for God's help in a military campaign he is about to embark on. They form the Christian's prayer as s/he puts on the armour of Christ and takes up the daily struggle against evil and injustice. The approaching dawn is a symbol of the light of God's presence coming to guide and direct us. (In popular mythology Dawn was pictured as a goddess who needed to be woken each day).

I will thank you, Lord, among the peoples,
among the nations I will praise you,
for your love reaches to the heavens
and your truth to the skies.
O God, arise above the heavens;
may your glory shine on earth!

The reason for the psalmist's praise and the whole basis for his confidence and joy is God's covenant loyalty, his *love* which *reaches to the heavens*; and his faithfulness (*truth*), his promise to save and bless his chosen people. In his exaltation the psalmist calls on God to *arise* as the sun rises in morning glory. As the glory of the sun lights up the whole earth, so he prays that the glory of the Lord will *shine* on *the nations.*

O come and deliver your friends;
help with your right hand and reply.

The psalmist prays that the Lord will come in might (his *right hand*) and answer his cry for help.

> *From his holy place God has made this promise:*
> *'I will triumph and divide the land of Shechem;*
> *I will measure out the valley of Succoth.*
> *Gilead is mine and Manasseh.*

The second part of the psalm (from Psalm 59(60)) is an ancient prophetic oracle setting the ideal boundaries of the promised land. The exiles reclaim the land they lost through disobedience, and they do so by reciting this ancient tradition of God's gift of the land to their forefathers. The oracle stresses that the land is the Lord's to divide how he wills: *I will . . . divide the land.*

Shechem was an ancient city north of Jerusalem. The *valley of Succoth* was a large territory on the east bank of the Jordan. They were the first places Jacob settled in on his return to Canaan, and together they represent the whole land, east and west of the Jordan, promised to Jacob and his descendants.

Gilead and Manasseh are territories east of the Jordan.

> *Ephraim I take for my helmet,*
> *Judah for my commander's staff.*
> *Moab I will use for my washbowl,*
> *on Edom I will plant my shoe.*
> *Over the Philistines I will shout in triumph.'*

The Lord is here dressed for battle! *Ephraim* was the northern kingdom of Israel and *Judah* the southern kingdom. *Ephraim,* the most powerful of the tribes, is his *helmet. Judah,* from which came the Davidic king, his *commander's staff.* Through these he will defeat Israel's traditional enemies. The Lord is pictured as a victorious general using *Moab* (east of the Dead Sea) as his *washbowl,* planting his *shoe* on *Edom* (south of Judah) as a sign of its total defeat, and shouting in victory *over the Philistines* (the peoples on the Mediterranean plain).

But who will lead me to conquer the fortress?
Who will bring me face to face with Edom?
Will you utterly reject us, O God,
and no longer march with our armies?

Perhaps here we have the particular crisis that prompted the psalm. *Edom* to the south of Israel was mountainous territory and several of its cities were impregnable. Taking them was like taking a *fortress. Edom* was one of Israel's most bitter foes, and harassed the nation for generations. Edom may have won some recent victory which sparks the question to God: *Will you . . . no longer march with our armies?* They recognize that without God's help they have no hope.

Give us help against the foe . . .

The psalm concludes with a direct cry for help as they go out to do battle with Edom.

The **sentence** interprets the psalm as an expression of Christ's victory at the resurrection and the subsequent claiming of the whole earth for him by the preaching of the Gospel. *Since the Son of God has been exalted above the heavens, his glory is preached over all the earth* (Arnobius). (Arnobius was a fourth century Christian scholar).

Isaiah 61:10—62:5

This canticle comes from the third part of Isaiah (chapters 56—66), which is a collection of prophecies given in the century following the exile. The canticle begins with thanksgiving for the promise of salvation given to the exiles, the promise that they will return to Israel, that Jerusalem will be rebuilt and the land restored. The second part of the canticle is a vision of the splendour of the new Jerusalem.

I will greatly rejoice in the Lord,
my soul shall exult in my God;
for he has clothed me with the garments of salvation,
for he has covered me with the robe of righteousness,
as a bridegroom decks himself with a garland,
and as a bride adorns herself with her jewels.

The reason for the prophet's exultant joy is the promise of salvation from captivity and the restoration of the nation in the verses immediately preceding this canticle. The joy of the people is like the joy of bride and groom on their wedding day. The promised *salvation* (deliverance from captivity and restoration) and *righteousness* (the saving justice of God in action) are like the beautiful wedding garments of the bride and groom.

For as the earth brings forth its shoots . . .

God's saving justice (his *righteousness*) is as certain as the steady growth of the crops, mysterious but sure. God's salvation of Israel will be obvious to *all the nations.*

For Sion's sake I will not keep silent . . .

The *I* in this section may be the prophet, who cannot possibly keep the good news of salvation to himself; or the *I* may be God, who has been silent for so long over the years of the captivity, but is now speaking out *for Jerusalem's sake* giving his word of hope. Jerusalem's *vindication* and *salvation* will be so startling that they will light up the night *as a burning torch.*

The nations shall see your vindication
and all the kings your glory;

These lines continue the theme of the previous verse.

and you shall be called by a new name
which the mouth of the Lord shall give.

The changing of a name in the Scriptures always signifies a

new status. The *new name* the Lord will *give* Sion will signify a new relationship between the Lord and Sion, a new status and honour for the city. The name is revealed later in the canticle.

You shall be a crown of beauty
in the hand of the Lord . . .

Instead of being a disgrace to the Lord, Sion will become like a dazzling *crown* for him, beautiful and precious.

You shall no more be termed Forsaken,
and your land shall no more be termed Desolate;
but you shall be called My delight in her,
and your land Married;
for the Lord delights in you,
and your land shall be married.

Here is revealed the *new name* which was previously announced. Sion had been *forsaken* by the Lord and her land laid waste, *Desolate*. Now God restores her and Sion's new name is: *'My delight in her'*, *'Married'*. In a particularly beautiful and intensely personal image the prophet describes Israel's salvation as her marriage to the Lord. The Lord's love for his people is like the love of a bridegroom for his new bride. (The Lord as Israel's bridegroom appears in other prophets too, in Hosea, Jeremiah and Ezekiel).

For as a young man marries a virgin,
so shall your sons marry you,
and as the bridegroom rejoices over the bride,
so shall your God rejoice over you.

The second line of this stanza is incomprehensible as it stands, and almost all scholars and modern translations emend the Hebrew to read:

For as a young man marries a virgin,
so shall your rebuilder marry you,

The *rebuilder* is the Lord. It is worthwhile writing in this emendation in the text of the canticle.

The image of the Lord marrying his people had a profound influence on the New Testament theology of the Church. The letter to the Ephesians speaks of the Church as the bride of Christ. 'Christ loved the Church and sacrificed himself for her to make her holy by washing her in cleansing water with a form of words, [baptism following proclamation of the Word], so that when he took the Church to himself she would be glorious, with no speck or wrinkle or anything like that, but holy, faultless' (Ephesians 5:25—27). In the book of Revelation the union of Christ with his Church is described as the marriage of the Lamb. *I saw the holy city, the new Jerusalem, as beautiful as a bride prepared to meet her husband* (Revelation 21:2), **sentence.** The whole canticle can be prayed as a prophecy of the relationship between Christ and his Church.

Psalm 145(146)

The psalm extols the power of God who comes with salvation for the oppressed and judgement for the wicked. God's will is unchangeable, in contrast to the plans of human rulers.

> *My soul, give praise to the Lord;*
> *I will praise the Lord all my days,*
> *make music to my God while I live.*

The psalmist regards the main purpose of his life as being the praise of God, a praise that will be lifelong.

> *Put no trust in princes,*
> *in mortal men in whom there is no help . . .*

The psalm makes a strong contrast between the *help* of the Lord which is sure and dependable, and the *help* of men, especially *princes,* which is uncertain and cut short by their death. A new prince brings a new policy. The *plans* of rulers shift with their whims and fancies.

He is happy who is helped by Jacob's God,
whose hope is in the Lord his God,
who alone made heaven and earth,
the seas and all they contain.

In contrast to human rulers, the help of the Lord can be counted on. Those who place their hope in him are always blessed. He is the creator God *who alone made heaven and earth,* and who has entered into covenant with his people. He is *Jacob's God.*

It is he who keeps faith for ever . . .

The Lord's faithfulness is especially seen in his commitment to the helpless and the weak: *the oppressed, the hungry, prisoners, the blind, those who are bowed down, the stranger, the widow, the orphan.* God's help for these helpless ones in Israel was demonstrated in the Law he gave his people, a law which sought to established a social structure where each of these needy groups was specifically cared for. The Pentateuch contains laws relating to the care of each group mentioned in the psalm. The tragedy was that the laws were often ignored and broken by the rich and powerful. In Jesus God acted again to bring 'Good news to the poor'. The Church was given the responsibility to enact God's justice and compassion, but often she has failed as Israel did. We long for that day when Christ will bring to fulfilment his kingdom of justice and peace. The psalm looks forward to that day, when *The Lord will reign for ever and ever, Sion's God from age to age.*

EVENING PRAYER

Psalm 138 is an profound meditation on the depth of God's knowledge and care for each of us, as well as being a prayer for integrity. The New Testament canticle takes us into the supreme revelation of God's love for the world, to Christ, *image of the invisible God.*

Psalm 138(139):1—18,23—24

The psalmist has been falsely accused of a capital offence, possibly idolatry, and he comes to the Temple to pray in the presence of the Lord who knows his innermost heart. The psalm is a plea for justice, but as the psalmist prays he becomes caught up in awe and wonder at the depth of God's knowledge of him.

> *O Lord, you search me and you know me,*
> *you know my resting and my rising,*
> *you discern my purpose from afar.*
> *You mark when I walk or lie down,*
> *all my ways lie open to you.*

The whole psalm could be described as a meditation on the first line: O *Lord, you search me and know me.* What does it mean to say that the Lord *knows me?* The psalm unfolds the amazing depth of that knowledge. God knows all the details of my daily life, from my *rising* to my *resting,* everywhere I go, all my plans and intentions, *my purpose.* In the original setting of the psalm, this means: 'You know I am not guilty of the charges brought against me.'

> *Before ever a word is on my tongue*
> *you know it, O Lord through and through.*
> *Behind and before you besiege me,*
> *your hand ever laid upon me. . . .*

The Lord not only knows the psalmist; he protects him

behind and before from those seeking his downfall. He lays his *hand* upon him in blessing.

O where can I go from your spirit. . . .

With this verse the psalmist begins a new line of thought. He asks: 'What if I was unwilling to accept God's knowledge of me, of every aspect of my life?' The answer comes in the next few verses: 'I cannot escape the Lord's presence and protection even if I tried.' In the most desperate circumstances, even in the *grave, you are there.* Even *at the sea's furthest end . . . your right hand would hold me fast.* Not even the dread *darkness* can hide me from the Lord's sight, for *even darkness is not dark for you.* The psalmist's trouble, his *darkness,* is never too much for God whom he knows can transform the worst tragedy into triumph.

This whole section is a wonderful affirmation of God's covenant love. Even if his people want to escape that love, no matter where they go they will meet it. In its original setting, the section is a further affirmation of the psalmist's innocence. He is not trying to run from God or from his guilt. He would feel secure and unafraid in God's presence wherever he went.

For it was you who created my being,
knit me together in my mother's womb . . .

The question now comes: 'How is it that God knows and cares for me so deeply?' The answer: because he created me. I am his creature. The next few verses spell out what that means to him. First of all, he reflects on his own birth, from the moment of his conception in his *mother's womb.* Then in a remarkable way he joins his own birth to the birth of the human race. A popular primaeval myth told of the birth of humankind from the womb of Mother Earth. In alluding to this myth (*when I was . . . moulded in the depths of the earth*) the psalmist states the meaning of creation: each person should understand and glory in the fact that they are created and cared for by God.

Your eyes saw all my actions,
they were all of them written in your book;
every one of my days was decreed
before one of them came into being.

From thinking of his birth the psalmist now thinks of God's knowledge of him right up to the present. The course of our life is an unfolding mystery, but God knows our destiny from the day we are born. The psalmist is not a theologian giving definitions on predestination, but a man at prayer overwhelmed by the mystery of God's knowledge. It was a common idea in the Old Testament that both our good and evil deeds are recorded by God in his *book*, and on the day of judgement 'the books will be opened.'

To me, how mysterious your thoughts . . .

The psalmist's meditation reaches its climax. Earlier in the psalm this conclusion was anticipated, now it bursts into full view. The extraordinary mystery of God's knowledge and love is more than the puny brain of man can comprehend.

O search me, God, and know my heart.
O test me and know my thoughts.
See that I follow not the wrong path
and lead me in the path of life eternal.

We return to where we set out, with the psalmist facing false accusations, turning to God for vindication, and praying for God to lead him in the *path of life eternal,* the way that is true to God.

Colossians 1:12—20

See Week 1, Wednesday Evening.

Week 4: Thursday

MORNING PRAYER

The first psalm is a prayer made in desolation, a prayer for God's salvation, guidance and healing. In the canticle which follows, the source of these blessings is revealed to be the Church, the Mother of God's people who nourishes her children. But the most startling revelation of the canticle is not that the Church is our Mother, but that the Lord God is our mother. As mother, God comforts her children, a theme which is continued in the final psalm. The Lord *heals the broken-hearted, binds up all their wounds.*

Psalm 142(143)

The psalmist has been crushed by his enemies and in his desolation he feels abandoned by God. He recalls God's faithfulness in the past and prays for deliverance. Above all he longs for a sense of God's presence. Psalm 143 is one of the seven Penitential Psalms.

> *Lord, listen to my prayer:*
> *turn your ear to my appeal.*
> *You are faithful, you are just; give answer.*
> *Do not call your servant to judgement*
> *for no one is just in your sight.*

The basis of the psalmist's plea for help is made plain in the opening verses and repeated throughout the psalm: it is the Lord's commitment to the covenant, his *faithfulness,* his saving justice. The psalmist is a member of God's covenant people, and it is for this reason that he can come and pray for help.

In many of the psalms the author bases his prayer for help on his own innocence and loyalty to God. This psalmist has a more profound sense of the weakness of our humanity. He knows that no one will be found blameless if measured against the standard of God's perfection. *No one is just in your sight.* His plea is for mercy rather than justice. St Paul echoed this psalm in the climax to his argument that 'all have sinned and fall short of the glory of God' (Romans 3:23, 20). The sentence from Galatians 2:16 may be another of his allusions to the psalm: *A man is made righteous not by obedience to the Law, but by faith in Jesus Christ.*

The enemy pursues my soul . . .

The psalmist is pursued by a ruthless enemy whose attacks have taken him to death's door. *He has made me dwell in darkness like the dead, long forgotten.* Relentless persecution has left him totally sapped of energy, depressed, almost beyond feeling. *My heart is numb within me.* In praying the psalm we pray for God's protection against the enemy of our souls, our 'adversary the devil [who] prowls around like a roaring lion, seeking someone to devour' (1 Peter 5:8).

I remember the days that are past:
I ponder all your works. . . .

In the depths of his despair, the psalmist turns his mind back to the past, to all that the Lord has done in Israel's history. This history is a history of the God who acts to save his people from their distress, and as he recalls God's action in the past hope begins to stir within him. As he reflects on what the *hand* of the Lord has *wrought* in the past he stretches out his own *hands, yearning* for the Lord to act again, thirsty for God's life-giving presence.

Lord, make haste and answer;
for my spirit fails within me . . .

If the Lord does not come to help him the psalmist knows he is finished. He will not survive the attacks made against him.

In the morning let me know your love
for I put my trust in you.
Make me know the way I should walk:
to you I lift up my soul.

The psalmist may have been praying in the Temple at night, and he waits for God's help as keenly as he waits for the morning sun to rise and banish the darkness. He may also have been waiting for a prophetic word from the priest assuring him of God's protection and giving him guidance for his life. The *way* of the Lord is the way to life but it can only be followed by those who *trust* in him.

Rescue me, Lord, from my enemies;
I have fled to you for refuge.
Teach me to do your will
for you, O Lord, are my God.
Let your good spirit guide me
in ways that are level and smooth.

For your name's sake, Lord, save my life;
in your justice save my soul from distress.

Having entrusted his life to the Lord the psalmist now prays for the Lord to *rescue* him, *teach* him, *guide* him and *save* him from death. In each case he acknowledges it is the Lord alone who can do this, and it is the *name* of the Lord which will receive honour through his servant's salvation.

Isaiah 66:10—14A

This canticle comes from the third part of Isaiah (Trito-Isaiah), and is a prophecy given against the backdrop of the condition of Jerusalem in the early years after the return from exile. The city was still in ruins but the prophet came with a message of hope, a promise assuring the people that the Lord would miraculously rebuild the nation. The canticle is a hymn of praise in response to the prophecy of hope. The New Testament took up the prophecy and applied it to the Church, the new Jerusalem. *The Jerusalem which is above is free and is our mother* (Galatians 4:26), **sentence**. It is in this sense that we pray the canticle today.

Rejoice with Jerusalem, and be glad for her . . .

The canticle begins with a call to the despondent inhabitants of Jerusalem to rejoice in the promise of salvation, of rebuilding, which the Lord has given. Those who *mourn* because of the desperate state of the city are called to rejoice because of what the Lord will do for them.

That you may such and be satisfied
with her consoling breasts. . . .

In a beautiful and tender image the future Sion is compared to a nursing mother giving *abundant* milk and *delight* to her children. Mother Church feeds and nourishes her children with God's grace given in his Word and in the Sacraments.

For thus says the Lord:
Behold, I will extend prosperity to her like a river,
and the wealth of the nations
like an overflowing stream;
and you shall suck, you shall be carried upon her hip,
and dandled upon her knee.

To Jerusalem in her extreme poverty the Lord promises *wealth* and *prosperity in abundance*, flowing like a river. Jerusalem will care for her citizens as a mother cares for a little child, feeding it, carrying it with care, playing with it. The Spirit is the river of life which flows from the Church to all her children.

As one whom his mother comforts,
so I will comfort you;
you shall be comforted in Jerusalem.

The image changes. Now it is not Jerusalem but the Lord who is the mother lovingly *comforting* her children. This *comfort* makes our *hearts rejoice* and our *bones flourish like the grass!*

Psalm 146(147)

This psalm of praise was inspired by the rebuilding of Jerusalem after the exile. The kernel of the psalm is the couplet: *Our Lord is great and almighty; his wisdom can never be measured.*

> *Praise the Lord for he is good;*
> *sing to our God for he is loving:*

The psalm begins with praise for God's nature, his goodness and love being revealed in the miraculous restoration of Israel.

> *The Lord builds up Jerusalem*
> *and brings back Israel's exiles,*
> *he heals the broken-hearted,*
> *he binds up their wounds.*

Each of these phrases applies to the restoration of city and people after the exile. The Lord *built up* the city again, he brought the *exiles back* home, he healed those who were *broken-hearted* by the long years of captivity and the devastation of the land, he bound up the *wounds* inflicted by their enemies.

> *He fixes the number of the stars;*
> *he calls each one by its name.*

Astrology flourished in Babylon, with the belief that the stars determined human destiny. In contradiction of these myths, Israel confesses her faith in the Lord. The stars are not gods, they have no influence on our destiny, they were created and put in their place by God.

Our Lord is great and almighty;
his wisdom can never be measured.
The Lord raises the lowly;
he humbles the wicked to the dust.

The Lord's greatness is the hub around which the whole psalm revolves. His greatness has been demonstrated in his deliverance of his people from captivity, a deliverance in which he *raised the lowly* and *humbled the wicked* Babylon.

He covers the heavens with clouds;
he prepares rain for the earth . . .

The Lord's greatness is also demonstrated in the gifts of nature, especially in the cycle of rain, growth, and harvest. Even animals and birds are in his care.

His delight is not in horses
nor his pleasure in warriors' strength.
The Lord delights in those who revere him,
in those who wait for his love.

The whole experience of the return from exile has underlined two fundamental convictions: that power belongs to the Lord, not to armies (*horses, warriors*); and those *who wait for his love* will surely be rewarded. Patience and reverence for the Lord are more powerful that the weapons of war.

EVENING PRAYER

The psalm is a prayer of the king as he goes into battle to defend his people. It is interpreted in the Office as the prayer of Christ as he prepared to do battle with 'the world', that is, with all the forces of evil aligned against him. *His arms are well trained for battle, since he has overcome the world, for he says, 'I have overcome the world'* (St Hilary), **sentence.** The second part of the psalm describes the blessings which follow the victory of the Messiah. The concluding New Testament canticle celebrates the victory of Christ over Satan, *the accuser of our brethren* who has been *thrown down.*

Psalm 143(144)

For the introduction to this psalm and comment of the first half, see Week 4, Tuesday Morning.

To you, O God, will I sing a new song;
I will play on the ten-stringed harp
to you who give kings their victory,
who set David your servant free.

The king concludes his prayer by making a vow to return to the Temple after the *victory* to *sing a new song* to God, a song of thanksgiving for God's deliverance. The deliverance of the successor of David will be the deliverance of *David* himself.

You who set him free from the evil sword . . .

The king's victory is anticipated and the psalm now becomes a prayer for the peace and prosperity of the land. This part of the psalm was later interpreted as a prophecy of the blessings of the messianic age.

Let our sons then flourish like saplings . . .

The future of the nation lies in its youth, and so the psalmist prays for a nation of strong young men who will be nurtured *like saplings* and not be left fatherless through war; and beautiful maidens fit to be princesses (*adorned as though for a palace*).

Let our barns be filled to overflowing . . .

The psalmist prays not only for protection from war, but from disease, plague and drought, so that the land will yield a superabundance of *crops, sheep,* and *cattle.* Peace and prosperity go hand in hand.

no ruined wall, no exile . . .
The horror of war is still in mind, but *the people whose God is the Lord* hope for his deliverance and their subsequent *blessing.*

Revelation 11:17—18, 12:10b—12a

See Week 1, Thursday Evening.

Week 4: Friday

MORNING PRAYER

The confession of sin (Psalm 50) is followed by a vision of the glory of the Church in heaven (Tobit 13) and a psalm of praise to God for the Church on earth, through whom God has *sent out his word to the earth.*

Psalm 50(51)

See Week 1, Friday Morning.

Tobit 13:8—11,13—15

The book of Tobit tells the story of an exile from Israel now living in Nineveh, capital of the Assyrian empire. Chapter 13, from which this canticle comes, is the song of the exile longing for Jerusalem and reflecting on the way the Lord has dealt with his people. The whole canticle is in the form of a psalm of praise, and the section of the canticle in Morning Prayer is an appeal to the people of Jerusalem to praise God because of the glorious future of the city. (We met another section of the same canticle in Week 1, Tuesday, Morning Prayer, where the commentary gives a little more background to the book of Tobit).

The author of Tobit was probably writing between 250—200 BC at a time when Jerusalem and the temple had been rebuilt, but the glory of the city was nothing like what it had been in the days before the captivity, and nothing like what the prophets of the exile and restoration (such as Isaiah) had promised. The author of Tobit writes to keep alive the glorious vision of the future which still awaits Jerusalem. The sentence tells us that this future will only be fulfilled in the heavenly Jerusalem: *He showed me the holy city of Jerusalem and it had all the radiant glory of God* (Revelation 21:10—11).

Let all men speak,
and give God thanks in Jerusalem.
O Jerusalem, the holy city,
he will afflict you for the deeds of your sons,
but again he will show mercy
to the sons of the righteous.

The *affliction* of which the canticle speaks was the capture of the city and the exile of its citizens. The *mercy* was the restoration and return from exile.

Give thanks worthily to the Lord,
and praise the King of the ages,
that his tent may be raised for you again with joy.

The Lord's *tent* is another name for the Temple. In the wilderness journey from Egypt to Canaan the presence of the Lord was focused in the tabernacle (or *tent*) which was erected at each stopping point. The *joy* which accompanied the building of the first Temple in the time of King Solomon will accompany the building of the new Temple. For Christians this prophecy points forward to Christ, who presented himself as the fulfillment and replacement of the Temple (John 2:13—22).

May he cheer those within you who are captives . . .
The rebuilding was a time of great hardship and struggle and the people often became despondent.

Many nations will come from afar
to the name of the Lord God
bearing gifts in their hands
gifts for the King of heaven.

Isaiah too prophesied that the nations would look to Jerusalem as the spiritual capital of the world and bring their gifts to the Lord as a sign of their allegiance to him. This vision was fulfilled in Jesus, firstly as the wise men from the east brought him gifts of gold, frankincense and myrrh; then as the Gospel spread to every nation of the world.

How blessed are those who love you! . . .
The canticle concludes with a promise of blessing to all those who at present mourn because of the *affliction* of Jerusalem. They will one day see *all your glory and they will be made glad for ever.* As the Eastertide antiphon states, this blessing will be experienced in the heavenly city, where God's children 'will be radiant with light.'

Psalm 147

See Week 2, Friday Morning.

EVENING PRAYER

Psalm 144 is one of the most beautiful psalms of praise in the whole psalter. It is simple and majestic, offering praise to God as creator and saviour. It is perfectly matched by the New Testament canticle of Revelation 15. *Great and wonderful are your deeds, O Lord God the Almighty!*

Psalm 144(145)

Psalm 144 is an incomparable hymn of praise which speaks for itself and needs little explanation. Its theme is the universal rule of God. In structure the psalm is an acrostic. The verses begin with successive letters of the Hebrew alphabet. It is one of the latest psalms in the psalter and brings together many phrases from the rest of the book of Psalms.

I will given you glory, O God my King . . .

The first line states the theme of the whole psalm: *God my king.* The psalm celebrates the reign of God as it is demonstrated in his creation and care for all the world.

The Lord is great, highly to be praised,
his greatness cannot be measured.

God's *greatness*, as this psalm reveals, is seen in his relationships with the world and its creatures, especially with humankind. His *greatness* as revealed in the psalms is not abstract or metaphysical but real and concrete, shown in his actions; but at the same time mysterious, beyond our comprehension. His *greatness cannot be measured.* To acknowledge his *greatness* is to recognize our relationship to him as his creatures.

Age to age shall proclaim your works,
shall declare your mighty deeds . . .

Each generation forges an unbroken chain of praise and each time we pray the psalm we are part of that chain, opening our lips to *proclaim your works.*

God's *greatness, splendour, glory, might, abundant goodness, justice, compassion* and *love* are shown in his *works, mighty deeds, wonderful works,* and *terrible deeds* (awesome *deeds*). It is in the *wonderful works* and *mighty deeds* of Jesus that *God my King* is supremely revealed.

The Lord is kind and full of compassion,
slow to anger, abounding in love.

This is the kernel of the psalm, the revelation of God's character as given at Mount Sinai when he made his covenant with his people, a revelation which is proved again and again in history and nature. It is to nature that the psalmist now turns.

All your creatures shall thank you, O Lord . . .

All creation joins the worshipping congregation to praise God's greatness.

The Lord is faithful in all his words
and loving in all his deeds.

God's covenant *faithfulness and love* are revealed in his *words* as well as his *deeds*, and particularly in the way he *supports all who fall and raises all who are bowed down.* While this is a general phrase, the experience of exile and restoration may be uppermost in the psalmist's mind.

The eyes of all creatures look to you . . .

The last section of the psalm offers praise to God as the source of all blessing and as the saviour. His blessing is universal, for *all creatures*. He sends his rain on the just and unjust, as Jesus reminded us (Matthew 5:45).

The Lord is just in all his ways
and loving in all his deeds.
He is close to all who call on him,
who call on him from their hearts.

God is not only the creator and sustainer of the world, he is our saviour. The one whose greatness cannot be measured is the one who *is close to all who call him.* He comes to *grant their desires* (provide all they need), to *save them*, to *protect all who love him.* But he is also a God of justice and *the wicked he will utterly destroy.*

Revelation 15:3—4

See Week 1, Friday Evening.

Week 4: Saturday

MORNING PRAYER

God is a God of new beginnings. He inspires a freshness and vitality in his saints right into old age (Psalm 91). He gives a new heart and a new spirit to those whose love has grown cold (Ezekiel 36). How great is his name in all the earth! (Psalm 8).

Psalm 91(92)

See Week 2, Saturday Morning.

Ezekiel 36:24—28

Ezekiel's prophecy given in this canticle is one of the high points of the Old Testament revelation. There is a direct link from this prophecy to Jesus as the one who baptizes in the Holy Spirit.

Ezekiel prophesied in the last years prior to the siege and fall of Jerusalem and in the early years of the exile that followed. According to Ezekiel the old covenant, the covenant made at Sinai, had failed, because the people had proved that they were unable to keep the Law given by God. Their long history since the Exodus had been a history of disobedience and rebellion against the Lord, a history which had come to a disastrous climax with the fall of the Jerusalem. But while Israel may have failed God had not, and his answer to their disobedience was to promise a new covenant not written on tablets of stone, as was the old covenant, but written on their hearts.

> *I will take you from the nations,*
> *and gather you from all the countries,*
> *and bring you into your own land.*

The prophecy begins with the promise that one day the exiles will return. Although it seemed utterly impossible to them at the time, the Lord promised that he would *gather* them from the countries into which they had been carried, and bring them home, to their *own land.*

> *I will sprinkle clean water upon you,*
> *and you shall be clean from all your uncleannesses,*
> *and from all your idols I will cleanse you.*

The sprinkling of water was an action used by the priest to symbolize cleansing from sin. The Lord himself would be their priest, he would *sprinkle clean water* on them and cleanse them from all their sin and in particular from the sin of idolatry. In its account of the reasons for the fall of Jerusalem, the Second Book of Chronicles singles out the persistent idolatry of 'all the leading priests and the people' (36:14).

> *A new heart I will give you,*
> *and a new spirit I will put within you;*
> *and I will take out of your flesh the heart of stone*
> *and give you a heart of flesh.*

The reason for the failure of the old covenant lay in the hearts of the people. Their hearts were stubborn and unresponsive to the Lord, hearts of *stone,* hard and cold. The only solution was a heart transplant, where the Lord would remove their hard heart and replace it with *a heart of flesh,* a heart sensitive to him and to his word, a heart ready to do his will, a heart given to him in love. This new heart is the foundation of the new covenant and is created by the gift of the Spirit.

> *I will put my spirit within you,*
> *and cause you to walk in my statutes*
> *and be careful to observe my ordinances.*

It is with the gift of the Holy Spirit that the promise of the new covenant became a reality. In response to the prayer of his Son, the Father filled the disciples with the Holy Spirit, the Spirit who gave them a new nature, making them sons and daughters of God, bringing them into a totally new relationship to the Father. Through faith and baptism we are born anew 'through water and the Holy Spirit' (John 3:5), and the prophecy of Ezekiel begins to be fulfilled in our own lives.

> *You shall dwell in the land*
> *which I gave to your fathers;*
> *and you shall be my people*
> *and I will be your God.*

The land which Ezekiel was thinking of was the land of Canaan, but Christ revealed that the new land of promise, the kingdom of God, is not a geographical territory but a community of those who have been reborn by the Spirit in baptism (John 3:5—8). This new community, the Church, will find its fulfilment in heaven, where *They shall be his people, and he will be their God; his name is God-with-them* (Revelation 21:3), **sentence.**

Psalm 8

See Week 2, Saturday Morning.

Commentary on the Psalmody of Night Prayer

AFTER EVENING PRAYER I OF SUNDAYS AND SOLEMNITIES

Psalm 4

This psalm is an evening meditation in which the psalmist asks the Lord for mercy. The psalmist's integrity has been questioned and he has become the butt of false accusations. The **sentence** directs us to pray the psalm with Christ, as his prayer from the darkness of the tomb. *The Lord raised him from the dead and made him worthy of all admiration* (St Augustine).

When I call, answer me, O God of justice;
from anguish you released me, have mercy and hear me!

The psalmist longs for the presence of the Lord, for God's answer to his prayer for help. In his anguish he holds on to two things: God is a *God of justice and mercy,* and will therefore come to help the needy. God has answered his prayers in the past, and will therefore answer him now. *From anguish you released me.*

O men, how long will your hearts be closed,
will you love what is futile and seek what is false?

The psalmist turns now to address those who are attacking him. He appeals to them to show compassion and understanding, not to close their hearts to him, to reject the *futile* and *false* charges that have been made against him.

It is the Lord who grants favours to those whom he loves;
the Lord hears me whenever I call him.

So confident is the psalmist of God's help that he no longer accuses his enemies of listening to lies, but he appeals to them on the basis of his own experience of God's *love* and *favour* and answered prayer.

Fear him; do not sin: ponder on your bed and be still.
Make justice your sacrifice and trust in the Lord.

The appeal to the psalmist's opponents continues. He knows how at night the heart can grow bitter over some injustice we think we have suffered, and so he warns them (and himself) not to give way to such feelings, but instead to follow a different path. This path is: to reverence God, to refuse to let bitterness turn into sin ('Even if you are angry, do not sin' (Ephesians 4:26)), to calm down (*be still*), to practice *justice,* to *trust in the Lord.* This is counsel we all need to hear at the end of each day.

'What can bring us happiness?' many say.
Let the light of your face shine on us, O Lord.

Happiness does not come from material prosperity but from the joy of knowing God's presence and blessing. 'Our hearts are restless until they rest in thee' (St Augustine).

You have put into my heart a greater joy
than they have from abundance of corn and new wine.

The greatest earthly pleasure, *abundance of corn and new wine,* cannot compare with the *joy* of knowing the presence of the Lord. Jesus said to his disciples: 'These things I have spoken to you, that my joy may be in you, and that your joy may be full' (John 15:11).

I will lie down in peace and sleep comes at once
for you alone, Lord, make me dwell in safety.

No matter what troubles surround him, the psalmist knows the blessed gift of sleep, because he trusts totally in the Lord. He does not toss and turn for hours before drifting off. *Sleep comes at once.* It is the Lord who protects him, makes him *safe* during the long night.

Psalm 133(134)

This psalm is a liturgical dialogue between priest and congregation, possibly used on the first evening of the feast of Tabernacles.

O come, bless the Lord,
all you who serve the Lord,
who stand in the house of the Lord,
in the courts of the house of our God.

To *bless the Lord* is to praise him for his goodness and love, shown especially in creation and redemption. The psalm begins with a call to all who *serve the Lord,* to join in offering him praise.

Lift up your hands to the holy place
and bless the Lord through the night.

The standard Jewish posture for prayer is to stand with hands lifted up to heaven. The stance of the priest during the Eucharistic Prayer derives from this custom. It is a sign of praise and an open-handed plea for grace. The *holy place* may refer to the Holy of Holies where the ark of the covenant rested.

May the Lord bless you from Sion,
he who made both heaven and earth.

This verse may be the priest's blessing on the congregation as they pray. It is the perfect end to the psalmody of Night Prayer.

Nunc Dimittis, Luke 2:29—32

Simeon is described in Luke 2 as 'an upright and devout man; he looked forward to the restoration of Israel, and the Holy Spirit rested on him' (2:25). The Holy Spirit had revealed to him that he would not die until he had seen the Messiah. Simeon was a watchman posted by God to watch for the arrival of the Christ. The Spirit led him into the temple at the very time of Jesus' presentation, and Simeon took the child Jesus in his arms and made this prayer:

At last, all-powerful Master,
you give leave to your servant
to go in peace, according to your promise.

Simeon has been the watchman-servant of the Lord, watching for the promised coming of the Messiah, and now that he has seen Jesus his task is over and he can be released to *go in peace.* The antiphon interprets this task of watching for the Lord as the task of every Christian who awaits the return of the Saviour: 'Save us, Lord, while we are awake; protect us while we sleep, that we may keep watch with Christ and rest with him in peace.' Sleep is a reminder of death, and as we go to sleep each night we thank God that we *go in peace.* We go to sleep with the same faith in which we hope to die.

For my eyes have seen your salvation
Which you have prepared for all nations,
the light to enlighten the Gentiles
and give glory to Israel, your people.

The first line echoes the prophecies of Isaiah, who promised that 'all flesh shall see God's salvation' (40:5). Jesus is to be the fulfilment of the long-awaited salvation which Luke's Gospel will reveal as the forgiveness of sins and the gift of the Holy Spirit.

This *salvation* is not just for Israel. It is *for all nations,* Jew and Gentile alike, as Isaiah prophesied (49:6). Again we have a distinctive emphasis of Luke, who reveals Jesus as *the light to enlighten the Gentiles* as well as Israel's Messiah. Jesus is Israel's crowning *glory,* the supreme gift of God to his people.

AFTER EVENING PRAYER II OF SUNDAYS AND SOLEMNITIES

Psalm 90(91)

A number of the psalms are called entrance liturgies because they involve a dialogue between priest and people at the entrance to the Temple. Part of the purpose of these psalms is to convey the blessings the Lord promises to those who come to worship him. Psalm 90 may be one of these entrance psalms. It is certainly best understood as a dialogue between priest and people. Unlike the psalms which wrestle with the problem of innocent suffering, Psalm 90 is content simply to affirm God's protection of the upright.

He who dwells in the shelter of the Most High
and abides in the shade of the Almighty
says to the Lord: 'My refuge,
my stronghold, my God in whom I trust!

This is the message of the whole psalm. In the Temple the worshipper is sheltered by the presence of the Lord. The Lord is like a tree shading a man from the burning desert sun, or like a strongly fortified castle giving refuge from an attacking army.

It is he who will free you from the snare
of the fowler who seeks to destroy you;
he will conceal you with his pinions
and under his wings you will find refuge.

In these next verses the priest speaks to the worshipper in a powerful series of images of the security he will find in the

Almighty. The psalmist is like a bird saved *from* ... *the fowler*; like a baby eagle sheltered under the wings ... mother.

You will not fear the terror of the night
nor the arrow that flies by day,
nor the plague that prowls in the darkness
nor the scourge that lays waste at noon.

These verses speak of more than man-made snares. They bring before us the power of evil spirits. The *terror of the night* may be a reference to the forces of evil which were believed to have free reign in the darkness, like wild animals on the *prowl*. Noon was also believed to be a dangerous time, possibly because at noon the fierce heat of the sun was at its most intense. The *arrow* and the *scourge*, evil spirits which threaten human life at noon, hold no fears to the one who *dwells in the shelter of the Most High*.

A thousand may fall at your side,
ten thousand at your right
you, it will never approach;
his faithfulness is buckler and shield.

From evil spirits the psalm moves to the terror of war. Despite destruction all around him, the psalmist is assured of safety because God's *faithfulness*, his covenant loyalty, will protect him from evil. A *buckler* is a small, hand-held shield.

Your eyes have only to look
to see how the wicked are repaid . . .

The lives of *the wicked* ultimately crumble and come to nothing.

Upon you no evil shall fall,
no plague approach where you dwell.
For he has commanded his angels,
to keep you in all your ways.

They shall bear you upon their hands
lest you strike your foot against a stone.
On the lion and the viper you will tread
and trample on the young lion and dragon.

Here we are at the heart of the mystery of which the psalm speaks. These are the words quoted by Satan in his attempt to persuade Jesus to throw himself off the pinnacle of the temple and so demonstrate God's miraculous power to save him. Jesus in his own life showed how the righteous are not protected from evil in the sense that they never suffer harm, but they are protected absolutely from eternal harm as they find their refuge in the Lord. Jesus promised his disciples power over all the forces of Satan when he said to them: *Behold, I have given you power to tread underfoot serpents and scorpions and the whole strength of the enemy* (Luke 10:19), **sentence.** God's faithful do experience physical suffering and tragedy (although some forms of popular piety try to make faith in God an insurance against trouble), but as we say to the Lord: '*My God in whom I trust*', we are delivered from the Enemy of our souls.

Since he clings to me in love, I will free him;
protect him for he knows my name.
When he calls I shall answer: 'I am with you.'
I will save him in distress and give him glory.

With length of life I will content him;
I shall let him see my saving power.

With this verse we hear the Lord himself speaking to the worshipper, possibly by way of a prophetic oracle given by the priest. The Lord assures his faithful that in the midst of *distress* he will be there to *save*. It is Christ's gift of eternal life and his promise of *glory* which come before the Christian who prays this psalm.

MONDAY

Psalm 85(86)

See Week 3, Wednesday Morning.

TUESDAY

Psalm 142(143)

See Week 4, Thursday Morning.

WEDNESDAY

Psalm 30(31):1—6

Psalm 30 has much in common with the confessions of Jeremiah, Jeremiah's laments to the Lord in the face of his rejection and suffering. The first part of the psalm (vv. 1—6) is a prayer for help in the face of vicious attack.

In you, O Lord, I take refuge . . .

In the face of attack by his enemies the psalmist flees to the Lord (to the Temple?) for refuge. His prayer for help is made on the basis of the Lord's *justice,* his faithfulness to his covenant.

Be a rock of refuge for me . . .

The psalmist prays that the Lord will protect him, *lead* him and *guide* him to safety.

Release me from the snares they have hidden
for you are my refuge, Lord.
Into your hands I commend my spirit.
It is you who will redeem me, Lord.

In Luke's Gospel Jesus' last words on the cross come from this verse: '*Father, into your hands I commend my spirit*'

(Luke 23:46), **sentence**. They are an expression of absolute trust in the Father, and as such have been used by countless Christians facing death. Night Prayer is a preparation for sleep and for death. *It is you who will redeem me, Lord.*

Psalm 129(130)

See Week 4, Sunday Evening I.

THURSDAY

Psalm 15(16)

See Week 2, Sunday Evening I.

FRIDAY

Psalm 87(88)

In this psalm we are confronted with the reality of unrelieved distress. The psalmist has suffered all his life. His friends have abandoned him and he feels that even God has forgotten him. The psalm takes us into the depths of Christ's suffering on the cross. *This is your hour; this is the reign of darkness* (**sentence**). It is a psalm which enables us to pray with those like the psalmist who feel utterly deserted and without hope. It is a psalm which enables us to pray with Christ at his death.

> *Lord my God, I call for help by day;*
> *I cry at night before you. . . .*

Although the psalmist receives no answer to his prayer, he still acknowledges that God is his only hope, the only one in whom he can find *help*.

> *For my soul is filled with evils;*
> *my life is on the brink of the grave . . .*

The psalmist is overwhelmed by his suffering and close to death. In Old Testament belief, the dead were permanently *cut off* from God, and can therefore expect nothing from him. They are *cut off from* his *hand* which alone can save. God *remembers* them *no more*. The psalmist understands his desperate situation to be a result of God's *anger* with him. He can find no other explanation.

You have taken away my friends . . .

His friends have deserted him, perhaps interpreting his great suffering as a sign that he must be a great sinner and therefore should be avoided. It is like being alone in a *prison*, locked up and unable to *escape*.

I call to you Lord, all the day long . . .

In his despair he cries to God to save his life. His situation is so desperate that it will take a *wonder* like the miracle of the Exodus to save him.

Will you work your wonders for the dead? . . .

The long series of questions all expect the answer 'No!' and are a further appeal to the Lord to come to his help while there is yet time. Christ by his resurrection enables us now to answer 'Yes!' to these questions.

As for me, Lord, I call to you for help . . .

Why, why, why? The psalmist confronts us with the impenetrable mystery of suffering with his relentless 'Why?'

Wretched, close to death from my youth . . .

The psalm builds towards a climax of anguish. The psalmist feels as if God has swept down on him like a roaring flood, before which he is utterly helpless. And the most bitter thing of all is that he is alone. The psalm finishes with the single cry: *My one companion is darkness.*

Index of Psalms

Index of Canticles